RAND ARROYO CENTER

The U.S. Army and the Battle for Baghdad

Lessons Learned—And Still to Be Learned

David E. Johnson, Agnes Gereben Schaefer, Brenna Allen,
Raphael S. Cohen, Gian Gentile, James Hoobler, Michael Schwille,
Jerry M. Sollinger, Sean M. Zeigler

Prepared for the United States Army
Approved for public release; distribution unlimited

For more information on this publication, visit www.rand.org/t/RR3076

Library of Congress Control Number: 2019940985
ISBN: 978-0-8330-9601-2

Published by the RAND Corporation, Santa Monica, Calif.
© Copyright 2019 RAND Corporation
RAND® is a registered trademark.

Limited Print and Electronic Distribution Rights

This document and trademark(s) contained herein are protected by law. This representation of RAND intellectual property is provided for noncommercial use only. Unauthorized posting of this publication online is prohibited. Permission is given to duplicate this document for personal use only, as long as it is unaltered and complete. Permission is required from RAND to reproduce, or reuse in another form, any of its research documents for commercial use. For information on reprint and linking permissions, please visit www.rand.org/pubs/permissions.

The RAND Corporation is a research organization that develops solutions to public policy challenges to help make communities throughout the world safer and more secure, healthier and more prosperous. RAND is nonprofit, nonpartisan, and committed to the public interest.

RAND's publications do not necessarily reflect the opinions of its research clients and sponsors.

Support RAND
Make a tax-deductible charitable contribution at
www.rand.org/giving/contribute

www.rand.org

Preface

This report documents research and analysis conducted as part of a project entitled *Lessons Learned from 13 Years of Conflict: The Battle for Baghdad, 2003–2008*, sponsored by the Office of Quadrennial Defense Review, U.S. Army. The project was intended to capture key lessons to help the U.S. Army and U.S. Department of Defense (DoD) retain institutional knowledge and capabilities, as well as to serve as a history of the U.S. Army's efforts in Iraq and Afghanistan from 2001 to 2016.

The Project Unique Identification Code (PUIC) for the project that produced this document is HQD146863.

This research was conducted within RAND Arroyo Center's Strategy, Doctrine, and Resources Program. RAND Arroyo Center, part of the RAND Corporation, is a federally funded research and development center sponsored by the United States Army.

RAND operates under a "Federal-Wide Assurance" (FWA00003425) and complies with the *Code of Federal Regulations for the Protection of Human Subjects Under United States Law* (45 CFR 46), also known as "the Common Rule," as well as with the implementation guidance set forth in DoD Instruction 3216.02. As applicable, this compliance includes reviews and approvals by RAND's Institutional Review Board (the Human Subjects Protection Committee) and by the U.S. Army. The views of sources utilized in this study are solely their own and do not represent the official policy or position of DoD or the U.S. Government.

Contents

Preface iii
Figures and Tables vii
Summary ix
Acknowledgments xxiii
Abbreviations xxv

CHAPTER ONE
Introduction 1
Study Approach 1
Organization of This Report 2

CHAPTER TWO
Prewar Planning 7
Civilian Prewar Planning 9
Prewar Military Planning 23
Lessons from This Era 38

CHAPTER THREE
Occupation 43
The Military Picture 44
ORHA's Short-Lived Tenure 54
Coalition Provisional Authority and the American Attempt at Occupation 59
CPA Orders 1 and 2 65
Rebuilding the Iraqi Security Forces: An Orphaned Mission 74
Lessons from This Era 81

CHAPTER FOUR
The Casey Period 89
Key Debates 89
Military Situation and Strategy: Actions on the Ground to Control Baghdad ... 91
Embassy Challenges: Reconstruction in a War Zone 99

Civilian Policy Views from Washington and Baghdad......... 103
Efforts to Create Iraqi Security Forces and Defense Institutions......... 109
Lessons from This Era......... 119

CHAPTER FIVE
The Surge......... 123
Key Debates: The Surge Versus the Iraq Study Group Report......... 123
Military Situation and Operations......... 125
A Tough Seven Months......... 126
Counterinsurgency and the Surge......... 130
Counterinsurgency Operations in Practice......... 131
Special Operations Command Ramps Up......... 136
Countering the Shia Element......... 137
The Battle of Sadr City......... 138
Civilians and the Surge: One Surge, Many Stories......... 142
Civilians and the Surge......... 149
Iraqi Security Forces Through 2008......... 152
Creating an Enterprise in Security Force Assistance—Changing MNSTC-I......... 154
Increased Training Efforts......... 157
Problems with MOI—Police, Corruption, and Security......... 159
Adviser Teams—Did the United States Get It Right?......... 162
Did the Surge Work?......... 163
Lessons from This Era......... 168

CHAPTER SIX
Withdrawal......... 171
The Military Story......... 172
SOFA: Tried and Failed......... 176
Politicization of the Iraqi Security Forces......... 188
Postmortem......... 191
Lessons from This Era......... 194

CHAPTER SEVEN
Overarching Lessons for the U.S. Army......... 197
The Nature of the Lessons from Iraq—and the Constraints on Learning......... 198
Overarching Lessons from the Iraq War and Recommendations for the Army......... 203
Final Thoughts......... 233

APPENDIX
Timeline of Major Events in the Battle for Baghdad......... 235

References......... 269

Figures and Tables

Figures

5.1.	Anbar Province, Iraq	127
5.2.	Baghdad Belts	134
5.3.	Intelligence, Surveillance, and Reconnaissance and Strike Assets Employed in the Battle of Sadr City	140

Tables

2.1.	Timetable of Civilian Prewar Planning for Phase IV	22
2.2.	Phase IV Troop-to-Task Analysis, May 2003	35
7.1.	Specific Lessons for the U.S. Army, by Chapter	201

Summary

This report tells the history of the Battle for Baghdad. But unlike most historical examples of combat in a large city, the Battle for Baghdad was not one but several sequential battles, each with its own focus and approach. Within the framework of the battle for that fabled city, this report describes U.S. adaptation to each new phase. As the enemy's tactics and techniques evolved, so too did those of the U.S. military. In doing so, U.S. soldiers and commanders learned many lessons, some specific to a given phase of the battle, others with a more universal application. It is important to chronicle those lessons because, as George Santayana noted, "Those who cannot remember the past are condemned to repeat it."[1] The goal of this report is to catalogue those hard-won lessons that are derived from action (and inaction) by both civilian and military leaders so that U.S. soldiers are better prepared in future conflicts and are less likely to repeat mistakes made in Iraq.

The story told here begins with the planning that went on during the run-up to combat operations in Iraq, because that planning dictated how the war, at least initially, was fought and how that shaped subsequent phases. The assumptions underpinning the prewar planning profoundly affected subsequent events. We then turn to major combat operations and recount the challenges that arose and how the United States and its coalition partners reacted when they unexpectedly found themselves in charge of Iraq. The report then transitions to what we call "the Casey period," named after the senior general in Iraq. The story next moves to the period dubbed "the Surge," during which the United States committed substantial additional forces to the fight, which GEN David Petraeus famously described to President George W. Bush as being "all in." The story then turns to the withdrawal from Iraq, which occurred under terms that surprised many and which many argue accounts for conditions that persist today. Each period has different lessons to teach, and we recount those lessons for each phase in this summary.

We also distill several overarching lessons in the hope that they will be shared widely both within the U.S. Department of Defense (DoD) and across the U.S. government and the nation. However, the lessons in this report focus primarily on the

---

[1] George Santayana, *The Life of Reason*, Vol. 1, New York: Charles Scribner's Sons, 1905, p. 284.

U.S. Army. In the Battle for Baghdad, the U.S. Army was the indispensable force. This is not to minimize the very important contributions of the other services and government agencies. But it is to acknowledge that the battle had to be won on the ground. And as this report stresses, winning on the ground entails far more than direct combat operations; it extends to stabilizing the city and the country after the initial direct combat phase. In this regard, the U.S. military failed.

The assumption of senior U.S. civilian policymakers and their military advisers was that once the Iraqi army was defeated and Saddam Hussein fled or was captured, the Iraqi national, provincial, and local governments would continue to function under new civilian leaders chosen and backed by the United States. The institutional failure was in not planning for potential contingencies should this fundamental assumption prove invalid, as it quickly did. There was a relatively narrow window of time following the capture of Baghdad when the country stood at a crossroads from which things could go in very different directions. One direction led to a defeated but functioning state that could still maintain order and carry out the basic functions of government. The other was a precipitous slide into chaos.

Because few political or military leaders envisioned the chaos and civil war that would soon follow the defeat of the Iraqi army and the collapse of the Saddam regime, the military was not instructed to plan for such a contingency. It also was not charged with rebuilding a defeated nation, especially because civilian and military policymakers did not envision the collapse of the entire Iraqi government at all levels. However, the U.S. Army was charged to provide forces to the combatant commanders to "occupy territories abroad and provide for the initial establishment of a military government pending transfer of this responsibility to other authority."[2] This report documents some of the challenges the U.S. Army faced in carrying out this mission.

Overarching Lessons from the Iraq War and Recommendations for the Army

The lessons described in this report fall into three broad categories: lessons the U.S. Army can institutionalize through its own internal processes, lessons the Army does not have the authority to institutionalize, and lessons the Army must institutionalize through a combined effort with other actors (for example, developing joint doctrine). The recommendations that follow all fall within the Army's authority to institutionalize. In some cases, and to its credit, the Army is already acting on the recommendations.

---

[2] DoD, *Functions of the Department of Defense and Its Major Components*, DoD Directive 5100.01, Washington, D.C., December 21, 2010b, p. 30.

Lesson 1: DoD War Plans Need to Include Actions to Ensure Long-Term Stability

The United States had to spend years countering an insurgency in Iraq. A key lesson from the Iraq War is that the combatant command, as the agent of DoD, is responsible for ensuring that chaos does not follow in the wake of initial combat success. The Army's role is central in this because one of its primary functions is to provide forces to the combatant commander that are trained, organized, and equipped to occupy and provide transitional military governance in the aftermath of major combat operations. This was—and remains—a primary function of the Army as specified in the August 1, 2002, DoD Directive 5100.1 and its superceding DoD Directive 5100.01, released in 2010.[3]

Recommendation: Resource and Prepare the Army to Provide Forces to the Combatant Commanders to Ensure Long-Term Stability

The U.S. Army needs to prepare forces to provide to combatant commanders following major combat operations. Regardless of whether the United States will ever want to pursue operations like those in Iraq or Afghanistan again, the Army must be resourced and prepared to provide the capabilities and capacity to execute such operations, if directed. Thus, an understanding of what happened in Iraq is central to preparing the U.S. Army for dealing with post–regime change operations. Particularly important is understanding that it will be the Army's responsibility to provide the majority of the capacity and capabilities in the aftermath of a regime change to prevent the slide into chaos that happened in Iraq in 2003.

As 2014's *The U.S. Army Operating Concept: Win in a Complex World* recognizes, "Compelling sustainable outcomes in war require land forces to defeat enemy organizations, establish security, and consolidate gains."[4] It also notes, "Wide area security includes the essential stability tasks including: establish civil security; [establish] security force assistance; establish civil control; restore essential services; support governance; and support economic and infrastructure development."[5] These are key tasks for which U.S. Army forces were neither resourced nor prepared to conduct in the aftermath of regime change in Iraq in 2003. Nevertheless, the operating concept recognizes the difficult challenges facing the Army in a time of constrained resources "to strike the right balance between current readiness and investment of future capabilities."[6]

Thus, it is essential that the U.S. Army retain and continue to develop the capabilities it will need to provide postconflict security and initial governance. This is in keeping with DoD guidance that while U.S. "forces will no longer be sized to con-

---

[3] DoD, *Functions of the Department of Defense and Its Major Components*, DoD Directive 5100.1, Washington, D.C., August 1, 2002; and DoD, 2010b.

[4] Department of the Army, *The U.S. Army Operating Concept: Win in a Complex World*, TRADOC Pamphlet 525-3-1, Washington, D.C.: Headquarters, Department of the Army, October 31, 2014b, p. 16.

[5] Department of the Army, 2014b, p. 23.

[6] Department of the Army, 2014b, p. 24.

duct large-scale prolonged stability operations," the services will "preserve the expertise gained during the past ten years of counterinsurgency and stability operations in Iraq and Afghanistan" and "protect the ability to regenerate capabilities that might be needed to meet future demands."[7] Congress and DoD have the responsibility to ensure that the Army is adequately resourced to preserve these capabilities and to provide the necessary capacity when so directed.

Lesson 2: Capacity and Capability Matter, and the "Whole of Government" Beyond the Military Could Not Provide Them in Iraq

The U.S. military did not have the capacity to secure Iraq at the end of major combat operations. The debate surrounding the number of forces that went into Iraq had been contentious even before the war. It came to a head when then–Army Chief of Staff GEN Eric Shinseki testified before the Senate Armed Services Committee about the sizeable number of forces that would be required to stabilize Iraq. What soon became clear during the early years of the war was that demands for capacity would fall largely on the U.S. military. Thus, a key lesson from Iraq is that the "whole of government" cannot compensate for insufficient boots on the ground, nor does it have the capabilities to provide what the military can.

Some stability operations and counterinsurgencies may be beyond the capacity of the U.S. military to execute once disorder breaks out. Again, the imperative is to ensure that, when the United States brings down a regime, the affected country does not erupt into chaos that quickly outstrips the military's capacity to establish order.

The U.S. military lacked key capabilities needed to occupy and secure Iraq and provide transitional military government. A complete plan for the postconflict period was not the only piece that was missing; the U.S. government and military did not have the capabilities and capacity to arrest the descent of Iraq into chaos or to adapt rapidly to the security environment following major combat operations. Planning alone could not have made up for this inherent capability deficit. Eventually, in 2007, President Bush surged five additional Army brigades to Iraq, which were essentially all of the forces available in an Army already heavily committed. Even this step required increasing Army deployments from 12 months to 15, a move that significantly increased stress on the force. It was not until the Surge that there were sufficient forces in Baghdad to do the job.

Recommendation: Build More Capacity for the Challenges the Army Will Likely Face in the Future

In the future, the U.S. Army will likely provide the majority of U.S. security forces to maintain order following conflict and natural disasters. It must provide security, as well as the bulk of the civil affairs and military government capabilities, until the transition to civil authority occurs. And that transition cannot occur until there is at least a modicum of order.

---

[7] DoD, *Quadrennial Defense Review 2014*, Washington, D.C., March 2014, p. viii.

The U.S. Army lacked key capabilities and the capacity needed to occupy, secure, and provide transitional military government in Iraq. A lack of capability and capacity across the U.S. government, coupled with short tour lengths for civilians, exacerbated the shortages of capacity in the military.

Recommendation: Continue Efforts to Provide Sufficient Military Government Capabilities

Historically, the U.S. Army has had to provide sufficient military government capabilities after almost every war it has fought, often with mixed results. World War II was the exception. Under the direction of the Civil Affairs Division in the War Department, the U.S. Army, learning from its experiences in World War I, manned, organized, trained, and equipped units for military government and civil affairs functions. Following the war, those capabilities withered. The United States and its coalition were unprepared for the responsibilities of administering Iraq and supporting the government of Afghanistan. Ad hoc efforts to deal with these problems were typically inadequate.

However, since then, some efforts are under way in the Army to deal with this issue. In August 2013, the commanding general of the U.S. Army Special Operations Command and the Chief of the Army Reserve partnered to establish the Institute for Military Support to Governance (IMSG) at the U.S. Army John F. Kennedy Special Warfare Center and School and plug the functional specialty capability gap in U.S. Army Reserve–Civil Affairs units. The mission statement of the institute shows that the civil affairs and military government lessons from Iraq and Afghanistan are being institutionalized by the Army: "The IMSG organizes, trains, and coordinates Governance Advisory Teams, integrates with U.S. Government and community of interest partners, and provides ongoing research and analysis to meet theater requirements across all operational phases in support of Unified Action."[8] The IMSG is a worthwhile investment to ensure that the capability gaps that the U.S. Army encountered in Iraq and Afghanistan are understood and ameliorated in the future.

Lesson 3: Robust and High-Quality Headquarters Are Critical

U.S. Central Command did not have a resourced plan to take charge in the early days following the collapse of the Iraqi regime, and U.S. policy suffered significantly as a result. The Joint Task Force organized around the V Corps Headquarters in Iraq was not capable of executing the mission it was assigned. Neither the V Corps Headquarters of LTG Ricardo Sanchez nor Ambassador L. Paul Bremer III's Coalition Provisional Authority were up to the challenges they faced. Their headquarters were not provided with the necessary capabilities for the problems at hand. Not until the creation of the Multi-National Force–Iraq, combined with the creation of Multi-National Corps–Iraq, did the headquarters on the ground have the talent and the horsepower to

---

[8] Hugh C. Van Roosen, *Military Support to Governance*, Version 7-Draft, white paper, January 12, 2015, p. 2.

link tactics and operations to strategy and policy. That said, these headquarters were not established until more than a year after the U.S.-led coalition intervened in Iraq, and much time had been lost.

In the aftermath of the war in Iraq, DoD directed end-strength reductions in the Army and other services as a result of the 2011 Budget Control Act. Facing these significant directed budget cuts, particularly under sequestration, the Army saw its authorized end strength drop from 563,600 Regular Army, 358,200 National Guard, and 205,000 Reserve soldiers in 2010 to a potential end strength in 2019 of 420,000 Regular Army, 315,200 National Guard, and 185,000 Reserve soldiers.[9] Headquarters at the two-star-general level and higher echelons, both institutional and operational, were targeted for a 25-percent aggregate reduction.[10] For division headquarters, the cuts amount to some 225 soldiers, and for corps-sized headquarters, around 222 soldiers.[11]

Recommendation: Provide Robust Division, Corps, and Theater Army Headquarters
As the U.S. Army has moved to a modular, brigade-centric force, it has spent considerable effort ensuring that its brigade-level headquarters are robustly staffed to accomplish their assigned missions. It should do the same for its higher operational headquarters. Rather than seeing headquarters as sources for manpower reductions, the Army should assess the need for more-robust division and corps headquarters—particularly for these large-scale stabilization missions that can operate simultaneously as deployed headquarters and as the parent organization for subordinate units that did not deploy.

Lesson 4: As the U.S. Military Continues to Perform the Training and Advising Mission, Developing Competent Advisers and Understanding Sustainable Outcomes Are Key
The initial intervention plan for Iraq did not envision a long-term occupation, including building a new Iraqi army from scratch. Without such direction from the President or Secretary of Defense, DoD did not resource the required forces, U.S. Central Command did not plan for the long term, and the Army was not tasked to provide the necessary forces. As in Afghanistan, this mission grew to include training and advising the new Iraqi Army, as well as training and reforming host-nation police.[12] DoD should address the train, advise, and assist mission in its defense strategy and provide the

---

[9] National Commission on the Future of the U.S. Army, *Report to the President and the Congress of the United States, January 28, 2016*, Arlington, Va., 2016, p. 122.

[10] Department of the Army, "2013 Focus Areas," memorandum, August 14, 2015.

[11] C. Todd Lopez, "Army to Realign Brigades, Cut 40,000 Soldiers, 17,000 Civilians," U.S. Army, July 9, 2015.

[12] Section 660 of the Foreign Assistance Act enacted in 1974 prohibited the United States from training foreign police forces, although in practice the United States often found work-arounds during stability operations. See Dennis E. Keller, *U.S. Military Forces and Police Assistance in Stability Operations: The Least-Worst Option to Fill the U.S. Capacity Gap*, Carlisle, Pa.: Army Strategic Studies Institute, Peacekeeping and Stability Operations Institute Paper, August 2010, p. 20.

direction and resources necessary to develop and sustain the skills and forces required for this mission. The DoD plan should also address requirements associated with all security forces, including police. The U.S. Army military police community would appear to be ideally postured to develop the plans and capabilities necessary to reform foreign police forces in the aftermath of military conflicts. Given recent force structure trends, the Army is deciding what is absolutely necessary and what is not. The trend, understandably, leans toward preparing for the most-consequential missions with a renewed focus on conventional war against advanced threats. Proposals about how to prepare the Army for conventional combat, stability operations, and advising have come and gone. The collapse of the Iraqi military when confronted by the Islamic State provides lessons for the future in several areas,[13] including determining what kind of military and police forces the host nation requires, and providing trainers and advisers for efforts that create sustainable outcomes.

Recommendation: Continue to Institutionalize Efforts to Prepare Trainers and Advisers

Proposals for how to train, advise, and assist foreign military and police forces frequently advance solutions for a specific problem within a larger problem set. They do not consider the totality of the demands on the U.S. Army in the current conflicts or the conflicts in which it may find itself in the future. Nevertheless, the Army needs to understand the problems that spawned the call for such solutions and how to learn from these experiences, and then it should institutionalize the relevant capabilities that were created for Iraq. The Army should ensure that it has adequate capacity to prepare trainers and advisers, particularly for advising on combined arms operations at battalion and higher echelons. It should also look to foreign examples, such as France, for different approaches.

In February 2017, the Army announced that it is establishing six security force assistance brigades and the Military Advisor Training Academy, beginning in October 2017. These initiatives have the potential to institutionalize the train, advise, and assist lessons from the Iraq War and ongoing efforts to bolster the Iraqi Security Forces (ISF) in the war against the Islamic State.

Lesson 5: The Goal of Building and Advising Foreign Military and Police Forces Should Be to Make Them Self-Sufficient

The ISF could not operate effectively without the continued support of U.S. enablers. On the eve of the U.S. departure from Iraq, DoD's view of Iraqi military capabilities was relatively optimistic. In reality, the ISF that broke and ran in the face of the

---

[13] The organization's name transliterates from Arabic as al-Dawlah al-Islamiyah fi al-'Iraq wa al-Sham (abbreviated as Da'ish or DAESH). In the West, it is commonly referred to as the Islamic State of Iraq and the Levant (ISIL), the Islamic State of Iraq and Syria, the Islamic State of Iraq and the Sham (both abbreviated as ISIS), or simply as the Islamic State. Arguments abound as to which is the most accurate translation, but here we refer to the group as the Islamic State.

Islamic State's offensive in 2014 did so because it was designed largely as an internal security force. The ISF could operate effectively only with significant U.S. assistance when facing anything other than moderate-scale internal threats. It was incapable of the combined arms maneuver required to defeat the Islamic State.

Causes for the failure of Iraq's army against the Islamic State were numerous. Perhaps most significant was rampant corruption within the ISF, which worsened after the U.S. departure. This occurred as Prime Minister Nouri al-Maliki used officers personally loyal to him to staff the ISF, which were dominated by Shia and mistrusted by Sunnis. Under these conditions, the Iraqi institutions created over several years by the U.S.-led coalition proved inadequate and fragile.

Thus, the ultimate lesson from this experience should be to design and develop foreign military and police forces and institutions that are appropriate to the challenges at hand and that are self-sustainable once U.S. forces are withdrawn. This may require U.S. trainers and advisers to support organizations and approaches that are significantly different from the U.S. model. Success lies in finding a solution that works for the indigenous forces, not imposing a U.S. solution that may be unsustainable.

Recommendation: When Designing Efforts to Build Indigenous Security Forces, Account for Their Ability to Operate Absent Large-Scale U.S. Support

U.S. military objectives and approaches for building institutions and security forces must work within the culture and situation at hand and not necessarily be designed to emulate U.S. approaches. Proposed solutions must be politically and economically feasible to the indigenous state. Achieving this objective requires a deep understanding of the capabilities of the host nation, which should help shape the type of adviser and foreign military sales strategies employed. Again, adviser and trainer preparation is a key ingredient for success.

Lesson 6: Military Transition Teams and Advisers Are Key to Developing Forces That Provide Sustainable Security

Training and advising the ISF was a key mission in Iraq—but one that the U.S. military was not initially prepared to execute. The U.S. military did not initially provide or adequately prepare advisers to create sustainable security forces in Iraq. In particular, U.S. civilian and military leaders did not anticipate having to train and advise the Iraqi military, and therefore the train and advise mission was slower to start and was superseded by the need to stabilize the country. The adviser mission did improve from 2004 through 2007 but still faced challenges, including the less-than-satisfactory performance of contractors who were hired to train the adviser team members prior to deployment. In addition, the Army did not institutionalize the skills acquired by advisers. The collapse of the Iraqi military when confronted by the Islamic State provides lessons for the future.

U.S. efforts to prepare advisers for what was the number one priority in Iraq for much of the war—build and train a competent Iraqi security force—were slow to get started and reminiscent of efforts in Vietnam, when advisory duty was not seen as career enhancing.[14] The new security force assistance brigades have the potential to address these issues.

Recommendation: Consider Institutionalizing Advisory Capabilities in Army Training, Culture, and Leader Development

A first step in ensuring that advisory capabilities survive within the U.S. Army as it continues to downsize is to incorporate and institutionalize those advisory capabilities into Army training, culture, and leader development.[15] This could include prioritizing advisory capabilities in leader development criteria and training. Currently, the U.S. Army selects brigade and battalion commanders through boards, rightly picking its best to lead soldiers. Prioritizing and recognizing advising as a skill that can enhance success in command has the potential to change a culture that views advising as a second-tier position. Directives, like those by GEN George W. Casey, Jr., in 2010 equating service in transition and provisional reconstruction teams with traditional Army key-development assignments for major theater wars, appear to have made little difference, because the philosophy runs counter to Army culture and the accepted model to advance in one's career.[16]

The U.S. Army, as already noted, is fielding six new security force assistance brigades. The competitiveness of those who serve in these units for promotion and key assignments will demonstrate how much the institution values this mission and could reshape Army culture.

Lesson 7: The Battle for Baghdad Offers Insights About How to Prepare for Future Urban Combat

The Battle for Baghdad offers many lessons for how the Army can prepare for potential future urban combat operations. There is increased awareness that future military operations will almost certainly have to contend with the challenges presented by large urban areas, including megacities with populations greater than 10 million people.

---

[14] On perceptions of advisory duty during the Vietnam War, see Andrew J. Birtle, *U.S. Army Counterinsurgency and Contingency Operations Doctrine, 1942–1975*, Washington, D.C.: U.S. Army Center of Military History, 2006, p. 451. Birtle writes,

> Many soldiers were also convinced, rightly or otherwise, that advisory duty was detrimental to their careers. Sincere and repeated efforts by the Army to dispel this belief, as well as to improve the quality of the advisory effort through career incentives and increased education, never succeeded in overcoming the officer corps' innate aversion for this key component of American policy.

[15] See Remi Hajjar, "What Lessons Did We Learn (or Re-Learn) About Military Advising after 9/11?" *Military Review,* November–December 2014. As Hajjar recommends, "Institutionalizing a concentration on military advising, including an effectual advisor training center, while preserving relevant soft-skill programs (such as culture centers, culture education and training, and other helpful culture-based initiatives) will help the military to remain balanced and well prepared for multifaceted future contingencies" (p. 74).

[16] Gina Cavallaro, "War Zone Training Will Garner Command Credit," *Army Times,* June 19, 2008.

Though not a megacity, Baghdad did have some 5–7 million residents. The final part of that battle—the battle of Sadr City—centered on a dense urban area containing about 2 million residents. Army forces gradually "shrank the problem" in Baghdad by using presence, walls to segregate neighborhoods and direct the flow of traffic in and out, integrated operations with conventional and special operations forces, highly integrated cross-agency intelligence, and a host of other innovative methods to secure the city and protect its population. In Sadr City, a brigade commander had resources at his disposal never imagined at that level before the Battle for Baghdad. This battle offers many insights and potential lessons for how the Army might fight in dense urban areas in the future.

Recommendation: Understand and Institutionalize Lessons from the U.S. Army's Recent Urban Warfare Experiences

The U.S. Army has undertaken a range of studies, both internally and in conjunction with external groups, on the broader question of urban operations and megacities. The Army should continue this work but understand that each city is an independent entity. Thus, the doctrine, organization, training, materiel, leadership and education, personnel, and facilities process should focus on specific cases of where the Army might be engaged in urban combat and of what types of adversaries it will likely face. Additionally, many of the solutions employed in Baghdad relied on infrastructure established over years that would not be available immediately during expeditionary operations and perhaps would make U.S. forces vulnerable if they were to face adversaries with greater capabilities than the insurgents had in Baghdad.

Lesson 8: Army Professional Military Education Is Critical in Preparing Army Leaders for the Future

The U.S. professional military education (PME) system, while extensive, did not prepare officers for the civil war and insurgency in which they found themselves following major combat operations in Iraq in 2003. This was most apparent at the senior levels, where operations had to be designed to achieve policy and strategic goals. Indeed, a U.S. Army study on Army training and leader development noted in 2003 that "officers are concerned that the officer education system does not provide them with the skills for success in full spectrum operations."[17] The report also noted that the officer education system has been "largely untouched since the end of the Cold War" and that it "is out of synch with Army needs."[18]

---

[17] Department of the Army, *The Army Training and Leader Development Panel Officer Study Report to The Army*, Arlington, Va., 2003, p. 6.

[18] Department of the Army, 2003, p. 22. See also Henry A. Leonard, J. Michael Polich, Jeffrey D. Peterson, Ronald E. Sortor, and S. Craig Moore, *Something Old, Something New: Army Leader Development in a Dynamic Environment*, Santa Monica, Calif.: RAND Corporation, MG-281-A, 2006.

Similarly, a 2002 RAND report prepared for the U.S. Army confirmed the Army report's finding, noting, "What appears to be missing from both the CGSOC [Command and General Staff Officer Course] and Army War College core curricula are any in-depth examinations of actual post–Cold War other-than-MTW [major theater war] experiences to provide students an understanding of the nondoctrinal realities these operations imposed on Army senior leaders."[19] In that same report, the perspectives of several general officers (Kevin Byrnes, William C. Crouch, Montgomery Meigs, Eric Shinseki) on their readiness for command in ongoing operations in Bosnia were both candid and concerning.

As they were in Bosnia, senior U.S. commanders were in a state of unpreparedness in the aftermath of major combat operations in Iraq, but operating in a much more lethal and complex environment. Their PME experiences had focused on preparing for operations against the same adversary encountered during Operation Desert Storm—the conventional military of Saddam—that had been so handily defeated by AirLand Battle doctrine. Neither the Army nor the other services and joint PME systems had done much to prepare leaders for military governance and rebuilding the institutions of a collapsed nation.

Another pattern emerged similar to what had happened in Bosnia. General Crouch started a program to pass on lessons learned from Bosnia, but it was not an Army-wide initiative, and the learning was local.[20] This is not dissimilar to General Casey starting the Phoenix Academy to "train the trainers" to work with the Iraqi army and the counterinsurgency academy to prepare incoming leaders for the fight in Iraq. Both of these initiatives were needed because the U.S. Army education and doctrine systems had not caught up to the problem Casey was facing.[21] In December 2006, the U.S. Army and Marine Corps published doctrine and adopted institution-wide approaches to the challenges of Iraq and Afghanistan.[22]

The institution at which the U.S. Army prepares the majority of its senior leaders is the U.S. Army War College, whose students are selected for attendance based on their potential for future service at the colonel and general officer levels.[23] A review of Army War College course directives shows that the institution eventually caught up to

---

[19] David E. Johnson, "Preparing Potential Senior Army Leaders for the Future: An Assessment of Leader Development Efforts in the Post–Cold War Era," Santa Monica, Calif.: RAND Corporation, IP-224-A, 2002, p. 19.

[20] Johnson, 2002, pp. 12–13.

[21] George W. Casey, Jr., *Strategic Reflections: Operation Iraqi Freedom—July 2004–February 2007*, Washington, D.C.: National Defense University Press, October 2012, pp. 61, 73–74.

[22] Field Manual 3-24, *Counterinsurgency*, Washington, D.C.: Headquarters, Department of the Army, December 2006.

[23] The majority of Army officers attend the Army War College, although many attend joint PME at the National Defense University, attend other service war colleges, or participate in a variety of fellowship opportunities. The Army War College, however, is the institution where the Army largely shapes the curriculum.

what was happening in the wars. It shifted from a focus on major theater war and military operations other than war in 2002 to a curriculum in 2005 that included counterinsurgency and counterterrorism.[24] The key question that still remains is: What needs to happen to Army PME to ensure that senior leaders are prepared for an environment like the one in Iraq following major combat operations?

Recommendation: Prepare Senior Leaders for the Full Range of Operations in Which They Will Operate

Studies on the need for PME and how it should be reformed are exhaustive. Thus, it is difficult to make a recommendation on what to do in PME, given that it has long been recognized and advertised that one of its central missions is to improve critical thinking. Then–Brigadier General David A. Fastabend commented on this in 2004: "Most Army schools open with the standard bromide: We are not going to teach you what to think . . . we are going to teach you how to think. They rarely do."[25] It is beyond the scope of this report to do much more than echo the observations made by James Carafano of the Heritage Foundation in his May 2009 testimony before the House Armed Services Committee's Sub-Committee on Oversight and Investigations:

> Military schools had changed only modestly since the end of the Cold War. Preparing to fight a known enemy required certain skills and knowledge, and professional education focused on those narrow areas. As a result, officer schools and development programs continued to train and promote leaders with skills and attributes to meet the needs of the 20th century, not future challenges.[26]

PME should use case studies and war games to teach officers vicariously about the U.S. Army's role across the range of operations. Since 2003, the focus has necessarily been on the irregular wars in which the Army was deeply engaged. Broadening the curricula is particularly important as the Army broadens its focus to preparing for high-end adversaries (for instance, Russia and China) while retaining the hard-won lessons of the past 15 years. For many officers, major combat operations against competent, well-armed adversaries are as unfamiliar as irregular warfare was in 2003. PME can provide future senior Army leaders with the intellectual underpinnings to be able

---

[24] See U.S. Army War College, "Directive Academic Year 2002: Core Curriculum Course 4: Implementing National Military Strategy," Carlisle Barracks, Pa., 2001; and U.S. Army War College, "Directive Academic Year 2002: Core Curriculum Course 4: Implementing National Military Strategy, Carlisle Barracks, Pa., 2005.

[25] David A. Fastabend and Robert H. Simpson, "'Adapt or Die': The Imperative for a Culture of Innovation in the United States Army," *Army Magazine*, February 2004, p. 20.

[26] James Jay Carafano, "20 Years Later: Professional Military Education," testimony before the Subcommittee on Oversight and Investigations, House Armed Services Committee, Washington, D.C., May 20, 2009.

to understand the tactical, operational, and strategic implications of a range of operational environments.[27]

This broader approach to PME should also improve the ability of senior Army leaders to advise civilian appointees and senior officers about whether a strategy will achieve policy objectives. Again, this is a perennial question and has been given exhaustive treatment in the literature on civil-military relations ever since Samuel Huntington's 1959 classic *The Soldier and the State: The Theory and the Politics of Civil-Military Relations*.[28]

PME should teach officers to understand the dynamics of what has happened in the past as a way to think about the future. Furthermore, PME should prepare officers to provide better military advice and plans to civilian policymakers based on empirical analysis, which enables policymakers to make better decisions or to at least understand the potential consequences of those decisions.

Final Thoughts

Over the past 14 years, the U.S. Army—largely trained, organized, and equipped in 2003 to "dominate land warfare," with the expectation that an army so prepared "also provides the ability to dominate any situation in military operations other than war"— has adapted in combat to meet the demands it faced on the ground after the collapse of the Saddam regime.[29] Tactical units generally adapted quickly, but they did not have a strategic or doctrinal framework to give that adaptation coherence and any linkage to policy objectives, which were initially unrealistic. Eventually, the U.S. Army as an institution caught up to practice in theater and provided the forces and capabilities needed to win the Battle for Baghdad.

These adaptations were extraordinarily broad-ranging: building and advising the ISF, advising Iraqi ministries, staffing provisional reconstruction teams, and accomplishing a host of other missions that DoD and other U.S. government agencies had not sufficiently prepared for before Operation Iraqi Freedom. The challenge now is to shape the U.S. Army for the future detailed in the Army Operating Concept, while institutionalizing the hard-learned lessons of the past 15 years. Instability and insurgency are almost certainly part of that future, and if history is any guide, the United States will look to the Army to deal with these challenges. More than the other ser-

---

[27] For a discussion of the implications of operating against a range of adversaries, see David E. Johnson, *Hard Fighting: Israel in Lebanon and Gaza*, Santa Monica, Calif.: RAND Corporation, MG-1085-A/AF, 2011a, pp. 148–181.

[28] Samuel P. Huntington, *The Soldier and the State: The Theory and Politics of Civil-Military Relations*, Cambridge, Mass.: Harvard University Press, 1957.

[29] Field Manual 3-0, *Operations*, Washington, D.C.: Headquarters, Department of the Army, 2001, p. vii.

vices, the Army is charged with providing security and transitional military governance in the aftermath of successful major combat operations. Thus, the ultimate goal of this report is to help the U.S. Army continue to institutionalize the lessons from the Iraq War and the Battle for Baghdad as it prepares for an uncertain future.

Acknowledgments

This report would not have been possible without the assistance of scores of people. They are too many to list here, but the extensive footnotes included in the report acknowledge them. They gave unstintingly of their time and helped us gain access to key documents. In particular, we thank those who gave their time to be interviewed by our research team, and we thank the Operation Iraqi Freedom Study Group, Office of the Chief of Staff, U.S. Army, which provided us with transcripts of hundreds of additional interviews.

We also thank Timothy Muchmore from our sponsor, the U.S. Army Quadrennial Defense Review Office, Office of the Deputy Chief of Staff, G-8, for providing essential and enthusiastic support for this project. He enabled us to gain access to important sources of information—both people and documentation.

We owe a particular debt of gratitude to our three reviewers: Richard Darilek, Walter Perry, and Gordon Rudd. Together, they brought a wealth of experience to the review of this report, some of it first-hand in Iraq, and their thoughtful and incisive comments have greatly improved this report. We remain, of course, responsible for any errors or omissions.

Abbreviations

AEI	American Enterprise Institute
BCT	brigade combat team
CA	civil affairs
CENTCOM	U.S. Central Command
CFLCC	Coalition Forces Land Component Command
CIA	Central Intelligence Agency
CJCS	Chairman of the Joint Chiefs of Staff
CJTF	Combined Joint Task Force
CMATT	Coalition Military Assistance Training Team
CPA	Coalition Provisional Authority
DoD	U.S. Department of Defense
EPW	enemy prisoner of war
ESG	Executive Steering Group
FIF	Free Iraqi Forces
IAG	Iraq Assistance Group
ICDC	Iraqi Civil Defense Corps
IED	improvised explosive device
I-MEF	I Marine Expeditionary Force
IMSG	Institute for Military Support to Governance
ISF	Iraqi Security Forces

JCS	Joint Chiefs of Staff
MNC-I	Multi-National Corps–Iraq
MNF-I	Multi-National Force–Iraq
MNSTC-I	Multi-National Security Transition Command–Iraq
MOD	Ministry of Defense
MOI	Ministry of Interior
NATO	North Atlantic Treaty Organization
NCO	noncommissioned officer
NSC	U.S. National Security Council
NSPD	National Security Presidential Directive
OIF Study Group	Operation Iraqi Freedom Study Group, Office of the Chief of Staff, U.S. Army
OPLAN	Operation Plan
ORHA	Office of Reconstruction and Humanitarian Assistance
OSD	Office of the Secretary of Defense
PME	professional military education
PRT	Provincial Reconstruction Team
SFAB	security force assistance brigade
SI	skill identifier
SOCOM	U.S. Special Operations Command
SOFA	Status of Forces Agreement
SSE	sensitive site exploitation
U.N.	United Nations
UK	United Kingdom
USAID	U.S. Agency for International Development
USF-I	U.S. Forces–Iraq
WMD	weapon of mass destruction

CHAPTER ONE

Introduction

Major combat operations in Iraq culminated for the U.S. Army with the now famous "Thunder Run," during which the 2nd Brigade of the 3rd Infantry Division dashed from the Baghdad airport into the heart of the city to secure the Republican Palace and other key government buildings. This dramatic exploitation in April 2003 ended the first phase of the Battle for Baghdad and ushered in a multiyear effort to secure Baghdad, install a functioning government, and repair infrastructure. During this period, the Multi-National Force–Iraq (MNF-I) and the newly created Iraqi Security Forces (ISF) tried many approaches to securing Baghdad and kept a record of attempts, most of which did not succeed, but all of which yielded important insights into urban warfare. Finally, in late 2006 and 2007, an approach was developed that succeeded, and over the following year or more, the city was brought under control for some time. However, Baghdad and Iraq as a whole later descended into chaos.

This report focuses on identifying lessons for the U.S. Army from the Battle for Baghdad. It is also the first effort in a research stream designed both to capture key lessons for helping the U.S. Army and the U.S. Department of Defense (DoD) retain institutional knowledge and capabilities (as addressed by the Quadrennial Defense Review) and to serve as an institutional history of the Army's efforts in Iraq and Afghanistan from 2001 to 2016.

Study Approach

The study on which this report is based consisted of the following four tasks:

1. Build the evidentiary base for a history of the battle and analysis of urban combat using primary and secondary sources.
2. Develop an initial historical outline and analytical framework for subsequent analysis.
3. Interview key players from all phases of the battle.
4. Finalize the history of the battle, draw key lessons for urban combat, and examine the strategic lessons learned from the conflict.

To complete these tasks, we drew on a wide variety of sources. The literature review included both primary sources (specifically, memoirs of the key participants) and secondary sources (consisting of previous RAND studies and journalists' accounts and histories). In addition, we consulted records from more than 100 interviews conducted by other researchers.[1] We also held discussions with 51 key military and civilian leaders, representing a cross-section of perspectives. Ultimately, the information from our literature review, our interviews, and transcripts from outside interviews helped us identify both lessons that the U.S. Army has already institutionalized and lessons that it has not institutionalized but should.

Two important caveats, however, should be noted. First, to this day, the Iraq War remains an emotional, highly polarizing event with widely divergent accounts among the central actors. When there is controversy among the key actors, we attempt to present the various sides of the debate.

Second, this report does not draw extensively on archival data for the simple reason that much of the documentation remains either classified or unavailable for research. Unfortunately, we could not overcome this constraint within the time frame and resources allocated to this study. Although we carried out extensive interviews, we acknowledge that there are still untapped data sources.

Organization of This Report

The Battle for Baghdad is not one homogeneous event, but rather a series of distinct phases. For the soldiers and civilians who directly participated in the war, the watershed moments of their experiences differ depending on where and when they were involved in the conflict. The soldiers who fought in the first stages of the Iraq War fought a vastly different battle from the one fought by soldiers deployed during the later Surge. Civilians involved in prewar planning in Washington, D.C., experienced a different war from the one of those who staffed the embassy as it was shelled from Sadr City.

The Iraq War had several major turning points—the formation of the Coalition Provisional Authority (CPA), the Samarra Mosque bombing, the appointment of GEN David Petraeus, and the 2008 Battle of Sadr City, to list only a few. Just as crucial to understanding this war are the minor events that occurred between landmark moments. This report captures both, and in doing so, it endeavors to create a full picture of this multiyear conflict.

---

[1] We thank the Operation Iraqi Freedom Study Group, Office of the Chief of Staff, U.S. Army (OIF Study Group) for providing transcripts of these interviews and giving us permission to cite them in our work. Many of those interviews were conducted by the OIF Study Group, and many were collected as part of its research efforts but conducted by others.

This report is divided into chapters based on the war's major phases: the prewar period and major combat operations; the occupation; GEN George W. Casey, Jr.'s, command; the Surge; and the withdrawal. The chapters not only present the war's major phases but also discuss the seemingly minor events without which the complete story of the Iraq War cannot be told.

The analysis is framed, therefore, by five distinct periods, and each is mined for lessons. Discussion ranges widely, describing events and actions from the national command level down to tactics and techniques employed by combat brigades. It also includes decisions and actions by both military and civilian leaders, because both had an effect on ground operations. However, the lessons focus on actions and events that the U.S. Army needs to anticipate and prepare for, even if the actions required might normally be considered within the purview of civilian authorities.

Our analysis begins in Chapter Two, with prewar planning. That period is important not only for what it focused on but also for what it did not include, which might be more significant. Several problems encountered after the intervention arose or were worsened because they were not anticipated and, as a result, got no attention in the planning phase. Many of the planning gaps occurred because of faulty assumptions made by both military and civilian leaders, sometimes over the objections of knowledgeable and experienced people. But when the unanticipated problems presented themselves, the U.S. military lacked the wherewithal to deal with them. The chapter discusses the planning that went on in both the U.S. government and U.S. Army.

The second period of interest was the occupation of Baghdad.[2] Chapter Three begins by describing the military situation after U.S. forces had taken control of key segments of the city. It chronicles the initial efforts to establish order and begin the reconstruction of damaged critical facilities. It also describes the civilian agencies established to assist in restoring the Iraqi government and some of the measures those offices implemented.

In addition to these topics, Chapter Three describes the early attempts to stabilize Baghdad. It focuses on the first year, from the occupation of the city until April 2004. It covers the shift from conventional operations to an urban counterinsurgency effort. It describes the two organizations set up sequentially to oversee the pacification and reconstruction operations and the effort to rebuild the Iraqi security forces.

Chapter Four describes events in Baghdad from the summer of 2004 until early 2007. It lays out key issues confronting both U.S. civilian and military leaders, describes the military situation in the city, and chronicles the key challenges facing

---

[2] We use the term *occupation* to describe the second phase of the Iraq War, for two reasons. First, the U.S. Army is specifically tasked with "occupation" by DoD Directive 5100.01 (DoD, *Functions of the Department of Defense and Its Major Components*, DoD Directive 5100.01, Washington, D.C., December 21, 2010b). Second, the United States was labeled as the "occupying power" in United Nations (U.N.) Security Council Resolution 1483, which authorized the CPA (United Nations Security Council, Resolution 1483 (2003) [on the Situation Between Iraq and Kuwait], New York, May 22, 2003a).

the embassy in Baghdad. It also discusses the differences in civilian policy views that existed in Washington and Baghdad. It describes the continued efforts to re-create the Iraqi security forces and security institutions during this period. It concludes with the lessons learned.

Chapter Five describes the oft-discussed "Surge," which sent an additional five combat brigades to Iraq. It describes the situation that prompted the Surge, the use of counterinsurgency techniques, and the battle for Sadr City, which crushed the forces of the young cleric Moqtada al-Sadr's Jaysh al-Mahdi militia (also known as the Mahdi Army). The chapter also describes the effort to create the new ISF and the issues that complicated that process. The chapter then provides the differing perspectives on the success of the Surge. It concludes with lessons drawn from this period.

The fifth period, addressed in Chapter Six, is the withdrawal of U.S. forces from Iraq. This chapter describes the aftermath of the Surge, how MNF-I transitioned into the United States Forces–Iraq (USF-I), and how the United States withdrew forces from Iraq. It provides an account of the negotiations conducted by civilians to try to keep an American presence in Iraq and describes the effect of the U.S. withdrawal on the ISF and its increased politicization. The chapter concludes by describing Iraq's collapse in 2014 and explaining why the Islamic State managed to capture large swathes of the northern half of the country a mere two years after American forces withdrew.[3]

Chapter Seven presents overarching lessons derived from the Battle for Baghdad. These are the most important ones for the Army—and DoD as a whole—to digest. The chapter categorizes the lessons from the previous chapters and then presents a series of cross-cutting lessons. These deal with the need to ensure long-term stability; the importance of capacity and capability; the need for high-quality headquarters; the importance of training and advising missions, including the importance of tailoring those efforts so that the force being advised can operate in the absence of U.S. capabilities; the contribution of transition teams and advisers to providing sustainable security; and the future of urban combat. For each lesson, the chapter offers both observations and recommendations.

In the appendix, we provide an overview of the timeline of events during the Battle for Baghdad. This timeline captures the varied experiences of military and civilian leaders involved in the battle's major events and creates an overarching view of a heterogeneous conflict. The timeline juxtaposes key U.S. political and military events and decisions to show the relationship between the two. In some ways, the timeline is a condensed version of the narrative contained within these chapters; it illustrates how

---

[3] The organization's name transliterates from Arabic as al-Dawlah al-Islamiyah fi al-'Iraq wa al-Sham (abbreviated as Da'ish or DAESH). In the West, it is commonly referred to as the Islamic State of Iraq and the Levant (ISIL), the Islamic State of Iraq and Syria, the Islamic State of Iraq and the Sham (both abbreviated as ISIS), or simply as the Islamic State. Arguments abound as to which is the most accurate translation, but here we refer to the group as the Islamic State.

each period of the war gave way to the succeeding phase. The timeline begins in June 2001, when Iraq first came up on the agenda of the U.S. National Security Council (NSC). It finishes in June 2009, when U.S. troops withdrew from Iraqi cities to forward operating bases.

CHAPTER TWO

Prewar Planning

On March 20, 2003, U.S. and coalition forces crossed the Iraqi-Kuwait border and forever changed the course of history, not just for Iraq, but potentially for the United States and the Middle East. The war was a culmination of a long series of events that started with Saddam Hussein's invasion of neighboring Kuwait in 1990 and the 1991 American-led intervention to expel Iraqi forces from the country. In 1991, during Operation Desert Storm, the United States responded by forcibly pushing the Iraqi military back across the border. Although Operation Desert Storm was successful, coalition partners opted not to continue the conflict. After Iraq's Shia and Kurdish population revolted, Saddam violently repressed the mass uprisings that followed. The U.N. intervened and imposed "no-fly" zones over northern and southern Iraq to protect both communities and instituted a series of weapon inspections to ensure that Iraq was dismantling its program for weapons of mass destruction (WMDs).

Throughout the Bill Clinton administration (1993–2001), tensions with Iraq remained high. Iraqi forces repeatedly fired at American pilots patrolling the no-fly zones, obstructed weapon inspections,[1] hid arsenals of WMDs from inspectors,[2] and blocked access to suspected WMD sites.[3] Meanwhile, Saddam provided financial support to families of Palestinian suicide bombers, as well as to families of Palestinians killed in attacks conducted by Hamas, by Islamic Jihad, or in military operations against Israel.[4] His government backed the Kurdistan Worker's Party, a separatist group in Turkey that the United States labeled a terrorist organization, as well as Palestinian splinter groups.[5] In April 1993, Iraq unsuccessfully attempted to assassinate

---

[1] Wright Bryan and Douglas Hopper, "Iraq WMD Timeline: How the Mystery Unraveled," NPR, November 15, 2005.

[2] Frontline, "Saddam Hussein's Weapons of Mass Destruction," Public Broadcasting Service, undated.

[3] CNN, "Journalists Given Tour of Huge Iraqi Palaces," December 19, 1997.

[4] Jarrett Murphy, "Palestinians Get Saddam Charity Checks," CBS News, March 14, 2003.

[5] Council on Foreign Relations, "Terrorist Havens: Iraq," *CFR Backgrounder*, December 1, 2005.

former President George H. W. Bush.[6] In late 1998, Congress passed and President Clinton signed the Iraq Liberation Act, making regime change in Iraq the official policy of the United States.[7]

Suspicions about Iraq's WMD program and frustration over Iraq's continued belligerence spilled over into the administration of President George W. Bush. His initial strategy for dealing with Saddam was to tighten economic sanctions, or, as Secretary of State Colin Powell phrased it, "keeping Saddam in his box."[8] Some Bush advisers pushed for an even more forceful policy. Paul Wolfowitz, who served as Deputy Secretary of Defense in the Bush administration, argued in 1998 that toppling Saddam was necessary to protect U.S. interests in the Gulf region and advocated a more aggressive approach to regime change in Iraq, including the presence of U.S. forces to create a safe haven where Saddam's opposition could organize.[9] Wolfowitz's voice, however, was a minority one until September 11, 2001 (9/11).

The terrorist attacks on New York City and Washington, D.C., fundamentally changed how the Bush administration viewed threats to national security. According to Bush's memoirs, before 9/11, he believed that the United States could manage Saddam.[10] After the attack, his view changed:

> I had just witnessed the damage inflicted by nineteen fanatics armed with box cutters. I could only imagine the destruction possible if an enemy dictator passed his WMD to terrorists. With threats flowing into the Oval Office daily—many of them about chemical, biological, or nuclear weapons—that seemed like a frighteningly real possibility.[11]

The prospect of another terrorist attack drove Bush to action:

> The stakes were too high to trust a dictator's word against the weight of evidence and the consensus of the world. The lesson of 9/11 was that if we waited for a

---

[6] David Von Drehle and R. Jeffrey Smith, "U.S. Strikes Iraq for Plot to Kill Bush," *Washington Post*, June 27, 1993.

[7] Douglas J. Feith, *War and Decision: Inside the Pentagon at the Dawn of the War on Terrorism*, New York: HarperCollins, 2008, p. 182. For a detailed history of this period, see Jefferson P. Marquis, Walter L. Perry, Andrea Mejia, Jerry M. Sollinger, and Vipin Narang, "Genesis of the War," in Walter L. Perry, Richard E. Darilek, Laurinda L. Rohn, and Jerry M. Sollinger, eds., *Operation IRAQI FREEDOM: Decisive War, Elusive Peace*, Santa Monica, Calif.: RAND Corporation, RR-1214-A, 2015.

[8] George W. Bush, *Decision Points*, New York: Crown Publishers, 2010, p. 228.

[9] Paul Wolfowitz, "Rising Up," *New Republic*, Vol. 219, No. 23, December 7, 1998.

[10] Bush, 2010, p. 229.

[11] Bush, 2010, p. 229.

danger to fully materialize, we would have waited too long. I reached a decision: We would confront the threat from Iraq, one way or another.[12]

That decision sent the United States down the road to war in Iraq.

In this chapter, we describe the planning for what would eventually be called Operation Iraqi Freedom. We begin by discussing the civilian planning that went on—and, in some cases, did not go on—inside DoD, NSC, the U.S. Department of State, and the U.S. Agency for International Development (USAID). We then turn to the military planning, which was a contentious process marked by disagreements between the civilian and military leadership over the size of the force to be committed. This discussion covers the guidance given and the various stages of the planning process for what would come to be called Cobra II, the name given to the war plan. We then discuss the planning effort that focused on activities required once Saddam's regime had been deposed. This discussion is followed by an account of Eclipse II, which subsumed much of the postcombat planning effort. As is the case with other chapters, this one ends with the lessons learned from this phase of the operation.

Civilian Prewar Planning

The ruins of the World Trade Center were still smoldering on September 26, 2001, when President Bush asked Secretary of Defense Donald Rumsfeld to examine the military's plans for war with Iraq.[13] With this request, the Bush administration initiated a planning process for a war that now defines his presidency. The planning process from 2001 until the March 2003 intervention involved multiple government agencies and became a complicated, somewhat ad hoc process. Faulty assumptions and insufficient prewar planning for postcombat operations, known as Phase IV, are often blamed for many of the problems that cropped up in the war's early years, and while the merit of this accusation is subject to interpretation, much can and should be learned from how the U.S. government planned for postwar operations prior to the major combat operations.

Central Command and DoD Take the Lead

Under the direction and close supervision of Rumsfeld, GEN Tommy Franks, the commander of U.S. Central Command (CENTCOM), led the planning for the American intervention in Iraq. Developing this plan consumed significant time and manpower, and CENTCOM found itself unable to allocate the personnel required for sufficient

---

[12] Bush, 2010, p. 229.

[13] Donald Rumsfeld, *Known and Unknown: A Memoir*, New York: Sentinel, 2011, p. 425.

Phase IV planning.[14] For this reason, GEN Richard B. Myers, Chairman of the Joint Chiefs of Staff (CJCS), directed Franks to create a special task force devoted to postwar planning. Joint Task Force–4 was stood up. Although plans were being made, civilians at the Pentagon and the State Department had limited access to information about postconflict military plans. One former senior DoD official we spoke with reported that the Office of the Secretary of Defense (OSD) was unable to obtain Phase IV plans from CENTCOM.[15] A former senior State Department official we spoke with found that CENTCOM was mostly focused on securing WMDs and oil fields and capturing Baghdad as quickly as possible, but it did not appear to be planning for certain postconflict scenarios. When this former official asked how the military intended to handle such issues as reprisal killings or sectarian violence, Admiral James Robb, who was CENTCOM's Director of Plans and Policy, frequently responded, "The war plan does not envision this eventuality."[16] Ultimately, Joint Task Force–4's work received little attention within the military.

While Joint Task Force–4 handled postwar planning for CENTCOM, civilians in the Pentagon also initiated a planning process. Around the time President Bush delivered his September 2002 speech to the U.N., in which Bush urged action if Iraqi President Saddam Hussein failed to comply with U.N. Security Council Resolutions, the Office of the Under Secretary of Defense for Policy formed a new office focused entirely on Iraq.[17] Located within the Office of Near East and South Asian Affairs, the Office of Special Plans was the civilian effort in the Pentagon for Phase IV planning. The office developed policy on issues ranging from building a coalition and supporting Iraq's oil sector to achieving de-Ba'athification and organizing a new Iraqi government.[18] The office's vague name was intended to disguise its true focus so as not to compromise the diplomatic efforts to encourage Iraq to surrender its WMDs.[19]

Much of the criticism of the postwar planning process centers on the DoD's Office of Special Plans. DoD claimed that the office was part of the interagency process, which will be discussed in detail later in this chapter, and that the office lacked the authority to dictate policy to other agencies. Feith noted, "The idea that my office

---

[14] Rumsfeld, 2011, p. 485.

[15] Former senior DoD official, interview with the authors, July 7, 2015.

[16] Former senior State Department and CPA official, interview with the authors, June 3, 2015.

[17] George W. Bush, speech delivered to the United Nations General Assembly, New York, September 12, 2002.

[18] Nora Bensahel, Olga Oliker, Keith Crane, Richard R. Brennan, Jr., Heather S. Gregg, Thomas Sullivan, and Andrew Rathmell, *After Saddam: Prewar Planning and the Occupation of Iraq*, Santa Monica, Calif.: RAND Corporation, MG-642-A, 2008, p. 24.

[19] Douglas J. Feith, interview with Gordon Rudd and Ginger Cruz, December 17, 2004, transcript provided to RAND by the OIF Study Group.

did all the postwar planning for Iraq is just a ridiculous over-simplification."[20] Outside DoD, however, many suggest that the office's opaque purpose, if not its very existence, confused normal government processes.[21]

On January 20, 2003, Bush signed National Security Presidential Directive (NSPD)-24, which officially charged DoD with responsibility for postwar Iraq.[22] This led to the creation of the Office of Reconstruction and Humanitarian Assistance (ORHA), which would lead postwar stability operations after the capture of Baghdad. In the years since NSPD-24 was issued, questions have arisen about why responsibility for post-Saddam Iraq was concentrated in the Defense Department.[23] The prominent explanation is that the State Department seemed opposed to the war and some in the Bush administration worried that the department would undermine government plans or policies.[24] For example, there were concerns that the State Department would allow the U.N. to assume control of post-Saddam Iraq.[25] Although the United States wanted U.N. involvement in reconstruction and humanitarian assistance, American officials did not want the U.N. hindering military efforts to hunt terrorists.[26] Given the objections that France and Russia, both Security Council members, raised about intervention, U.N. influence in postwar Iraq beyond reconstruction and humanitarian assistance could have significantly affected the strategy of the United States.

Other accounts suggest that President Bush always intended the Defense Department to lead postwar Iraq. According to Condoleezza Rice, who was the National Security Adviser at the time,

> There was never a question in anyone's mind that the President wanted a single chain of command, and that meant that Defense had to have authority over both the civilian and military side. . . . This became a very post hoc point of contention. . . . But that operations on the ground, both civilian and military, would be under the Defense Department was clear from day one.[27]

---

[20] Douglas J. Feith, interview with Gordon Rudd and Ginger Cruz, December 17, 2004, transcript provided to RAND by the OIF Study Group.

[21] Bensahel et al., 2008, p. 28.

[22] L. Elaine Halchin, *The Coalition Provisional Authority (CPA): Origin, Characteristics, and Institutional Authorities*, Washington, D.C.: Congressional Research Service, RL32370, June 6, 2005.

[23] Charles H. Ferguson, *No End in Sight: Iraq's Descent into Chaos*, New York: Public Affairs, 2008, pp. 71–72. For a comprehensive examination of ORHA, see Gordon W. Rudd, *Reconstructing Iraq: Regime Change, Jay Garner, and the ORHA Story*, Lawrence, Kan.: University of Kansas Press, 2011.

[24] Bensahel et al., 2008, p. 30.

[25] Former senior national security official, interview with the authors, May 21, 2015.

[26] Rumsfeld, 2011, p. 482.

[27] Condoleezza Rice, interview with Jason Awadi and Jeanne Godfroy, U.S. Department of State, Office of the Historian, July 12, 2014, p. 4, transcript provided to RAND by the OIF Study Group.

While the performance of ORHA and its successor, CPA, is often used to discredit DoD's handling of postwar Iraq and to claim that the Department of State should have been in charge, according to Rice, at the time, the interagency did not dispute DoD receiving this responsibility.

After NSPD-24 was issued, Phase IV planning in the Pentagon stalled.[28] According to one source, "Rumsfeld did not seem anxious about the lack of momentum. His assumption was that he and his department would not be organizing a massive nation-building program, but facilitating Iraqi efforts to secure and reconstruct their own country, using their own oil exports to finance whatever was needed."[29] In March 2001, Rumsfeld wrote a short paper describing guidelines that he hoped the administration would adopt when deciding when and how to use military force. The goal of this paper was to encourage President Bush not to use the military to achieve nonmilitary objectives, such as resolving another country's domestic political disputes, overseeing a period of reconstruction, providing domestic security in another nation, and democracy-building.[30] Rumsfeld was not alone in his dislike for nation-building: Rice, another architect of George Bush's foreign policy and the National Security Adviser during his first term, famously stated, "Carrying out civil administration and police functions is simply going to degrade the American capability to do the things America has to do. We don't need to have the 82nd Airborne escorting kids to kindergarten."[31] Consequently, postwar planning at the Pentagon assumed that nation-building was unnecessary and instead focused on transitioning responsibility for Iraq to Iraqis whenever possible.

Rumsfeld also feared that extensive postwar planning would undermine the administration's other efforts: "This could signal that America considered war inevitable and derail President Bush's diplomatic efforts, which continued almost until the day the war began."[32] Exactly to which diplomatic efforts Rumsfeld referred is unclear, because two lines of action were being conducted simultaneously. First, the Bush administration expended significant effort to garner support for the war from the international community while pursuing the passage of U.N. Security Council Resolution 1441, which passed on November 8, 2002, and stated that this was Saddam's final opportunity "to comply with international demands regarding Iraq's WMD program."[33] It was possible that potential allies could have been less likely to support

---

[28] Michael R. Gordon and Bernard E. Trainor, *Cobra II: The Inside Story of the Invasion and Occupation of Iraq*, New York: Vintage Books, 2006, pp. 141–142.

[29] Gordon and Trainor, 2006, pp. 141–142.

[30] Rumsfeld, 2011, pp. 481–482.

[31] Michael R. Gordon, "The 2000 Campaign: The Military; Bush Would Stop U.S. Peacekeeping in Balkan Fights," *New York Times*, October 21, 2000.

[32] Rumsfeld, 2011, p. 486.

[33] Rumsfeld, 2011, p. 441.

American actions or contribute to the war effort if they viewed extensive postwar planning as a sign that the United States had decided to go to war regardless of where its allies stood on the issue. The other diplomatic effort Rumsfeld may have alluded to was the effort to convince Saddam to abandon his WMD program. If Saddam became aware of postwar planning, he also might have concluded that war was inevitable, thereby making him less willing to comply with U.N. or American demands.

The lack of postwar planning for reconstruction hurt the United States once rebuilding Iraq and establishing democratic institutions became an objective. Whether nation-building was the appropriate approach to take in Iraq is beside the point; DoD was unprepared to lead postwar Iraq once the administration decided not to hand authority over to Iraqis immediately. Moreover, DoD's assertion that Iraqi police forces would maintain domestic security was flawed, and in the absence of a military-like power able and willing to maintain order, destructive looting broke out in Baghdad. Although many of the problems experienced after the fall of Baghdad are attributable to DoD's philosophy on postwar planning, other actors in the interagency also failed to varying extents.

The Absent State Department

The State Department was marginalized from much of the planning occurring within DoD and CENTCOM. Consequently, the State Department had little influence over the plans that were made. Officials from the Bureau of Intelligence and Research, the State Department's intelligence apparatus, reported being ignored by DoD in meetings focused on postwar scenario planning and being excluded from a DoD-sponsored war game about Iraq in the summer of 2002.[34] Aside from one important line of effort, the Future of Iraq Project, the State Department had minimal sway over the postwar planning process.

Even within the State Department, the Future of Iraq Project was a little-known effort,[35] and yet it was "the broadest assessment of postwar requirements that would be conducted within the U.S. government."[36] As Special Adviser to the Assistant Secretary of State for the Bureau of Near Eastern Affairs, Thomas S. Warrick headed up the Future of Iraq Project. He claimed,

> The purpose of the Future of Iraq Project was to engage in a process of practical planning and to try to tap into the pool of Iraqi American ex-pats . . . Iraqi Americans, Iraqi Europeans, people from northern Iraq, people who had lived in the Middle East. We were reaching out to doctors, engineers, lawyers, business people,

---

[34] Bensahel et al., 2008, p. 30.

[35] Bensahel et al., 2008, p. 31.

[36] Bensahel et al., 2008, p. 29.

people who . . . had, in many cases, consciously not participated in the Iraqi political opposition.[37]

These individuals were separated into 17 working groups broken down by topic, such as transitional justice, public finance, democratic principles, defense policy, local governance, and technical issues, such as agriculture and water.[38] Each working group comprised 15–20 Iraqis representing many different opposition groups, as well as several international experts. American officials from various agencies moderated the working groups, which produced reports, plans, briefings, and so on for each group's topic. For example, the transitional justice group produced more than 700 pages of recommended modifications to Iraq's legal code, including the criminal code, nationality law, penal code, and civil code, as well as draft reforms for the judiciary, prison system, and de-Ba'athification.[39] In anticipation of U.S. action in Iraq, the State Department began the process of developing the Future of Iraq Project in October 2001, and the first working group met in July 2002. Working groups continued to meet until the spring of 2003.

Interestingly, the approximately 200 Iraqis and 40 international experts involved in the project identified many of the reconstruction and governance issues that the United States confronted after the collapse of the Ba'athist regime. For example, the transitional justice working group predicted that looting would be a major problem. The public finance working group warned that job creation, rather than other financial issues (such as currency stability), would be an instrumental economic tool for preserving peace. The democratic principles working group emphasized the importance of transitioning to an Iraqi-led government as quickly as possible,[40] although there was debate about whether the government should be led by Iraqi exiles or composed of Iraqis who had stayed in the country. As discussed later, this debate also took place among the State Department, Central Intelligence Agency (CIA), and DoD. The democratic principles group also agreed that Iraq should be democratic, federal, and governed by the rule of law, all of which would come to be enshrined in the 2005 Iraq constitution. Moreover, the democratic principles working group warned against

---

[37] Thomas S. Warrick, interview with Gordon Rudd, November 10, 2004, transcript provided to RAND by the OIF Study Group.

[38] Thomas S. Warrick, interview with Gordon Rudd, November 10, 2004, transcript provided to RAND by the OIF Study Group.

[39] Thomas S. Warrick, interview with Gordon Rudd, November 10, 2004, transcript provided to RAND by the OIF Study Group.

[40] The view was shared by the Defense Department, although DoD believed that Iraqi exiles should lead post-Saddam Iraq because internal leaders were unknown to the U.S. government and would have to be vetted for Ba'athist ties.

appointing an American general to govern Iraq after Saddam fell, but it did not discuss the prospect of an American civilian governing the country.[41]

The project's influence on the broader planning process was limited, however. Secretary Rumsfeld acknowledged the project's utility in the abstract, but he claimed that the lack of concrete plans curtailed the project's usefulness in practice. He asserted,

> In fact, senior DoD officials did review and consult those papers, finding some of them to be helpful. But the Future of Iraq project—outlining broad concepts—did not constitute postwar planning in any sense of the word. There were no operational steps outlined in them nor any detailed suggestions about how to handle various problems.[42]

Feith agreed. He described the products from the project as a series of papers that contained nothing immediately executable.[43] Former Ambassador Robin L. Raphel echoed DoD's position: "To say there was a blueprint out there, which we should have followed, that's simply not the case."[44] However, not everyone at the State Department shared Warrick's view of the purpose of the Future of Iraq Project. A former senior State Department official we spoke with described the Future of Iraq Project as "an effort to keep the opposition occupied so that they weren't calling for regime change all the time,"[45] which may have contributed to why the Future of Iraq Project's effort was not considered more seriously by the broader policy community.

Another potential factor that undermined the influence of the Future of Iraq Project was its inclusion of non-Americans and other individuals who lacked security clearances. For example, Rumsfeld tasked Michael Mobbs to prepare for dealing with Iraq's oil infrastructure. Mobbs met with Warrick once to discuss the Future of Iraq Project's insights, but he then claimed, "It would have been, in my judgment, completely inappropriate for me, or anybody in my group, to go and talk to anybody who did not have the clearances [i.e., the Iraqi expatriates on the Future of Iraq project] or the need to know about our small part of the pre-war planning."[46]

Even after ORHA and CPA were created and tasked with managing post-Saddam Iraq, the Future of Iraq Project's influence remained only moderate. Warrick spent

---

[41] Thomas S. Warrick, interview with Gordon Rudd, November 10, 2004, transcript provided to RAND by the OIF Study Group.

[42] Rumsfeld, 2011, p. 486.

[43] Douglas J. Feith, interview with Gordon Rudd and Ginger Cruz, January 27, 2005, transcript provided to RAND by the OIF Study Group.

[44] Robin L. Raphel, interview with Gordon Rudd, November 15, 2005, transcript provided to RAND by the OIF Study Group.

[45] Former senior State Department and CPA official, interview with the authors, June 3, 2015.

[46] Michael Mobbs, interview with Gordon Rudd, December 12, 2005, transcript provided to RAND by the OIF Study Group.

only a week at the Pentagon working with retired LTG Jay Garner, who was appointed to lead ORHA in late January 2003.[47] Warrick was supposed to join Garner's team, but he was subsequently nixed from the team—allegedly for political reasons.[48] It is unclear how much Garner incorporated Warrick's insights into his plans, and Garner was unsuccessful in bringing Warrick onto ORHA's staff. Both Raphel and a former senior State Department official we spoke with, who coordinated war planning between DoD and the State Department, noted that the materials produced by the Future of Iraq Project were useful in their work for CPA.[49] Whether other CPA officials consulted these documents is not known.

While multiple people involved in postwar planning criticized the Future of Iraq Project's recommendations for their inability to produce actionable plans, much of the project's work seems to have been disregarded entirely. There are two reasons many of the problems the project predicted were not planned for. First, Warrick's counterparts in other agencies were not inclined to collaborate with him because they saw no actionable items in the Future of Iraq Project's work. Second, the State Department did not press other officials involved in postwar planning to take seriously the potential problems that the project identified. Had the State Department and other agencies recognized the value of the Future of Iraq Project's insights and more actively promoted them, the project's influence on the planning process could have been more profound.

The National Security Council: The "Primary" Coordinator

The NSC intended to coordinate the interagency's approach to postwar Iraq, and DoD, the State Department, and USAID did in fact participate in the interagency process run through the NSC. This planning process began at the behest of the Joint Chiefs of Staff (JCS), which wanted to include the interagency in the Iraq exercises being run by the JCS and CENTCOM.[50] Then-LTG George Casey, who at the time was the JCS's Director of Strategic Plans and Policy (J5), formed the Executive Steering Group (ESG), which served as a coordination body for the Joint Staff, Office of the Vice President, the State Department's Bureau of Political-Military Affairs, the CIA, and the Office of the Under Secretary of Defense for Policy. The NSC's Frank Miller was assigned to lead the ESG, which began meeting in August 2002. The ESG met three times each week, and attendance grew to include the State Department's Bureau of Near Eastern Affairs and Bureau of European and Eurasian Affairs, the Office of the Under Secretary of Defense (Comptroller), and the Joint Staff Directorate of Logis-

---

[47] Thomas S. Warrick, interview with Gordon Rudd, November 10, 2004, transcript provided to RAND by the OIF Study Group.

[48] Former ORHA official, interview with the authors, May 12, 2016.

[49] Former senior State Department and CPA official, interview with the authors, June 3, 2015.

[50] Bensahel et al., 2008, pp. 21–22.

tics (J4), as well as representatives from various offices within the NSC.[51] The ESG was supposed to coordinate plans among these agencies, and, when its members could not reach a consensus, issues were passed to the Deputies Committee for approval. If consensus could not be reached at that level, issues were then passed to the principals.

The ESG focused mainly on war planning and dealt with political-military issues, such as securing basing and overflight rights.[52] However, the ESG also served as an umbrella for several working groups, one of which was the Iraq Relief and Reconstruction group led by the NSC's Elliot Abrams and Robin Cleveland of the Office of Management and Budget. It is unclear to what extent the Iraq Relief and Reconstruction group worked with the Future of Iraq Project. Moreover, Miller met with Warrick only once for a briefing on the project's work.[53] According to Miller, no actionable items came out of that briefing, and Warrick did not recommend further collaboration between the NSC and the Future of Iraq Project. Whether this was a symptom of problems with the Future of Iraq Project or with the ESG's struggles, the interagency process is still subject to debate, and both sets of problems likely contributed to the absence of the Future of Iraq Project in the NSC's planning process.

Two factors undermined the effectiveness of the ESG.[54] First, the same agencies or the same people within each agency did not always attend ESG meetings. Second, the ESG focused too heavily on war planning. As a result, no agreed-on plan for post-Saddam Iraq that had gone through a thorough interagency process ever emerged.

USAID: Underdeveloped Planning

USAID initiated its planning for post-Saddam Iraq later than did DoD or the State Department. Informal planning began in the summer of 2002, and plans made in the fall were revised until major combat operations began.[55] The agency did not receive formal tasking to start planning until 2003.[56] USAID's plans focused on postconflict humanitarian assistance and reconstruction—including electricity, water, sewers, public health, education, local governance, agriculture, infrastructure, and food—but were hindered by time constraints and a lack of information about conditions in Iraq.

USAID carries out most of its projects through contracting, and the contracting process was well under way by the time the war started. The director of USAID, Andrew Natsios, authorized $63 million for local procurement of Iraqi relief and recon-

---

[51] Bensahel et al., 2008, p. 22.

[52] Gordon and Trainor, 2006, p. 148.

[53] Franklin C. Miller, interview with Gordon Rudd, November 20, 2007, transcript provided to RAND by the OIF Study Group.

[54] Bensahel et al., 2008, p. 23.

[55] Bensahel et al., 2008, p. 33.

[56] Bensahel et al., 2008, p. 33.

struction on January 16, 2003.[57] Most contracts focused on humanitarian assistance, such as refugee aid, rather than reconstruction projects, such as electricity generation.[58] According to Wendy Chamberlain, who worked on postwar planning for USAID, this was because of the NSC's assertion that funding for reconstruction was not necessary because Iraq would be able to fund its own reconstruction.[59] Chamberlain herself asserts that USAID was nearly left out of the NSC planning process, stating that USAID was not included until Robin Cleveland, who trusted Chamberlain, reached out to her and brought USAID into the process.[60]

It is difficult to judge USAID's performance in prewar planning because it appears to have been hindered by the NSC's assumption that reconstruction planning and funding would not be necessary. In retrospect, this assumption turns out to have been false, and it is unknown how effective USAID planning might have been on reconstruction issues.

The Unsettled Debate: Governing Iraq After Saddam

As plans for Iraq moved forward, disagreement emerged over how Iraq should be governed after the fall of the Ba'ath regime. This difference of opinion was evident even at the cabinet and subcabinet levels. The Defense Department wanted to return control of Iraq to Iraqis as quickly as possible and establish a government composed of "externals," Saddam's exiled opponents. The State Department wanted to form a democratic government chosen by the Iraqi people themselves, even if this required American rule over Iraq until such a government could be formed. These two positions proved irreconcilable, and in the words of Secretary Rumsfeld, "trying to achieve a bridge or compromise between the two different approaches was not a solution."[61]

From DoD's perspective, creating a government composed of Iraqi exiles, similar to what the United States had done in Afghanistan, would enable the military to withdraw from Iraq as quickly as possible. Rumsfeld believed that Iraqi exiles were capable of running Iraq: "These Iraqi 'externals,' many living in the United States or London, included some highly educated and skilled professionals. Some clearly had ambition. While by no means monolithic in their politics or their views, they shared an interest in Iraq's freedom and success."[62] This government could temporarily and, in DoD's opinion, legitimately govern Iraq until elections could be scheduled. Another reason DoD

---

[57] Bensahel et al., 2008, p. 34.

[58] Bensahel et al., 2008, p. 34.

[59] Wendy Chamberlin, interview with the Middle East Institute, April 18, 2007, p. 1, interview notes provided to RAND by the OIF Study Group.

[60] Wendy Chamberlin, interview with the Middle East Institute, April 18, 2007, p. 1, interview notes provided to RAND by the OIF Study Group.

[61] Rumsfeld, 2011, p. 487.

[62] Rumsfeld, 2011, p. 490.

favored a government formed of externals was because this approach avoided the time-consuming process of vetting local Iraqi candidates for their ties to the Ba'athists.[63]

Consequently, the Office of Special Plans spent considerable time throughout the summer and fall of 2002 collaborating with exiles and Kurdish groups, which were also considered externals. This effort culminated in a large conference held with Iraqi opposition groups in London in December 2002. Although DoD wanted to transition governing authority to the Iraqis as quickly as possible, Rumsfeld claims that he did not promote above other exiles the leadership of Ahmed Chalabi, the controversial leader of the Iraqi National Congress, who had significant political influence leading up to the intervention.[64]

In an effort to put an Iraqi face on the war, the Office of Special Plans also sought to create the Free Iraqi Forces (FIF).[65] This program would train Iraqi externals to operate under CENTCOM during the intervention—to act as translators and fight alongside American troops. The FIF never came to fruition, which Rumsfeld blamed on two specific agencies: "At least in part because of a lack of cooperation from the State Department and the CIA," he wrote in his memoir, "we were unable to recruit and train enough Free Iraqi Forces to show that Iraqis were involved in the military campaign to rid their country of Saddam."[66] Despite Rumsfeld's intentions, CENTCOM viewed the FIF as a liability, especially if they were not properly vetted.[67]

By contrast, the State Department was skeptical of giving control of Iraq to externals and was particularly suspicious of Ahmed Chalabi. Richard Armitage, the Deputy Secretary of State under Colin Powell, claimed, "The notion that [we] can put a diaspora Iraqi in who had been out of the country for 30 years to lead a nation [which had] been under that much trauma for so many years was laughable and remains laughable."[68] A State Department paper from March 2002 characterized Chalabi as "autocratic" and accused him of not cooperating with other opposition groups.[69] Armitage also cut off the Iraqi National Congress's funding from the State Department, citing the group's inability to account for how this money was spent.[70]

The State Department, however, did not clearly favor another option. From DoD's perspective, the State Department was torn between its desire for Iraqis to

---

[63] Bensahel et al., 2008, p. 27.

[64] Rumsfeld, 2011, p. 490.

[65] Douglas J. Feith, interview with Gordon Rudd and Ginger Cruz, December 17, 2004, transcript provided to RAND by the OIF Study Group.

[66] Rumsfeld, 2011, p. 490.

[67] Bensahel et al., 2008, p. 28.

[68] Frontline, "Interviews: Richard Armitage," Public Broadcasting Service, December 18, 2007.

[69] Feith, 2008, p. 243.

[70] Frontline, 2007.

govern themselves and its desire to retain control over the postwar situation by installing a U.S.-led interim government long enough to exclude Iraqi externals.[71] While Armitage's papers that were presented to the Deputies Committee warned against a U.S.-led occupation, they also seemed to endorse the idea of a gradual transition back to an Iraqi-led government.

The conflict between the approaches of DoD and the State Department was not resolved before major combat operations started. As a result, the United States had no clear plan for how to handle Iraq in the aftermath of the war. As will be seen in Chapter Three, this lack of a coherent plan created significant challenges for the United States once the Ba'athist regime had been toppled.

Overall Critiques of the Prewar Planning Process

The lack of a comprehensive postwar planning process is often blamed for many of the problems the United States later encountered in Iraq. However, reviews from government insiders are more nuanced. Some point to the glaring deficiencies in planning. For example, Rumsfeld claimed, "Postwar planning for Iraq lacked effective interagency coordination, clear lines of responsibility, and the deadlines and accountability associated with a rigorous process."[72] A former senior State Department official we spoke with, who coordinated war planning between DoD and the State Department, expressed similar sentiments to Rumsfeld's: "Postwar planning was a mess in part because no one knew who was in charge. Once a decision was made by Bush that DoD was in charge of postwar planning, the State Department stopped engaging," although some cooperation continued at lower levels.[73] A former senior national security official, who witnessed Phase IV planning from the perspective of the Vice President's office, argued that the planning focused too much on Iraq circa 1991 rather than 2003: "The planning is open and subject to the criticism that it was planning for the last war, if you will, by civilians, not just military, which is to say people were worried about a lot of phenomena that appeared after the first Gulf War," such as refugee flows and oil infrastructure destruction.[74]

Others defend certain elements of the interagency process. For instance, one former senior national security official we spoke with suggests that the planning process deserves more credit for avoiding problems in Iraq. "It's not accurate to say there was no planning for the postwar," he said. "There was lots of planning that went on in the process, and in fact much of it was successful. . . . [T]he fact that nobody talks

---

[71] Feith, 2008, p. 277.

[72] Rumsfeld, 2011, p. 487.

[73] Former senior State Department and CPA official, interview with the authors, June 3, 2015.

[74] Former senior national security official, interview with the authors, May 21, 2015.

about it I think is a tribute to its success."[75] In particular, he cited the lack of both a food shortage and a refugee crisis as successes of prewar planning. Feith echoed this belief, although he claims that the successes in postwar planning are mostly the result of CENTCOM's war plan: "Some serious problems were anticipated: sectarian violence, a power vacuum, severe disorder. Some other serious problems—including large numbers of refugees pouring across Iraq's borders, mass hunger, and environmental disasters—were averted, in large part because of Franks' war plans, which focused on speed in order to diminish their likelihood."[76] Like any counterfactual, however, it is difficult to prove this conclusively.

Based on these analyses of the main entities (DoD and the Office of Special Plans, the Future of Iraq Project, the NSC and its ESG, and USAID), several problems clearly plagued postwar planning. First, there was a tendency to disregard the work of other organizations. The insights gained by the Future of Iraq Project were largely overlooked because they did not come with actionable solutions. No process was in place to turn these insights into operational plans. Likewise, had CENTCOM identified such potential issues as a power vacuum and sectarian violence, as Feith claims, it is unclear why explicit plans were not available to deal with them. Creating actionable plans based on insights from various agencies and organizations should have been a collaborative effort among DoD, State, and USAID. A second consistent problem was that the plans were based on assumptions that were later revealed to be unfounded, and no contingency plans existed. Planners assumed that Iraq could fund its own reconstruction and subsequently did not make contingency plans in case that assumption turned out to be false. DoD also assumed that the military coalition would not engage in nation-building, which the President ultimately tasked DoD to do, or domestic security, which was sorely needed to stop looting. Unfounded assumptions and a lack of contingency plans caught many government agencies flat-footed after Saddam was overthrown.

Another problem with planning, which none of the participants could change, was the short time frame between the initiation of combat and the implementation of Phase IV plans. The Future of Iraq Project's first working group met in July 2002, and the ESG was formed in August; the Office of Special Plans was also formed in August and took shape over the first few weeks of fall. The intervention began on March 19, 2003, and just three weeks later, footage of U.S. Marines pulling down statues of Saddam was broadcast around the world. This timing left these organizations with mere months to prepare for postwar Iraq. This short time frame, combined with the dearth of intelligence about conditions in Iraq, undermined each agency's ability to conceive of comprehensive, effective plans. This forces one to question the wisdom of delaying Phase IV planning. It is important that government

---

[75] Former senior national security official, interview with the authors, May 21, 2015.

[76] Feith, 2008, p. 275.

agencies support a president's diplomatic efforts, but in the case of the Iraq War, this support came at the cost of effective planning that could have made the war go more smoothly.

Table 2.1 summarizes the timeline of the civilian prewar planning process.

Table 2.1
Timetable of Civilian Prewar Planning for Phase IV

Organization	July 2002	August 2002	Fall 2002
State Department: Future of Iraq Project	First working group meets (planning for Future of Iraq Project began in October 2001). Formed to gain insights from Iraqi international experts and Iraqi expatriates on topics ranging from transitional justice to agriculture and public finance.		
DoD: Office of Special Plans		Formed in August and took shape over fall of 2002. Formed to coordinate Iraq policy on a range of issues, including building a coalition, supporting Iraq's oil sector, achieving de-Ba'athification, and organizing a new Iraqi government.	
NSC ESG		Formed to coordinate planning between the Joint Staff, Office of the Vice President, the State Department's Bureau of Political-Military Affairs, the CIA, and the Office of the Under Secretary of Defense for Policy. Focused primarily on acquiring basing and overflight rights.	
USAID			Postwar planning began in fall 2002, but formal tasking was not provided until 2003. Planned postconflict humanitarian assistance and reconstruction, including electricity, water, sewers, public health, education, local governance, agriculture, infrastructure, and food.

Prewar Military Planning

As Washington was trying to grapple with the strategic questions involved in planning for the war, a parallel effort to plan for major combat operations on an operational level was under way at CENTCOM in Tampa, Florida. On November 27, 2001, the Secretary of Defense tasked CENTCOM with planning to remove Saddam Hussein from power.[77] Planning, however, proved a contentious process. The source of much tension resulted from Secretary of Defense Rumsfeld's rejection of a standing war plan that called for a large buildup of ground forces, followed by a large-scale ground operation similar to Operation Desert Storm. Rumsfeld viewed the standing plan as "the product of old thinking and the embodiment of everything that was wrong with the military."[78] By contrast, from the military perspective of BG Vincent K. Brooks, then serving in the Pentagon as a deputy in the Army G3 operations section, the military was being asked to do things on the cheap, "well beyond the scope of military logic."[79] The net result of this tension was not creative friction, but rather incoherence that left much of the planning for what happened after the United States got to Baghdad vague at best.

A Slow, Iterative Process

Franks developed his concept for the Iraq intervention on December 8, 2001, and, after fleshing it out over the course of several weeks with Rumsfeld, briefed it to President Bush on December 28.[80] As Franks originally envisioned, the plan included four phases. In a nutshell, Phase I created an air bridge that would allow the United States to deploy troops into theater. Phase II shaped the battlespace before the start of ground combat operations. Phase III consisted of combat operations leading to the downfall and capture of the regime. Phase IV was to restore Iraqi sovereignty under a representative government. While the concept provided only the broad brushstrokes of the major combat operation, Bush approved the plan.[81]

On January 7, 2002, CENTCOM's senior planners met to design Operation Plan (OPLAN) 1003V, the war plan for major combat operations in Iraq. The plan was grounded in the commander's concept and call for a "generated start" plan, in which the United States deployed the necessary forces for regime change before begin-

---

[77] Bensahel et al., 2008, p. 6.

[78] Gordon and Trainor, 2006, p. 4.

[79] Personal email from Brigadier General Brooks to COL Kevin Benson, U.S. Army (Ret.), August 2002, in Kevin C. M. Benson, unpublished personal war journal and files compiled while serving as the Director of Plans, C/J-5, Coalition Forces Land Component Command (CFLCC), 2002/2003, provided to RAND by the author.

[80] Tommy Franks and Malcolm McConnell, *American Soldier*, New York: HarperCollins, 2004, pp. 340–348.

[81] Bensahel et al., 2008, pp. 6–7.

ning the ground war.[82] By contrast, Rumsfeld worried that Saddam might preempt an American combat operation and wanted to keep the overall force small.[83] In response, CENTCOM planners developed a "running-start" plan. It envisioned starting the war with as small a force as feasible and deploying follow-on forces as needed. The challenge of a "running start" was getting enough forces into Kuwait before the decision to start the war and convincing Rumsfeld, Feith, and the rest of OSD how many forces were "enough."[84] To aid in this effort—or to monitor it—Feith sent two of his aides, Abram Shulsky and Bill Bruner, to integrate into CENTCOM's efforts.[85]

Over the next several months, Franks and his staff continued to develop OPLAN 1003V. In March 2002, CENTCOM held its first planning session with all component commanders—ground, air, naval, and special operations—in Germany, and later that month, Franks briefed the plan to the JCS in the Pentagon.[86] CENTCOM developed plans for beginning the war, if necessary, with a 45-day air war and a ground war beginning as soon as 25 days into operations, with as few forces as two Army brigades and a Marine Expeditionary unit.[87] CENTCOM planners, however, viewed these and other light-footprint options as risky—as did key allies, such as Sir Michael Boyce, the then–head of the British defense staff.[88] Eventually, planners developed a compromise, or a "hybrid" solution—with five days of "quiet" mobilization, 11 days of a buildup of forces and materials, 16 days of air war, and then the invasion itself lasting up to 125 days.[89] Simultaneous with this planning, Franks was personally involved with helping coordinate with partners in the region. He traveled around the region to meet with leaders in Bahrain, Jordan, Oman, Qatar, and the United Arab Emirates, paving the way for the American military buildup necessary to execute the plan.[90]

On August 4, 2002, Franks briefed the plan again to President Bush and the NSC in Washington, D.C. The briefing touched on a variety of subjects, including the buildup of forces in the region to contend with a variety of potential catastrophes—from Iraqi use of WMDs to "catastrophic success" in areas where the Iraqi regime

---

[82] Franks and McConnell, 2004, p. 361.

[83] Franks and McConnell, 2004, p. 353; Gordon and Trainor, 2006, pp. 57–58.

[84] Franks and McConnell, 2004, pp. 361–362; and former senior military planner, interview with the authors, October 14, 2015.

[85] Gordon and Trainor, 2006, pp. 37, 52–54. See also Walter L. Perry, "Planning the War and the Transition to Peace," in Walter L. Perry, Richard E. Darilek, Laurinda L. Rohn, and Jerry M. Sollinger, eds., *Operation IRAQI FREEDOM: Decisive War, Elusive Peace*, Santa Monica: RAND Corporation, RR-1214-A, 2015, pp. 31–35.

[86] Franks and McConnell, 2004, p. 382–384.

[87] Gordon and Trainor, 2006, p. 57.

[88] Gordon and Trainor, 2006, pp. 57–58, 62.

[89] Gordon and Trainor, 2006, pp. 67–68.

[90] Franks and McConnell, 2004, p. 386.

imploded early. One of the issues that Bush asked about was how Franks planned to deal with "Fortress Baghdad"—that is, all the Special Republican Guard units and Republican divisions positioned outside the city. Franks's answer was that he intended to erode resistance in Baghdad from "inside out"—striking targets inside the city to push Saddam forces to the outer cordon. Finally, at the tail end of the meeting, Franks briefed the Phase IV, or stability, operations—in which he called for the standing up of a new Iraqi army and new institutions. And while there was widespread agreement among Bush and the NSC that Phase IV was necessary, the meeting concluded before such operations could be discussed in depth.[91]

Back in Tampa, plans continued toward war. On August 15, 2002, Franks entered a room in a secure facility on MacDill Air Force Base in Tampa. The conversation quickly turned to the current situation in Iraq. Lt Gen Mike "Buzz" Moseley dominated the room. His Ninth Air Force was the basis of the Combined Force Air Component Command. His pilots were flying increasingly dangerous missions up to the limits of the U.N.-mandated no-fly zone over southern Iraq. Moseley made a pitch at this conference for an even more aggressive scope of operations. He wanted to begin attacking the Iraqi air defense command and control system in the west of the country starting at the conclusion of the conference. Attacking the command and control nodes outside the no-fly zone, in Iraqi-controlled airspace, really was an act of war, not covered by U.N. mandate, but in keeping with the aggressive series of actions that CENTCOM was taking in preparation for war.[92]

After Moseley's presentation, Franks leaned back in his chair, looked around the room, and said, "Approved." It appeared that as long as U.S. actions remained below a certain level, they would essentially be invisible to the media, which was exactly the intended effect. In August 2002, Franks implemented a pattern of peaks of action followed by inaction that were ever gently increased. The intended effect was to acclimatize both the media and the Iraqis to patterns of activity and attacks that would appear normal over time.[93]

In the meantime, back in Washington, another member of the Bush administration—former CJCS turned Secretary of State Colin Powell—voiced other concerns about Franks's plan. Powell thought that the number of troops was too small and Iraq too large for the task at hand. More broadly, he worried that if the United States "broke" Iraq, it would need to commit up to 40 percent of the U.S. Army there for years on end.[94] He raised these concerns privately with the President at a dinner at the White House in August 2002 and then again with the full NSC

---

[91] Franks and McConnell, 2004, pp. 384–393.

[92] Former senior military planner, interview with the authors, October 14, 2015.

[93] Former senior military planner, interview with the authors, October 14, 2015.

[94] Gordon and Trainor, 2006, p. 81.

and Franks at a meeting in September 2002 at Camp David.[95] At the Camp David meeting, however, Franks defended the plan and believed he had managed to assuage many of Powell's misgivings.[96]

Cobra II

While Franks was shuttling back and forth between Washington and Tampa, LTG David McKiernan, then commander of CENTCOM's Coalition Forces Land Component Command (CFLCC), was working on the plan for the ground operation. As CFLCC commander, McKiernan was responsible for integrating the contributions to the war effort from the Army (in this case, the V Corps) and Marine Corps (I Marine Expeditionary Force [I-MEF]). To help with the task, according to a former senior military commander, McKiernan was given a dream team—with hand-selected general officers to fill out his staff.[97] The name they gave the nascent ground plan was Cobra II, an allusion to American forces' breakout from the Normandy beachhead shortly after the invasion of Europe during World War II.[98]

Cobra II called for a two-pronged assault into Iraq. I-MEF would attack in the east and take the oil fields, while the Army's V Corps—the main effort—would attack in the west toward Baghdad.[99] It marked a departure from the OPLAN 1003V hybrid plan. While Franks would still refer to it as the hybrid plan, Cobra II did not have an 11-day deployment to theater or a 16-day air campaign before the start of the ground war.[100] More contentiously, perhaps, it presumed a larger force than under the original hybrid plan. In the words of one history of the early Iraq war, "McKiernan's plan was closest to Franks's Generated Start, which had drawn stern objections from Rumsfeld a year earlier."[101] Even so, when McKiernan briefed Franks and Rumsfeld on the plan during a December 2002 rehearsal, or "rock drill," Rumsfeld accepted it.[102]

While Rumsfeld may have accepted the shift to Cobra II, he did not cease scrutinizing CENTCOM and CFLCC's requested forces. Cobra II originally called for 86,000 troops, including 17,000 reservists—far more than the 18,000 troops in Rumsfeld's preferred running-start plan.[103] And this would be just a fraction of the

---

[95] Gordon and Trainor, 2006, p. 81; Franks and McConnell, 2004, pp. 393–397.

[96] Franks and McConnell, 2004, p. 397.

[97] Former senior military commander, interview with the authors, April 17, 2015; see also the description of McKiernan's team in Gordon and Trainor, 2006, pp. 89–91.

[98] Gordon and Trainor, 2006, p. 88.

[99] Gordon and Trainor, 2006, p. 102.

[100] Gordon and Trainor, 2006, p. 108.

[101] Gordon and Trainor, 2006, p. 107.

[102] Gordon and Trainor, 2006, p. 108.

[103] Gordon and Trainor, 2006, pp. 102, 111.

total forces in theater (but not engaged in the ground war per se). When Rumsfeld heard these numbers from CENTCOM, he was not pleased. According to an email sent on January 7, 2003, from CENTCOM to a CFLCC lead planner, Rumsfeld "had a cow." The CENTCOM planner then asked if a British division could substitute for an American division to lower the numbers of American troops deployed to theater.[104] For its part, CFLCC pushed back on these force requests, but for the better part of the next couple of months, McKiernan, Franks, Army Chief of Staff Eric Shinseki, and Rumsfeld battled over force numbers and their flow into theater.[105]

To further complicate decisions about force sizing, CFLCC also was wrestling with how large the coalition contribution would be. Some in CENTCOM—including Franks himself—wanted a repeat of the Afghanistan model, with a minimal American footprint working primarily with coalition partners.[106] Not until February 14, 2003, did CFLCC receive a draft CENTCOM J5 fragmentary order to incorporate coalition units from Europe, ranging from Slovakia to Ukraine. The units were mostly combat support (engineers, military police, and chemical weapon specialists) and combat service support (truck companies, water and fuel tankers), with some promise for unspecified combat troops. Even then, many of these units did not have projected arrival dates. More problematic, no predominantly Muslim countries were providing forces. CENTCOM planners had hoped to use the Gulf Cooperation Council and Pakistan to help guard Muslim holy sites, even though most of these sites were Shia, and most of these troops—if they came—would be Sunni, as CFLCC planners pointed out.[107]

In the end, however unpleasant the process of negotiating was, McKiernan got closer to his number of forces than did Rumsfeld's running-start plan.[108] Ultimately, some 222,500 troops deployed to theater to support the Iraq War in March 2003, and some 93,900 troops entered Iraq by April 2003.[109] The plan, however, included a series of "off ramps"—where forces would prepare to go but could be stood down in relatively short order if they were not needed. For CFLCC, CENTCOM, and Army staff in Washington, it was a frustrating and imperfect solution. As Army Chief of Staff Shinseki told CFLCC leaders on February 15, 2003, OSD had "constipated

---

[104] Former senior military planner, interview with the authors, October 14, 2015; see also Gordon and Trainor, 2006, p. 112.

[105] Gordon and Trainor, 2006, pp. 112–116.

[106] See Perry, 2015, p. 41.

[107] Former senior military planner, interview with the authors, October 14, 2015.

[108] For a clear description of the final plan, see Perry, 2015, Figure 3.2, p. 39.

[109] Amy Belasco, *Troop Levels in the Afghan and Iraq Wars, FY2001–FY2012: Cost and Other Potential Issues*, Washington, D.C.: Congressional Research Service, R40682, July 2, 2009, p. 64.

the hell out of the process" and reserve-component mobilization in particular nearly ground to a halt.[110]

Rehearsing the Plan

On February 14, 2003, CFLCC conducted a combined arms rehearsal of Cobra II.[111] The rehearsal was conducted on a huge terrain model constructed by CFLCC noncommissioned officers (NCOs) under the guidance of the command sergeant major, John Sparks, before the faculty of the Sergeants Major Academy. The NCOs' model covered Iraq's terrain from Kuwait to the Turkey border in the north and from the Iraq border to the Syria and Jordan borders. The rehearsal covered the Cobra II plan through the end of Phase III, which concluded at the arrival of V Corps and I-MEF in and around Baghdad.

After McKiernan gave a briefing on the operational scheme of maneuver, MG James "Spider" Marks, the CFLCC J2, or primary intelligence officer, assessed how the Iraqis would fight coalition forces all the way to Baghdad, as well as the effect that sand storms and other weather phenomena could have on the operation. Major General Marks stressed that higher-level Iraqi command and control would be shattered by the coalition air offensive. As a result, the Iraqi forces—including Fedayeen Saddam and other irregular forces known to operate in some Iraqi cities—would likely mount uncoordinated actions along CFLCC lines of communication. Marks also outlined the three potential areas where the Iraqis could use chemical weapons: near An Nasiriyah, in the Karbala area, and in and around Baghdad. At the first two targets, American forces would be concentrated, forming an attractive target for a chemical attack, although the use of chemicals in and around Baghdad was seen as an act of desperation. Because the actual use of chemical weapons would confirm U.S., U.N., and coalition statements that Saddam indeed possessed WMDs, Marks concluded that the Iraqis would most likely use chemical weapons only as a last resort. Marks also argued that while American psychological operations would have some effect on Iraqi forces, he could not predict the full success of these operations. Finally, Marks argued that Iraqis would take every measure, conventional and unconventional, to contest the CFLCC advance and delay its arrival in Baghdad, hoping that with time, international pressure would build and force the United States and its coalition to halt operations and enter into negotiations.

Following Marks during the rehearsal was the J3, or lead operations officer, MG James D. Thurman. Thurman presented a more detailed explanation of the con-

---

[110] Former senior military planner, interview with the authors, October 14, 2015; also see Gordon and Trainor, 2006, pp. 116–117. Of note, one of CFLCC's subordinate units, the V Corps, had conducted smaller-scale rehearsals of previous plans, but this was the first full CFLCC plan (former senior military commander, interview with the authors, April 16, 2015).

[111] This "Rehearsing the Plan" subsection is drawn from former senior military planner, interview with the authors, October 14, 2015.

cept of the operations. This was a straightforward presentation of the corps and I-MEF zones, how fires would be coordinated and allocated, how the Combined Force Air Component Command would support the advance to Baghdad, what the CFLCC-level decisions were, and when the commander anticipated they might be carried out. The J4, or chief supply officer, MG Chris Christianson, followed Thurman and delivered another straightforward presentation on the flow of logistics in support of the advance.

LTG Scott Wallace, the V Corps commander, then discussed how the corps would apply fire and maneuver to reach Baghdad with the major combat elements of the 3rd Infantry Division. He spoke of the first major operation that would support the I-MEF crossing of the Euphrates River to the west of An Nasiriyah and how the V Corps would expand the bridgehead line and then hand over the area to I-MEF. Wallace said that the main effort of the corps would be west of the river, but to maintain contact with the I-MEF forces in that zone, he would place the cavalry squadron of the 3rd Infantry Division on the east bank of the river. Wallace then moved on to anticipated actions in the Karbala Gap, where terrain favored an Iraqi defense in some depth, as well as a possible use of chemical weapons to disrupt the corps advance, as Marks outlined. Wallace concluded with his assessment of how he would control operations in Baghdad in accordance with the plan at the time. The plan called for the establishment of so-called lily-pads, where CFLCC would call for Iraqi civilians to assemble as they fled the city. These areas would be supported by nongovernmental humanitarian organizations and coordinated by civil affairs (CA) units from the United States and the coalition. Combat actions would be in the form of intelligence-driven raids based on where centers of resistance would be inside the city. The commonly shared feeling was that CFLCC would take measures to avoid street-by-street fighting, which might call to mind images of the Israelis in Jenin in the occupied territories of the West Bank.

LTG James Conway, the commander of the I-MEF, followed Wallace and explained how I-MEF would attack in its zone and support the V Corps' main effort. Conway talked about the anticipated corps-forward passage of lines, which would take place near An Nasiriyah and how he expected that there would be opportunities to accelerate that passage of lines by using bridges around the city. Lieutenant General Conway covered how he expected to use the broad zone given him once across the river, remaining aware of the buffer area in his zone, which would keep U.S. ground units well away from the Iran-Iraq border. Conway would rely on Marine air to observe the area and to suppress any Iraqi units trying to exploit the buffer area as maneuver space. Conway stressed that once operations began, his Marines would maintain unrelenting pressure on Iraqi forces in the zone; exploiting the shattered Iraqi chain of command and keeping forces in the zone off balance.

Ultimately, the February 14, 2003, rehearsal brought together many of the major components in the Cobra II plan and synchronized many of the major moving pieces for the invasion. Perhaps most important in this rehearsal was what it did not cover: the plan for what came after Saddam fell from power.

Task Force IV

At a CENTCOM war game called "Internal Look" in December 2002—which, like the later CFLCC game, did not focus on Phase IV—retired GEN Gary Luck asked about what the military's role was during Phase IV. Recognizing that there was not a good answer to this question, the chief planner on the JCS, then-LTG George W. Casey, Jr., turned to the Standing Joint Force Headquarters Concept, developed by Joint Forces Command.[112] Ultimately, this led to the creation of Task Force IV under BG Steven Hawkins to begin planning the postwar effort. The task force arrived at CENTCOM headquarters in the middle of January 2003 and set to work.[113]

Almost from the beginning, Task Force IV suffered from a series of woes. It was a small, ad hoc cell—only 58 personnel strong—and staffed by officers who often lacked the required experience. For example, the political adviser had expertise in China rather the Middle East. It was also commanded by a one-star general officer and a reservist, well junior to Franks, McKiernan, and the other major players in the Iraq War planning process. Finally, Task Force IV was an orphan: Directed by Casey and formed by Joint Forces Command, it was assigned to Franks, who in turn passed it to McKiernan, who passed control down to his deputy for postconflict operations, MG Albert Whitley from the United Kingdom (UK). At the same time, Task Force IV was also physically removed from ORHA under retired Lieutenant General Garner, who was leading the civilian side of the planning effort. The net result was that Task Force IV never played much of a role in postwar planning, with much of the planning falling to either ORHA on the civilian side or CFLCC's own planning effort on the military side. At the end of March 2003, over the objections of Hawkins, McKiernan ended the task force's postwar planning tasks and ordered Hawkins to begin work on the narrower, if still herculean, task of getting Iraq's electrical system working again.[114]

Eclipse II

While most of the planning for the campaign to defeat the Iraqi military and remove Saddam's regime focused on Phase III (decisive maneuver), a small group of officers at CFLCC looked at what to do after getting to Baghdad. They also received limited guidance. Their formal guidance consisted of a single line in a message that went to

---

[112] Bensahel et al., 2008, p. 42; Perry, 2015, p. 43.

[113] Bensahel et al., 2008, p. 42.

[114] Bensahel et al., 2008, pp. 46–52; Gordon and Trainor, 2006, pp. 537; and Walter L. Perry, Richard E. Darilek, Laurinda L. Rohn, and Jerry M. Sollinger, eds., *Operation IRAQI FREEDOM: Decisive War, Elusive Piece*, Santa Monica, Calif.: RAND Corporation, RR-1214-A, 2015, p. 43. Perry and colleagues (2015) also cover the operations of the U.S. Marine Corps during Operation Iraqi Freedom, which is beyond the scope of this report, and include lessons from the Marine Corps' experience that the Army should examine.

all regional combatant commands: to be prepared to support interagency efforts and coalition nations in responding to stabilization and support requirements as a result of decisive combat operations against Iraq. These included Phase IV tasks: humanitarian assistance and civil-military operations.[115] Despite these limitations, the group labored on.

On February 16, 2003, CFLCC Phase IV planners met with McKiernan and UK Major General Whitley. This was the first exclusively Phase IV meeting with McKiernan. He began the meeting by stating, "No one wants to get a grip on this thing [Phase IV] at CENTCOM." He noted that LTG John Abizaid, the deputy CENTCOM commander, was worried that he would be stuck with running Iraq. He also noted that he did not place much confidence in Task Force IV's abilities to handle planning. McKiernan thought that the planning would fall on CFLCC.[116]

Several ideas were advanced for who should run Phase IV. McKiernan preferred turning over the post-hostilities administration of Iraq to a coalition headquarters, perhaps built around the North Atlantic Treaty Organization (NATO)'s Allied Rapid Reaction Corps headquarters, to signal NATO and European support of the effort in Iraq. The planners prepared a message for McKiernan to send to Franks outlining the value of this type of coalition headquarters and asking Franks to work on getting DoD and Secretary Rumsfeld to support the idea. Realistically, McKiernan knew this option might not be feasible and directed the planners to prepare a range of proposals for a post-hostilities headquarters built around the existing corps headquarters. Not wanting to talk the Army into a job, however, he admonished the planners to not mention V Corps as a possible Phase IV headquarters, stating, "Nothing leaves CFLCC that says V Corps" in the range of possibilities. Ultimately, this led to CFLCC's Phase IV plan—Eclipse II.[117]

In the words of Whitley, the CFLCC deputy commanding general, Eclipse II was an attempt to "bring coherence to chaos" in postwar Iraq planning.[118] It divided Phase IV into three stages: (1) stabilization, (2) recovery, and (3) transition. Phase IVa focused on establishing security conditions and completing emergency repairs to vital infrastructure. For a period of up to six months, McKiernan and CFLCC would remain

---

[115] Former senior military planner, interview with the authors, October 14, 2015.

[116] Former senior military planner, interview with the authors, October 14, 2015.

[117] Former senior military planner, interview with the authors, October 14, 2015. CLFCC drew the name from the plan for post–World War II Germany, called Eclipse (Gordon and Trainor, 2006, p. 165).

[118] Albert Whitley, "Statement by: Major General Albert Whitley CMG, CBE, Senior British Land Advisor to the Commander the Coalition Forces Land Component Command (CFLCC) Kuwait and Iraq from November 2002 to May 2003; and Deputy Commanding General (with Particular Responsibility for Post Hostilities) DCG CFLCC, February 2003 to May 2003," in *Report of the Iraq Inquiry: Report of a Committee of Privy Counsellors*, London, 2010.

in charge of all forces in Iraq, so long as McKiernan was in place.[119] In Phase IVb, CFLCC would transition to Combined Joint Task Force (CJTF)–Iraq or, preferably, to a civil authority (although the latter would depend largely on how quickly these civil authorities ramped up).[120] Finally, the United States would transition to Iraqi sovereignty in Phase IVc.

While the plan seemed neat and orderly, it hinged on the Iraqi government remaining mostly intact after the conclusion of major combat operations. It assumed that Iraq's police force and judicial system would still function, as would most of the ministries. And it assumed that other American agencies would do much of the reconstruction work after the war. This approach matches General Franks's reflections on postwar planning in his memoirs:

> One thing was certain, however: Phase IV would require civilian leadership. In addition to boots on the ground, we would need *wingtips* on the ground—hundreds, perhaps thousands, of civilians from America and the international community, from governmental advisers to eager investors. Key to all of this, of course, would be security. But security would not be possible in Iraq without immediate reconstruction and civic action.[121]

Finally, the CFLCC Phase IV plan assumed that much of the Iraqi military could be recalled, and the bulk of the task of reforming the institution would eventually fall to the new Iraqi government. In sum, while the military would assist these efforts, much of the work—particularly in the later phases—would fall to someone else.[122]

In fairness to CFLCC's planners, however, as we discuss in Chapter Three, de-Ba'athification and dissolution of the former Iraqi army were not yet official American policy; furthermore, the man who would later implement these policies in Iraq—Ambassador L. Paul Bremer III—was not yet selected for his position. Although CFLCC expected that the coalition would detain the top Ba'ath officials (the so-called deck of cards) for war crimes after the war, CFLCC, CENTCOM, and even the Joint Chiefs did not know the extent of this policy.[123]

---

[119] Gordon and Trainor, 2006, p. 165.

[120] Former senior military planner, interview with the authors, October 14, 2015.

[121] Franks and McConnell, 2004, p. 422.

[122] Gordon and Trainor, 2006, p. 166. See also Samuel R. Berger and Brent Scowcroft, eds., *In the Wake of War: Improving U.S. Post-Conflict Capabilities*, Report of an Independent Task Force, Washington, D.C.: Council on Foreign Relations, 2005, p. 4, which notes, "In Iraq, pre-war inattention to post-war requirements—or simply misjudgments about them—left the United States ill-equipped to address public security, governance, and economic demands in the immediate aftermath of the conflict, seriously undermining key U.S. foreign policy goals and giving early impetus to the insurgency."

[123] Former senior military planner, interview with the authors, October 14, 2015.

Eclipse II also had significant gaps. Most notably, it did not give a firm estimate for the number of troops required for Phase IV. Task Force IV had concluded that the United States would need at least 200,000 troops for stability operations, with some estimates as high as 500,000.[124]

The debate surrounding the number of forces required for postwar Iraq became publicly contentious when then–Army Chief of Staff Shinseki testified on February 25, 2003, before the Senate Armed Services Committee about the number of forces that would be required to stabilize Iraq after an invasion. In response to Senator Carl Levin, Shinseki stated,

> Something on the order of several hundred thousand soldiers are probably, you know, a figure that would be required. . . . We're talking about post-hostilities control over a piece of geography that's fairly significant, with the kinds of ethnic tensions that could lead to other problems. . . . And so it takes a significant ground force presence to maintain a safe and secure environment, to ensure that people are fed, that water is distributed, all the normal responsibilities that go along with administering a situation like this.[125]

Deputy Secretary of Defense Paul Wolfowitz and Secretary Rumsfeld publicly rebuked Shinseki for his testimony. Wolfowitz was particularly dismissive, saying that Shinseki was "wildly off the mark. . . . The notion that it would take several hundred thousand American troops just seems outlandish."[126] After his testimony, Shinseki would remain in the Army until his scheduled retirement in June 2003. Additionally, the contemptuous response by DoD leadership to Shinseki's troop estimates had a stultifying effect on other senior military officers. Kori Schake, the director for defense strategy on the NSC staff from 2002 to 2005, recalled that it "sent a very clear signal to the military leadership about how that kind of military judgment was going to be valued. . . . So it served to silence critics just at the point in time when, internal to the

---

[124] Bensahel et al., 2008, p. 43. Franks himself told Rumsfeld that Phase IV would require 250,000 troops (Perry, 2015, p. 41).

[125] Thom Shanker, "New Strategy Vindicates Ex-Army Chief Shinseki," *New York Times*, January 12, 2007. See also Cullen Murphy and Todd S. Purdum, "Farewell to All That: An Oral History of the Bush White House," *Vanity Fair*, February 2009. In this article, LTG Jay Garner recalled,

> When Shinseki said, Hey, it's going to take 300,000 or 400,000 soldiers, they crucified him. They called me up the day after that, Wolfowitz and Rumsfeld. They called me the next day and they said, Did you see what Shinseki said? And I said yes. And they said, Well, that can't be possible. And I said, Well, let me give you the only piece of empirical data I have. In 1991, I owned 5 percent of the real estate in Iraq, and I had 22,000 trigger pullers. And on any day I never had enough. So you can take 5 percent—you can take 22,000 and multiply that by 20. Hey, here's probably the ballpark, and I didn't have Baghdad. And they said, Thank you very much. So I got up and left.

[126] Center for American Progress, "Questions for Paul Wolfowitz," April 20, 2004.

process, you most wanted critical judgment."[127] For Rumsfeld and many in the Bush administration, this size was simply too much. Indeed, they argued that Iraq would look more like Afghanistan, and by this model, it would need closer to 13,900.[128]

CFLCC was caught in the middle of this debate. To mitigate the risk and boost its numbers, it counted on a significant coalition contribution, but, as already noted, such a contribution was not readily forthcoming.[129] More significantly, CFLCC also counted on recalling large parts of the Iraqi security forces to help establish security—at that point a possible, though far from guaranteed, option. As a result, as late as March 2003, when CFLCC planners briefed MG Peter Chiarelli, then in Army G3 in Washington, planners still did not have a definitive troop number because it depended on how Phase III ended.[130]

Ultimately, CFLCC did settle on a minimum force size. Table 2.2 represents what the CFLCC C5 thought was needed to establish a secure environment for the restoration of Iraqi control and free operation of nongovernmental organizations, the U.N., and similar agencies. In a comparison of the ratios between land mass and security forces, CFLCC planners determined that CFLCC had fewer troops than then-Governor Arnold Schwarzenegger had police to provide security for the state of California.[131]

Whatever its faults, though, the Eclipse II process caused planners to begin to think through some of the challenges that the United States would face in a post-Saddam Iraq. On April 3, 2003, the CFLCC J5, Colonel Benson, wrote to the CFLCC command group about the nature of the threat to Phase IV:

> Believe we should explore asking the TRADOC [Training and Doctrine Command] Threat Directorate to review ECLIPSE II and red team the plan based on how the Saddam Fedayeen fought in [Phase] III. Given de-Ba'athification is US policy we must think through the potential problem this could cause us as an asymmetric threat. We could face an insurgency problem or at least a terror problem in [Phase] IV.[132]

According to a former senior military planner, CFLCC believed that the Sunni minority, primarily represented by the remnants of the regime-sponsored paramilitary (Fedayeen Saddam and Ba'ath Party Militia), might threaten the stability of Iraq and

---

[127] Shanker, 2007. See also Bensahel et. al, 2008, p. 17. This report suggested that if Kosovo had been used as a benchmark, then Iraq, for its size and population, could require as many as 526,000 security forces.

[128] Gordon and Trainor, 2006, p. 119.

[129] Gordon and Trainor, 2006, p. 120.

[130] Former senior military planner, interview with the authors, October 14, 2015.

[131] Former senior military planner, interview with the authors, October 14, 2015. In practice, the United States never reached this number of brigades in Iraq. Even during fiscal year 2008, the United States averaged only 17.5 brigade combat teams (BCTs) (Belasco, 2009, p. 12).

[132] Personal journal of Colonel Benson, April 3, 2003 (see Benson, 2002/2003).

Table 2.2
Phase IV Troop-to-Task Analysis, May 2003

Priority	Governance	Population	Units Required	Comment
1	Baghdad	6.2 million	6 brigades	Score settling, capital of Iraq, large population, sensitive site exploitation (SSE) site
2	Basra/Maysan	2.4 million	2 brigades	Rumalia oil field, score settling, border crossing with Iran, Supreme Council for Islamic Revolution in Iraq
3	At Ta'Mim/Arbil	2.1 million	3 brigades	Kirkuk oil field, Kurdistan Democratic Party/Patriotic Union of Kurdistan intentions, border crossing with Iran
4	Salah ad Din	1.1 million	2 brigades	Tikrit, SSE sites
5	Ninawa	2.4 million	1 brigade	Mosul, Kurdistan Democratic Party/Patriotic Union of Kurdistan intentions, border crossings with Syria
6	As Sulaymaniyah	1.4 million	1 brigade	Al Qaeda enclave, Patriotic Union of Kurdistan
7	Anbar	1.2 million	1 brigade	Border crossing with Jordan and Syria, SSE sites, Logistics Support Area Copperhead
8	Babil	1.7 million	2 battalions	Population merge with Baghdad, SSE sites
9	An Najaf	900,000	3 battalions	Shia holy city, Logistics Support Area Bushmaster
10	Karbala	700,000	2 battalions	Shia holy city
11	Dhi Qar	1.4 million	1 brigades	Al-Nasiriyah, Supreme Council for Islamic Revolution in Iraq, Logistics Support Area Adder
12	Wasit	860,000	2 battalions	Mujahadeen-e-Khalq, border crossing with Iran
13	Diyala	1.4 million	1 battalion	Mujahadeen-e-Khalq, border crossing with Iran, SSE sites
14	Dahuk	450,000	1 battalion	Border crossing with Turkey
15	Al Qadisiyah	850,000	1 battalion	
16	Al Muthann	480,000	—	
Total		25.5 million	20 brigades	

SOURCE: Donald P. Wright and Timothy R. Reese, *On Point II: Transition to the New Campaign—The United States Army in Operation Iraqi Freedom, May 2003–January 2005*, Fort Leavenworth, Kan.: Combat Studies Institute Press, 2008, p. 75.

could provoke a broader ethnic sectarian conflict among the Sunnis, Kurds, and Shia as the groups fought for power in post-Saddam Iraq. CFLCC also believed that the long-oppressed Kurdish and Shia populations might retaliate against Sunnis, and particularly Ba'athists. Additionally, CFLCC was concerned about the role that outside state actors (e.g., Syria and Iran) and terrorist groups (e.g., the Mojahedin-e-Khalq, Supreme Council for the Islamic Revolution in Iraq, and Ansar al-Islam) might play in post-Saddam Iraq.[133]

Also, in this former senior military planner's view, CFLCC believed that the coalition would probably face opposition from a range of forces in a post-Saddam Iraq. The regime-sponsored paramilitary groups would continue to try to retain a stranglehold on the civilian population as a whole and continue to attack "soft" or nonmilitary targets (e.g., reconstruction efforts). A rash of internal, factional territorial claims and score-settling could lead to local rioting and violence in major urban centers. In Baghdad, in particular, CFLCC felt that competition for leadership in the postregime government, and wresting control of the city between Shia and Sunnis, could lead to factional violence. CFLCC also expected to see an increase in Islamic fundamentalist groups attempting to infiltrate Iraq, particularly along the Syrian border, to attack coalition efforts. Overall, however, CFLCC anticipated popular support for the coalition effort, provided the population's basic needs were met and Iraqi lives continued to improve.[134]

Combat

McKiernan held a final commanders' huddle at 3:30 p.m. (Zulu time) on March 18, 2003, telling his commanders and key staff that it was a historic day. D-Day, H-Hour would be 6:00 p.m., March 19, 2003. The execution order would be by verbal order of the commander.[135] CFLCC would cross the line of departure as a full-scale operation, not a limited one.

Overall, the initial operation went well. Although coalition forces faced irregular Fedayeen fighters in cities, a sand storm, and other challenges, many of the possible disasters that could have occurred never materialized. Chemical weapons were not used. Oil wells were not set alight. "Scud" missiles (the Western name for the early Soviet missile series) were not fired at Israel, provoking geopolitical woes for the coalition. By April 3, less than three weeks after the initial assault, coalition forces reached the airport on the outskirts of Baghdad—far faster than the 125 days presumed by Cobra II.[136] Perhaps unsurprisingly then, the fight for Baghdad also did not go according to plan.

---

[133] Former senior military planner, interview with the authors, October 14, 2015.

[134] Former senior military planner, interview with the authors, October 14, 2015.

[135] Former senior military planner, interview with the authors, October 14, 2015.

[136] Thomas E. Ricks, *Fiasco: The American Military Adventure in Iraq*, New York: Penguin Press, 2006a, p. 125.

The V Corps envisioned surrounding Baghdad. Safe-haven areas would be established for civilians evacuating the city. While this took place, a combination of special operations forces and conventional force raids, based on developed intelligence, occurred. The thought was that this methodical approach would avoid the U.S. military becoming ensnared in a protracted urban warfare battle in "Fortress Baghdad." Also, with Baghdad and the means of regime control cut off from the country, CFLCC would transition into Phase IVa, establishing military authority in Iraq while completing regime removal.[137]

A former senior military commander we spoke with had a different perspective. He knew that the Iraqis had a deeper understanding of the urban terrain than did his units. Although his units were equipped with Blue Force Trackers, he knew his soldiers could not learn the city better than the Iraqis. He told us, "So we needed to figure out how to make [the Iraqis'] knowledge irrelevant."[138] He also did not want to risk losing momentum on the attack. After capturing several Iraqis, he stated that the Iraqis "were very central and localized." By striking into the heart of the regime, he also realized his operation had a strategic message.[139] He decided to take his brigade into Baghdad in a series of attacks.

COL David Perkins, the commander of the 2nd Brigade of the 3rd Infantry Division, decided to take his brigade into Baghdad in a series of attacks. Those raids became known as the "Thunder Runs." Franks came up with the label in an April 4, 2003, consultation with McKiernan about the impending assault. Franks got the name "Thunder Run" from a tactic he saw in Vietnam in 1968, where armored and infantry forces would move through a city at high speed to surprise or overpower enemy forces.[140]

Perkins launched the first Thunder Run on April 5, 2003. The brigade fought along Route 8 for about eight hours before returning to the airport. The brigade met stiff resistance, encountering a fusillade of rocket-propelled grenades and small arms fire. By some estimates, the brigade killed up to 2,000 enemy combatants during the mission.[141] Aside from the casualties it inflicted, the first Thunder Run had significant psychological effects. On the way out of Baghdad, the 2nd Brigade captured an Iraqi brigadier. According to one former senior military commander we spoke with, "As we are attacking, this car comes out on the road [and] sees a tank column coming down

---

[137] Gordon and Trainor, 2006, pp. 428–429.

[138] Former senior military commander, interview with the authors, July 21, 2015.

[139] Former senior military commander, interview with the authors, July 21, 2015.

[140] Franks and McConnell, 2004, p. 517.

[141] Ricks, 2006a, p. 126.

the road. So he stopped and he got out and surrendered. The Iraqi one star was driving to work; he thought they were winning the war."[142]

The capture of the Iraqi general taught the former senior military commander we spoke with that "our lack of having a visible strategic symbol [of victory] emboldened the Iraqis to continue fighting."[143] Perkins intended to deliver just such a symbol. On April 6, 2003, Perkins and his brigade conducted another Thunder Run. This time, the brigade struck Saddam's palace in the heart of Baghdad. More importantly, unlike during the previous raid, the brigade decided to stay.[144] Despite the intense fighting, it seemed that the predictions of "Fortress Baghdad" were overblown and the Iraq War was entering its final phases. As *Washington Post* correspondent Thomas Ricks noted, "The American military believed it had taken Baghdad."[145] As it turned out, however, the Battle for Baghdad had just begun.

Lessons from This Era

In a postwar interview, the commander of V Corps, LTG William S. Wallace, gave what arguably has become the consensus view of prewar planning:

> The military did their job in three weeks. I give no credit to the politicians for detailed Phase Four planning. But I don't think that we, the military, did a very good job of anticipating [that] either. I don't think that any of us either could have or did anticipate the total collapse of this regime and the psychological impact it had on the entire nation. When we arrived in Baghdad, everybody had gone home. The regime officials were gone; the folks that provided security of the ministry buildings had gone; the folks that operated the water treatment plants and the electricity grid and the water purification plants were gone. There were no bus drivers, no taxi drivers; everybody just went home. I for one did not anticipate our presence being such a traumatic influence on the entire population. We expected there to be some degree of infrastructure left in the city, in terms of intellectual infrastructure, in terms of running the city infrastructure, in terms of running the government infrastructure. But what in fact happened, which was unanticipated at least in [my mind], is that when [we] decapitated the regime, everything below it fell apart.[146]

While much of the blame for the shortcomings of postwar planning rightly falls on senior rungs of the Bush administration, the truth of the matter is that there is more

---

[142] Former senior military commander, interview with the authors, July 21, 2015.

[143] Former senior military commander, interview with the authors, July 21, 2015.

[144] Ricks, 2006a, p. 127; Gordon and Trainor, 2006, pp. 454–455.

[145] Ricks, 2006a, p. 127.

[146] Bensahel et al., 2008, p. 18.

than enough blame to go around, up and down the chains of command in military and civilian planning.

To begin with, contrary to popular misconception, the problem was not that postwar planning did not occur. Indeed, several organizations—in the State Department, DoD, CENTCOM, and CCFLCC—engaged in postwar planning to some effect. As Whitley later testified,

> ECLIPSE II had some local practical effect: military teams and locals working on sanitation plants, jury rigging the national power grid, recommissioning power stations, repairing and opening the Baghdad – Umm Qasr – Basra railway (essential to bring bottled gas from Kuwait into the country so people could cook), hospitals and so on. ECLIPSE II was inadequate and so were the resources available but it did achieve something.[147]

Rather, the true problem behind the postwar planning effort was that it was disjointed, poorly organized and structured, and often largely ignored by senior leadership.[148]

The remainder of this section identifies and describes the lessons learned from the U.S. experience in Baghdad during the prewar planning period.

Start Planning Early, Remain Focused, and Expect Policy to Cause Friction

Many of the problems in planning for post-Saddam Iraq stemmed from the time frame available for this effort. Iraq planners had only a few months to plan before major combat operations began—and then only a few weeks before plans needed to be implemented. Moreover, while the buildup to the war lasted about 18 months, early planning efforts were hampered by the Bush administration's insistence that war was not a foregone conclusion until just before major combat operations began.

To add to these difficulties, much of planning time—particularly on the military side of the operation—focused on Phase III (decisive or combat operations), not Phase IV. Commanders at CFLCC and CENTCOM were often preoccupied with approving the reports sent back to Washington.[149]

Establish Unity of Command

Government officials from multiple agencies described the planning process as unorganized and confusing, with no clarity over who ultimately had authority over plans. It is unclear where the division of labor was laid among DoD, the State Department,

---

[147] Whitley, 2010.

[148] Frederick W. Kagan, *Finding the Target: The Transformation of American Military Policy*, New York: Encounter Book, 2006, p. 335.

[149] For a similar set of recommendations in greater detail, see Perry, Darilek, et al., 2015, pp. 373–376.

the NSC, and USAID, and it was even less certain what, if any, role the Future of Iraq Project had.

Arguably, the same lesson could be applied to the military. While Task Force IV was created to plan for the aftermath of the war, it was not clearly integrated with the Joint Staff, CENTCOM, or CFLCC. CFLCC and CENTCOM also had a hand in postwar planning, but these efforts were not coordinated with ORHA and the civilian effort. As a result, plenty of planning was going on, but no single, actionable plan for Phase IV could be generated.

Resolve Disputes Among Principals
Disputes between senior officials in DoD and the State Department about the type of government that should replace Saddam undoubtedly impeded planning for Phase IV. Consequently, the prewar creation of cohesive postwar plans that could have been implemented on the ground in Baghdad never came to fruition. Ideally, this should happen without much military involvement, but if not, senior military officers must ask for, even demand, such guidance before execution.

A similar lesson applies to the military side regarding force numbers and the war plan. The endless debates among Rumsfeld, Franks, Powell, McKiernan, and others about "generated," "running," and "hybrid" starts focused on how the military would start the war. While the focus on major combat operations is understandable, these leaders arguably overlooked postwar planning—how to end the war—in the process.

Question Assumptions and Plan for Contingencies
Many of the key actors—from the Future of Iraq Project and CFLCC's postwar planning team to Rumsfeld and Feith in their 2002 "Parade of the Horribles" memo outlining all possible problems that could occur in postwar Iraq—identified the possibility of terrorism, if not a full-blown insurgency.[150] And yet, despite all the people who claimed that they predicted the coming disaster in Iraq, there was remarkably little outcry that something was amiss. Only Marine LtGen Gregory Newbold, the Joint Staff Director of Operations (J-3), retired in October 2002 in silent protest of Iraq War planning.[151] And yet, aside from this one act, few senior leaders publicly challenged the assumptions or resigned in protest of what many believed was an impending catastrophe. At the same time, there was no coherent attempt to plan for such contingencies.

Combined Arms Training and Mobile Protected Firepower Are the Essential Ingredients of Combat Operations
With 3rd Infantry Division's offensive into Iraq, its Thunder Runs into the heart of Baghdad in early April 2003, and 1st Armored Division's dispersion of small combat

---

[150] Feith, 2008, pp. 332–335.

[151] David Margolick, "The Night of the Generals," *Vanity Fair*, April 2007.

outfits throughout Baghdad in 2003, combined arms training and mobile protected firepower enabled these two divisions to adjust and adapt to the demands and challenges of the urban combat environment they confronted in the march to Baghdad and the initial combat operations there.

Combined arms training enabled Perkins and his brigade task force to invade Iraq, carry out some difficult tactical fighting against enemy elements along the way, and make an assault into Baghdad during the Thunder Runs. If 3rd Infantry Division had been a light infantry–only force, especially during the Thunder Runs, it likely would have taken significantly higher casualties. Army units premised on mobile-protected firepower and trained in combined arms from the squad through division levels enabled freedom of movement and the gaining and maintaining of the tactical initiative. The problems later faced in Baghdad and throughout Iraq had less to do with the tactical performance of Army ground units than with a failure of strategy and policy.

CHAPTER THREE

Occupation

With the fall of Baghdad in April 2003, the United States confronted an unpleasant reality: It was an occupying power. Accepting this fact did not come easily to anyone—in Washington or Iraq, military or civilian. As then–National Security Adviser Condoleezza Rice remarked in a postwar interview, "To be fair, we Americans don't like the notion of occupation, and I remember very well having this discussion with the British, who said, 'You're going to be occupying the country whether you like it or not. You should just accept it and act in that way.'"[1] Prior to the war, Washington had expected the Iraqi government to continue to function after Saddam Hussein's fall, albeit without the senior Ba'athist leadership.[2] To the extent that outside supervision was necessary, much of the Washington policy community believed that someone else would pick up the responsibility for the postwar stabilization. As Thomas Warrick, head of the State Department's Future of Iraq Project, noted, "The realization should have dawned in February, but I think it really didn't sink in until March of 2003, but everyone assumed that there would be some major role for the international community in the governing of Iraq itself after Saddam was taken down."[3] And this is despite the fact that the Bush administration viewed the U.N. with skepticism, if not hostility.[4] A former senior State Department official we spoke with similarly noted, "The military wanted to put a civilian face on it while the civilians wanted to put an Iraqi face on it, and meanwhile there were 150,000 troops on the ground and a U.N. order saying it was an occupation."[5] Indeed, on May 22, 2003, the U.N. Security Council adopted Resolution 1483, recognizing the United States and the United Kingdom as "occupy-

---

[1] Condoleezza Rice, interview with Jason Awadi and Jeanne Godfroy, U.S. Department of State, Office of the Historian, July 12, 2014, p. 5, transcript provided to RAND by the OIF Study Group.

[2] Nora Bensahel, "Mission Not Accomplished: What Went Wrong with Iraqi Reconstruction," *Journal of Strategic Studies*, Vol. 29, No. 3, June 2006, pp. 457-458. See also Bensahel et al., 2008.

[3] Thomas S. Warrick, interview with Gordon Rudd, November 17, 2004, p. 5, transcript provided to RAND by the OIF Study Group.

[4] Thomas S. Warrick, interview with Gordon Rudd, November 17, 2004, p. 5, transcript provided to RAND by the OIF Study Group.

[5] Former senior State Department and CPA official, interview with the authors, June 3, 2015.

ing powers" with all the "authorities, responsibilities, and obligations under applicable international law."[6] And so, the United States was arguably caught flat-footed and now confronted the hard reality of needing to establish an occupation government.

This chapter describes the first critical year of the Battle for Baghdad, from April 2003 through the end of CPA in June 2004. It first describes how U.S. forces gradually shifted from conventional combat into counterinsurgency operations. Next, it provides an overview of the two principal civilian organizations in Baghdad—the Office of Reconstruction and Humanitarian Assistance and its successor organization, CPA—with special attention given to its two most critical decisions to disband Iraq's army and rid governing bodies of Ba'thists. It describes the disjointed effort to rebuild Iraq's security forces. Finally, it concludes with lessons learned from this period of the war.

The Military Picture

On April 7, 2003, only three weeks after the American-led major combat operations had begun, M1 tanks of the American 3rd Infantry Division were thundering through the streets of Baghdad, securing the main palaces that were the seat of Saddam's power. The air offensive had destroyed Saddam's command and control systems and had caused him and his key subordinates to flee Baghdad for the countryside. It would be five months before Saddam was finally tracked down and captured. Instead of fighting organized Iraqi infantry and armor, although there were these kinds of engagements at various points, the advancing American and British forces confronted an irregular foe that was made up of Saddam's loyal militia (the Fedayeen) combined with regular army troops who had abandoned their posts. It was an enemy, as American senior general Wallace noted, that differed from "the one we war-gamed" or had planned to fight against.[7]

Once Colonel Perkins's 2nd Brigade Task Force, 3rd Infantry Division had secured the area in the center of Baghdad that had many of the Saddam regime's palaces and government buildings (this area would eventually become known as the Green Zone and then the International Zone), the brigade, along with other elements of the 3rd Infantry Division, began initial operations in Baghdad. As a heavy brigade, Perkins's outfit did not have a lot of dismounted infantry, so it used tanks and Bradley fighting vehicles to secure road intersections in the center of Baghdad that gave it mobility throughout parts of the city and the ability to begin rebuilding Iraqi institutions.[8]

---

[6] United Nations Security Council, 2003a.

[7] Fred Kaplan, "War-Gamed: Why the Army Shouldn't Be So Surprised by Saddam's Moves," *Slate*, March 28, 2003; see also Franks and McConnell, 2004, pp. 485–516.

[8] Former senior military commander, interview with the authors, July 21, 2015; former senior military commander, interview with the authors, September 18, 2015; Gregory Fontenot, E. J. Degen, and David Tohn, *On Point: The United States Army in Operation Iraqi Freedom*, Fort Leavenworth, Kan.: Combat Studies Institute

Major combat operations in Iraq in March 2003 accomplished their goal of toppling the Saddam regime with a minimum number of forces. However, two key assumptions that drove force planning for the war proved highly problematic. First was the expectation by the Bush administration that coalition forces would be "greeted as liberators instead of occupiers." Second was that the Iraqi government would

> continue to function after the ministers and their closest advisors were removed from power. Since Saddam's regime depended on a highly centralized government structure, where all important decisions were made in Baghdad, U.S. officials assumed that government ministries were largely effective state structures. If that were the case, then the top leadership of each ministry could be replaced, leaving the remaining technocrats and civil servants—the vast majority of the ministry staff—to continue running the state. No large-scale reconstruction would therefore be necessary, since the new leadership of Iraq would inherit a functioning and capable governance structure. The United States would only need to help the ministries continue their work for a short time during the transition of power.[9]

These erroneous assumptions had three principal effects. First, they precluded the United States from recognizing what kind of war it was getting into. Second, Iraqi institutional mechanisms that the United States was relying on to prevent the slide of Iraq into chaos were not there. What was left of the Iraqi security apparatus was later swept away by the administrator of CPA, L. Paul Bremer III, when he directed the disbanding of the Iraqi military and de-Ba'athification.[10] Third, when looting and disorder began, the United States had insufficient forces on the ground to establish security, and those forces

> were not directed to establish law and order—and may not have had sufficient capabilities to do so—they stood aside while looters ravaged Iraq's infrastructure and destroyed the facilities that the military campaign took great pains to ensure remained intact, creating greater reconstruction requirements than existed when major combat ended. Because U.S. forces have had to focus far more on providing security for U.S. personnel (both military and civilian) than on providing security for Iraqis, ordinary Iraqis started growing frustrated with the lack of law and order in their country soon after Saddam was removed from power.[11]

Press, 2004; and Williamson Murray and Robert H. Scales, *The Iraq War: A Military History*, New York: Belknap, 2003. See also Bing West and Ray Smith, *The March Up: Taking Baghdad with the United States Marines*, New York: Bantam, 2004; Seth W. B. Folsom, *The Highway War: A Marine Company Commander in Iraq*, Washington, D.C.: Potomac Books, 2006; and David Zucchino, *Thunder Run: The Armored Strike to Capture Baghdad*, New York: Grove Press, 2004.

[9] Bensahel, 2006, pp. 457–458. See also Bensahel et al., 2008.

[10] Bensahel et al., 2008, p. 71.

[11] Bensahel et al., 2008, pp. 240–241.

That this descent into lawlessness was not planned for is apparent in the recollections of GEN Richard B. Meyers, CJCS in 2003:

> After a few days of joyous outbursts at the overthrow of Saddam's regime, crowds of looters took to the streets. Small-scale looting by "couch pushers" stealing furniture from government buildings quickly gave way to organized bands of vandals stripping anything of value they could lay their hands on in ministries and hospitals—even museums. Coalition forces should have done more to stop this.[12]

Journalists, such as Thomas Ricks, later used the looting as an example of the military's lack of understanding that its mission had changed from offensive operations to remove the regime to now securing the Iraqi people and rebuilding Iraq's institutions.[13]

These post facto assessments from Washington and the Fifth Estate show the immense gulf between prewar expectations and planning and what commanders actually encountered on the ground. As a former senior military commander noted in a 2015 interview,

> [The looting] started right away, we come into Baghdad with 1,000 guys in tanks and Bradleys and that FOB [forward operating base] area becomes the Green Zone since it is the best interior lines of communication for a tank brigade. So you have a huge amount of oppressed Iraqis. So what happened was that the Americans are actually here and Saddam is gone, so they saw this as a chance to get even. And General Wallace is here and we are in my 113 [M-113 armored personnel carrier] and there is a guy pushing a couch, giving the thumbs up. They saw looting as an act of solidarity. It was the least they could do. So I am not advocating for looting, but here is the deal—I have 1,000 soldiers and can't stop millions of people from looting. So, I can start shooting them; I don't have handcuffs, I have sabot [120-mm tank round]. I can't kill all of these people, and they are with me at this point, and I am surrounded by 6 million people.
>
> . . . [The looting] wasn't the [tipping point]. . . . I also don't see it as looting; I see it as wealth redistribution, since no one was allowed to go in there. They weren't killing other Iraqis; it was an act of defiance against the regime. They weren't killing their neighbors; it was incredibly targeted wealth redistribution, and that is what they went after. So the decision was not something we desire but the alternative would have been much worse. They never turned on us, and we didn't have a Mogadishu with the crowds jumping on us. But if we started arresting and kill-

---

[12] Richard B. Myers, *Eyes on the Horizon: Serving on the Front Lines of National Security*, New York: Simon and Schuster, 2009, p. 249.

[13] See, for example, Ricks, 2006a, pp. 135–138; and Frontline, "Interviews: Frederick W. Kagan," Public Broadcasting Service, February 26, 2004.

ing people, we would have had a huge problem since it would have been seen as defending the regime. That was a strategic calculation not to shoot looters.[14]

If senior military commanders were less concerned about looters at this point in the war, Washington seemingly was, too. The perceived success of major combat operations sufficed to allow U.S. political leaders to consider the "mission accomplished" in May 2003.[15]

However, the President's "mission accomplished" speech was premature. A former senior military commander who visited Baghdad in May 2003 remembered hearing the President's speech and that the security situation in Baghdad had the appearance of looking "promising. . . . There weren't many attacks from the end of April through May." Yet he also realized that Baghdad was not in any way "stable" and that, in other parts of the country, such as Tikrit, the 4th Infantry Division was already fighting a growing Sunni insurgency by May of that year.[16]

Washington also watched the decay in the security situation with growing alarm. During a trip to Baghdad on April 28, 2003, Secretary of Defense Rumsfeld decided that the CFLCC commander, Lieutenant General McKiernan—who led American ground troops through the major combat operations in Iraq—was not up to the job of running the occupation.[17] In June 2003, the 1st Armored Division commander, the newly promoted LTG Ricardo Sanchez, replaced McKiernan as V Corps commander and commander of the newly created CJTF-7, responsible for the military forces in Iraq.

The change in leadership added a layer of confusion to an already muddled situation. Replacing McKiernan with Sanchez functionally meant changing out a seasoned three star for the most junior one in the Army. Worse yet, when McKiernan left, he took his staff with him—all hand-chosen generals, leaving Sanchez with a colonel-level staff.[18] On a deeper level, however, U.S. military and civilian leadership were wrestling with a more profound strategic dilemma. If removing the Saddam regime was "mission accomplished," what should come next? Should the United States leave Iraq quickly as planned, or should it stay for an extended period to rebuild the country's institutions

---

[14] Former senior military commander, interview with the authors, July 21, 2015.

[15] Robert Brigham, *The United States and Iraq Since 1990: A Brief History with Documents*, Chichester, UK: Wiley-Blackwell, 2013, p. 149.

[16] Former senior military commander, interview with the authors, July 29, 2015; and John Abizaid, interview with the OIF Study Group, September 19, 2014, transcript provided to RAND by the OIF Study Group.

[17] Rumsfeld, 2011, p. 494.

[18] Michael R. Gordon, "Occupation Plan for Iraq Faulted in Army History," *New York Times*, June 29, 2008a; and former senior military commander, interview with the authors, April 17, 2015.

and provide security for the Iraqi people while it was doing so?[19] To further complicate matters, Washington was split over which approach to take—with many in DoD pushing for the former course of action and many in the NSC backing the latter option.[20]

A former senior military commander we spoke with sensed this confused strategy on the ground in Baghdad. Either U.S. strategy was to keep the American forces in Baghdad for an extended period to do armed nation-building or it was to put someone else in charge and leave by the end of 2003. For him,

> all of the planning/discussions before the war were about tactical and operational challenges like crossing the berm, resupplying large forces, taking down Baghdad and the regime. There were never discussions, at least at my level, about what would we do if we accomplished regime change. How would we exploit success? What would the next phase look like? The two most daunting words in military planning are, "What then?"[21]

The following month, the 1st Armored Division arrived in Baghdad to relieve 3rd Infantry Division of operations in the city. A former senior military commander we spoke with also sensed this uncertainty over the duration that the United States would remain in Iraq. Within a few months of operations, he concluded that transitioning things over to Iraqis would take a long time, but his senior military leaders told him differently. He recalled that in the "July 2003 time frame, there was a level of violence in Baghdad, but it was mostly crime," and it had yet to reach any significant level. Still, he could tell that there was resistance to the American occupation by former Saddam regime members and various Shia groups. He also got the sense from his higher headquarters that the U.S. forces "should be prepared to take as much risk getting out [of Baghdad and Iraq] as they did getting in to it."[22] He noted that the perception was that "the time horizon was probably measured in months, not years. There was an expectation of the troops in the 3rd Infantry Division that they would leave before Labor Day" and that the 1st Armored Division "probably had a sense that we'd be home by Christmas."[23]

Despite this strategic incoherence and confusion, units from platoon through division began to adapt to the challenging dynamics of Baghdad in the first year of

---

[19] Reidar Visser, "An Unstable, Divided Land," *New York Times*, December 15, 2011; and Joel Wing, "Rethinking the Surge in Iraq," *Musings on Iraq*, August 22, 2011. For an excellent analysis of how American strategy has evolved with Iraq, see Steven Metz, *Iraq and the Evolution of American Strategy*, Washington, D.C: Potomac Books, 2008.

[20] Gordon and Trainor, 2006, pp. 475–485; and L. Paul Bremer III, *My Year in Iraq: The Struggle to Bring a Future of Hope*, New York: Simon and Schuster, 2006.

[21] Former senior military commander, interview with the authors, July 21, 2015.

[22] Former senior military commander, interview with the authors, May 13, 2015.

[23] Former senior military commander, interview with the authors, May 21, 2015; and former senior military commander, interview with the authors, July 29, 2015.

the American occupation. Reflecting on his year in Baghdad in command of a combat brigade from 2003 to 2004, COL Ralph O. Baker realized from his first days on the ground an important principle of counterinsurgency operations: accurate intelligence on insurgent activities. Colonel Baker figured out very early on that without specific information on insurgents, his brigade—2nd Brigade Task Force of the 1st Armored Division—would be floundering around in the dark. He therefore quickly put into place processes that developed the kind of intelligence he needed to hunt down and capture or kill insurgents.[24]

Another brigade commander in Baghdad during 2004 in then-BG Martin Dempsey's 1st Armored Division, COL Peter Mansoor, noted that even though his 1st Brigade, 1st Armored Division had been trained for "high intensity combat," it had quickly made the transition to effective counterinsurgency operations in Baghdad. The original concept of "rapid, decisive operations" for the intervention in Iraq had overlooked the possibility of guerilla attacks against American forces, and it gave only perfunctory treatment to the possibility of terrorist attacks.[25] Mansoor also described the broader ways in which the inadequacies of prewar planning and doctrine became apparent in the early months and years of the war. Not only did the coalition not have the requisite force, it "lacked imagination and insight," he argued. In fact, "Without an operational concept to guide the conduct of the war," Mansoor recounted later in his book, "Lieutenant General Sanchez and CJTF-7 lacked the link between strategic ends and tactical means."[26] Criticizing this "conceptual shortfall" further, he maintained that there was no "comprehensive plan" at the time, other than "ad hockery in action" and a ramping up of offensive operations to eliminate an enemy conceived simply as leftover Ba'athist elements.[27]

Mansoor described in detail the recurring and complex operations designed to flush out and interdict insurgent networks early in the occupation, the challenge of protecting forward operating bases from indirect fire, and the maneuvers undertaken in Operation Sherman, a monthlong operation designed to locate and destroy insur-

---

[24] Ralph O. Baker, "The Decisive Weapon: A Brigade Combat Team Commander's Perspective on Information Operations," *Military Review*, May–June 2006; and Peter A. Mansoor, *Baghdad at Sunrise: A Brigade Commander's War in Iraq*, New Haven, Conn.: Yale University Press, 2008a, pp. 356–357.

[25] By early 2004, some analysis had pursued this dilemma somewhat further, concluding in part that "it is not clear that [rapid, decisive operations are] either useful or necessary" in the fight against terrorist groups (Douglas A. Ollivant, *Rapid, Decisive, or Effective? The Applicability of Rapid Decisive Operations in the Enforcement of the Bush Doctrine*, Fort Leavenworth, Kan.: School of Advanced Military Studies, April 21, 2004).

[26] Mansoor, 2008a, p. 109.

[27] Mansoor, 2008a, p. 109. This assessment was made most memorably by Rumsfeld in his comments about "regime dead-enders." See Brian Bennett, "Who Are the Insurgents?" *Time*, November 16, 2003. The debate is also discussed elsewhere in this report, and it was discussed increasingly widely during the early years of the war; see, for example, Michael Eisenstadt and Jeffrey White, "Assessing Iraq's Sunni Arab Insurgency," *Military Review*, May–June 2006.

gent mortar firing positions that had been harassing American positions in the Green Zone. While facilities were eventually hardened, he emphasized that "offensive operations, engagement with the population, and control of the [surrounding] battlespace" were ultimately more-important measures.[28] Most operations focused on route clearances and cordon-and-search missions, as coalition forces sought to cleanse their areas of insurgent safe houses and disrupt the staging of attacks and production and supply of weapons and improvised explosive devices (IEDs).[29]

Mansoor also recounted how a lack of quality human intelligence sometimes forced coalition troops to engage in more-general and less-targeted house-to-house sweeps in the face of insurgent attacks: "The key was to treat the local population with dignity and respect in order to mitigate the hard feelings that could emerge as a result of the intrusive building searches." While not a foundation of operations, such sweeps were only to be used sparingly and with subsequent "consequence management."[30]

Even though tactical units in Baghdad were adapting to the situation that confronted them in Baghdad, a former senior military commander realized after his arrival that his units were trained for high-intensity combat operations and not for military occupation duties against a growing virulent insurgency. His units were "exquisitely prepared and exquisitely trained for maneuver warfare. . . . Our maneuver warfare tactical operation centers . . . were generally designed to pull intel and information from the top down."[31] He quickly realized that, in Baghdad, the best information was coming from the bottom up, so he began fixing his intelligence fusion and all source analysis centers to adapt to this new reality.

The commander's units were not alone in this regard. From May 2003 on, other combat outfits in Baghdad and throughout Iraq were slowly adapting to their new mission set. For example, a former senior military commander we spoke with largely used the *battlefield framework*—or the way in which military units on the ground delineate areas of responsibility for given units—first developed by the 82nd Airborne when it arrived in Baghdad shortly after the collapse of the regime. He recalled that the plan was "well thought out" and noted,

> It was in large measure based on demographics of the population, geographic terrain feature[s], road networks, bridges and so forth. I earned as I went. For the first three months I played the hand I was dealt and then adapted as the enemy adapted. There is a notion that living among the population was new in 2006, but

---

[28] Mansoor, 2008a, pp. 121–123.

[29] Field Manual (FM) 3-24, *Counterinsurgency*, Washington, D.C.: Headquarters, Department of the Army, December 2006, and other texts have emphasized the patience and resolve required by the counterinsurgency practitioner. See U.S. Interagency Counterinsurgency Initiative, *U.S. Government Counterinsurgency Guide*, Washington, D.C., January 2009.

[30] Mansoor, 2008a, p. 172.

[31] Former senior military commander, interview with the authors, May 21, 2015.

when I got to Baghdad, I had combat outposts adjacent to major buildings. I had little pockets of troops living among the population.[32]

His last point describes how combat units in Baghdad operated in 2004: They were dispersed into the population, which gave them better situational awareness and made them more effective in carrying out operations to suppress the insurgency and, at the same time, rebuild Iraqi institutions.

MG Peter Chiarelli's 1st Cavalry Division, which took over responsibility for most of Baghdad from Dempsey's 1st Armored Division in February 2004, also adapted to its new operating environment. Building on lessons learned from the 1st Armored Division, the 1st Cavalry Division learned to collect intelligence and operate in Baghdad's diverse and religiously heterogeneous neighborhoods, while ensuring the visibility of Iraqi forces to demonstrate Iraqi control and focusing increasingly on "nonkinetic" operations.[33] In southwest Baghdad and the huge district known as West Rasheed, COL Stephen Lanza's 5th Brigade, 1st Cavalry Division navigated mixed areas of both Sunni and Shia populations, as well as some areas that were mostly Sunni. Tied to combat operations against insurgent forces in Baghdad, the American forces carried out reconstruction efforts, such as building or rebuilding city infrastructure.[34] Writing with MAJ Patrick R. Michaelis, Chiarelli argued in mid-2005 for "full-spectrum operations," stating that "it is no longer sufficient to think in purely kinetic terms" and that the military must embrace "economic pluralism," governance, and the "restoration/improvement of essential services" alongside more-traditional combat operations and the training of local security forces.[35] Thus, at this time, an inchoate program of building Iraq's security forces—namely, the Iraq Police and the Iraqi Army—began.[36]

Despite Chiarelli's optimism for softer operations, however, trouble was brewing on his arrival. Furious at the muzzling of a newspaper for incitement and arrest of an adviser for murder, the radical cleric Moqtada al-Sadr's Jaysh al-Mahdi militia "exploded into violence."[37] Within two days, insurgents emplaced 28 IEDs across the

---

[32] Former senior military commander, interview with the authors, May 21, 2015.

[33] Bruce R. Pirnie and Edward O'Connell, *Counterinsurgency in Iraq (2003–2006): RAND Counterinsurgency Study—Volume 2*, Santa Monica, Calif.: RAND Corporation, MG-595/3-OSD, 2008, pp. 41–42.

[34] Scott Wilson, "A Different Street Fight in Iraq: U.S. General Turns to Public Works in Battle for Hearts and Minds," *Washington Post*, May 27, 2004.

[35] Peter W. Chiarelli and Patrick R. Michaelis, "Winning the Peace: The Requirement for Full-Spectrum Operations," *Military Review*, July–August 2005.

[36] Stephen Lanza, interview with Peter Connors, Contemporary Operations Study Team, Combat Studies Institute, November 2, 2005, transcript provided to RAND by the OIF Study Group; Brian J. McKiernan, interview with the Contemporary Operations Study Team, Combat Studies Institute, April 29, 2006, transcript provided to RAND by the OIF Study Group; and Wright and Reese, 2008, pp. 87–88, 567–568.

[37] Michael R. Gordon and Bernard E. Trainor, *The Endgame: The Inside Story of the Struggle for Iraq, from George W. Bush to Barack Obama*, New York: Vintage Books, 2012, p. 67.

country, and within the week, 10,000 supporters of Sadr were protesting in the streets of Baghdad.[38] An ambush in Sadr City left eight U.S. soldiers dead,[39] and parts of Iraqi National Guard battalions began mass desertions. As he would do again several times, Sadr eventually declared a cease-fire to avoid further losses. The victory was pyrrhic for U.S. forces, however, as losses had been relatively heavy and the cleric retained the ability to play a spoiling hand at times of his choosing.[40]

In the southwestern quadrant of Baghdad centered on the district of al Dora, MAJ Douglas Ollivant, then an operations officer in one of the 1st Cavalry Division's combat battalions, reduced his battalion's lessons learned to the following five essential operating principles:

1. Successful counterinsurgency operations require assistance from the community.
2. A static unit with responsibility for a specific area of responsibility is preferable to a mobile unit moving from area to area.
3. No one approach can defeat an insurgency.
4. The principle of unity of command is even more important in counterinsurgency than it is in conventional warfare.
5. Effective counterinsurgency requires a grid of embedded units.[41]

In applying these five essential principles to their part of Baghdad, Ollivant and his battalion discerned the "vexing problem" that armed nation-building presents to a conventionally trained army:

> The Army fights and wins America's battles through land dominance, not by establishing civic, security, and economic institutions in failed states. Such nation-building requires the strategic and operational application of national power (a subject well beyond the scope of this paper), but at the tactical level, [counterinsurgency] and nation-building tasks are the same: Both call for grassroots support and require Soldiers to win popular approval by solving practical problems: turning on electricity, keeping the streets safe, kinetic coercion, while others benefit from less. It is the counterinsurgent, living among the population and working with local security forces and opinion-makers, who must integrate the operations to achieve the desired effect.[42]

---

[38] Mansoor, 2008a, pp. 280–281.

[39] For a detailed account of this engagement, see John C. Moore, "Sadr City: The Armor Pure Assault in Urban Terrain," *Armor*, November–December 2004.

[40] Center for Military History, "The April 2004 Battle of Sadr City," April 21, 2014.

[41] Douglas A. Ollivant and Eric D. Chewning, "Producing Victory: Rethinking Conventional Forces in COIN Operations," *Military Review*, July–August 2006.

[42] Ollivant and Chewning, 2006, pp. 51–52; see also Douglas A. Ollivant, "Producing Victory: A 2007 Post-Script for Implementation," *Military Review*, March–April 2007.

Ollivant captured what his battalion—and many other battalions like his—learned in Baghdad in 2004.

The 1st Cavalry Division's time in Baghdad, however, is best known for its operations in the Shia stronghold of Sadr City. Soon after arriving, Chiarelli designed a plan to combine security operations in order to capture and kill Shia militia loyal to Moqtada al-Sadr and still improve the infrastructure in Sadr City and form new Iraqi governmental institutions. A former senior military commander we spoke with gave Chiarelli a "lot of credit" for the work his division was doing in Sadr City.[43] The former commander noted that in preparing for the 1st Cavalry Division's deployment to Baghdad, Chiarelli took his senior leaders to Austin, Texas, so that they could at least get a sense of "how to run a city whether it is paving roads or [managing] sewage" or running a police force and understanding the duties of city managers.[44]

Not all units adjusted to counterinsurgency and nation-building operations as successfully as the 1st Cavalry Division. While Chiarelli had figured out what it took to "run a city" at the "civil level" of a million people in his area of Baghdad, a former senior military commander recalled that there was a "gap . . . between what other American civilian agencies were trying to do and with the [military] unit that owned the territory. It was hard to track down where the money went to" in a given area of operation.[45] He also lamented the fact that in his subordinate units, reconstruction work would often have to take a "back seat" to combat operations.[46]

Especially during that first year of the American intervention, Baghdad was a difficult place to plan and conduct military operations. A sprawling, heterogeneous city estimated at well over 5 million people,[47] the relative newness of the mission and the strategic confusion at the upper echelons only added to the complexity of the task for tactical units. To further complicate matters, the Army brigades deployed to Baghdad were not the only actors in the city at the time. Between 2003 and 2004, these Army units shared their mission of rebuilding Iraq with a civilian agency—first ORHA and then CPA.

---

[43] Former senior military commander, interview with the authors, June 2, 2015.

[44] Former senior military commander, interview with the authors, June 2, 2015; former senior military commander, interview with the authors, April 7, 2015; and Chiarelli and Michaelis, 2005.

[45] Former senior military commander, interview with the authors, June 2, 2015.

[46] Former senior military commander, interview with the authors, June 2, 2015.

[47] Accurate estimates of Baghdad's size are difficult to come by, owing to the lack of accurate census data and the ongoing conflict spurring population transfers. In 2005, the U.N. estimated that Baghdad had about 5.9 million people (Louay Bahry, "Baghdad," *Encyclopedia Britannica*, undated).

ORHA's Short-Lived Tenure

"It was stillborn. It never got off the ground,"[48] judged Secretary Condoleezza Rice on the ill-fated ORHA. Led by retired LTG Jay Garner, ORHA had a short, four-month existence from January 20 to May 11, 2003. On paper, Garner seemed like the perfect candidate. As a senior military officer, he led the assistance effort to the Kurds after the first Gulf War. In theory, ORHA had a similar mission. It was supposed to reconstruct Iraq, rebuild its infrastructure, and help it recover from the war. But as a former senior national security official remarked to us, the United States quickly found out that *reconstruction* was a misnomer: "The word reconstruction itself reveals the misconception of the situation in Iraq at the time. There was no reconstruction; there was a war going on. The enemy blew up whatever you built."[49] And so, rather than leading a humanitarian mission, ORHA found itself as the nucleus of an occupation government.[50]

ORHA was created at the order of Secretary of Defense Rumsfeld and initially had a direct line to the Secretary of Defense through the Under Secretary of Defense for Policy.[51] In addition to the retired military officers, there were senior diplomats and policy hands. Although ORHA's staff was eventually about three-quarters civilian, in the words of ORHA's semiofficial historian Gordon Rudd, "the real methodology in ORHA was predominantly military."[52] ORHA was subdivided into three "pillars" for humanitarian assistance, reconstruction, and CA (charged with setting up the ministries) and three regions (north, central, and south), with a military-like staff to oversee the operations.[53] Seemingly, it should have been a good fit to work with the military and create the underpinnings of a successful occupation. And yet, in practice, it ran into significant difficulties.

To begin with, ORHA was thrown together just before the invasion. Ambassador Robin Raphel, who served as Senior Adviser to the Ministry of Trade and later as Coordinator for Iraq Reconstruction, recounted to Rudd that she was asked to join

---

[48] Condoleezza Rice, interview with Jason Awadi and Jeanne Godfroy, U.S. Department of State, Office of the Historian, July 12, 2014, p. 5, transcript provided to RAND by the OIF Study Group.

[49] Former senior national security official, interview with the authors, April 8, 2015.

[50] For an additional discussion of ORHA's tenure, see Nora Bensahel, Olga Oliker, Keith Crane, Heather S. Gregg, Richard R. Brennan, Jr., and Andrew Rathmell, "The Aftermath: Civilian Planning Efforts and the Occupation of Iraq," in Walter L. Perry, Richard E. Darilek, Laurinda L. Rohn, and Jerry M. Sollinger, eds., *Operation IRAQI FREEDOM: Decisive War, Elusive Peace*, Santa Monica, Calif.: RAND Corporation, RR-1214-A, 2015, pp. 328–329.

[51] Former senior DoD official, interview with the authors, July 7, 2015.

[52] Gordon Rudd, interview, February 27, 2006, p. 7, transcript provided to RAND by the OIF Study Group.

[53] Former ORHA official, interview with the authors, May 12, 2016; and former ORHA official, email correspondence with the authors, May 9, 2016.

ORHA "rather last moment."[54] Similarly, former ORHA and CPA official Meghan O'Sullivan recounted to Rudd that she deployed to Qatar within five days of hearing that she was selected to participate.[55]

A former ORHA official also recalled that,

> when ORHA deployed from Washington, D.C., to Kuwait on 16–17 March 2003, it had 179 personnel. By 26 March ORHA had 227 personnel in Kuwait. In mid-April when ORHA deployed into Iraq, it had about 350 personnel. Once in Baghdad, it was augmented by an Army Military Police Company and part of a Signal Company with about 160 Army personnel altogether (not enough). It had a dozen contractors from Raytheon for communications and about 100 personnel from KBR for general support in the Palace. For external security around the Palace it had a Florida National Guard rifle company with about 100 soldiers. For internal security it had 100 contract soldiers from Nepal. A group of Iraqi ex-pats joined from the USA and the UK. While in Iraq, ORHA continued to have additional people join from the United States and a few from other coalition countries. By the end of April, ORHA had about 1,000 personnel altogether. Close to 90% of these were located in the Palace in Baghdad, to include Region Central. Region North and Region South each had about 50 personnel at their respective locations; each would continue to grow. Although the numbers would seem close to what was needed, ORHA had many senior and critical subordinate positions unfilled through May, notably for the Ministry of Defense [MOD], which was to be held by Walter Slocombe, who chose not to deploy until Bremer arrived.[56]

Part of the reason for ORHA's ad hoc creation was that, officially, the Bush administration did not decide to go to war with Iraq until relatively shortly before the conflict began. Without an official decision to go to war, many in the bureaucracy felt that they could not plan—much less resource—for the period after major combat operations. O'Sullivan recalled that ORHA official and diplomat Lewis Luck said, "We have plans for . . . I am just using the terms loosely . . . like $2.7 billion worth of work, and we have a shortfall of 2.5 billion. And people kept saying, 'That is because the President hasn't made a decision to go to war'; and therefore, there's been no supplemental request."[57] Only on March 20, 2003, did President Bush sign an executive order unfreezing Iraqi funds, giving Garner and his team access to some

---

[54] Robin L. Raphel, interview with Gordon Rudd, November 15, 2005, p. 8, transcript provided to RAND by the OIF Study Group.

[55] Meghan O'Sullivan, interview with Gordon Rudd, December 29, 2003, pp. 3–4, transcript provided to RAND by the OIF Study Group.

[56] Former ORHA official, email correspondence with the authors, May 9, 2016.

[57] Meghan O'Sullivan, interview with Gordon Rudd, December 29, 2003, p. 5, transcript provided to RAND by the OIF Study Group.

$1.7 billion.[58] Moreover, at least according to some accounts, the Bush administration applied ideological litmus tests to ORHA employees, and Garner needed to fight to get certain members of his team on board, further slowing the staffing process.[59] As a result, unlike military units, ORHA could not train together extensively before the major combat operations in Iraq.

The hurried timeline also meant that ORHA never established a close relationship with the military. A former senior military official recounts wanting to colocate ORHA with CFLCC in Kuwait prior to major combat operations, but by the time ORHA got on the ground, there was no room. As a result, ORHA had to rent villas separate from CFLCC—eliminating any opportunity for a habitual relationship between the two.[60] The ambiguous command and control relationship between Garner and CFLCC Lieutenant General McKiernan further complicated matters. Rather than being under McKiernan or CENTCOM commander GEN Tommy Franks organizationally, Garner reported directly to Rumsfeld, complicating unity of command and laying the foundation for—as one observer at the time recalled—a "dysfunctional" command relationship.[61] In this sense, Garner's own military background likely complicated the situation. McKiernan was junior to Garner (when Garner was a three-star general in the mid-1990s, McKiernan was still a colonel),[62] and Garner and McKiernan's boss, Franks, had commanded battalions in the same division in the 1980s.[63] Consequently, the question of who should report to whom became even more muddled.

Underfunded and without a strong organizational relationship with the military, ORHA found itself paralyzed, unable to move around Iraq. Even getting to Baghdad after major combat operations began took longer than expected. As one former senior military official recounted, ORHA lacked helicopters to move around the country, much less engineers, military police, and all the other assets it needed to do its job effectively.[64] He also described that Franks supported providing ORHA with security contracts, but CENTCOM was able to provide troops to protect ORHA staff and facilitate their work in Iraq.[65] As a former senior State Department and CPA official,

---

[58] Dov S. Zakheim, *A Vulcan's Tale: How the Bush Administration Mismanaged the Reconstruction of Afghanistan*, Washington D.C.: Brookings Institution Press, 2011, p. 196; see also Ferguson, 2008, p. 91.

[59] Meghan O'Sullivan, interview with Gordon Rudd, December 29, 2003, pp. 9, 11–12, transcript provided to RAND by the OIF Study Group; and Gordon and Trainor, 2006, p. 475.

[60] Former senior military commander, interview with the authors, June 9, 2015.

[61] Former senior military commander, interview with the authors, April 17, 2015.

[62] Gordon Rudd, interview, February 27, 2006, pp. 33–34, transcript provided to RAND by the OIF Study Group.

[63] Gordon Rudd, interview, February 27, 2006, p. 35, transcript provided to RAND by the OIF Study Group.

[64] Former senior military commander, interview with the authors, June 9, 2015; see also Ferguson, 2008, p. 92.

[65] Former senior military commander, interview with the authors, June 9, 2015.

who went to Iraq in May 2003, recounted, "Garner was trying to do a job he didn't have the resources or authority for."[66]

Even if ORHA had been better resourced, it is not clear how much of a difference it would have made. Thanks to the hurried timeline, ORHA's prewar planning was both cursory and based on strategic assumptions that eventually proved invalid. As its name implied, ORHA was prepared to conduct reconstruction and humanitarian assistance—not occupation and governance.[67] Indeed, the very selection of Garner to lead ORHA belied a governance mission. As a former senior national security official remarked, "Garner wasn't prepared for or really a good candidate for leading an occupation as a political matter instead of a technical, humanitarian, administrative matter."[68] In a 2007 *Foreign Affairs* article, British Prime Minister Tony Blair essentially admitted as much: "Real worry back in 2003 was a humanitarian crisis," which drove much of the postwar planning.[69] ORHA—and postwar planning—also did not anticipate the rapid fall of the regime. As a former senior State Department and CPA official remarked, "The whole war plan envisioned that Garner would have months in southern Iraq to prove to people in Baghdad and beyond what Iraq would look like if they walked away from the regime. Instead, Garner was there overnight and was soon asked to put a civilian face on the occupation."[70]

ORHA—or any part of the U.S. government for that matter—also had different expectations about the state of Iraqi society. Before the war, many in the administration thought Iraq was a coherent state and was one of the most progressive and westernized in the Arab world before the Saddam regime. And so, when Saddam fell, many assumed that there could be an orderly and relatively stable transition to a postwar regime.[71] As mentioned, this assumption turned out to be invalid. As a former senior national security official recounted, "What I didn't appreciate enough was the degree

---

[66] Former senior State Department and CPA official, interview with the authors, June 3, 2015.

[67] In a PBS interview from 2006, Garner recounted that much of his planning while in Kuwait was aimed at what he (and many others) believed were the most likely postwar crises—oil wells being set on fire, mass refugee flows possibly in conjunction with the use of chemical weapons against civilians, and epidemic brought on by a collapse of the water infrastructure. Fortunately, none of these events occurred (Frontline, "Interviews: Lt. Gen. Jay Garner (ret.)," Public Broadcasting Service, August 11, 2006a). See also James Dobbins, Seth G. Jones, Benjamin Runkle, and Siddarth Mohandas, *Occupying Iraq: A History of the Coalition Provisional Authority*, Santa Monica, Calif.: RAND Corporation, MG-847-CC, 2009, p. 4.

[68] Former senior national security official, interview with the authors, May 21, 2015.

[69] Tony Blair, "A Battle for Global Values," *Foreign Affairs*, Vol. 86, No. 1, January–February 2007, p. 85.

[70] Former senior State Department and CPA official, interview with the authors, June 3, 2015.

[71] Indeed, this assumption partially drove coalition forces to surround Baghdad originally, assuming that once it was surrounded, Saddam would be toppled and the coalition could then conduct an orderly transition to the new regime. Bruce R. Pirnie, John Gordon IV, Richard R. Brennan, Jr., Forrest E. Morgan, Alexander C. Hou, Chad Yost, Andrea Mejia, and David E. Mosher, "Land Operations," in Walter L. Perry, Richard E. Darilek, Laurinda L. Rohn, and Jerry M. Sollinger, eds., *Operation IRAQI FREEDOM: Decisive War, Elusive Peace*, Santa Monica, Calif.: RAND Corporation, RR-1214-A, 2015, p. 95.

to which Saddam had smashed and atomized Iraqi society. Others didn't realize it either."[72] And so, when Baghdad fell to coalition forces in April 2003, the city plunged into chaos.

Indeed, descriptions from civilians present at that time paint a vivid picture of the turmoil and destruction that engulfed Baghdad. Ambassador Raphel, for example, recounted how much of the government infrastructure had collapsed: "The Ministry of Trade had several sites around town, all of which were trashed."[73] In noting his initial impressions of the city, a former CPA official stated, "Looting was going on everywhere. You could see the looting from the air and on the streets. Ministry buildings were burning or damaged in some way. It was hot. Everyone worked out of the palace. It was chaotic."[74] Other senior diplomats viewed the city similarly. A former senior State Department official recounted how his initial impressions of Baghdad shortly after arriving in May 2003 were that it was "chaotic" and how "there was a tremendous amount of damage in the city not caused by the invasion, but by the postinvasion looting."[75]

Upon getting to Bagdad, ORHA tried to reestablish the Iraqi ministries. In describing the initial attempts to stand up the ministries, Raphel said, "In that respect, there wasn't much guidance to be had because we [were] all playing it by ear. And the key in the beginning was to get people to make contact with Iraqis in the ministry."[76] At times, ORHA representatives went into the street trying to find bureaucrats and piece the ministries together. Because of a lack of functioning Iraqi communications gear, facilities, and adequate security, it was slow, difficult, and frustrating work.[77]

Ultimately, ORHA's progress was not fast enough for Washington. Frustrated with the disintegration of law and order in Iraq and what it perceived as ORHA's slow pace to get to Baghdad (also a function of ORHA's lack of mobility), the Bush administration decided to change leadership.[78] According to Rumsfeld, the administration always planned to transition the lead for the reconstruction task to a civilian, most likely a State Department official, after the end of the conflict.[79] And yet, no one—and certainly not Garner—expected it to be this soon.[80] A mere day after Garner arrived in

---

[72] Former senior national security official, interview with the authors, May 21, 2015.

[73] Robin L. Raphel, interview with Gordon Rudd, November 15, 2005, p. 26, transcript provided to RAND by the OIF Study Group.

[74] Former CPA official, interview with the authors, March 30, 2015.

[75] Former senior State Department official, interview with the authors, April 16, 2015.

[76] Robin L. Raphel, interview with Gordon Rudd, November 15, 2005, p. 25, transcript provided to RAND by the OIF Study Group.

[77] Former senior military commander, interview with the authors, June 9, 2015.

[78] Ricks, 2006a, p. 155; Zakheim, 2011, p. 202.

[79] Rumsfeld, 2011, p. 503.

[80] Rumsfeld, 2011, p. 503.

Baghdad, he received a call from Rumsfeld saying that Bush had selected diplomat and Republican foreign policy hand L. Paul Bremer III as Garner's successor.[81] A few weeks later, on May 12, 2003, Bremer arrived in Baghdad, and shortly thereafter, Garner headed home. While the hand-off between Garner and Bremer was conducted "in the most productive manner possible" according to Raphel, the circumstances made the transition an awkward one for both men.[82]

Ultimately, ORHA's story is one of seemingly small, early mishaps having outsized effects. Because the United States was unable to admit publicly that it was going to war in Iraq, ORHA was stood up late and formed on an ad hoc basis. Because it was ad hoc, it never hammered out the critical civil-military relationship between it and CFLCC, nor did it thoroughly plan for missions. Because ORHA did not have an established relationship with the military, it lacked assets to move around the country and provide the substantial support needed to stabilize Iraq. Because it was formed quickly and in ad hoc fashion, it lacked robust contingency plans if Iraq needed something other than humanitarian assistance.

Coalition Provisional Authority and the American Attempt at Occupation

Despite the name change and the new leadership, CPA was not a new organization. Indeed, a former CPA official, for his part, noted that CPA was based on the structure that Lieutenant General Garner had established for ORHA and that Bremer reshaped and reorganized that existing structure.[83] For the most part, the original ORHA members agree. As ORHA historian Rudd remarked, "ORHA kind of blended into CPA. A lot of ORHA people transitioned out, a lot of CPA people came in, and the overall task greatly expanded."[84] What Bremer brought to CPA that was new was a dramatically different conception than the one Garner, Rumsfeld, and many senior military officers had about how to govern Iraq.

Before Bremer's arrival, the theory for postwar Iraq was that American forces should leave Iraq and transition control of the government to Iraqis as quickly as possible. This "light footprint" conception of Iraq (heralded by Rumsfeld, among others) rested on an overly optimistic prediction about the state of Iraqi society in a post-Saddam Iraq, as well as a more sophisticated argument—the *antibody thesis*. According to this theory, the longer that large numbers of American forces stayed in Arab lands

---

[81] Former senior military commander, interview with the authors, June 9, 2015.

[82] Robin L. Raphel, interview with Gordon Rudd, November 15, 2005, p. 34, transcript provided to RAND by the OIF Study Group.

[83] Former CPA official, interview with the authors, March 30, 2015.

[84] Gordon Rudd, interview, February 27, 2006, p. 5, transcript provided to RAND by the OIF Study Group.

in the heart of the Muslim world, the more likely it was to breed resentment. In other words, the half-life between Americans being viewed as "liberators" rather than "occupiers" was a very short one, and so it was far better to reduce American presence as quickly as possible to avoid spurring a backlash.[85]

Bremer approached the problem somewhat differently. He argued that political and economic progress was predicated on securing and stabilizing Iraq.[86] As a result, contrary to what the Pentagon thought, he and CPA argued that the nascent Iraqi Army was incapable of substituting for an American presence in Iraq—a 15-brigade rotation in the spring of 2004.[87] Additionally, Bremer privately recommended to the Secretary of Defense an increase of two divisions to cope with the deteriorating security situation. In hindsight, even some military officers—such as GEN Jack Keane—believe that Bremer's basic instinct here was correct.[88] Ultimately, Bremer saw his task as establishing a caretaker government that would eventually create the conditions for the return of Iraqi sovereignty.

Soon after arriving in Baghdad, Bremer tried to fix some of the perceived problems of ORHA. As Rudd recounted, "ORHA did not project or perceive the weight of the task that was the future."[89] Bremer tried to change this perception. He met with ORHA-turned-CPA employees from all levels and projected an authoritative, if imperial, tone about the scale and gravity of the task ahead.[90] And at least according to some, he succeeded in this regard. Another former senior CPA official remarked that, initially, "Bremer certainly did [have standing among the Iraqi people]. People greeted him as a hero."[91] The new tone, however, did not sit well with everyone, most notably Garner, and observers from the time recount that there was considerable friction between the two.[92]

Bremer set about streamlining the CPA bureaucracy. As another former CPA official recounted to us,

> It didn't transform overnight, but Bremer brought to the CPA a sense of how you need to construct a decisionmaking process. For instance, he created an executive secretariat and institutionalized a process by which papers could flow. He stood up regular senior staff meetings and regularized a lot. Bremer set the priorities

---

[85] Douglas Lute, interview with Mathew Wharton, undated, p. 3, transcript provided to RAND by the OIF Study Group.

[86] Dobbins, Jones, et al., 2009, p. xxi.

[87] Former CPA official, interview with the authors, March 30, 2015.

[88] Former senior military commander, interview with the authors, April 17, 2015.

[89] Gordon Rudd, interview, February 27, 2006, p. 5, transcript provided to RAND by the OIF Study Group.

[90] Former CPA official, interview with the authors, March 30, 2015.

[91] Former CPA official, interview with the authors, June 1, 2015.

[92] Former ORHA official, email correspondence with the authors, May 9, 2016.

through those leadership syncs. It didn't take long, but Bremer imposed a process that clarified how decisions would be made. This happened pretty quickly and was a clear objective of Bremer.[93]

Earlier in his career, Bremer had served as Executive Secretary of the State Department under Alexander Haig, and in Baghdad, he brought some of the same skills to bear.[94]

Bremer also managed to leverage the resources of the State Department. Despite the postwar impression of CPA being staffed by junior, inexperienced hands who owed their positions to political connections rather than expertise, at its senior rungs, CPA attracted high-caliber personnel. As a former senior national security official recounted, "there were very serious people at the higher levels, such as [Ambassador] Robert Ford, [Ambassador Ryan] Crocker, [former British Ambassador to the United Nations Jeremy] Greenstock, etc. These people at the top were dedicated and smart and had good relations with Iraqis, but they were put in a difficult situation."[95] And so, while CPA's staff included inexperienced but politically well-connected civilians, viewed holistically, CPA's composition proved a mixed bag.

Despite these advances, however, many of the other problems that plagued ORHA persisted under CPA. The creation of CPA did not solve the interagency animosity back in Washington, and if anything, CPA exacerbated it. CPA fell outside both the State and Defense Departments' chains of commands. A senior DoD official was at one point supposed to assume the role of Bremer's deputy, but Bremer supposedly vetoed the idea, not wanting to have DoD looking over his shoulder.[96]

At the same time, Bremer and CPA also fell outside the State Department's reporting channels.[97] Indeed, the reason that Bremer, a former diplomat, was picked for the position—as opposed to a currently serving diplomat—was because some in the Bush administration felt that the State Department could not be trusted with the task. As one former senior national security official recounted,

> There was a bias in the White House and DoD against having anyone in the State Department's Near East Asia bureau, which had a reputation of being against

---

[93] Former senior State Department and CPA official, interview with the authors, June 3, 2015.

[94] Dobbins, Jones, et al., 2011, p. 11.

[95] Former senior national security official, interview with the authors, September 25, 2015. For this depiction of CPA, see Rajiv Chandrasekaran, *Imperial Life in the Emerald City*, New York: Vintage Books, 2006a; Rajiv Chandrasekaran, "Who Killed Iraq?" *Foreign Policy*, Vol. 156, September–October 2006b; and Ricks, 2006a, pp. 203–208. James Dobbins has a somewhat more charitable view: "The CPA operation became an exercise in heroic amateurism, in which hundreds of dedicated, courageous Americans went and filled positions for which they had not the slightest preparation" (Frontline, "Inside the Green Zone," Public Broadcasting Service, October 17, 2006b).

[96] Former senior DoD official, interview with the authors, July 7, 2015.

[97] Dobbins, Jones, et al., 2011, p. 19.

Bush's policies, head the CPA. There was a sense they weren't with the program and that you needed to have someone who supported the war and wanted this to succeed head the CPA. It wasn't just bias or political differences; you wanted someone who was committed to the war.[98]

Perhaps unsurprising given this environment, some in CPA blamed Washington infighting for its problems in the field. As one former CPA official noted, CPA's principal problem "wasn't from lack of understanding but from lack of nonfinancial resources. The fight between State/NSC and Defense was endless."[99]

While Bremer claims that it was a "myth" that he and his military counterpart CJTF-7 commander, LTG Ricardo Sanchez, were at loggerheads, other firsthand accounts suggest that the civil-military divide extended beyond Washington to Baghdad.[100] A Defense Policy Board member who visited Iraq during this period recalled that Baghdad at that time "was dysfunctional. It was clear the military and civilians didn't like each other and weren't talking to each other."[101] A member of CJTF-7 who spoke with us remembered that many CJTF-7 senior officers thought—and wanted to prove—that Sanchez was senior to Bremer.[102] Sanchez himself rejected any notion of being subordinate to Bremer.[103] Nonetheless, while Bremer talked directly to President Bush and Prime Minister Blair, Sanchez had to go through the CENTCOM commander, JCS, and Rumsfeld before getting to the President.[104]

Even if Bremer and Sanchez were actually united, the appearance of dysfunction proved deeply problematic. While Bremer may have had the ear of the President, Sanchez still had the resources. Indeed, formally, Bremer had no authority over 98 percent of the American personnel in Iraq.[105] As a former CPA official noted, "The problem, which was also the problem for Bremer, was Garner had no authority. There were 150,000 troops in country and a hundred civilians. CPA eventually grew to 3,000 civilians if you count all contractors, including cooks."[106] He recalled one heated exchange he had with then–Major General Petraeus, who was commanding the 101st Airborne

---

[98] Former senior national security official, interview with the authors, May 21, 2015. For confirmation of DoD personnel's widespread skepticism of the State Department, and the Near East Bureau in particular, see Zakheim, 2011, p. 198.

[99] Former CPA official, interview with the authors, June 1, 2015; see also, Dobbins, Jones, et al., 2011, p. 29.

[100] See Bensahel, 2006, pp. 465–466; and Ricks, 2006a, pp. 209–212.

[101] Former Defense Policy Board member, interview with the authors, June 10, 2015. The Defense Policy Board is a body of former high-ranking civilian and military officials that provides counsel to the Secretary of Defense.

[102] Former military commander, interview with the authors, April 17, 2015.

[103] Dobbins, Jones, et al., 2011, p. 17.

[104] Former military commander, interview with the authors, April 17, 2015.

[105] Dobbins, Jones, et al., 2011, p. xiii.

[106] Former senior State Department and CPA official, interview with the authors, June 3, 2015.

(Air Assault) Division at the time; the conversation ultimately concluded when Petraeus remarked to him, "I have more JAG [judge advocate general, or military lawyer] officers than you have people."[107] Celeste Ward, the former Director of National Security Policy, similarly argued that there was a mismatch between CPA's mandate and its capacity, which led some military officers to refer to it as "Can't Provide Anything."[108] With only 56 percent of its required personnel and little ability to move independently around the country, CPA needed military resources to perform even the most basic activities.[109] A former CPA official noted that CPA even needed to buy old Iraqi taxis to get around because there were too few military vehicles to escort them given all the missions they had to take on and, in any case, traveling discreetly in taxis was safer than traveling in Humvees. CPA lacked other options to move around Baghdad.[110]

Aside from the civil-military challenges, it is not clear how well CPA understood the threat environment. Another former CPA official recalled identifying the growing Iraqi insurgency by October 23, 2004 (as opposed to former regime "dead-enders" that Rumsfeld described, for example), but others disagree.[111] That said, a former senior national security official argued that, when he arrived in Iraq right after the CPA period, he thought CPA had been slow to realize that Iraq was in an insurgency.[112] A former senior State Department official, who served in Iraq during the transition from Bremer to John Negroponte and later under Negroponte at the embassy, agreed. He believed that CPA did not have a good sensing of the nature of insurgency. In particular, it missed the significance of the Jaysh al-Mahdi militia and did not connect the dots between the tactical intelligence that the CIA and others were gathering at the time and the broader Shia aspect of the insurgency.[113]

In fairness to CPA, however, the evidence was conflicting. In the immediate aftermath of major combat operations, Iraq descended into chaos, with widespread criminal behavior but less organized resistance to the American occupation.[114] In a June 18, 2003, interview, then-MG Raymond T. Odierno, commander of the 4th Infantry Division responsible for the Sunni stronghold of Tikrit, told reporters, "This is not guerilla warfare. It is not closer to guerilla warfare because it is not coordinated, it's not

---

[107] Former senior State Department and CPA official, interview with the authors, June 3, 2015.

[108] Celeste J. Ward, *The Coalition Provisional Authority's Experience with Governance in Iraq: Lessons Identified*, United States Institute of Peace, Special Report 139, May 2005, p. 10.

[109] See Bensahel, 2006, pp. 462–463.

[110] Former senior State Department and CPA official, interview with the authors, June 3, 2015.

[111] Former CPA official, interview with the authors, March 30, 2015.

[112] Former senior national security official, interview with the authors, April 8, 2015. In fairness, the entire U.S. government—including Rumsfeld, Wolfowitz, and others—shied away from even using the term *insurgency* (Ricks, 2006a, pp. 168–172).

[113] Former senior State Department official, interview with the authors, April 9, 2015.

[114] Ferguson, 2008, pp. 104–138.

organized, and it's not led."[115] A former senior State Department official recounted that although there was chaos and rampant vandalism in Baghdad when he joined CPA, "there was no organized resistance" and he personally felt safe driving around in unarmored vehicles.[116] Moreover, at the time, most people in Washington—or Baghdad—were not better informed. CPA deputy and senior adviser to MOD Walter Slocombe recalled that before departing for Iraq, he "got a lot of information about offensive capabilities and weapons and stuff, but it's harder to [understand] the sociology, what the people were like, what the problems were, and how it fit into the society as a whole from the intelligence community. But we did have lots of people at CPA with deep knowledge of the region."[117]

And the Washington policy community was not more coherent in terms of its understanding of the threat. A former senior DoD official remarked,

> Even now, I'm not sure I understand what an insurgency is. When's the difference between insurgency and lawlessness and problems—who's leading the insurgency? At the time, you had eight different power centers. No coordinated strategy, differing ideologies. I think it was a really messy opaque security situation. To me, an insurgency is when there's a political purpose, a power structure, and a critical mass of capability that wants change in a discernible direction; that wasn't apparent at the time.[118]

A former member of the Defense Policy Board similarly recalled briefings to the Defense Policy Board in which DoD would suggest that the violence in Iraq was caused by a "few thousand dead-enders," to which he replied, "You've killed them all at least once or maybe twice if I add up the numbers, so why are there still 5,000 of them still out there?"[119]

Despite its limitations and structural problems, CPA managed to rack up an impressive number of accomplishments during its year of existence from May 2003 to June 2004. It stood up the Iraqi Governing Council to provide the first steps to a return to Iraqi self-government, and it continued ORHA's work in reconstituting the Iraqi bureaucracy. It formulated the Transitional Administrative Law, which became the basis for the Iraqi constitution. CPA helped on the economic front as well, heading off concerns about the dollarization of Iraq's economy and initially trying to priva-

---

[115] Ricks, 2006a, p. 170. These impressions, according to media accounts, only began to change in the summer and fall of 2003. See, for example, CNN, "Time Reporter: Iraqi Resistance Getting Smarter," November 20, 2003e.

[116] Former senior State Department official, interview with the authors, April 16, 2015.

[117] Walter B. Slocombe, interview with Gordon Rudd, July 18, 2003, p. 5, transcript provided to RAND by the OIF Study Group; for a similar critique, see Ferguson, 2008, p. 93.

[118] Former senior DoD official, interview with the authors, July 7, 2015.

[119] Former Defense Policy Board member, interview with the authors, June 10, 2015.

tize many of the Iraqi state-run enterprises before realizing that such a program was impractical.[120] CPA also made progress on the security front. CPA officials reached agreements with all the major militia—the Kurdistan Democratic Party and Patriotic Union of Kurdistan Peshmergas, the Badr corps, the Sunni militia (Iraqi Islamic Party), and the major Iraqi Shia militias that were not Jaysh al-Mahdi units—to bring their people into programs, such as job training, police and army positions, or pensions. These programs were ultimately not implemented, because neither the U.S. embassy nor MNF-I was willing to see it to fruition.[121] Despite all of CPA's actions—good and bad—none looms as large today as its two initial orders.

CPA Orders 1 and 2

With the possible exception of going to war in Iraq in the first place, no decisions remain as controversial today as CPA Order Number 1, mandating that all Ba'ath party members be excluded from the new government, and Order Number 2, disbanding Iraq's existing army.[122] Both orders were signed by Bremer two months after CPA was established—on May 16, 2003, and May 23, 2003, respectively.[123] Both orders functionally upended and reshaped Iraqi society, throwing the once-ruling military and political elites out of power and forcing the coalition to create a new cadre of elites to fill their places. And while the significance of CPA Orders 1 and 2 is undisputed, at least four active debates surround both orders: (1) who gave the orders, (2) how were they supposed to be implemented, (3) were they necessary, and, most importantly, (4) what was their effect?

---

[120] Robin L. Raphel, interview with Gordon Rudd, November 15, 2005, p. 21, transcript provided to RAND by the OIF Study Group.

[121] Former official at the U.S. embassy in Baghdad, interview with the authors, May 26, 2015.

[122] For example, for the controversy surrounding the orders playing out in the policy sphere, see Farnaz Fassihi, Greg Jaffe, Yaroslav Trofimov, Carla Anne Robbins, and Yochi J. Dreazen, "Early U.S. Decisions on Iraq Now Haunt American Efforts Officials Let Looters Roam, Disbanded Army, Allowed Radicals to Gain Strength," *Wall Street Journal*, April 19, 2004; Frontline, "Key Controversies of the Post-War Period: Debaathification," Public Broadcasting Service, October 17, 2006c; Sebastian Usher, "Baathist Mistake Corrected Amid Concern," BBC News, January 12, 2008; and Liz Sly, "The Hidden Hand Behind the Islamic State Militants? Saddam Hussein's," *Washington Post*, April 4, 2015. For the debate about de-Ba'athification in the academic arena, see Daniel Byman, "An Autopsy of the Iraq Debacle: Policy Failure or Bridge Too Far?" *Security Studies*, Vol. 17, October 2008; and James P. Pfiffner, "US Blunders in Iraq: De-Baathification and Disbanding the Army," *Intelligence and National Security*, Vol. 25, No. 1, March 2010.

[123] L. Paul Bremer III, "Iraq Coalition Provisional Authority Order Number One: De-Ba'athification of Iraqi Society," May 16, 2003a; L. Paul Bremer III, "Coalition Provisional Authority Order Number 2: Dissolution of Entities," May 23, 2003b.

Who Gave the Orders?

Perhaps the most basic of all the debates was about who made the decision to rid the Iraqi government of Ba'thists and disband the army. This policy marked a dramatic shift from ORHA days. Rudd recounted Garner saying in February 2003 not to worry about Ba'athists because the hardcore ones would be either dead or gone, the mid-level Ba'athists would be turned in and jailed by the Iraqis, and the rest could be dealt with on a case-by-case basis.[124] Garner assumed that the worst Ba'athists would simply run away. And so, when Garner and his team got to Baghdad, they vetted the top people in the various Iraqi ministries to make sure they were not war criminals and moved forward from there.[125] When Garner and his team visited MOD, they found that the building had been ransacked and most of the documentation—including lists of exactly who was in the security forces—in disarray.[126]

One of ORHA's lead planners started work on a more comprehensive approach to dealing with the former Iraqi army. Shortly after getting to Baghdad, he was introduced to a group of five former Iraqi officers who had compiled a list of 9,000 former regime officers across the country and offered to help demobilize the Iraqi security force in exchange for their back pay. At his instruction, the group began to expand the list of names. Eventually, the list grew to more than 102,000 officers, soldiers, and civilians. Simultaneously, the ORHA planner began discussions with defense contractor Ronco to set up a "disarmament, demobilization, [and] reintegration" process for former regime officials. With Garner's permission, he flew back to the United States to work toward setting up the contract. While the ORHA planner was in the United States, Bremer took over Garner's role. It is unclear whether it was a deliberate policy shift or that the planner's efforts simply got lost in the leadership, but one way or another, before he could sign the contract with Ronco, Bremer had disbanded the Iraq army.[127]

Perspectives on who drafted the orders vary. One former CPA official recounted that Bremer arrived in Baghdad with drafts of both orders that he received from Under Secretary of Defense for Policy Douglas J. Feith and later implemented.[128] Moreover, he circulated drafts of the orders, and apart from Garner, no senior military or civilian

---

[124] Gordon Rudd, interview, February 27, 2006, pp. 23–24, transcript provided to RAND by the OIF Study Group.

[125] Meghan O'Sullivan, interview with Gordon Rudd, December 29, 2003, p. 18, transcript provided to RAND by the OIF Study Group. For a similar account of Garner's approach to de-Ba'athification, see Gordon and Trainor, 2006, pp. 476–477.

[126] Former ORHA official, interview with the authors, May 12, 2016.

[127] Former ORHA official, interview with the authors, May 12, 2016; Ronco, "Decision Brief to Department of Defense Office of Reconstruction and Humanitarian Assistance on the Disarmament, Demobilization and Reintegration of the Iraqi Armed Forces," briefing, March 2003, provided to RAND.

[128] Former CPA official, interview with the authors, March 30, 2015. Interestingly, in a 2007 editorial, Bremer claimed that both orders were based on policy he got from Washington and were well vetted by Washington prior to submission. See L. Paul Bremer III, "How I Didn't Dismantle Iraq's Army," *New York Times*, September 6, 2007.

official objected.[129] Conversely, from Washington's perspective, Bremer got out in front of the policymaking process. Condoleezza Rice—then National Security Adviser—argued that although the NSC discussed both orders, no formal order had been issued.[130] She noted that "someplace between what was decided in Washington and what happened in Iraq, there were some missed signals, and de-Ba'athification went much, much deeper than it should have."[131] For his part, Feith, in his memoirs, similarly recounted that his staff briefed Bremer on de-Ba'athification policy, but the final version of both orders was left up to Bremer. In fact, Feith remembered CPA Deputy and Senior Adviser to MOD Walter Slocombe handing him the final version of CPA Order 2 in a May 9, 2003, meeting.[132] Feith promised to review it, but before that happened, Bremer announced it as policy.[133] Because large parts of historical archives remain classified, verifying which of these two narratives is correct is difficult.

How Were They Supposed to Be Implemented?
A second controversy surrounds the reach of both orders. According to former CPA officials, Rice, and other senior policy officials at the time, the orders were not intended to be draconian measures. Only former senior regime officers and Ba'ath party officials were intended to be banned from military and government positions.[134] Indeed, while the orders were modeled after denazification following World War II, they were designed to affect only 0.1 percent of Iraq's population (compared with 2.5 percent in post–World War II Germany).[135] Even these senior officials would be pensioned off at twice the rate under the Saddam regime, rather than simply kicked out of the office.[136] Bremer also retained the right to grant exceptions and granted all sorts of waivers that came to his desk.[137]

---

[129] Dobbins, Jones, et al., 2009, p. 57.

[130] Condoleezza Rice, interview with Jason Awadi and Jeanne Godfroy, U.S. Department of State, Office of the Historian, July 12, 2014, p. 7, transcript provided to RAND by the OIF Study Group. For a similar account from DoD's perspective, see Zakheim, 2011, p. 205; and Ricks, 2006a, pp. 162–164.

[131] Condoleezza Rice, interview with Jason Awadi and Jeanne Godfroy, U.S. Department of State, Office of the Historian, July 12, 2014, transcript provided to RAND by the OIF Study Group.

[132] Feith, 2008, p. 428.

[133] Feith, 2008, p. 429.

[134] Condoleezza Rice, interview with Jason Awadi and Jeanne Godfroy, U.S. Department of State, Office of the Historian, July 12, 2014, p. 6, transcript provided to RAND by the OIF Study Group; former CPA official, interview with the authors, March 30, 2015; and former senior State Department and CPA official, interview with the authors, June 3, 2015.

[135] Dobbins, Jones, et al., 2011, p. xxvi.

[136] Former CPA official, interview with the authors, March 30, 2015.

[137] Meghan O'Sullivan, interview with Gordon Rudd, December 29, 2003, p. 24, transcript provided to RAND by the OIF Study Group; and former CPA official, interview with the authors, March 30, 2015.

In practice, however, CPA Orders 1 and 2 ended up as far more invasive and far-reaching: The former Iraqi army never reconstituted by units (although individuals rejoined the new ISF), bureaucrats down to local teachers were thrown out of work, and promised pensions were slow to be paid.[138] Several competing explanations exist for why the orders were implemented with a heavier hand than originally intended. First, Bremer argued that Iraqi politicians and particularly the expatriates, such as Ahmed Chalabi, applied CPA Order 1 (de-Ba'athification) in a more draconian manner than Bremer intended.[139] Indeed, after Chalabi's death, the *New York Times* labeled him as "an architect of the country's de-Ba'athification policy," and the person who "became its champion and quickly seized the reins as the implementer of the new policy."[140] In general, according to some CPA officials, these Iraqi expatriates tended to have a more black-and-white view of Ba'ath party membership than those Iraqis who remained in Iraq and interacted with Ba'ath party officials on a more routine basis.[141] That said, other officials there at the time counter that CPA Order 1 was initially enforced by CPA, and only later turned over to Chalabi and the Iraqi expatriates.[142]

Still other CPA officials blame the implementation of the policies rather than the policies themselves. In a December 2003 interview, then–CPA official Meghan O'Sullivan commented, "The real de-Ba'athification story is outside of this building. It's in the field. It's with the military, and how the military did or did not implement de-Ba'athification."[143] By contrast, some in the military counter that CPA Orders 1 and 2 took them by surprise. Indeed, some of the lead planners for postwar Iraq—such as COL Paul Hughes at ORHA and COL Kevin Benson at CFLCC—recount how neither expected such a move and how both reacted with shock to Bremer's announcement.[144]

Bremer also claimed that CPA delayed announcing the pension program with CPA Order 2 because the organization lacked a good list of who constituted the former Iraqi army and the program's costs, although CPA's documents suggest that even after CPA Order 2 was issued, there still was considerable debate about the pension program.[145] Finally, some of the policy failure stemmed from a basic lack of understanding about Iraqi society. CPA officials did not know how rampant rank inflation was

---

[138] Gordon and Trainor, 2006, p. 491.

[139] Former CPA official, interview with the authors, March 30, 2015.

[140] Alissa J. Rubin, "Ahmad Chalabi and the Legacy of De-Baathification in Iraq," *New York Times*, November 3, 2015.

[141] Meghan O'Sullivan, interview with Gordon Rudd, December 29, 2003, p. 35, transcript provided to RAND by the OIF Study Group.

[142] Former ORHA official, email correspondence with the authors, May 9, 2016.

[143] Meghan O'Sullivan, interview with Gordon Rudd, December 29, 2003, p. 24, transcript provided to RAND by the OIF Study Group.

[144] Ricks, 2006a, pp. 161–164.

[145] Former CPA official, interview with the authors, March 30, 2015; and Dobbins, Jones, et al., 2011, pp. 58–60.

in the Saddam-era military or how many relatively low-level bureaucrats had become Ba'ath party members to prove their ideological loyalty so that they could get jobs. For instance, anyone wishing to be a teacher had to be Ba'ath party member.[146]

Were the Orders Necessary?

The third debate surrounding CPA Orders 1 and 2 centers on why CPA issued the orders in the first place. Bremer argued that if he left the Ba'ath party intact and recalled Saddam's army, the Kurdish population would have seceded from Iraq and Shia would have revolted en masse.[147] Given Saddam's treatment of both groups, neither was about to accept a return to the old regime. Others agree with Bremer's analysis. A former senior State Department official noted that when the British took over Iraq after the collapse of the Ottoman regime at the end of World War I and tried to reconstitute Ottoman rule, it prompted a Shia revolt that took years for the British to suppress.[148] Feith similarly wrote, if it had not been for de-Ba'athification, "people might now be asking how President Bush could have failed to foresee that soft-pedaling de-Ba'athification would trigger an uprising by more than 80 percent of the Iraq population."[149] And then-BG Martin Dempsey, whose 1st Armored Division controlled Baghdad, said that if it were not for de-Ba'athification, "it would have gone easier for us in the near term, but less well for the Iraqi population in the long term."[150]

These intuitions about Iraqi public opinion seem at least partially grounded in fact. One academic analysis of polling conducted in December 2004 showed a sharp sectarian divide, with Kurds and Shia still supportive of de-Ba'athification and Kurds still supportive of disbanding Iraq's army, notwithstanding all the violence in the ensuing year and a half after CPA Orders 1 and 2 were issued.[151] Another poll that was conducted at the behest of ABC News and other international news agencies found that even four years later, in March 2007, only 35 percent of Shia and 31 percent of Kurds believed that former Ba'athists should be allowed to hold government positions.[152] Not until a February 2008 poll did a majority of Shia support allowing low- and mid-level Ba'athists back into government positions, and even then, 50 percent of Kurds opposed

---

[146] Former senior State Department and CPA official, interview with the authors, June 3, 2015. See also Robin L. Raphel, interview with Gordon Rudd, November 15, 2005, p. 28, transcript provided to RAND by the OIF Study Group; and Ricks, 2006a, p. 163.

[147] Former CPA official, interview with the authors, March 30, 2015.

[148] Former senior State Department official, interview with the authors, April 16, 2015.

[149] Feith, 2008, p. 431.

[150] Ricks, 2006a, p. 161.

[151] Mansoor Moaddel, Mark Tessler, and Ronald Inglehart, "Foreign Occupation and National Pride: The Case of Iraq," *Public Opinion Quarterly*, Vol. 72, No. 4, Winter 2008.

[152] ABC News, "ABC/BBC/ARD/NHK Poll—Iraq Five Years Later: Where Things Stand," March 17, 2008.

the measure.[153] Unfortunately, these polls did not ask what the population would have done had it not been for CPA Orders 1 and 2 and, therefore, cannot test whether concerns about a Shia revolt or Kurdish separatism were valid.

Moreover, some noted that CPA did not disband the former Iraqi army; the army had melted away during U.S. major combat operations and functionally self-disbanded.[154] Then–deputy CENTCOM commander GEN John Abizaid had informed Washington on April 17, 2003, that "there are no organized Iraqi military units left."[155] Another CPA official agreed:

> The fact is by the time the conventional fighting had ended . . . by the fall of Tikrit, there were no organized units of the Iraqi Army in existence. . . . So the assumption which had prevailed during the prewar period that we would be dealing with an intact institutional Iraqi Army simply turned out to be untrue. So we . . . had to start from a clean slate.[156]

And as seen from the effort needed to recall employees to the civilian ministries, reactivating the former Iraqi military would have been an equally intensive task. CPA authorized the resumption of payments to Iraqis who had been receiving pensions before the war. CPA set up a separate system to pay monthly stipends (which were much more generous than pensions paid through the Iraqi system) to the 80,000 or so officers who had been on the rolls as active duty when the war started (and also made a one-time payment to some 400,000 conscripts). Very early in the occupation, there were demonstrations in Baghdad and other cities by officers demanding to be paid. When the military payment program was instituted, these protests stopped.[157] If finding former soldiers to send them their pension checks was difficult, the argument goes, recalling them as an effective fighting force would be all the more difficult.

By contrast, Bremer's critics doubt his narrative for three reasons. First, they suggest that Iraq's army was not as uniformly despised as sometimes portrayed. While certain units (such as the Special Republican Guard or the Fedayeen Saddam) needed to go, along with the senior leadership, one Council on Foreign Relations and Rice University prewar study concluded, "The army remains one of the country's more

---

[153] ABC News, 2008.

[154] Former CPA official, interview with the authors, March 30, 2015; former senior State Department official, interview with the authors, April 16, 2015; and Condoleezza Rice, interview with Jason Awadi and Jeanne Godfroy, U.S. Department of State, Office of the Historian, July 12, 2014, p. 7, transcript provided to RAND by the OIF Study Group.

[155] Former CPA official, interview with the authors, March 30, 2015; and Dobbins, Jones, et al., 2009, p. 53.

[156] Former CPA official, interview with the authors, June 1, 2015.

[157] Former CPA official, interview with the authors, June 1, 2015; and former CPA official, interview with the authors, November 5, 2015.

respected institutions."[158] The military played multiple roles in Iraqi society. The former Iraqi army was a vast social and economic institution; by almost any measure, it was the nation's foremost corporate entity—with a significant presence in the health sector, housing, and construction. Many Iraqi men of a certain age served in the army during the Iran-Iraq war. It also was both a promoter of nationalist values and a tool of domestic repression. These mixed roles account for the public's complex and contradictory attitude toward it. A 2003 report by the International Crisis Group, for example, describes the Iraqi populace's stance toward its former military as "ambivalent."[159]

Second, some critics downplay the negative consequences of keeping the Iraqi army in place.[160] For example, one former senior military commander we spoke with disputes whether the Kurdish northern area of Iraq would have seceded. According to him, the Kurdish senior leadership recognized that Iran and Turkey—both of which have sizable Kurdish minority populations—would not have allowed an independent Kurdistan to exist, and he contends that Kurdish leaders would have remained firmly committed to the coalition, even without CPA Orders 1 and 2.[161]

Third, multiple accounts suggest that recalling the army was practical. One former senior military commander counters that the Iraqi military did not self-disband, rather "at our instructions, they went home. The military dropped leaflets telling them to go home, which they did, but the United States never brought them back like the leaflet said."[162] If the United States wanted to recall the Iraqi army, it was possible to do so. Other figures agree that the former Iraqi army could and should have been recalled.[163] To these critics, both orders smacked of poor strategic thinking, if not ideologically induced naïveté, in which evils of the Saddam regime could be purged in one fell swoop.

For some, the real problem of CPA Orders 1 and 2 was less the policy and more its verbalization. A former general officer deployed to Iraq during the CPA years commented,

> Everyone understood that [Bremer] had to demobilize the military, but did he have to *say* it? There was just mass devastation of the army. They had self-demobilized.

---

[158] Edward P. Djerejian and Frank G. Wisner, eds., *Guiding Principles for U.S. Post-Conflict Policy in Iraq*, Report of an Independent Working Group, Washington, D.C.: Council on Foreign Relations and the James A. Baker III Institute for Public Policy of Rice University, 2002, p. 5.

[159] International Crisis Group, "Iraq: Building a New Security Structure," Middle East Report No. 20, Baghdad/Brussels, December 23, 2003.

[160] For the widespread support for keeping the Iraqi military around in some form and its positive effects, see Ricks, 2006a, pp. 162–164.

[161] Former senior military commander, interview with the authors, June 9, 2015.

[162] Former senior military commander, interview with the authors, June 9, 2015.

[163] Gordon and Trainor, 2006, p. 480; Zakheim, 2011, p. 205; and former senior military commander, interview with the authors, April 17, 2015.

> The demobilization order was a psychological body blow to men who were very proud. We unnecessarily disenfranchised Saddam's army, air force, and navy. Whatever the political reasons were at the time, it was a terrible decision. [Bremer] didn't need to say it. It had already happened.[164]

Even if it was impossible to recall Iraq's army, the United States could have avoided unnecessary ill will by not formally disbanding the force.

What Were the Orders' Effects?

Finally, and perhaps most controversially, there is a dispute over the effects of CPA Orders 1 and 2. For many, these orders were one of the principal drivers of the insurgency. Rice reflected, "By going ahead and doing it [disbanding the army], it caused some problems for us politically with the Iraqis, and I think made things harder going forward. I think the disbandment of the army probably is the origin of the insurgency initially."[165] And many in the military agree. One general officer commented that not disbanding the Iraqi army "would have changed everything, from a psychological perspective and as an insurgency generator. It would have been a good-faith response."[166] Even if recalling the army was not feasible, making some attempt to recall the soldiers might have changed Iraq's dynamics, making a symbolic gesture to Iraq's Sunni community that it would not be excluded from the postwar regime. As with any counterfactual, it is impossible to say for sure.

More specifically, these orders had at least two downsides. First, they robbed the United States of what the U.S. military identified as "our best partners in preserving security" and forced the United States to rebuild both the military and Iraqi institutions from the ground up—a slow and several-years-long process.[167] In the words of a former senior military commander, "the U.S. had fired the only respected Iraqi institution without telling them what their future would be . . . and then announced there would only be nine battalions in the new Iraqi Army."[168] Second, it upset Iraq's precarious ethnic balance of power—unseating Sunnis in favor of Kurds and Shia.[169]

---

[164] Former senior military commander, interview with the authors, April 4, 2015.

[165] Condoleezza Rice, interview with Jason Awadi and Jeanne Godfroy, U.S. Department of State, Office of the Historian, July 12, 2014, p. 7, transcript provided to RAND by the OIF Study Group.

[166] Former senior military commander, interview with the authors, April 4, 2015.

[167] Meghan O'Sullivan, interview with Gordon Rudd, December 29, 2003, p. 29, transcript provided to RAND by the OIF Study Group.

[168] Former senior military commander, interview with the authors, July 31, 2015.

[169] In a relatively early piece about what went wrong in Iraq, Larry Diamond, political sociologist and former CPA governance advisor, argued that CPA "failed to grasp" the implications of de-Ba'athification and disbanding the Iraqi army in the context of Iraq's sectarian divide. See Larry Diamond, "What Went Wrong in Iraq," *Foreign Affairs*, Vol. 83, No. 5, September–October 2004, p. 43.

In response to these criticisms, a former CPA official offered several counter-arguments. First, he noted that when the United States tried in a limited fashion to bring back the former Iraqi army, with the Fallujah brigade in 2004 led by a former Republican Guard general, the effect was not more security but a mass defection to the insurgency.[170] Second, he noted that even after de-Baʻathification, the principal problems confronting the ministries were not a lack of senior people but a lack of computers, Internet, and other facilities, in addition to a bureaucracy with an entrenched culture of extreme caution in order not to ruffle any senior regime officials.[171]

Ultimately, it is impossible to say definitively how the Iraq War would have progressed differently without CPA Orders 1 and 2. What can be known is how Iraq reacted to the orders. As Meghan O'Sullivan recounted, the de-Baʻathification order was initially peaceful:

> And what happened in most cases was pretty amazing is that people literally got up and left the room. People, you know, identified themselves and . . . and left. . . . They didn't lie about, you know, what affiliation they had with the party; and they didn't try to protest it and they certainly, you know, didn't become, you know, violent or obstreperous. A lot of people just sort of either one, never came back into the office after the policy was announced on the radio or two, left once the senior advisor described it. That was sort of remarkable.[172]

Alas, the peace was not to last. As O'Sullivan later remarked, "A very different approach [to de-Baʻathification apart from ORHA's policy] to what happened when the CPA order number 1 happened, and that was May 16. So, it's funny, I think about that period as being an eternity but it was really only a month."[173] Baghdad had become a noticeably different—and more violent—place after de-Baʻathification. Indeed, some even suggest that only after de-Baʻathification and the disbanding of the former Iraqi army did the "real war in Iraq—the one to determine the future of the country" begin.[174]

Once issued, CPA Orders 1 and 2 could not be undone. As later–Ambassador to Iraq Zalmay Khalilzad remarked,

> Everybody agreed [de-Baʻathification] had gone too far and had affected too many people negatively and had been a source of hostility and resentment and instabil-

---

[170] Former CPA official, interview with the authors, March 30, 2015. Some outside analyses also make this point. See, for example, David C. Hendrickson and Robert W. Tucker, "Revisions in Need of Revising: What Went Wrong in the Iraq War," *Survival*, Vol. 47, No. 2, 2005, p. 22.

[171] Former CPA official, interview with the authors, March 30, 2015.

[172] Meghan O'Sullivan, interview with Gordon Rudd, December 29, 2003, pp. 21–22, transcript provided to RAND by the OIF Study Group.

[173] Meghan O'Sullivan, interview with Gordon Rudd, December 29, 2003, p. 19, transcript provided to RAND by the OIF Study Group.

[174] Thomas E. Ricks, "In Iraq, Military Forgot the Lessons of Vietnam," *Washington Post*, July 23, 2006b.

ity and that it needed to be adjusted. But, you couldn't just undo it because there were some people who had been involved, senior Ba'athists and others, in major abuses.[175]

Functionally, the United States found itself trapped in a no-win situation. It could not reverse the orders for fear of angering the Shia and Kurds, not to mention excusing senior Ba'ath party officials for war crimes. Neither could the United States "buy off" these Sunni ex-leaders with alternative jobs, because Baghdad's estimated unemployment rates were 50 percent at the time and the United States could not justify giving senior Ba'athists jobs when many average Iraqis were out of work.[176] And yet, keeping the status quo functionally meant leaving the United States with a growing Sunni insurgency. Arguably, it would take years—until the Sons of Iraq program and the Sunni Awakening—for the coalition to find a solution to this conundrum.[177]

CPA Order 2 also forced the United States' hand in rebuilding Iraq's army. Without a previous army to reform, the United States would need to build a new one, unit by unit, from the bottom up. A former CPA official reiterated this point: "The only way to go tactically, and from a political and mission point of view, was to start a new army. Rather than attempt to recall the old army, we would start training and start small, with the idea that you can't create a huge new military with no infrastructure or facilities."[178]

Rebuilding the Iraqi Security Forces: An Orphaned Mission

The story of how U.S. forces came to build up the ISF and especially the new Iraqi Army begins with the four assumptions underpinning planning for the intervention in Iraq. First, planners assumed that U.S. combat forces would be in Iraq for a relatively short period of about six months. This limited time frame would prevent the United States from building a new Iraqi Army (which was fundamentally a long-term proposition), and as a result, CENTCOM did not plan for this possibility. Second, planners assumed that Iraq's army would survive intact, similar to the Japanese and German militaries at the end of World War II. Third, planners assumed that after the fall of Saddam, the security environment would be relatively benign, and Iraq's police force would be capable of maintaining order. As a result, the United States needed to field

---

[175] Zalmay Khalilzad, interview with Peter Connors, Contemporary Operations Study Team, April 30, 2008, p. 13, transcript provided to RAND by the OIF Study Group.

[176] Former CPA official, interview with the authors, March 30, 2015.

[177] The Sons of Iraq program is also known as the Sunni Awakening movement and the Anbar Salvation Council (DoD, *Measuring Stability and Security in Iraq*, Washington, D.C., September 2008b, p. 23).

[178] Former CPA official, interview with the authors, June 1, 2015.

only a limited number of advisory teams.[179] And when Iraq turned out to be more confused and violent than expected, and even the police proved underequipped and not up to the task of keeping order, the coalition had to adapt and rebuild Iraq's security forces on the fly.[180] Fourth, planners assumed that the principal role of the Iraqi Army in a post-Saddam Iraq would be to defend against foreign threats, not provide internal security. As a result, it could be significantly smaller than Iraq's prewar military. When events in Iraq proved these assumptions invalid, the military and its civilian overseers struggled over how to adjust a process exacerbated by a growing civil-military gap, especially between Baghdad and Washington.

The U.S. military's formal role in rebuilding Iraq's army essentially began with the establishment of the Coalition Military Assistance Training Team (CMATT), commanded by MG Paul Eaton. On May 11, 2003, Eaton received a phone call from his commanding general at Training and Doctrine Command, GEN Kevin Byrnes, informing him that the Army Chief of Staff had selected him to lead CMATT. Apart from a short meeting with his future boss in the field (Slocombe) and a series of cultural preparation briefings on the Middle East, the two-star general had essentially no time to prepare for his new mission. He also had no prior experience in the Middle East. On June 13, 2003, two months after the fall of Saddam's Ba'athist regime, Eaton arrived in Iraq via transport for individual augmentees into the theater. His task—as the commanding general of CMATT—was to stand up the new Iraqi Army.

Eaton's arrival was marked by a significant amount of confusion. On arrival in Kuwait and in civilian clothes (as stipulated in his orders), he handed over his military identification card to a young soldier, who responded, "Oh Sir, we weren't expecting *you*." The specialist's comment epitomized Eaton's next several weeks in Iraq as he attempted to get his command off the ground.[181] He essentially hitchhiked from Kuwait City to Baghdad, riding northbound in a UH-60 helicopter from the 101st Airborne. Once in Baghdad, he had to find transport into the Green Zone. In fact, on the night of his arrival in Baghdad, there was not even a room reserved for him. An unlucky colonel would give up his bunk so that Eaton could get some sleep in an air-conditioned trailer.

---

[179] Andrew Rathmell, Olga Oliker, Terrence K. Kelly, David Brannan, and Keith Crane, *Developing Iraq's Security Sector: The Coalition Provisional Authority's Experience*, Santa Monica, Calif.: RAND Corporation, MG-365-OSD, 2006.

[180] For a description of the police in Baghdad at the time, see Ricks, 2006a, pp. 182–183. CPA planners were also forced to readjust their time frame considerably for reconstructing Iraq's national security apparatus after the November 15, 2003, agreement paved the way for CPA turnover to the Iraqis in the summer of 2004. A former CPA official noted, "It was a bit of an afterthought—the idea that you needed an MOD. We weren't going to build an MOD until 2006, and then suddenly we had six months" (former CPA official, interview with the authors, November 5, 2015).

[181] Former senior military commander, interview with the authors, April 4, 2015.

In Iraq, Eaton's command reported directly to CPA and was officially under the direction of Slocombe, the senior director for national security within CPA. As the de facto minister of defense, Slocombe was the CPA civilian in charge of the Iraqi military, all internal security forces, Iraqi intelligence, and the country's criminal justice system.[182] As a CPA entity, CMATT would not be under the control of the U.S. military command in Iraq, CJTF-7. Eaton's initial team of five officers came on loan from CENTCOM staff. According to Eaton, as focused as the CENTCOM commander, General Franks, was on wrapping up the fight, he did not want the responsibility to rebuild Iraq's army: "General Franks, specifically, rejected the . . . mission, and pushed it into the CPA."[183] A former CPA official also noted that the CJTF-7 did not want the task of training the new Iraqi Army and consequently placed it under CPA and its new CMATT initiative.[184]

Eaton received an initial budget of $173 million and a Microsoft PowerPoint briefing outlining planning for the training, staffing, and equipping of what was ultimately to be a three-division Iraqi Army, composed of 27 battalions.[185] According to Eaton, the briefing was prepared by CENTCOM in likely consultation with CPA.[186] While the original aim was to construct an overall force of approximately 50,000 to 60,000 personnel over three years, the initial mission was to generate nine battalions in the first year, followed by nine battalions of light motorized infantry the following year and nine more in the third year.[187] In many ways, this was an unambitious goal, given that Iraq's army in 1990 stood at more than 1 million men.[188] This bottom-up approach, however, ran against the top-down mentality of the Saddam regime. A senior military adviser to new Iraqi forces attached to CPA noted that this produced a leadership problem. On the one hand, most Iraqis at the time looked to a strong leader to tell them what to do, and yet the years under Saddam's control had effectively decapitated Iraqi leadership in the country and left an intellectual void. Most Sunnis capable of filling these positions were often tainted by their connections to the former regime, and there were few Shia capable of filling senior positions.[189]

---

[182] By July 2003, Slocombe's remit would narrow to include oversight of the Iraqi military and the intelligence agencies.

[183] Paul Eaton, interview with Gordon Rudd, December 27, 2004, transcript provided to RAND by the OIF Study Group.

[184] Former CPA official, interview with the authors, June 1, 2015.

[185] Wright and Reese, 2008, pp. 87–88, 433, 567–568.

[186] Paul Eaton, interview with Gordon Rudd, December 27, 2004, transcript provided to RAND by the OIF Study Group.

[187] Paul Eaton, interview with Gordon Rudd, December 27, 2004, transcript provided to RAND by the OIF Study Group.

[188] Sharon Otterman, "Iraq: Iraq's Prewar Military Capabilities," *CFR Backgrounder*, April 24, 2003.

[189] Former military adviser to Iraqi forces, interview with the authors, June 12, 2015.

Moreover, unlike the former Iraqi army, the new army was to include all volunteers and be ethnically reflective of Iraqi society, with units comprising roughly 60 percent Shia, 20 percent Sunnis, and 20 percent Kurds. There were to be no Ba'athists recruited, nor former colonels or general officers from Saddam's army. CPA determined that the new army should focus on foreign, rather than internal, threats, and CMATT recruited new members based on this premise. Once it became clear that the new Iraqi Army would have responsibility for internal security, several members deserted.

Not wanting responsibility for the mission, the U.S. military made the explicit decision to use contractors in Iraq to train the new Iraqi forces. This represented a departure from what the U.S. military had done in Afghanistan, where a brigade commander from a Regular Army division would develop a table of personnel requirements to conduct the training mission and serve as the commander. Because the intent was to begin training straight away, the contract for training the first nine battalions was fast-tracked.[190] The winning bid had to commit to taking charge of the first recruits by July 10, 2003. Vinnell Corporation won the contract and subsequently subcontracted some of the recruitment and staffing to Science Applications International Corporation, or SAIC, and Military Professional Resources Inc., or MPRI.

The process was remarkably swift. Eaton located a training installation in Kirkush, a desert base located 20 miles from the Iranian border. Elements of the 4th Infantry Division provided security, and a Czech contractor helped build barracks and infrastructure. SAIC helped establish recruiting centers in Baghdad, Basra, and Mosul, with temporary trips to Irbil to attract Kurds. The first class of recruits arrived in late July; by late August, a second battalion was being trained. The enlisted soldiers of the first Iraqi battalion graduated from training at the Kirkush installation on October 4, 2003; the second battalion graduated from a rebuilt base in Taji, north of Baghdad, on January 6, 2004; and by late January, CMATT had trained the enlisted soldiers of the first three battalions of the new Iraqi Army.[191]

While this process was notionally a success, it suffered from a lack of infrastructure, food, equipment, and personnel. CMATT was woefully understaffed and underequipped for the training mission. Reluctant to burden CJTF-7 with its requests, CMATT had to contract for nearly everything, including weapons, vehicles, personal protective equipment, uniforms, and food.[192] Washington often withheld approval for funds and programs with little or no explanation. A former senior military com-

---

[190] According to a former CPA official, the time between issuing the Request for Proposal and granting the award was eight days (former CPA official, interview with the authors, June 1, 2015).

[191] Wright and Reese, 2008, p. 435.

[192] A former senior military commander said that General Sanchez would "do what he could." But the former commander was sensitive to the fact that any resources that might have gone to CMATT would mean that much less for U.S. Army forces in Iraq (former senior military commander, interview with the authors, April 4, 2015).

mander recounted that when CMATT and CPA contracting selected the winning bid to equip the Iraqi Army with everything from individual soldier equipment to weapons, communications, and vehicles, a competing company challenged the selection. The Pentagon supported the challenge and created a huge task for CMATT to equip the nascent Iraqi Army. Barracks spaces and other buildings were also in total disrepair and required complete refurbishment. According to this former senior military commander, the Deputy Secretary of Defense withheld funding for this effort on account of his dissatisfaction with the Iraqi police training program.[193] The infrastructure, equipment, and food challenges proved so vexing that Eaton was forced to "backdoor" acquisitions any way possible. AK-47s arrived from Jordan and Egypt.[194] Most of the equipment that eventually arrived came from NATO allies. Reflecting on the unconventional nature of these early acquisitions, a former senior military commander said, "Things happened that just made no sense—Russian aircraft would roll in with stuff from Bulgaria. Angels made it happen, but it certainly wasn't pretty!"[195]

Part of CMATT's difficulties stemmed from command structure problems. CMATT belonged to CPA. Major General Eaton worked under Slocombe, who in turn worked for Bremer. Bremer therefore represented Eaton's official link to the Pentagon. But according to a former senior military commander, Bremer had larger concerns than bringing Eaton's problems to the Secretary of Defense. (Eaton's chain of command ran from Bremer to the Secretary of Defense.) The fact that the Secretary of Defense did not appoint a service executive agent (and a four-star general and staff to run interference in the Pentagon) created what was basically a two-star command that was essentially "an orphan," with no command responsibility at CJTF-7 or at CENTCOM. A former senior military commander would further note that Eaton's "problems" tended to linger on the Deputy Secretary of Defense's desk.[196] There was no clear reporting channel for CMATT to relay difficulties or seek guidance and assistance. The chain of command left CMATT without a four-star or service chief to champion its mission and cause. A former CPA official also noted that even General Sanchez was puzzled by the fact that a two-star general charged with standing up the Iraqi Army worked below two civilians and not in the military chain of command. According to the former official, Sanchez felt that Eaton's entity should fall within his own chain of command and that, from the beginning, the CJTF-7 should have been

---

[193] Former senior military commander, interview with the authors, April 4, 2015. The police training program arguably was in even worse shape than the Iraqi army, with shortages of vehicles, uniforms, and bulletproof vests, among other items (see Ricks, 2006a, pp. 210–211). This may, however, have been due to legal confusion over whether the United States could train foreign police forces (Dennis E. Keller, *U.S. Military Forces and Police Assistance in Stability Operations: The Least-Worst Option to Fill the U.S. Capacity Gap*, Carlisle, Pa.: Army Strategic Studies Institute, Peacekeeping and Stability Operations Institute Paper, August 2010).

[194] Former senior military commander, interview with the authors, April 4, 2015.

[195] Former senior military commander, interview with the authors, April 4, 2015.

[196] Former senior military commander, interview with the authors, April 4, 2015.

in charge of training the military forces that were going to replace it.[197] But a change in the command structure would not occur until the following year.

CMATT moved quickly to develop the training platform. Within months, Eaton had nearly 20 officers and NCOs overseeing the Vinnell Corporation's training efforts and personnel. Vinnell provided planners, operations officers, unit trainers, and translators. However, Vinnell did not provide drill instructors, which were not in its contract, and CENTCOM did not task CJTF-7 to provide them either.[198] The absence of drill instructors proved to be an acute shortfall. While the civilian contractors could teach recruits basic soldier tasks, such as how to operate equipment or organize a fire team, they could not impart or develop the ethos of being a soldier. "It is easy for an American [to develop]; he believes in his constitution, and his leadership, etc. That was not the case in Iraq," a former senior military commander recounted.[199]

Eaton proposed an alternative training plan based on the cohesion, operational readiness, and training (or COHORT) battalions.[200] Eaton enlisted the Jordanian Army's Chief of Training to assist CMATT with training up to 2,000 Iraqi officers in Jordan and briefed the plan to Secretary Rumsfeld in September 2003. With Rumsfeld's approval, in December 2003, CMATT sent to Jordan the first 750 Iraqi officers, who then returned to Iraq in March the following year. Simultaneously, the new NCO academy in Taji worked to train 750 NCOs. The idea was for graduates of both officer and NCO schools to link up with Iraqi recruits subsequent to the recruits' completion of basic training to form new Iraqi Army battalions.[201] Taji and Kirkush were to become the Fort Jacksons of the Iraqi military (that is, the sites of basic training).[202] Funding delays, however, prevented CMATT from fully implementing this plan.

In parallel to General Eaton's effort with the Iraqi Army, CJTF-7, with approval from CENTCOM, started building the Iraqi Civil Defense Corps (ICDC) for internal security. The ICDC force was born out of the need for occupation forces to put an Iraqi face on operations and, specifically, to help with translation, interpretation, static defense, human intelligence, and joint patrolling. Each division was ordered by CJTF-7 to stand up a single ICDC battalion. The initial plan for the ICDC was presented to CPA and Pentagon officials in the summer of 2003.[203] ICDC units

---

[197] Former CPA official, interview with the authors, June 1, 2015.

[198] Wright and Reese, 2008, p. 435.

[199] Former senior military commander, interview with the authors, April 4, 2015.

[200] This concept keeps units together from initial training through their operational deployments. An experienced cadre of officers and NCOs trains the units.

[201] On this design, see Wright and Reese, 2008, pp. 436–437.

[202] Blaise Cornell-d'Echert, interview with Steven Clay, Combat Studies Institute, October 31, 2006, transcript provided to RAND by the OIF Study Group.

[203] Rathmell et al., 2006, p. 38.

received only minimal training and largely lacked the capability to act without coalition forces. By August 21, 2003, CENTCOM commander General Abizaid reported that 23,000 ICDC members were working with the coalition.[204] In early 2004, the CJTF-7 expanded the program to include one ICDC battalion for each of Iraq's 18 provinces. By the end of the year, the program grew to more than 60 battalions and was renamed the Iraqi National Guard. Each U.S. brigade developed its local ICDC force, and as a result, these units' effectiveness varied greatly. Some brigade commanders embraced the concept, while others saw it as a distraction.[205] Division commanders received the mission but lacked resources and sufficient training to execute it properly. Consequently, the results of the ICDC initiative were, according to a former senior military commander, "a mixed bag."[206]

Especially by 2004, the ICDC became a point of contention between CPA and CJTF-7.[207] Bremer believed that the initiative by the U.S. military inflated the numbers of Iraqis engaged in security work and resulted in forces that were inadequate substitutes for coalition troops.[208] A former CPA official felt that the military overestimated the ICDC's capabilities. According to him, "The fallacy was that Iraqis under arms and in uniform would help turn the situation around, and that pure numbers of Iraqis would solve the problem."[209] Another former CPA official similarly expressed disappointment with the ICDC's results: "Since [the United States doesn't] use the Army for internal threats—and that is what Iraq was facing—we had a vision for what was required to defend Iraq and we wanted the ICDC to be the internal security force. But ultimately they were a huge disappointment."[210] LTC Blaise Cornell-d'Echert, one of the original CMATT staffers, went a step further. While he sympathized with CJTF-7's need to provide security, he argued that the locally organized ICDC undermined CMATT's efforts to stand up the new Iraqi Army and Iraqi Police force:

> [The CJTF-7] would be creating a parallel military structure that would compete with the Ministry of Interior [MOI] and the police, and who will owe allegiance to their mukhtars or their sheiks and will be tribally aligned. Thus, [ICDC] won't do anything for you in terms of the overall security of the provinces themselves, because now you're going to have multiple armed entities with different allegiances

---

[204] Wright and Reese, 2008, p. 439.

[205] Wright and Reese, 2008, pp. 438–439.

[206] Former senior military commander, interview with the authors, April 4, 2015.

[207] On this point, see Dobbins, Jones, et al., 2009, pp. 61–65.

[208] Wright and Reese, 2008, p. 439.

[209] Former CPA official, interview with the authors, October 22, 2015.

[210] Former CPA official, interview with the authors, November 5, 2015.

within a province and then you magnify that throughout the whole country. All you've done now is really increased the scope of the problem.[211]

From their inception, ICDC forces were a "strange hybrid," and precisely where this intentionally impermanent institution fit in and who would ultimately control it was an open question.[212] By the spring of 2004, it became apparent that having the ICDC as a parallel military structure was not an optimal solution. On April 22, 2004, CPA issued Order 73, transferring authority of the ICDC over to MOD as part of a larger reorganization. This move effectively transitioned the ICDC into the Iraqi National Guard and paired it with coalition forces.[213] CPA also slowly recognized that ISF training needed to be under military, rather than civilian, control. Eventually, this realization paved the way for the establishment of the Multi-National Security Transition Command–Iraq (MNSTC-I), commanded by Lieutenant General Petraeus in June 2004.

Lessons from This Era

Ultimately, the first year of the Iraq intervention proved critical for defining Iraq's future. Stumbles during this year—by both the military and civilian organizations, in the field and in Washington—inflicted huge damage on the U.S. effort in Iraq and took years to undo (if they ever were undone). The stumbles also left unresolved the great question of who should run an occupation government. Arguably, the task does not fit neatly into any existing bureaucratic lane within the U.S. government. The United States does not have a colonial office charged with governing captured territories. Indeed, even the concept of retaining such a capability within the American government seems, at best, like a historical anachronism and, at worst, antidemocratic and sharply at odds with Western liberal values. And yet, the United States took on the task of creating an occupation government in Iraq, sparking a debate about whether the State Department or the military should have been in the lead.

On the one hand, the State Department comes closer than any other government agency to training a new government. As Ambassador Gary Grappo, who later served in the U.S. embassy in Iraq, remarked,

> The State Department does governance. . . . So this is the type of work we have people doing for a living. Unfairly, this responsibility was thrust on the US military, everywhere from the commanding officer all the way down to frontline

---

[211] Blaise Cornell-d'Echert, interview with Steven Clay, Combat Studies Institute, October 31, 2006, transcript provided to RAND by the OIF Study Group.

[212] Rathmell et al., 2006.

[213] Rathmell et al., 2006, p. 39.

troops. "Go out and do good governance." Well, it is great if you have taken a high school civics class or a college class in political science. But what does that actually mean when you are in a country with no history of democracy; very little regard for or tradition of human rights; speaks a language that few of us speak; has just come through a very oppressive regime; and, of course, has no culture of good governance, of democracy, respect for human rights, or rule of law? How do you do that? Well, there are a few people in the State Department who have done it before. I cannot say always successfully, but have done it. We have some experience. We know what works and what does not work.[214]

To a degree, Grappo has a point. The United States does regularly report on the state of foreign elections and, along with international and nongovernmental organizations, assists in building democracies the world over. In most cases, these professionals reside in the State Department rather than in the military.

On the other hand, Grappo's critics counter that the military, despite its obvious limitations, must be in the lead for governance in war zones, at least temporarily, for two reasons. First, there are the resource constraints. The entire Foreign Service, which is about the size of an Army brigade, is already spread across the entire world and lacks the capacity to surge into places like Iraq. Even if it did, it would still need to rely on the military to provide logistics, transportation, and other basic necessities. Second, and more fundamentally, critics differentiate between diplomacy and governance and argue that the skills necessary to broker international agreements successfully do not necessarily overlap with the skills needed to run cities, provinces, or countries successfully.[215] As ORHA historian Rudd commented, "The State Department's fundamental world is one of diplomacy, it is not the world of executive management. We don't use this term for DoD, but the world of DoD is most distinctly in the world of executive-level management."[216] For Rudd, the principal trait needed to run an occupation is management expertise, and this is where the military excels. Others agree. A former senior State Department official, for example, argued that the State Department should provide political advisers down to the BCT level to offer political and governance advice to the lowest levels. That said, the lion's share of occupation governance and reconstruction must—for reasons of capacity and skill set—fall to the Defense Department and the military.[217]

The remainder of this section identifies and describes the lessons learned from the U.S. experience in Baghdad during the occupation of Iraq.

---

[214] Gary Grappo, interview with Lynne Chandler Garcia, Contemporary Operations Study Team, July 30, 2012, p. 8, transcript provided to RAND by the OIF Study Group.

[215] Gordon Rudd, interview, February 27, 2006, p. 9, transcript provided to RAND by the OIF Study Group.

[216] Gordon Rudd, interview, February 27, 2006, pp. 9–10, transcript provided to RAND by the OIF Study Group.

[217] Former Defense Policy Board member, interview with the authors, June 10, 2015.

Plan Early for an Occupation and for a Full Range of Contingencies

As described in Chapter Two, the United States planned for a series of contingencies that did not occur, such as the mass movement of refugees and oil wells being set alight.[218] Missing in all of this was any long-term preparation for occupation. ORHA was a slapdash, poorly resourced organization assembled mere months before major combat operations. On the military side, CJTF-7 was no better. The fatal flaw of this lack of planning was that, for the most part, it was a self-inflicted wound. While the United States was headed to war, military staff planning for the postwar period started relatively late in the game and then did not plan for what to do if Iraq's institutions disintegrated and the United States faced a full-blown insurgency.[219]

Stabilize a Situation as Quickly as Possible After Combat Operations Are Complete

In Baghdad, Army units did not stop Iraqis from looting and engaging in other criminal activity immediately after the regime fell. While there are many reasons why this did not happen, including some beyond these units' control (e.g., the insufficient numbers of troops), this instability arguably bred more instability that ultimately allowed the insurgency to grow. In the future, the military forces need to capitalize on the window of time immediately after combat ends and restore order as quickly as possible to cut off any potential cycles of violence.

Embrace the Training of Security Forces and Tailor the Approach to the Society

Part of this failure to plan was due to the United States not embracing the training of Iraqi defense forces early on. On the civilian side, critics accuse DoD of being late to assemble and then deploy Slocombe and his team on the ground to stand up the Iraqi Ministry of Defense.[220]

A second set of issues stemmed from U.S. leaders' lack of understanding of Iraqi society. The bottom-up approach to rebuilding the new Iraqi Army did not recognize that the army was historically a highly hierarchical institution. Similarly, by disbanding Iraq's former army, the United States did not recognize that it had created a leadership gap in the senior ranks.

Finally, U.S. forces arguably paid even less attention to the new Iraqi Police than to the Iraqi Army, presuming that the police force was both relatively benign and could help maintain law and order after the fall of the regime. Part of this may have had to

---

[218] Former senior national security official, interview with the authors, May 21, 2015.

[219] Former senior military commander, interview with the authors, April 17, 2015. Other analyses have found similar conclusions. For example, as Perry and colleagues describe, "When a desired endstate (such as regime change) has been established, a robust interagency process should take the lead in planning to achieve that end. The planning process should begin with the endstate—i.e., planning should be 'inverted'—so that all political and military, diplomatic and economic, intelligence and information operations directly support the end to be achieved" (Perry, Darilek, et al., 2015, pp. 373–374).

[220] Former ORHA official, interview with the authors, May 12, 2016.

with legal confusion about whether the United States could train police forces, and if so, in what form.[221] The American military was slow to accept the training of police forces as a military—rather than a civilian—task. The Department of State's Bureau of International Narcotics and Law Enforcement Affairs and the Department of Justice's International Criminal Investigative Training Assistance Program had the authority to train and reform police forces in another country, but in Iraq, those agencies lacked deployable formations for such a task and thus proved incapable of properly executing it. Without functional police formations in a host nation, counterinsurgency tasks are far more formidable, which can lead to violence and destruction. In 2005, the 42nd Military Police Brigade (I Corps) with two or three military police battalions trained for and provided training and reform for the police forces in Baghdad. Training and reforming police forces during a postconflict phase is a critical task. Given the lack of capacity in other U.S. government agencies, military police will have to take the lead in this critical area.[222]

Promote Unity of the Chain of Command and Positive Civil-Military Relations

One of the themes seen in the training of the ISF, as well as throughout the CPA period, is the importance of both unity of command and, conversely, civil-military relations. The conflicts during this period show just how tremendously damaging a civil-military rift is to operations. In Washington, the "poisonous relationship between State and Defense" effectively undermined the planning for postwar Iraq and left those tasked with executing it—in CJTF-7, ORHA, and CPA—without firm institutional support back home.[223] This situation is beyond the realm of the U.S. Army to change directly, but such interagency relationships, if they resemble those during the Iraq War, will adversely affect the larger institutional environment in which the Army will operate in the future if they continue.

In Baghdad, the Garner-McKiernan relationship—and, later, the Bremer-Sanchez relationship—proved equally problematic. It also consisted of two distinct chains of command, leaving one with all authority and the other with the lion's share of the resources.[224] Perhaps this relationship could have worked if the two had gotten along better—or at least were perceived by their subordinates as doing so—but this was not the case, and the CJTF-7 and CPA relationship suffered as a result. As a former CPA official remarked, in hindsight, "it would have been better to have Sanchez work for

---

[221] Section 660 of the Foreign Assistance Act enacted in 1974 prohibited the United States from training foreign police forces, although, in practice, the United States often found work-arounds during stability operations. See Keller, 2010, p. 20.

[222] Former ORHA official, email correspondence with the authors, May 9, 2016.

[223] Former Defense Policy Board member, interview with the authors, June 10, 2015.

[224] Dobbins, Jones, et al., 2011, p. 17.

Bremer or the other way around rather than having no common superior short of Secretary Rumsfeld."[225]

Focus on Nonmilitary Intelligence

While much of the focus on the intelligence failures during the Iraq War centers on Iraq's WMD program, perhaps the larger issue was the failure to understand the state of Iraqi society and how Iraqis would respond to the end of the Saddam regime.[226] There are any number of explanations for this intelligence failure, mostly focusing on the intelligence community being distracted by other priorities: the general al Qaeda threat, the Iraqi WMD program, and Iraqi military behavior during conflict.[227] Moreover, the belief was that the occupation would be brief and the United States would leave Iraq soon after. One way or another, however, much of the postwar planning problems stemmed from an inability to predict accurately what postwar Iraq would look like and a failure to rapidly adapt to the dynamic conditions on the ground.

Embrace the Military's Role in an Occupational Government

Running an occupation government does not fit neatly into any existing bureaucratic lane within the U.S. government. While the State Department regularly reports on the state of foreign elections and, along with international assistance, builds democracies the world over, the military must be in the lead for governance in war zones. As already noted, the State Department and other non-DoD government agencies do not have the capacity or capabilities to establish an occupational government.[228] While the State Department and other U.S. agencies should advise these efforts, the lion's share of occupation governance and reconstruction should fall to the Defense Department and the military services, particularly the U.S. Army.

DoD Directive 5100.01, *Functions of the Department of Defense and Its Major Components*, specifies that one of the functions of the U.S. Army, for which it "shall develop concepts, doctrine, tactics, techniques, and procedures, and organize, train, equip, and provide forces with expeditionary and campaign qualities" is to "occupy territories abroad and provide for the initial establishment of a military government pending transfer of this responsibility to other authority."[229] Army forces and leaders

---

[225] Former CPA official, interview with the authors, June 1, 2015.

[226] Former senior national security official, interview with the authors, May 21, 2015.

[227] George Tenet and Bill Harlow, *At the Center of the Storm: My Years at the CIA*, New York: HarperCollins, 2007, p. 301.

[228] Gordon Rudd, interview February 27, 2006, p. 9, transcript provided to RAND by the OIF Study Group.

[229] DoD, 2010b, p. 30. See also Conrad C. Crane and W. Andrew Terrill, *Reconstructing Iraq: Insights, Challenges, and Missions for Military Forces in a Post-Conflict Scenario*, Carlisle Barracks, Pa.: Strategic Studies Institute, U.S. Army War College, 2003, pp. 11–18.

will—like it or not—have the lead in an occupational government. The Army needs to build the force structure and capabilities to accomplish this mission—from military governance specialists to training teams, local security forces, and military police units capable of running prisons.

Anticipate Abnormality

One of the recurring problems throughout this period came from the desire to be "normal." According to Rice, the decision to transition back to Iraqi sovereignty in early 2004 was in part attributable to a desire for "normal relations with the Iraqis."[230] Similarly, according to Slocombe, the 60,000-man ISF came from what could be sustained based on a budget of 2–3 percent of gross domestic product, consistent with world averages.[231] These policies miss the fact that Iraq was not "normal." While returning to normal diplomatic relations and right-sizing Iraq's military are admirable long-term goals, Iraq was still reeling from the relatively sudden removal of its longtime dictator and was in the midst of a deteriorating security situation.

Balance Justice and Pragmatism

Finally, the story behind CPA Orders 1 and 2 raises troubling, if unresolved, questions about how to balance justice and pragmatism. Although it is easy in hindsight to pillory Bremer for issuing the orders, it is impossible to prove what Iraq would have looked like had it not been for de-Ba'athification and the disbanding of Iraq's former army. The orders could have been more deftly handled on a tactical level (e.g., waiting to announce both orders until the pension program for former regime officials was in place), but the basic strategic problem would have remained. The prewar Iraqi elite were majority Sunni, but the Iraqi population was overwhelmingly not. And given Saddam's past, it is doubtful that any of Iraq's persecuted ethnicities and religious groups would have blithely accepted a restoration of large portions of the old regime. Although the groups rightly wanted justice for the abuses of the former regime, unscathing former regime members would leave large numbers of disenfranchised elites, historically a volatile and violent combination.[232] Therefore, the occupiers' challenge is striking the right balance between the desire for justice and the need for pragmatism. Ultimately, despite the short planning time frame, strategic confusion, and scale of the task, U.S. Army units, on a tactical level, began to adapt to their new mission relatively soon after getting to Baghdad—sometimes with significant success, as was the case

---

[230] Condoleezza Rice, interview with Jason Awadi and Jeanne Godfroy, U.S. Department of State, Office of the Historian, July 12, 2014, p. 8, transcript provided to RAND by the OIF Study Group.

[231] Walter B. Slocombe, interview with Gordon Rudd, July 18, 2003, p. 13, transcript provided to RAND by the OIF Study Group.

[232] See Edward D. Mansfield and Jack Snyder, *Electing to Fight: Why Emerging Democracies Go to War*, Cambridge, Mass.: MIT Press, 2005.

with the 1st Armored Division and 1st Cavalry Division. One can only conjecture how Baghdad might have looked different if policy, strategy, and tactics were better aligned into a united, more focused effort. As with any counterfactual, however, it is impossible to say for sure.

CHAPTER FOUR

The Casey Period

This chapter covers events from the summer of 2004 until early 2007. It begins by sketching out some of the key issues confronting both civilian and military leaders. These include establishing security in the city, setting up governance structures to fill the vacuum created in the wake of deposing Saddam, dismantling the Iraqi military, and restoring infrastructure damaged during the wars. It describes the military situation in the city and chronicles the key challenges facing the embassy in Baghdad. It then describes the civilian policy views from two perspectives: Baghdad and Washington. Next, it discusses the efforts to re-create Iraq's security forces and security institutions. It concludes with the lessons learned.

Key Debates

The transition of sovereignty to the Iraqi government in June 2004 marked the beginning of a new chapter in the Iraq War. The 14-month tenure of Bremer and CPA, along with that of Lieutenant General Sanchez and CJTF-7, had been tumultuous, with the growing insurgency providing a backdrop to the political saga playing out in Baghdad. Although the handover of sovereignty fostered a sense of optimism about Iraq's future, the following years proved to be a difficult and dangerous phase of the war. Insecurity in Baghdad created enormous challenges for American military and civilian leadership in the city.

After assuming command in June 2004, GEN George W. Casey, Jr., carried out a strategy that ultimately rested on the premise of an eventual turnover of security and governing responsibilities to the Iraqis. The operational framework that supported this strategy was a combination of counterinsurgency operations that fought the various insurgent groups—both Shia and Sunni—intertwined with multiple efforts to build up Iraqi institutions. The idea underpinning the strategy was that American forces would gradually turn over responsibility to increasingly competent and capable Iraqi governing, military, and economic institutions. To provide a common framework for understanding nation-building operations, General Casey established the Counterinsurgency Academy at Camp Taji, located just northwest of Baghdad, in late 2005. The academy was run by selected officers from a U.S. Army special forces battalion and was designed to teach the principles of counterinsurgency to the leaders of Casey's tactical outfits that would be carrying out his strategy on the ground.[1]

By the end of 2006, however, the situation in Baghdad became acute. The Sunni-Shia sectarian civil war caused widespread death and destruction throughout the country. In December 2006, nearly 1,500 Iraqi civilians were killed in sectarian violence in Baghdad alone.[2] At that point, President Bush decided to change command and strategy. The new commander, GEN David Petraeus, arrived in February 2007, and with him came a newly written Army doctrine for counterinsurgency, FM 3-24.[3] Over the course of 2007, violence would drop significantly so that by the end of the year, the "tide had turned," according to Army COL Peter Mansoor (who had commanded a BCT in Baghdad in 2004 and later was General Petraeus's executive officer), and, thanks in large part to "the Surge,"[4] Iraq was finally on the path to peace.[5]

Yet the cause for the decrease in violence became a fiercely debated topic in the years following the Surge. One school of thought that emerged even during the Surge was that violence dropped because General Petraeus fundamentally changed the strategy from his predecessor Casey and that Petraeus's troops also changed their operational approach to a new form of counterinsurgency operations.[6] This school of thought acknowledged that other conditions (described below) on the ground were certainly important for the decrease in violence; however, without the new and enlightened generalship of Petraeus and the change in operations and strategy that he brought about, those conditions would have never led to the drop in violence that occurred. In countering this idea, another school of thought emerged arguing that there really was no significant difference in strategy and operations between

---

[1] For Casey's Iraq strategy, see George W. Casey, Jr., *Papers of George W. Casey*, National Defense University, various years. Specifically, see *Campaign Plan: Operation Iraqi Freedom*; *Partnership, from Occupation to National Elections*, August 5, 2004; "Campaign Progress Review," Multi-National Forces–Iraq, December 5, 2004; and "MNF Update, 29 December 2004." See also George W. Casey, Jr., *Command Report: Multi-National Force Iraq, July 2004–February 2007*, Washington, D.C.: National Defense University Press, undated, draft copy provided to RAND; and George W. Casey, Jr., *Strategic Reflections: Operation Iraqi Freedom—July 2004–February 2007*, Washington, D.C.: National Defense University Press, October 2012, pp. 73–74. For contemporary media coverage, see Eric Schmitt, "U.S. to Intensify Its Training in Iraq to Battle Insurgents," *New York Times*, November 2, 2005.

[2] Iraq Body Count, "Civilian Deaths from Violence in 2007," webpage, January 1, 2008.

[3] FM 3-24, 2006.

[4] "The Surge" refers to the dramatic increase in the number of U.S. troops in Iraq, especially Baghdad, announced by President Bush during a television speech in January 2007.

[5] See, for example, Peter Mansoor, *Surge: My Journey with General David Petraeus and the Remaking of the Iraq War*, New Haven, Conn.: Yale University Press, 2013.

[6] Peter Mansoor, "How the Surge Worked," *Washington Post*, August 10, 2008b; see also Octavian Manea, "The Philosophy Behind the Iraq Surge: An interview with General Jack Keane," *Small Wars Journal*, Vol. 7, No. 4, April 5, 2011.

Casey and Petraeus during the Surge. Instead, according to this line of thinking, the key factors in lowering the violence by the end of 2007 were the critical conditions that led to the spread of the Anbar awakening, the aligning of Sunni tribes with the U.S. Army to fight al Qaeda, and the decision by the Shia militia to stand down their attacks against Sunni civilians.[7]

Debates around fundamental questions underlying different theories of victory in Iraq spanned the Casey and Petraeus years. Does security allow political stability to grow and develop, or does political stability, created though the establishment of political institutions, produce a secure environment? What is probable, and what this chapter and Chapter Five highlight, is that elements of both theories of victory were meshed in the approaches used, first by Casey and then by Petraeus.

Military Situation and Strategy: Actions on the Ground to Control Baghdad

The installation of a new military commander and the first American ambassador to Iraq alleviated much of the tension on the ground in Baghdad that stemmed from Lieutenant General Sanchez and Ambassador Bremer's somewhat difficult relationship. General Casey, who took command of MNF-I in July 2004, and Ambassador John Negroponte, who became the U.S. ambassador to Iraq around that time, held each other in a high regard. Casey has described Negroponte as a seasoned and capable ambassador with significant experience leading embassies.[8] As examples of Negroponte's savvy approach to being ambassador, Casey noted the appointment of former military officers to high-ranking positions in the embassy—specifically James Jeffrey,[9] a former artillery officer who became the deputy chief of mission and would serve as ambassador to Iraq during the Barack Obama administration, and Ronald Neumann,[10] a former infantry officer who, as a political-military officer, became a key interface between MNF-I and the embassy. Neumann went on to become ambassador to Afghanistan. Negroponte has expressed similar praise for Casey, claiming that the two developed a close relationship before deploying to Iraq and that they, along with their families, became good friends.[11]

---

[7] See Bob Woodward, "Why Did Violence Plummet? It Wasn't Just the Surge," *Washington Post*, September 8, 2008b; Dylan Matthews, "How Important Was the Surge?" *The American Prospect*, July 25, 2008; and DoD, *Measuring Stability and Security in Iraq*, Washington, D.C., March 2008a, p. 18.

[8] Former senior military commander, interview with the authors, September 30, 2015.

[9] "Biography: James F. Jeffrey," U.S. Department of State, November 21, 2006.

[10] "Biography: Ronald E. Neumann," U.S. Department of State, August 1, 2005.

[11] Former senior national security official, interview with the authors, April 8, 2015.

On arriving in Iraq, Casey and Negroponte colocated their offices in the embassy, creating a joint headquarters to capitalize on the political, economic, and media effects of events that could improve the security situation. They met together frequently throughout the workday, and Casey made a point of bringing key embassy staff with him when he visited troops in the field in an effort to convey to the forces that the military and State Department were "in this together."[12] Negroponte, in turn, accepted several hundred military officers in the embassy. Moreover, the two often met outside the office at General Casey's quarters, where they mulled over the problems that the military and embassy faced.[13] Casey and Negroponte subsequently drafted a joint mission statement for MNF-I and the U.S. embassy and then set aside 30 days to conduct field research on Iraq that informed the reshaping of the mission statement into a document that reflected the objectives of both the military and the embassy.[14]

Casey and Negroponte created a joint red team composed of military officers, embassy staff, and CIA personnel, which enhanced civil-military relations at lower ranks and exposed both Casey and Negroponte to the concerns of both civilians and military officers.[15] The red team examined the nature of the war and the nature of the enemy, assessed the military strategy and its chances for success, evaluated intelligence, and recommended ways ahead for MNF-I and the embassy.[16] The red team's recommendations were particularly useful early on in helping Casey expand his knowledge about Iraq and think of the future differently—and thus in informing his decisionmaking.[17]

The establishment of Provincial Reconstruction Teams (PRTs) in Iraq was another development brought about early in the tenures of Casey and Negroponte. PRTs incorporated Foreign Service officers and staff from USAID, the U.S. Departments of Justice and Agriculture, contractors, and Iraqi experts. They were designed to improve Iraqi governance, aid in the reconstruction effort, and promote development.[18] Although, in practice, State Department employees led PRTs, the teams were often subordinated to the "land-owning" brigade commander, thereby maintaining a clear chain of command and enhancing civil-military cooperation at the low levels.[19] Ambassador Zalmay Khalilzad, Negroponte's successor in Baghdad, agreed with the

---

[12] Former senior military commander, interview with the authors, September 30, 2015.

[13] Former senior national security official, interview with the authors, April 8, 2015.

[14] Former senior national security official, interview with the authors, April 8, 2015.

[15] Casey, 2012, p. 24.

[16] Former senior military commander, interview with the authors, September 30, 2015; and Gordon and Trainor, 2012, p. 160.

[17] Former senior military commander, interview with the authors, September 30, 2015.

[18] United States Institute of Peace, "Provincial Reconstruction Teams in Iraq," March 20, 2013.

[19] Condoleezza Rice, interview with Jason Awadi and Jeanne Godfroy, U.S. Department of State, Office of the Historian, July 12, 2014, p. 12, transcript provided to RAND by the OIF Study Group.

concept of PRTs in Iraq based on his experience from 2002 to 2003 as U.S. ambassador to Afghanistan, where PRTs enabled economic reconstruction on a local level throughout the country. From his perspective, this was the economic component of winning the war and facilitated civil-military cooperation by decentralizing reconstruction.[20] Secretary of State Rice noted that the creation of the PRT structure was an achievement from her time at the State Department.[21]

By 2005, there were some indicators that the strategy that Casey and Negroponte had developed might be working. The Iraqis held a nationwide election in January that put into place a representative body that in the months ahead would form a governing parliamentary structure.[22] Images of Iraqi women with their index finger painted purple to indicate that they had voted seemed to confirm President Bush's vision that Iraq was on the path to democracy. An uncomfortable fact, however, was that the Sunni minority in Iraq did not take part in this election because they perceived it as a sham to ensconce a Shia-dominated government that would continue to oppress them.[23]

Also, lurking beneath the façade of a budding Iraqi democracy was a growing Iraqi civil war, combined with ongoing resistance to the American occupation. The American strategy for Iraq was to build up its state institutions and, most importantly, its security forces, and then relatively quickly turn the responsibilities of governance and security over to the Iraqis. As President Bush often said, "As the Iraqis stand up, we will stand down."[24] Yet demographics and post-Saddam politics meant that "standing up" the Iraqi government meant empowering a Shia sectarian government that was bent on crushing the Sunnis in Iraq.[25] By 2005, a civil war was brewing in Iraq that was fought by Sunni insurgent groups against the Iraqi government and its various Shia militia allies.[26]

---

[20] Zalmay Khalilzad, interview with Peter Connors, Combat Studies Institute, April 30, 2008, p. 10, transcript provided to RAND by the OIF Study Group.

[21] Condoleezza Rice, interview with Jason Awadi and Jeanne Godfroy, U.S. Department of State, Office of the Historian, July 12, 2014, p. 12, transcript provided to RAND by the OIF Study Group.

[22] Cal Perry, "Milestone Elections Begin in Iraq," CNN, January 30, 2005.

[23] For a positive portrayal of the elections and the promise of a better future with the Iraqi elections, see Bartle Bull, "Iraqi Elections: Looking for Purple Fingers in Sadr City," *New York Times*, January 31, 2005. On the downside of the Iraqi elections and the fact that the majority of Sunnis did not vote in it, see John F. Burns and Dexter Filkins, "Shiite Alliance Adds to Leads as More Are Counted in Iraq," *New York Times*, February 4, 2005.

[24] Bush, 2010, p. 356. There is a clear turnaround in the years following 9/11 when, prior to the global war on terror, President Bush, his policy advisors, and military leaders were arguing against having the U.S. military involved in nation-building. However, the wars in Iraq and Afghanistan brought about a change of mindset, which thereby allowed a full embrace of armed nation-building as an operational method to try to achieve policy aims.

[25] Visser, 2011.

[26] Nicholas Sambanis, "It's Official: There Is Now a Civil War in Iraq," *New York Times*, July 23, 2006.

General Casey's strategic approach aimed to deal with these growing levels of sectarian violence. In so doing, he continued his close partnership with Ambassador Khalilzad, who succeeded Negroponte in July 2005.[27] Casey and Khalilzad knew each other from when Casey was the chief of strategic plans and policy on the JCS and Khalilzad worked for the NSC.[28] They developed a constructive working relationship in Baghdad. Because the campaign plan created at the beginning of Casey's and Negroponte's time in Iraq was due to expire in December 2005, Casey and Khalilzad collaborated on a bridging strategy to guide the military and embassy from October 2005 to May 2006, when they expected to have an Iraqi government in place.[29] Casey and Khalilzad released this plan to assist new units entering Iraq after September 2005.[30] Afterward, Casey and Khalilzad began developing a five-year campaign plan that was to take effect after an Iraqi government was formed in the spring of 2006.[31]

Carrying out Casey's military strategy in Baghdad in 2005 presented complex problems for senior commanders in Baghdad. A former senior military commander whose units operated in the southwestern part of Baghdad described his operations revolving around a handful of difficult challenges. One was the rising level of al Qaeda activity, including the increased use of IEDs, including vehicle-borne IEDs against Shia civilians.[32] Another aspect of the former commander's operations was to conduct raids targeting al Qaeda cells in the Dora section of southwest Baghdad. He was better able to target these cells because, as he recalled, before his BCT's deployment to Baghdad in 2005, he had spent time in New York City, understanding how urban systems and networks work.[33] Tied to al Qaeda attacks against Shia civilians were the infiltration of Shia militiamen into the Iraqi Police and National Police battalions that he was tasked to train and partner with. What he was starting to experience in 2005, and what would come to its brutal fruition in 2006, was the essence of the Shia-Sunni civil war and the way in which it was playing out in Baghdad. Acting independently and in cooperation with Iraqi Police and, at times, Iraqi Army units, Shia militia would kill and capture Sunnis in a given area; then, in reprisal, al Qaeda would attack Shia popu-

---

[27] Office of the Historian, "Zalmay Khalilzad (1951–)," U.S. Department of State, Bureau of Public Affairs, undated.

[28] Zalmay Khalilzad, interview with Peter Connors, April 30, 2008, p. 2, transcript provided to RAND by the OIF Study Group.

[29] Former senior military commander, interview with the authors, September 30, 2015.

[30] Former senior military commander, interview with the authors, September 30, 2015.

[31] Former senior military commander, interview with the authors, September 30, 2015; and Wright and Reese, 2008, pp. 177–180.

[32] Although tactical weapons, IEDs had strategic and political effects, which resulted in the creation of the Joint Improvised Explosive Device Defeat Organization and the fielding of thousands of mine-resistant ambush-protected vehicles.

[33] Former senior military commander, interview with the authors, July 24, 2015.

lation centers, usually with car bombs, killing scores in the process. Thus, a vicious circle of sectarian violence repeated itself with action, then reaction, then counteraction on a huge scale.[34] American combat outfits like the former commander's were in the middle of this sectarian civil war trying to use their operations to curb it so that the Iraqi government could gain credibility with the Iraqi people: a tall order not least because parts of the Iraqi government had already taken sides in the civil war.[35]

A former senior military commander we spoke with remembered that the complexity of the problem that U.S. Army units were dealing with in Baghdad was shaped by the early policy decisions by Bremer. By the end of 2005, for example, this former commander had noticed an important shift in the Sunni side of the sectarian civil war. Initially, in the immediate months after the removal of the regime, the resistance was primarily to the American occupation, and former Ba'athists and regime members dominated the developing Iraqi government. The shift he noticed by late 2005 was to a new government that was dominated by Sunni extremists, often from foreign countries—for example, Abu Musab al-Zarqawi from Jordan. The former commander noted that while he agreed with the way the government had been formed, he also saw a growing sectarian division between the Shia government and the Sunnis of the country:

> With each election, you had the country becoming less violent but more sectarian. The problem of Iraq was endemic of the larger problem in the Middle East. The long war was the war against violent Sunni extremist elements. It was poorly understood in D.C. that the number one theater problem in 2004–2005 shifted from Iraq-centric to extremist-centric. Sunni Islamic extremism was on the rise in Iraq.[36]

Even within this complex environment that he described, encouraging signs emerged in 2004 and 2005 that U.S. operations in Baghdad were working and that they were having the desired effect of improving government services, infrastructure, and security forces to better the lives of Iraqi civilians and build trust with their new government. One example was the experience of the 1st Cavalry Division in Sadr City under then-MG Peter Chiarelli that suggested promising results if the U.S. forces applied multiple synchronized lines of effort in building Iraqi institutions and improving security.[37] Other areas outside of Baghdad also were apparently showing

---

[34] See, for example, Ashraf Khalil and Patrick J. McDonnell, "Iraq Violence Taking a Sectarian Twist," *Los Angeles Times*, May 16, 2005; and International Crisis Group, "The Next Iraqi War? Sectarianism and Civil Conflict," Middle East Report No. 52, February 27, 2006.

[35] James A. Baker, Lee H. Hamilton, Lawrence S. Eagleburger, Vernon E. Jordan, Jr., Edwin Meese III, Sandra Day O'Conner, Leon E. Panetta, William J. Perry, Charles S. Robb, and Alan K. Simpson, *The Iraq Study Group Report*, December 2006, p. 13.

[36] Former senior military commander, interview with the authors, July 29, 2015.

[37] Chiarelli and Michaelis, 2005, p. 7.

progress. Then-COL H. R. McMaster's 3rd Armored Cavalry Regiment was posted to Talafar in northwestern Iraq to stop or at least slow the flow of Sunni fighters and IED materiel from Syria into places like Baghdad.[38] There was also the tactically successful second assault on Fallujah by the 1st Marine Division in November 2004 that paved the way for the ISF backed by American combat units to take over security of the city.[39]

Just as events and actions occurring outside of Baghdad affected Baghdad itself, so too were operations in one area of Baghdad affecting other areas of the city. Then–COL Stephen Lanza, who commanded a BCT,[40] noticed this connection in 2004 and 2005. Lanza recalled that operations in other parts of Baghdad would affect his area of operations in southern Baghdad:

> What's interesting is that what happened in Sadr City would have an impact on our area [al Rashid, often referred to as West Rashid, which is the southwestern region of Baghdad proper], because of the linkage of the Shiite population. And we had a very large Shiite population in our areas so that what happened in Sadr City affects Al Rashid and vice versa. Al Rashid is a very diverse population; a very poor population. So, actions in other parts of Iraq and other areas had a significant impact on what we were doing in Al Rashid.[41]

Thus, by the beginning of 2006, General Casey believed that the combination of American operations over the course of the two previous years, such as those of Colonel Lanza in southern Baghdad, and Iraqi elections had laid the foundations of an independent government such that U.S. forces would be able to start drawing down as early as that summer.[42]

However, the al Qaeda bombing of the Shia al-Askari shrine in Samarra brought into sharp relief for General Casey the ambitious nature of his timeline for an Ameri-

---

[38] George Packer, "The Lesson of Tal Afar: Is It Too Late for the Administration to Correct Its Course in Iraq?" *New Yorker*, April 10, 2006; see also Ricks, 2006a.

[39] On Fallujah, see Timothy S. McWilliams and Nicholas J. Schlosser, *U.S. Marines in Battle: Fallujah*, Quantico, Va.: U.S. Marine Corps, 2014, p. 2. See also Gerald de Lira, Jr., *The Anger of a Great Nation: Operation Vigilant Resolve*, thesis, Quantico, Va.: Marine Corps University, 2009, pp. 6–7; Rick Herrera, "Brave Rifles at Talafar," in William G. Robertson, ed., *In Contact: Case Studies in the Long War*, Vol. 1, Fort Leavenworth, Kan.: Combat Studies Institute, 2006; and Chris Gibson, "Battlefield Victories and Strategic Success: The Path Forward in Iraq," *Military Review*, September–October 2006.

[40] Lanza's BCT was formerly the 1st Cavalry Division's Artillery Brigade but had adapted and converted to a BCT in order to conduct counterinsurgency operations; see Wright and Reese, 2008, pp. 177–178.

[41] Stephen Lanza, interview with the Contemporary Operations Study Team, Combat Studies Institute, November 2, 2005, transcript provided to RAND by the OIF Study Group.

[42] "Rumsfeld, Casey Hold Press Conference on Iraq," CNN Transcripts, June 22, 2006. For Casey's Iraq strategy, see Casey, various years—specifically, *Campaign Plan: Operation Iraqi Freedom; Partnership, from Occupation to National Elections*, August 5, 2004; "Campaign Progress Review," Multi National Forces Iraq, December 5, 2004; and "MNF Update, 29 December 2004."

can drawdown. Before the bombing, General Casey saw as his primary threat the Sunni insurgents made up of former Saddam regime members who refused to accept the American occupation of their country in support of establishing a Shia-dominated government.[43]

Yet the fundamental problem that General Casey identified by spring and early summer of 2006 was, in his words, that the violence in Iraq was over the "division of political and economic powers among Iraq's ethnic and sectarian groups." He noted that this evolving conflict was moving away from "an insurgency" against the American occupation toward a civil war fought between the Iraqi people.[44] Thus, General Casey confronted a paradox: On the one hand, during 2004–2005, the operational construct put into place by Casey's strategy in Baghdad seemed to be working; but on the other hand, the Samarra bombing showed the limits of these operations when set in the middle of a growing Iraqi sectarian civil war.

The aftermath of the Samarra bombing made clear to some senior military commanders in Baghdad that they were not simply dealing with a Sunni insurgency against the U.S. presence and Iraqi government. In the weeks and months after the Samarra bombing, some began seeing other indicators of the sectarian civil war that had been barely visible to previous Baghdad commanders.[45] The growing scale and sectarian nature of the crisis became clearer as bodies of kidnapping victims began to appear on the streets of increasingly homogeneous Sunni and Shia districts in the city.[46]

By mid-2006, some senior military commanders had also become concerned about the performance of the ISF and their readiness to take over responsibility for parts of Baghdad.[47] Even though by summer of 2006, General Casey's strategy of drawing down American forces as the ISF stood up seemed to be on track, MG James D.

---

[43] In Casey, various years, see "Campaign Progress Review, December 2004–December 2005," Multi-National Forces–Iraq, December 20, 2005.

[44] In Casey, various years, see, for example, "Pocket Day-Timer Notes," January 20, February 22, March 1, March 9, and March 11, 2006; "Talking Points for POTUS SVTC," February 7, 2007; and General Casey's interview with David Cloud and Greg Jaffe, September 27, 2008. Casey made a similar statement at a briefing with Khalilzad on October 23, 2006 (see CQ Transcriptions, "Iraq Briefing," *Washington Post*, October 24, 2006).

[45] Former senior military commander, interview with the authors, July 30, 2015.

[46] Joshua Thiel, "The Statistical Irrelevance of American SIGACT Data: Iraq Surge Analysis Reveals Reality," *Small Wars Journal*, April 12, 2011; and John Agnew, Thomas W. Gillespie, Jorge Gonzalez, and Brian Min, "Baghdad Nights: Evaluating the U.S. Military Surge Using Nighttime Light Signatures," Los Angeles: California Center for Population Research, CCPR-064-08, December 1, 2008.

[47] Former senior military commander, interview with the authors, August 12, 2015. During the interview, the former commander also stated, "I knew that in 2006, our job going in there, when I was told by General Casey, was to turn the job over to the Iraqis. That is what Generals Chiarelli and [John R.] Vines told me too. All of the division commanders had the experience, but our mission was to build capacity and transition to Iraqi security, but we didn't have the capacity."

Thurman and his commander, Lieutenant General Chiarelli, began to question if they were actually ready to take over. As a former senior military commander noted,

> when you look at the overall strategy during this time period, when you don't have security conditions right (and we were under a lot of pressure to turn these areas over) and we had some . . . we were tracking everything . . . but at the end of the day, if they can't do the job, then you can't pull Americans out of there; and so, you've got to keep American forces in there long enough to allow them to build the capacity that they need in order to provide adequate security.[48]

In an effort to halt or at least slow the spiraling levels of sectarian violence in Baghdad, the U.S. Army's 4th Infantry Division and the Iraqi 6th Infantry Division conducted an operation called "Together Forward." The concept behind Together Forward was to increase the number of ISF troops in Baghdad and the number of American combat troops by bringing the American 172nd Infantry Brigade down from Mosul to carry out more clearing operations and establish a larger ISF presence on the streets. After nearly four months of Together Forward operations, by fall of 2006, the results were disappointing.[49] The Iraq Study Group, which provided President Bush an independent assessment of the situation in Baghdad, noted, "The results of Operation Together Forward II are disheartening. Violence in Baghdad—already at high levels—jumped more than 43 percent between the summer and October 2006 and U.S. forces continued to suffer high casualties."[50]

Ultimately, Together Forward proved unsuccessful largely because the sectarian civil war was raging and growing; it had not yet peaked, but would do so by early 2007 and the start of the Surge. It was at that point when levels of violence started to drop precipitously.[51]

General Casey noted in late 2006 that the greatest problem in Iraq was sectarian violence, because it made resolving the key issues dividing Iraq more difficult. Until the violence was reduced, argued Casey, the chances for reconciliation were slim to none. It was in his conception of how to proceed in this milieu of Iraqi sectarian violence that Casey anticipated what would come with Petraeus and the Surge of troops in 2007. Casey noted that the United States should not walk away from the violence and hunker down in its forward operating bases, awaiting a precipitous American with-

---

[48] Former senior military commander, interview with the authors, August 12, 2015.

[49] Baker et al., 2006, p. 15.

[50] Baker et al., 2006, p. 15.

[51] Iraq Body Count, 2008; Paul Von Zielbauer, "Iraqi Violence Ebbed in September, Reports Say," *New York Times*, October 2, 2007.

drawal from Iraq. Instead, the American military had a role to play in helping to curb sectarian violence so that reconciliation among Iraqis might proceed.[52]

In December 2006, then-LTG Raymond T. Odierno became the commander of Multi-National Corps–Iraq (MNC-I), taking over from Lieutenant General Chiarelli. Later, in written answers to questions from the Senate Armed Services Committee in May 2008, Odierno recalled his initial guidance from General Casey:

> General Casey challenged me to take a look at different ways to break the cycle of sectarian violence in Baghdad. As a result of the assessment, we confirmed that Baghdad was the most important piece of terrain and ethno-sectarian violence, fueled by extremist elements[,] was the primary cause of the problem. We conducted crisis action planning and through our assessment and analysis determined that we must first and foremost protect the population first in Baghdad and then the other ten cities. We also determined that there was an opportunity in Anbar to exploit some initial success that was created by the reconciliation efforts with the tribes. We developed tactics, techniques, and procedures to push coalition and ISF forces out into the neighborhoods in small Joint Security Stations (JSS) and combat outpost (COP). In the past we would clear areas but would not be able to hold these areas. We knew we must secure the population; we must deny the enemy sanctuaries and eliminate the support zones in the so called Baghdad Belts. We then developed the operational plan and requested the surge forces. This plan was briefed to General Casey and the Secretary of Defense for approval, and later to General Petraeus upon his arrival.[53]

The execution of this approach, eventually resourced with five additional combat brigades, is discussed in Chapter Five.

Embassy Challenges: Reconstruction in a War Zone

The violence in Baghdad directed at Americans posed an enormous challenge for the State Department and the embassy. One former senior national security official noted that the security situation made the embassy in Baghdad unique and described the violence as "systematic," noting that the embassy was bombed the day after his arrival in Iraq.[54] American civilians were also being attacked outside the Green Zone, but the military seemed unable to provide adequate security to embassy staff outside the embassy compound. Civilians were being shot, particularly along the perilous road

---

[52] In Casey, various years, see "Guiding Principles," November 11, 2006; and "MNF-I Commanders Conference," December 15, 2006.

[53] U.S. Senate, *Nominations Before the Senate Armed Services Committee, Second Session 110th Congress*, Committee on Armed Services, Washington, D.C., 2008, p. 192.

[54] Former senior national security official, interview with the authors, April 8, 2015.

between the embassy and the Baghdad airport, known as Route Irish, which became a prime example of Baghdad's instability.[55] Eventually, Route Irish became so dangerous that embassy personnel stopped using it and insisted that the military transport people to and from the airport in helicopters. This helicopter transportation requirement became so onerous that the military finally established security along the route, but only at night.[56] In addition to the personal safety risk that violence posed to State Department personnel, Baghdad's security situation infringed on the ability of Foreign Service officers to work effectively. In a 2006 survey of Foreign Service officers who had served in Baghdad, many cited the inability to travel outside the Green Zone without guards, as well as the burdensome, though necessary, security precautions as limiting their ability to work and accomplish their missions in Iraq.[57]

Recruiting sufficient numbers of qualified staff to work in the embassy was another enduring problem for the State Department. It was not accustomed to maintaining high staff levels in war zones.[58] An often-cited criticism of the State Department's performance during the war is that the department did not send an adequate number of staff to Baghdad. To a certain extent, this is true. According to a former senior State Department official, approximately 40 percent of staff were absent or slots were unfilled at the embassy at any given time. Causes for these absences included staff being on rest and recuperation or sick leave, gaps as personnel rotated through, the inability to find personnel to fill billets, and personnel cutting their tours short.[59] Secretary Rice noted that recruiting midcareer Foreign Service officers was particularly difficult because their children, who normally attend schools in host nations, would go to a school in the United States instead while their parents were deployed to Baghdad, causing great disruption to families.[60] A former senior State Department official who spent two years at the embassy spoke with us about the personal toll that serving in Iraq took on his family, because he was absent during his children's teen years.[61] Interestingly, the State Department foresaw staffing issues stemming from family separation and, in 2005, sought ways to ameliorate the effect of serving in Baghdad on the families of Foreign Service officers, such as granting leaves back to the United States

---

[55] John F. Burns, "On Way to Baghdad Airport, Death Stalks Main Road," *New York Times*, May 29, 2005.

[56] Former senior State Department official, interview with the authors, April 9, 2015.

[57] Shawn Dorman, "Desire to 'Serve My Country' Cited by Volunteers for Duty in Iraq," *Washington Post*, March 23, 2006.

[58] Former senior State Department official, interview with the authors, June 12, 2015.

[59] Former senior State Department official, interview with the authors, June 12, 2015.

[60] Condoleezza Rice, interview with Jason Awadi and Jeanne Godfroy, U.S. Department of State, Office of the Historian, July 12, 2014, p. 12, transcript provided to RAND by the OIF Study Group.

[61] Former senior State Department official, interview with the authors, June 12, 2015.

whenever possible, but unfortunately, problems persisted.[62] Given the personal sacrifices required of diplomats who served in Iraq and the difficulty of serving in this dangerous environment, it is not surprising that the State Department struggled to maintain adequate staff levels in the embassy.

The sheer mismatch between the size of MNF-I and a significantly smaller embassy presence further exacerbated the State Department's staffing difficulties in Iraq. The U.S. military manpower in Iraq dwarfed that of the embassy and so, in general, could devote far more resources to any given issue.[63] A former official at the U.S. embassy in Baghdad observed that the average staff section in MNF-I was about ten times larger than its embassy counterpart, highlighting why the embassy could not keep up with MNF-I's demands and expectations with respect to what the embassy staff could accomplish.[64] Secretary Rice has responded in interviews to critiques of staff levels in Iraq during the war. In 2014, she discussed how the State Department is limited by the number of Foreign Service officers that could be sent to Iraq and Afghanistan, which is an unusual posting for most diplomats. She said,

> The fact of the matter is Foreign Service officers are not military officers. They needed a blueprint for how to operate in war zones. We hadn't done that since Vietnam, and there frankly aren't that many of them. . . . [W]e had to cover not just Iraq and Afghanistan; we couldn't put our weight of effort there in the way that the military could put its weight of effort there, because we had to run every other country in the world.[65]

The Foreign Service not only is smaller than the military but it also does not have the ability to focus the majority of its resources on one or two countries, thereby limiting what it could devote to Iraq and Afghanistan.

The embassy also faced frequent staff turnover. One former senior national security official noted that military officers returned to Iraq for multiple tours, while civilians rotated in and out of Iraq quickly.[66] He contrasted this with Vietnam, where civilians spent a long time in country during the war or returned for multiple postings. A former senior State Department official noted that the military developed systems that facilitated the transition of command, responsibility, and information and that incoming and outgoing military personnel overlapped for a short period of time, but the civil-

---

[62] U.S. Department of State and the Broadcasting Board of Governors, Office of the Inspector General, *Review of Staffing at U.S. Embassy Baghdad*, Report No. ISP-IQO-05-57, March 2005.

[63] Former senior State Department official, interview with the authors, June 12, 2015.

[64] Former official at the U.S. embassy in Baghdad, interview with the authors, May 26, 2015.

[65] Condoleezza Rice, interview with Jason Awadi and Jeanne Godfroy, U.S. Department of State, Office of the Historian, July 12, 2014, p. 11, transcript provided to RAND by the OIF Study Group.

[66] Former senior national security official, interview with the authors, April 8, 2015.

ians did not adopt this practice.[67] Consequently, institutional knowledge evaporated when staff members left.

Another challenge that the State Department faced was conducting reconstruction in a war zone. One former senior national security official noted that anytime the embassy would make progress on infrastructure projects, the insurgents would attack them. Furthermore, the absence of security undermined the embassy's reconstruction efforts. The official stated, "There is a lot of stuff that is happening in the security situation that impinges on your ability to grow the economy."[68] Secretary Rice echoed this sentiment: "The truth of the matter is you can talk all you want to about politics and economic development and those things, but if people are running for their lives, they're not going to actually stop and do political development."[69] These comments reaffirm sentiments that RAND researchers heard from many civilians: Reconstruction could not be achieved until security had been established.

Reconstruction in Iraq was also hindered by a problem that plagues international development around the world: sustainability challenges. According to a former senior State Department official, the United States pushed sophisticated reconstruction projects that often outstripped the capacity of the Iraqis to maintain without U.S. assistance. As an illustration, he claimed that the United States could build advanced power plants, but it was entirely possible that the Iraqi staff at the plant had never used a computer before.[70] The $5.5 million sewage treatment plant in Najaf exemplifies his characterization of this sustainability problem. Funded by USAID, the plant was completed in February 2005, only to remain closed until August 2005 because no one in Najaf was qualified to operate it.[71] A similar situation occurred with a plant in Diwaniya, which sat idle for ten months after its completion in December 2004. The former official also noted that the U.S. government and civilian contractors directed projects, but a lack of a sense of ownership often led to the collapse of these projects after they were handed over to Iraqis.[72] The embassy addressed this problem by engaging Iraqi ministries and encouraging them to take on more responsibility for implementing projects.

---

[67] Former senior State Department official, interview with the authors, June 12, 2015.

[68] Former senior national security official, interview with the authors, April 8, 2015.

[69] Condoleezza Rice, interview with Jason Awadi and Jeanne Godfroy, U.S. Department of State, Office of the Historian, July 12, 2014, p. 13, transcript provided to RAND by the OIF Study Group.

[70] Former senior State Department official, interview with the authors, June 12, 2015.

[71] Craig S. Smith, "Poor Planning and Corruption Hobble Reconstruction of Iraq," *New York Times*, September 18, 2005.

[72] Former senior State Department official, interview with the authors, June 12, 2015.

Civilian Policy Views from Washington and Baghdad

By the summer and fall of 2006, nightly news broadcasts in the United States were filled with images of bazaars being bombed, bodies littering Iraq's dusty streets, and the distraught families of fallen American soldiers laying their loved ones to rest. The civil war raged in Baghdad and uncertainty paralyzed Washington. Although many government officials were convinced by mid-2006 that something needed to be done in Iraq, seeds of doubt about the military's strategy had been sown long before. Could the U.S. military stand up an Iraqi Army that was capable of providing security? Could the Iraqi Army stand up so that the U.S. military could stand down? As early as 2004, civilians in the State Department and NSC began questioning whether the military had a winning strategy in place. The resounding answer from many was "no."

When a former senior State Department official arrived in Baghdad in 2004 to become an official at the U.S. embassy, he quickly assessed that the military did not have an effective strategy in place. In describing the chaos that gripped Baghdad, he bluntly stated, "We had no strategy."[73] He suggested that the political leadership in Washington was responsible: "The U.S. military was totally clueless, not because they hadn't done it—I saw them do counterinsurgency before in Vietnam—but because the political leadership was in a state of trauma. This had been George Bush's dream to bring democracy to the Middle East."[74] The former official claimed that General Casey was capable of conducting an effective counterinsurgency strategy, but Rumsfeld prevented him from doing so. Furthermore, "Then the luck ran out because there was not a real commitment to conduct a 'no s---' counterinsurgency in Washington."[75]

Another former senior State Department official also realized early on that the military strategy in Iraq was insufficient and became increasingly concerned throughout his tenure at the State Department that the United States was losing the war. He traveled extensively throughout Iraq from late 2004 until he left government in 2006. After visiting Iraq in the spring and summer of 2005, he concluded that the military did not have a coherent overarching strategy for winning the war.[76] He noted,

> By the summer of 2005, I realized that the strategy of what we were actually doing in Iraq radically varied from unit to unit rather than my initial assumption that there was some central strategy guided from Camp Victory. I learned several months in that that was not the case and then learned that actually Camp Victory had no coherent strategy.[77]

---

[73] Former senior State Department official, interview with the authors, April 9, 2015.
[74] Former senior State Department official, interview with the authors, April 9, 2015.
[75] Former senior State Department official, interview with the authors, April 9, 2015.
[76] Former senior State Department official, interview with the authors, March 23, 2015.
[77] Former senior State Department official, interview with the authors, March 23, 2015.

In the fall of 2005, Secretary Rice announced in a congressional hearing that the military strategy in Iraq was to "clear, hold, and build," which meant to clear insurgents from an area; reestablish, or hold, governance in that area; and build protection for the population.[78] The creation of the phrase began with Philip Zelikow, who served on an interagency review team in 2005 and then as counselor to Secretary Rice in 2005 and 2006. In preparation for his work on Iraq, Zelikow familiarized himself with literature on the Vietnam War, including reading Lewis Sorley's *A Better War*, in which the author claims that the military was too late to adopt a "clear and hold" strategy.[79] Ultimately, Zelikow came to believe that in some of the areas he visited in Iraq, commanders were clearing and holding positions with Iraqi brigades and then establishing a permanent presence to hold the battle space. For example, this appeared to be the strategy executed by COL H. R. McMaster to retake the city of Talafar from insurgents.[80] When writing Secretary Rice's testimony for a September 2005 congressional hearing, Zelikow characterized the military's strategy in Iraq as "clear and hold." General Odierno, who was the assistant to the CJCS at the time, recommended to Zelikow that he add the word "build" to capture the military's effort to then build Iraqi institutions in areas free from insurgent presence.[81] Thus, the phrase "clear, hold, build" was born for its use in Iraq.

Because Odierno had consulted on the writing of Rice's testimony and GEN Peter Pace, who served as CJCS at the time, had cleared it with no comment, Rice and Zelikow believed that the testimony had the approval of the military. Furthermore, the testimony had been provided to Secretary Rumsfeld, who never responded one way or the other before the hearing.[82] Unfortunately, neither General Abizaid, the CENTCOM commander, nor General Casey, the MNF-I commander, was notified that Rice would be outlining military strategy in her testimony. Casey felt that "clear, hold, build" did not adequately reflect the military's strategy, because it overlooked the training of the ISF.[83] Moreover, Casey felt that Zelikow had personally double-crossed him by not clearing the phrase with him first, after Casey had facilitated Zelikow's trips around Iraq. Rumsfeld was also surprised by the testimony, and, although he had been sent an advanced copy, he was unable to focus on it because of his travel sched-

---

[78] Colin Ahern, "Clear, Hold, Build: Modern Political Techniques in COIN," Fort Huachuca, Ariz.: University of Military Intelligence, 2008.

[79] Gordon and Trainor, 2012, p. 176.

[80] Condoleezza Rice, *No Higher Honor: A Memoir of My Years in Washington*, New York: Crown Publishers, 2011, p. 373.

[81] Former senior State Department official, interview with the authors, March 23, 2015.

[82] Former senior State Department official, interview with the authors, March 23, 2015.

[83] Bob Woodward, *The War Within: A Secret White House History, 2006–2008*, New York: Simon and Schuster, 2008a, p. 32.

ule.[84] On account of this breakdown in communications, the military's relationship with the State Department suffered, and Zelikow found his access to the American military in Iraq diminished going forward.

The NSC also shared concerns about the lack of a coherent, winning military strategy and whether the war had spiraled out of control. According to a former senior national security official, the NSC developed the National Strategy for Victory in Iraq in the fall of 2005, partly because it felt that there was no coherent strategy guiding the war in Iraq.[85] This document outlined the administration's strategy for winning the war, provided an update on progress toward that goal, and discussed remaining challenges.[86] The strategy also was meant to establish benchmarks against which the public could measure progress. The very fact that the NSC felt motivated to write the strategy demonstrates how unclear the military strategy had become to Washington-based civilians in government involved in Iraq policy.

Outside of government, the civilians serving on the Defense Policy Board also questioned whether the military's strategy could succeed. In particular, some expressed significant concern about the state of the war as early as 2004.[87] Worried that the briefers sent to the Defense Policy Board were not accurately depicting the perilous nature of the situation on the ground, one member of the board sought out Derek Harvey, an Army colonel directing a small Iraq task force on the Joint Staff, whose ground-based investigation of the insurgency had produced a different interpretation of the insurgency at that time.[88] With the encouragement of the Defense Policy Board, Harvey would later brief his interpretation of the situation in Iraq to Rumsfeld, Rice, National Security Adviser Stephen Hadley, and, in December 2004, President Bush.[89] Although the Defense Policy Board continued to focus on Iraq throughout 2004, 2005, and 2006, Rumsfeld would counter the board's pessimism about the security situation and military strategy by asserting that its assessments were wrong.[90]

The Defense Department and military defended the strategy of training Iraqi forces to take on the insurgents throughout this phase of the war, but as time wore on, civilian voices arguing that the military's strategy was failing grew louder and louder. What started as a small group of skeptics grew into a major push within the government for the military to reevaluate how it would win the war. As described in

---

[84] Gordon and Trainor, 2012, p. 177.

[85] Former senior national security official, interview with the authors, September 25, 2015.

[86] National Security Council, *National Strategy for Victory in Iraq*, November 30, 2005.

[87] Former Defense Policy Board member, interview with the authors, June 10, 2015.

[88] Former senior military commander, interview with the authors, April 17, 2015.

[89] Gordon and Trainor, 2012, pp. 132–133.

[90] Former senior military commander, interview with the authors, April 17, 2015.

the following chapter, this pressure would eventually lead to the adoption of a new military strategy.

One common critique of DoD, the NSC, the State Department, and the military during General Casey's command was the overemphasis on metrics or measurements of operational progress. This emphasis led to a confusing combination of the efforts used to achieve progress and the achievements purportedly made. The U.S. government emphasized quantitative measurements of inputs and outputs, but civilians claimed that this clouded the perception of outcomes. A former senior State Department official who served at the U.S. embassy in Baghdad observed that the U.S. government had difficulty moving "beyond quantitative measurement of input and output to what really matters, which was the qualitative judgment of outcomes." He described the sheer amount of information, data streams, and reports coming out of Baghdad as a "fire hose" and asserted, "This enormous tension between putting more and more people, more and more money, all of which were carefully measured and monitored, into an area where that application would not and could not translate into meaningful outcomes was the bedevilment of Iraq policy from word go."[91] The utility of these metrics in revealing what was actually happening on the ground is debatable.

Furthermore, the amount of information being produced distracted policymakers from addressing the core issues of the war, because the interagency process began to focus more on the production of reports and information than on what those reports and information were or were not revealing about the war and the military's strategy. Another former senior State Department official echoed this critique. He described the weekly interagency and NSC meetings as taking on a repetitive format, opening with a situation report and briefing slides with little time for discussion of substantive issues and actual decisionmaking.[92] Broad strategy was assumed, but not discussed, because it was presumed that everyone in the interagency already knew what the strategy was.[93]

During a 2006 visit to Iraq, one member of the Defense Policy Board also noticed that the military's focus on metrics clouded an understanding of what was happening on the ground. After meeting with General Casey, this member thought the general was overly focused on turning battle space over to Iraqis as a principal measure of success.[94] There did not seem to be an appreciation that the security situation on the ground was deteriorating despite the amount of battle space placed in the hands of the ISF, the member said.[95]

---

[91] Former senior State Department official, interview with the authors, June 24, 2015.

[92] Former senior State Department official, interview with the authors, March 23, 2015.

[93] Former senior State Department official, interview with the authors, March 23, 2015.

[94] Former Defense Policy Board member, interview with the authors, June 10, 2015.

[95] Former Defense Policy Board member, interview with the authors, June 10, 2015.

By contrast, a former senior national security official noted that tracking metrics helped the NSC expose the inconsistences in the military's strategy. In response to DoD's insistence that the problems in Iraq were political and economic, the NSC tracked metrics.[96] Tracking security-related metrics enabled the NSC to challenge the military's claim that Iraq did not have a security problem, which opened the door to questioning the core assumptions of the military's strategy. For example, Meghan O'Sullivan, an NSC staffer on the Iraq portfolio, kept a chart in her office that tracked levels of violence in Baghdad's neighborhoods to demonstrate visually the problems of the military's strategy.[97] To bring the President around to the same conclusion, the NSC sent him memos on a nightly basis outlining the flaws in the strategy and analytically showing that when the U.S. military applied force, violence declined.[98] The evidence that the NSC presented to Bush contradicted the military's strategy, which was to bring down levels of violence by standing up the ISF. These memos prompted discussions that became "the nucleus of the surge."[99]

As the situation in Iraq in 2006 grew in complexity with the increasing violence of the civil war, select military officers, along with a battery of retired military and civilian experts, were constructing what they saw as potential military solutions to the problem in Iraq. A February 2006 meeting at Fort Leavenworth, Kansas, began the discussion of the writing of what would become the Army's new counterinsurgency doctrinal manual. Led by then–Lieutenant General Petraeus, the Combined Arms Center commander at Fort Leavenworth, this weeklong meeting brought together high-profile civilian and military experts, along with notable media luminaries. In the months after this initial meeting, in fall 2006, a small writing group led by retired Army officer and historian Conrad Crane produced a draft of the Army's new doctrine on counterinsurgency or armed nation-building. Although the United States had been performing armed nation-building to win Iraqi hearts and minds from the early days after the collapse of the Saddam Hussein regime, the manual marked a shift by the Army and Marine Corps as institutions. As discussed earlier in this report, soldiers and Marines were adapting to the challenges of the war. This learning from the bottom up was happening in Iraq, and the manual turned the developing approach into Army and Marine Corps policy and doctrine.

At the same time that the manual was being finalized for publication, a growing bevy of voices could be heard from the NSC, certain military experts, and retired Army officers arguing that Iraq was burning in civil war because the U.S. forces under Casey

---

[96] Former senior national security official, interview with the authors, September 25, 2015.

[97] Woodward, 2008a, p. 68.

[98] Former senior national security official, interview with the authors, September 25, 2015.

[99] Former senior national security official, interview with the authors, September 25, 2015.

did not do counterinsurgency operations correctly. In this worldview, Iraq demanded a new strategy because Casey's was apparently failing.[100]

The November 2006 congressional elections, in which the Republicans lost both houses to the Democrats, were seen as a referendum of criticism against the war in Iraq. Secretary of Defense Rumsfeld's quick resignation after the elections only furthered the sense among administration officials that something needed to be done in Iraq to turn the war around.[101] In the official memoirs of his tenure of command in Iraq, General Casey offered a profound observation about the relationship between strategy and policy during American wars. This observation was based on his personal research through his own papers and other sources. He commented on those tumultuous final months in command when he was trying to contain a civil war in Iraq while simultaneously dealing with a bureaucratic insurgency from his own government to discredit his strategy for domestic political purposes. Looking back on those months, General Casey wrote that, with all of the video teleconferences, discussion groups, and visits by NSC groups, what his President was really looking for was something that appeared different in terms of strategy and operations. The general noted that this "was an intense period as it was clear that Washington was looking for something different from what I was recommending to them." In the end, Casey offered the President his best plan for achieving American objectives in Iraq. But as he reflected years later on those final days in 2006, it became clear to him that he "should have offered the President a broader range of options . . . in Iraq." What Casey did not fully understand was that Bush wanted to clearly demonstrate that he was embarking on a different approach so that he could maintain domestic support for the war. The problem that General Casey had in these closing months of 2006 was that nobody, from the President on down, had really conveyed to him the President's need for options to show to a skeptical American public and political constituency that the war could be won. Casey was left in the dark and did not really figure it all out until well after he departed.[102]

Nevertheless, President Bush was clear about what he wanted. In his recent memoir, he described a meeting with his national security team, including General Casey, General Abizaid, and Ambassador Khalilzad, on August 14, 2006. General Casey believed "we could succeed by transferring responsibility to the Iraqis faster."

---

[100] Ricks praises certain individuals, such as General Keane for circumventing military command channels by going directly to the President and other key officials arguing for the Surge and calling Casey's strategy a failure; see Thomas E. Ricks, *The Gamble: General David Petraeus and the American Military Adventure in Iraq, 2006–2008*, New York: Penguin Press, 2009, pp. 74–105. For an alternative explanation of the efforts of Keane and others in putting together the Surge, see Woodward, 2008a; and Peter Feaver, "The Right to Be Right: Civil Military Relations and the Iraq Surge Decision," *International Security*, Vol. 35, No. 4, Spring 2011.

[101] Sheryl Gay Stolberg and Jim Rutenberg, "Rumsfeld Resigns as Secretary of Defense After Big Election Gains for Democrats," *New York Times*, November 8, 2006.

[102] Casey, 2012, p. 122–146. See also Casey's interview with David Cloud and Greg Jaffe, July 28, 2008, and with Tom Ricks, October 13, 2008, in Casey, various years.

Secretary Rumsfeld believed "we needed to 'help them help themselves.' . . . That was another way of saying that we needed to take our hand off the bicycle seat." The President made it clear that he wanted another approach:

> I wanted to send a message to the team that I was thinking differently. "We must succeed," I said. "If they can't do it, we will." If the bicycle teeters, we're going to put the hand back on. We have to make damn sure we do not fail.[103]

The President was committed to doing whatever it would take to succeed in Iraq. He made clear to the American people the objective of U.S. troops in Iraq in the upcoming months during the Surge: "to help Iraqis clear and secure neighborhoods, to help them protect the local population, and to help ensure that the Iraqi forces left behind are capable of providing the security that Baghdad needs."[104]

Efforts to Create Iraqi Security Forces and Defense Institutions

New Organizations

Casey's military strategy from June 2004 until his departure in January 2007 was premised on the need for the ISF to take over combat operations from American and coalition forces. For his strategy to succeed, Casey realized early on the importance of building the right framework for the training of the new ISF by American forces. But it was not just about the tactical training of Iraqi soldiers and policemen; it was also about the more difficult task of creating new institutions from scratch that in a short amount of time could act independently and effectively. When this effort began in force in the early months of Casey's command tenure, building such institutions from the rubble of ones destroyed by major combat operations and earlier decisions of U.S. policymakers proved to be a formidable task.

The transition from CJTF-7 to MNF-I reflected a change in strategy, from a short-term occupation to long-term nation-building. MNF-I's role was to deliver security, economic, diplomatic, and information operations with the U.S. embassy and the new Iraqi government.[105] As a four-star-level command, MNF-I had two subordinate commands led by three-star generals: MNC-I, which controlled tactical-level military operations, and MNSTC-I, which oversaw programs that were organizing, equipping, training, and advising the ISF, as well as rebuilding Iraq's MOD and other military infrastructure.[106] The creation of MNSTC-I brought many security training efforts

---

[103] Bush, 2010.

[104] CQ Transcriptions, "President Bush Addresses Nation on Iraq War," *Washington Post*, January 10, 2007.

[105] Wright and Reese, 2008, p. 173.

[106] Wright and Reese, 2008, p. 173.

under one command, yet issues remained. With the transition of commands and new leadership—including General Casey and General Petraeus in June 2004—the U.S. government signaled its commitment to the war effort, even as violence in Iraq continued to mount.

In the fall of 2004, it was clear to Casey and Negroponte that getting Iraq to a place where the United States could realistically pass control to the Iraqis was going to take much longer than the 18 months envisioned in the U.N. timeline. Negroponte wrote a cable to Secretary of State Powell at that time, noting that stabilizing Iraq was going to take a long time—at least five years—and insurgency and sectarian violence would still exist.[107] This personal assessment was contrary to the timeline that Casey was getting from Washington, which stated that the goal for handing over security responsibilities to the Iraqis was 18 months.[108]

By the middle of 2004, the contradiction between a swift withdrawal of U.S. forces and the long-term endeavor to stand up the Iraqi military had largely resolved itself. The United States and coalition forces were committed to Iraq for an extended period. Critical to stabilizing Iraq would be the training of ISF and putting an Iraqi face on the security sector. To do this, Casey and Negroponte put together a joint mission statement and campaign plan outlining the minimum conditions necessary for U.S. withdrawal from Iraq: a government perceived as representative of all Iraqis and security forces that could maintain domestic order and "keep the terrorists out" of Iraq.[109]

Both tasks outlined in the campaign plan were ambitious. The governance goal was difficult on account of numerous turnovers in the Iraqi government; within the first two years of Saddam's removal from power, there were three different Iraqi governments, and building a relationship between U.S. forces and the government of Iraq was difficult and continuous.[110] Establishing domestic order and securing the borders were equally difficult tasks for the nascent ISF. U.S. forces' role in training the ISF is discussed in detail below.

Evolution of Training Organizations

The transition between security training organizations occurred throughout the spring and summer of 2004, coinciding with U.S. congressional approval to expand the funding and training mission of the ISF. On March 9, 2004, MG Paul Eaton became the head of the new Office of Security Cooperation–Iraq, which oversaw the operations of

---

[107] Former senior military commander, interview with the authors, September 30, 2015.

[108] Gordon and Trainor, 2012, p. 278.

[109] Former senior military commander, interview with the authors, September 30, 2015.

[110] Former senior military commander, interview with the authors, September 30, 2015.

CMATT and the Civilian Police Assistance Training Team.[111] In May 2004, MNF-I replaced CJTF-7, which quickly led to the transition of the Office of Security Cooperation–Iraq into MNSTC-I on June 6, 2004.

This transition coincided with the departure of Eaton and the arrival of Petraeus. While many of the stated goals of CMATT remained unmet by the time Eaton left Iraq, CMATT had established a solid foundation by mid-2004 on which Petraeus could build.[112] Issues with funding, command and control, logistics, procurement, and personnel all remained. However, under Petraeus, the effort to train the ISF rose in prominence and became a primary effort of coalition forces. A former senior military commander summed up the shift in attitude just before BG Martin Dempsey's departure from Iraq in July. The commander described a recognition on the part of U.S. forces that standing up the indigenous forces and establishing a viable security architecture would enable the United States to leave Iraq, and Petraeus (in his capacity as commander of MNSTC-I) was tasked to add "industrial strength and speed [to the training effort] and get Iraqis on the street."[113]

With a successful transition behind MNSTC-I, the training of the ISF slowly progressed under Petraeus, remaining a dispersed operation. MNSTC-I had training centers throughout Iraq, the Jordanians were training Iraqi Army officers, multiple adviser teams were embedded with the ISF, and conventional and special forces were training other ISF units. Before MNSTC-I, six ICDC brigades were trained across Iraq by coalition forces. However, local ICDC forces lacked standardization in the training they received, because each unit received training based on the decisions of U.S. forces at each location. These brigades were in addition to the three divisions that were being trained under CMATT throughout 2004.[114] The number of ICDC brigades being trained would grow to six and would eventually be folded into the Iraqi Army, and each brigade became the center for an Iraqi Army division by the end of 2004. With the addition of one mechanized division, these ten Iraqi Army divisions formed the core fighting force of the army for the next four years.[115]

MNSTC-I was wholly responsible for every aspect of the new ISF—police and military, along with their ministries and all associated structures, bases, and infrastructure—which led to incredible demands on the organization. What type of security forces should be created: air force, navy, marine unit, border police, national police, customs and immigration unit, and so on? What doctrine should govern them? What would the systems to support the ISF look like (e.g., personnel, logistics, health

---

[111] Wright and Reese, 2008, p. 450.

[112] Wright and Reese, 2008, p. 451.

[113] Former senior military commander, interview with the authors, May 13, 2015.

[114] Former senior military commander, interview with the authors, April 23, 2015.

[115] Wright and Reese, 2008, pp. 451–452.

care, pensions)?[116] All these questions needed to be addressed by MNSTC-I, yet most personnel on the staff had little or no experience in security force assistance, let alone security sector reform. Further complicating matters, MNSTC-I's organizational structure was filled with personnel in an ad hoc fashion, and replacements from all of the services trickled into the command piecemeal. In an effort to address the ad hoc nature of replacements, the 98th Division (U.S. Army Reserve) was mobilized to support the MNSTC-I mission. On paper, the 98th Division appeared to be a good selection to help staff MNSTC-I. It was an institutional training unit that had the stateside mission to train soldiers from basic training through qualification schools up to advanced military schooling. While the 98th had many of the necessary skills needed to train the new Iraqi Army and willing soldiers, it was not fully prepared, trained, or equipped for the mission. For instance, the division was asked to both train and advise the Iraqi Army in ten-person teams, yet these teams were small and not well suited to the institutional structure of the division, which existed to conduct training of U.S. reserve-component soldiers and leaders. As a result, and through no fault of their own, the soldiers of the division were not fully prepared for the mission they were asked to accomplish.[117]

Throughout 2004, the focus continued to be on training tactical-level units, especially for the operations to stabilize Fallujah in November 2004. By the time Petraeus left and Dempsey took over command of MNSTC-I in the summer of 2005, training had been streamlined and capacity increased, but little progress had been made in the development of Iraqi Army command-and-control structures. In the late summer of 2005, Petraeus emphasized this point to Dempsey, noting that his job as incoming commander for MNSTC-I would be to develop the institutions at the top of the rapidly developing ISF. Dempsey's task was to develop the MOD, MOI, and institutional training base with logistical capability and infrastructure to support the fighting force.[118] This proved to be even more difficult than the training of tactical-level units.

As one senior military commander transitioned into command and began to focus his efforts on the development of the MOD, MOI, and headquarters elements of the Iraqi Army, he observed one immediate issue with the ISF: loyalty. As the coalition continued to establish security institutions and train the ISF, it became apparent to him that the forces trained by U.S. personnel were more loyal to the United States than to the government of Iraq. In Iraq, the United States paid the Iraqi soldiers' salaries, and that fact alone generated loyalty. The commander therefore began to stress the transition aspect of the MNSTC-I mission: "It was about transition and getting the

---

[116] Former senior military commander, interview with the authors, July 31, 2015.

[117] Former senior military commander, interview with the authors, July 31, 2015.

[118] Former senior military commander, interview with the authors, May 13, 2015.

Iraqi government to take responsibility for its own military and police forces. That was going to be the strategy to get the United States out of Iraq."[119]

Evolution of U.S. Trainers

As new units began to rotate into Iraq, they started to expand their focus beyond combat operations. The 1st Squadron, 7th Cavalry of the 1st Cavalry Division had rotated into Iraq in April of 2004 and witnessed firsthand the shift in priorities. Of the unit's five core tasks, the first was combat operations and the second was partnering with the ISF. To train the ISF, this unit took some of its own soldiers and formed adviser teams to work with the Iraqi Army 5th Division; units assigned to this task reported mixed success.[120] These adviser teams helped to set up training, mentor their Iraqi counterparts, and run joint patrols with the Iraqi Army but were never fully integrated with the host-nation army. The training regime that was established was never truly a partnership with the Iraqi Army. Most training efforts continued in an ad hoc and mostly uncoordinated fashion. They also tended to emphasize the operation at hand rather than develop training for the future Iraqi trainers. The priority was often the immediate operational mission rather than fostering a sustainable Iraqi training regime.

With the establishment of MNF-I in June 2004 and MNSTC-I to coordinate the training of the Iraqis, both commands distributed guidance to American combat units in an effort to align all the divergent efforts throughout the country. One of the first plans to coordinate the training of the ISF and improve security across Iraq was what Casey called the "15 cities plan." Under this plan, the U.S. military and its ISF partners had to secure 15 cities that contained 60 percent of the Iraqi population by the January 2005 election. With this goal established, U.S. forces continued to train with their ISF partners throughout the summer and fall of 2004. By and large, the plan secured many of the cities, absent Mosul and Fallujah, and helped to put an Iraqi face on the security establishment for the first Iraqi elections in 50 years.[121] While security did improve enough to hold national elections in January 2005, the training of the ISF remained a convoluted affair, and U.S. forces still had the lead for security throughout most, if not all, of the country.

Violence in Iraq continued to escalate after the elections in January 2005, and the inability of Iraqi leaders to form a consensus government throughout the early months of 2005 only exacerbated the situation. When Prime Minister Ibrahim al-Jaafari was sworn into office in May 2005, violence continued to increase. Simultaneously, U.S. intelligence changed the assessment of the main threat to U.S. strategic objectives in Iraq away from Sunni-Arab rejectionists and toward Islamic extremism. To directly

---

[119] Former senior military commander, interview with the authors, May 13, 2015.

[120] Former military commander, interview with the authors, May 18, 2015.

[121] Former senior military commander, interview with the authors, September 30, 2015.

counter this threat, Casey launched the Western Euphrates Campaign to disrupt the terrorist facilitation networks and make the western border more secure.[122] Thus began the recruitment and deployment of U.S. military adviser teams on a large scale.

The selection and training of these adviser teams was conducted in a similar fashion to the training of the ISF—it was ad hoc, uncoordinated, and tended to change from one training rotation to the next. The adviser teams typically comprised 10–15 officers and enlisted personnel with a variety of military skills. Although all of the services contributed to the missions, the bulk of the personnel came from the Army; as a result, most of the adviser training facilities located in the United States were on Army instillations. Training was initially conducted at Fort Carson, Colorado, but transitioned to Fort Hood, Texas, then to Fort Riley, Kansas, in October 2006.[123] (It would eventually end up at Fort Polk, Louisiana.) Teams would train together for several weeks before deploying to Camp Buehring, Kuwait, where they would receive another week of preparation. From there, they would report to the Phoenix Academy, at Camp Taji, Iraq, where they draw their equipment and were supposed to receive advanced-level training specific to the region to which they were to deploy with their designated ISF unit. Unfortunately, there were many issues with the way that the U.S. military established and ran the adviser training program, and success varied widely by team and individual.[124]

Additional Education for U.S. Army Forces Involved with ISF Training in Iraq

While new brigade and battalion commanders and their staff rotating into Iraq were attending the in-country counterinsurgency academy, other efforts were under way to bring in additional adviser teams to augment the training of the ISF, including the establishment of the Phoenix Academy, where adviser teams received in-country training. This academy was under the control of the Iraq Assistance Group (IAG).

The establishment of several educational institutions in Iraq was an effort to educate the U.S. force on the nature of its partners in the ISF, as well as the nature of the enemy. However, the institutions and the academies were stopgap measures conducted by the necessity of the situation in Iraq. Throughout Casey's time at MNF-I, units would rotate into Iraq not understanding counterinsurgency, with preconceived notions of combat in Iraq shaped by years of conventional training.[125]

---

[122] Former senior military commander, interview with the authors, September 30, 2015.

[123] Former military commander, interview with the authors, July 10, 2015.

[124] These issues included problems with recruiting, establishing proper training regimes, acquiring equipment, shifting advised ISF units, rotating operational areas, and establishing the chain of command for reporting and personnel actions, among others.

[125] Former senior military commander, interview with the authors, September 30, 2015.

Iraq Assistance Group and Responsibility for the Adviser Teams

The adviser teams enjoyed mixed success across Iraq, with results largely depending on the personalities of the team members and their backgrounds. Throughout 2005, the U.S. military struggled to embrace the adviser mission, and unity of command was a pressing issue for those teams.[126] Once a team rotated into Iraq, it fell under the administrative control of the IAG, a one-star-level command that reported to MNC-I, not MNSTC-I.[127] However, once embedded with its partnered unit, the team came under operational control of the local U.S. ground force commander. This was often a convoluted process, and not many clear procedures were established for teams; as a result, communication among U.S. forces was at times lacking. Initially, advisers who were embedded with their ISF counterparts and separated from U.S. units received limited support, which created some tension among U.S. forces. For example, requests for support could go to different units, such as a U.S. battalion or brigade or directly to the IAG, and it often took time to figure out whom to ask for support.[128]

Also complicating the effort was the fact that brigades rotating into Iraq were being tasked to provide additional adviser teams; these were to be carved out of the incoming brigade. When commanders of U.S. brigades were tasked with providing these teams out of their own units, they had to make a judgment call on how to staff the teams. A former military commander we spoke with was responsible for the adviser teams in the brigade's area of operation in eastern Baghdad. While in that position, he helped to select brigade staff, officers, and NCOs to serve on adviser teams. He said it was a tough call to make and that some battalions within the brigade put strong officers on the teams while others did not; it was a judgment call.[129] Having adviser teams on the battlefield that were sourced in different ways created issues for battle space owners. The brigade commanders who owned battle space often were not invested in the teams that did not come from their own units and, with limited resources, tended to take care of their own soldiers first. A former senior military commander summed up the problem by noting, "The issue with adviser teams from outside the brigade was trust and unity of command, and it dramatically impacted operations."[130]

Need for Additional Advisers

The effort to train the ISF continued to gather momentum throughout 2006. In November and December, with the main security focus on Baghdad, the adviser program began to show signs that it was insufficient to stand up the required amount

---

[126] Former military commander, interview with the authors, July 27, 2015.

[127] Former military commander, interview with the authors, July 10, 2015.

[128] Former commander of a military transition team, interview with the authors, May 26, 2015; and former military commander, interview with the authors, July 27, 2015.

[129] Former military commander, interview with the authors, July 10, 2015.

[130] Former senior military commander, interview with the authors, April 7, 2015.

of ISF troops.[131] Additionally, there were often problems with the teams themselves, especially staffing, leadership, and military bearing and discipline. Within the overall framework for the advisory mission set within General Casey's strategy, each team, ultimately, was left to determine for itself what it was going to do and to what degree it was going to train its respective ISF outfits.

The adviser program did not have enough advisers in Iraq. In 2006, the United States had approximately 3,600 advisors in Iraq, but it needed more.[132] The U.S. Army alone estimated that it needed to train up to 2,000 mid-grade officers as advisers every two months to fill demand in Iraq and Afghanistan.[133] The services, and the U.S. Army in particular, were having a difficult time finding personnel to fill the billets they were tasked to provide. To illustrate this point, the U.S. Army began to take graduates out of the Command and Staff College as early as January 2006 to fill adviser teams. By the middle of 2007, it was becoming routine to take officers from the class early to fill teams; and of the remaining officers graduating from the college, a substantial percentage were selected to serve on adviser teams.[134] Even as additional officers were pulled for adviser assignments, MNSTC-I continued to add end strength to the ISF personnel rosters, continuing to drive upward the demand for even more teams. The outcome was that more Iraqi Army units at the battalion and brigade levels were without U.S. advisers to assist them.

Both the mentality of individuals on the teams and the mix of military occupational specialties and particular skill sets within them were important factors that affected adviser team success. The teams needed to have both the breadth and depth of military knowledge, because advisers were called on to teach a vast array of subjects. While certain skill sets were easy to come by, others were more difficult, leading to shortfalls and difficulty in adequately staffing the teams. Commenting on the staffing of the adviser teams, a senior military commander woefully noted, "If we had got that right, we would have made a bigger difference."[135]

When a team had all the necessary personnel and skill sets, not only was advising the Iraqis feasible, it worked well. For example, a former military commander's team consisted of a trained medic, mechanic, drill instructor, logistical expert, and other soldiers representing diverse experiences. The former commander attributed his team's success in Iraq to the breadth of technical and operational experience within it.[136] However, other teams were less fortunate in their composition, oftentimes lacking

---

[131] Former senior military commander, interview with the authors, July 30, 2015.

[132] Peter Spiegel, "Army Is Training Advisors for Iraq," *Los Angeles Times*, October 25, 2006.

[133] Spiegel, 2006.

[134] Former military commander, interview with the authors, May 19, 2015.

[135] Former senior military commander, interview with the authors, August 7, 2015.

[136] Former military commander, interview with the authors, May 19, 2015.

the kind of diversity found on the former commander's team. These teams struggled to instruct the Iraqis on a variety of tasks and usually found their credibility compromised as a result.

The teams in country were often undermanned and underresourced. While not having the right composition of soldiers and skills on a team was an issue, not having enough soldiers to fill a vehicle for a patrol with their Iraqi counterparts was another issue entirely. A senior adviser to the 9th Iraqi Army Division from 2005 to 2006 reflected that to increase trust, the teams had to show partnership, facilitated through functional expertise. Some of the ten- or 15-man teams did not have enough personnel to cover the subject matter needed, which indirectly degraded U.S. credibility.[137]

From Training to Operations

The tempo of operations in Iraq did not slow down at all during 2005 and 2006. Operation Together Forward I (summer of 2006) and Operation Together Forward II (fall of 2006) both revealed the ineptness of the ISF. As ISF units completed their training, soldiers were placed into ongoing operations, whether or not they were ready. Many of the institutional checks that U.S. forces use when progressing through a training pipeline were omitted from Iraqi training. One former military commander captured this idea by stating, "When you build an aircraft in flight, like the U.S. was doing with the [Iraqi Army], you miss some of the key readiness gates. Some of the collective tasks don't get trained in a field environment before the unit was thrust into operations."[138] As a consequence, many of the Iraqi Army units relied heavily on U.S. assistance during operations.

Throughout the ISF, and particularly the Iraqi Army, the caliber of training continued to vary. Many U.S. officers considered the training by 2005 as better than the early efforts of 2004, which should come as no surprise because the shift in strategy from quick withdrawal to building the ISF brought with it a huge increase in funding. But the fact remained that under MNSTC-I, training was still not consistent and the level of effectiveness of Iraqi Army units varied greatly once they joined the operational force.

The Iraqi Army leadership continued to be a problem during this period, and many units that were moved from a training to an operational status were thrown into a situation that they were ill-prepared to handle. U.S. soldiers were continuing to train the ISF, but without the right Iraqi leadership, all the training would be for naught.[139] Some units at the tactical and operational levels had good leadership, but those units were in the minority. At the highest levels of the ISF, Prime Minister Nouri al-Maliki was ultimately in charge. One reason that Operation Together Forward I did not suc-

---

[137] Former military commander, interview with the authors, July 27, 2015.

[138] Former military commander, interview with the authors, July 27, 2015.

[139] Former senior military commander, interview with the authors, August 7, 2015.

ceed was because Maliki was not committed either politically or militarily to the operation, while at the same time, the ISF were still beholden to U.S. forces for equipment, ammunition, and leadership.[140] Additionally, it was not unheard of to have the prime minister intervene in operations by calling an Iraqi Army brigade commander directly and ordering him to follow a course of action.[141]

Also problematic, the United States trained the ISF to perform various operations but did not train the forces to be fully functioning and self-sustaining.[142] The ISF lacked many of the basic institutional capacities that modern armies require. The institutional force had severe deficiencies, with personnel recruitment, initial training, equipping, and pay all suffering from problems and the lack of effort needed to properly address them. Sustainment training was another issue for Iraqi Army soldiers. Finally, there were few opportunities to continue professional military education.

Along with the increased training effort came an additional scrutiny to show how many forces had been trained and ready, therefore showing how close the United States was to transitioning responsibility to the ISF. The U.S. forces generated multiple metrics to measure the numbers of Iraqi soldiers trained and to assess progress. For the Iraqi Army, the metrics included evaluating which forces were fully manned, when they reached that point, when they received equipment, when they reached proficiency, when they were organized from battalions to brigades and from brigades to divisions, when their barracks were built, and when their depots were built. These metrics were generally inputs because that was MNSTC-I's role.[143] While many of these metrics looked good on paper, they did not convey the true status of the Iraqi Army once initial training was concluded. This became all too apparent once Iraqi Army units were responsible for an area of operations and asked to conduct offensive actions against a determined foe and failed.

In a high-level strategic planning document distributed at the end of 2006, General Casey recognized that reducing the sectarian violence and protecting the Iraqi population were important requirements to compete with transitioning control of security operations to the Iraqis.[144] Casey also acknowledged that at least two or three more combat brigades might be useful to help quell the violence.[145] American military presence would need to remain large because the training of the ISF had not reached a point where Iraqi forces could take over operations from the Americans. Thus, as

---

[140] Former senior military commander, interview with the authors, September 30, 2015.

[141] Former military commander, interview with the authors, May 18, 2015.

[142] Former official at the U.S. embassy in Baghdad, interview with the authors, May 26, 2015.

[143] Former senior military commander, interview with the authors, May 13, 2015.

[144] In Casey, various years, see "Joint Campaign Plan: Transition of Security Responsibility," January 2007.

[145] Michael R. Gordon, "U.S. Troop 'Surge' Took Place Amid Doubt and Debate," *New York Times*, August 31, 2008b.

Casey viewed things, Baghdad would require continued American combat presence to conduct operations and continue training with ISF well into 2008 and beyond. To be sure, Casey and his planners believed that any additional American brigades should come with agreements from the Iraqi government in exchange for reconciliation and other forms of progress. But by late 2006 and on the eve of the Surge, General Casey and his staff were not looking to depart from Iraq anytime soon.

Lessons from This Era

This section identifies and describes the lessons learned from the U.S. experience in Baghdad from the summer of 2004 until early 2007, when General Casey was the force commander.

Operational Lessons
In Complex Urban Environments, the Factors Causing an Insurgency Will Have a Powerful Effect on Whether Military Operations Succeed or Fail
The Casey years indicate that the course that Iraq took was heavily determined by the policy decisions of Ambassador Bremer and, before Bremer, the strategic confusion and incoherence that defined the U.S. invasion of Iraq and its following phases. The key insights and lessons for the U.S. Army during these years are that tactical action will be shaped by those decisions of strategy and policy. The most innovative and creative use of tactical force in these kinds of wars will be limited by the larger elements of strategy and policy and the conditions on the ground where tactical action is being applied.

Tactical Adaptation and Creativity Are Important
What the Casey years also emphasize is that tactical adaptation and innovation remain important elements if strategy and policy are to succeed. During the Casey years, there was a clear evolution of tactical progression based on innovation and adaptation. In Baghdad, battle-space-owning units learned from previous units and made important adaptations during their year on the ground. Instead of viewing the Surge in 2007 under General Petraeus as a radical change from past practices, it ought to be seen as an evolutionary event that built on the innovation and adaptations of the years that preceded it.

Lessons from the Civilian Experience in Iraq, 2004–2007
Strong Civil-Military Cooperation Requires a Concerted Effort from All Parties
The strong relationship that General Casey shared with both Ambassadors Negroponte and Khalilzad smoothed civil-military relations on the ground. This relationship took effort and constant cultivation. The open lines of communication between Casey and the ambassadors made resolving civil-military tensions more likely and set a precedent for further cooperation between civilians and military officers in lower ranks, such as

when Jeffrey and General Chiarelli were able to work together to find a manageable solution to the security problems along Route Irish.

The State Department Has Limited Resources
As of 2013, the Foreign Service comprised approximately 13,000 officers,[146] compared with the contemporary Regular Army's approximately 540,000 soldiers and the hundreds of thousands of soldiers in the Army National Guard and the Army Reserves. The State Department and its cadre of Foreign Service officers are responsible for maintaining diplomatic relations with every nation in the world except for three (North Korea, Iran, and Bhutan), while the U.S. military is active in significantly fewer places.[147] Given the disparity in human resources and the vast nature of the State Department's responsibility, the Foreign Service cannot match the resources allocated by the military during wartime.

That being said, recruiting and minimizing turnover in Iraq were problems for the State Department. Secretary Rice made significant changes to the department's personnel system later in the war, but changes should have been made earlier to ensure that postings that needed to be filled were not left vacant for long periods. Moreover, as one former national security official we spoke with noted, during the Vietnam War, Foreign Service officers returned to Saigon for numerous tours. This enabled institutional memory developed during earlier postings to be applied later in the war. This did not occur to the same extent in Baghdad.

Outcome-Based Metrics Need to Be Precisely Tailored to the Conflict
The purpose of metrics should be to inform decisionmaking and allow for an honest assessment of performance. Although some civilians found utility in metrics, the majority of civilians interviewed for this report felt that the overemphasis on metrics became a distraction that prevented deeper discussion of the U.S. strategy in Iraq. Moreover, so many reports were produced that they lost their utility and ultimately served to feed a bureaucratic process that made little contribution to achieving U.S. objectives. In future conflicts, identifying the metrics that accurately measure progress and success and using those to spur debate about strategy and objectives will help ensure that floods of information do not take the place of a deep strategy discussion. Which metrics are appropriate will differ depending on the conflict. For example, level of violence was a good metric to use in Iraq to determine the success of the military's strategy, but number of insurgents killed or battle space turned over to Iraqi forces was not. Measurements of electricity produced in Iraq can be useful in judging the success of reconstruction efforts, but they do not have much meaning if the metric distracts

---

[146] Olga Khazan, "Being a Foreign Service Officer Became Much, Much Harder After 9/11," *The Atlantic*, April 9, 2013.

[147] Matt Schiavenza, "After Cuba: The Only Three Countries That Have No Relations with the U.S.," *The Atlantic*, July 1, 2015.

from the fact that insurgents continuously attacked power lines or that Iraqis were not capable of maintaining sophisticated power plants. During this time, it was problematic that the suite of metrics used focused on inputs or, at best, performance (e.g., how many Iraqi soldiers trained) and not on outcomes (e.g., how many units demonstrated combat effectiveness).

Lessons from Creating the Iraqi Army and Defense Institutions

Build Institutions Around Existing Organizations Rather Than in an Ad Hoc Fashion

With the creation of MNSTC-I, the United States signaled that it was going to be in the business of training and equipping the totality of the ISF. The new command was granted additional personnel, funding, and a commitment from MNF-I to be the main effort moving forward in Iraq. Unfortunately, the structure of MNSTC-I was not formed from an existing military structure and was cobbled together in an ad hoc fashion. When asked to reflect on what changes might have improved the U.S. Army's experience with MNSTC-I, a former senior military commander suggested that the establishment of the command should have been designed around an existing organization: "The way to form MNSTC-I should have been to take a brigade, division, or even a corps and reshape it around the MNSTC-I mission." Creating the new command from the ground up was therefore not the optimal solution. It was akin to "building the world's largest aircraft, while it is being designed, while in-flight, and while being shot at."[148]

Personnel rotated into the command continually. Oftentimes, the Joint Manning Document used to fill positions would not specify a service to source the position. As a result, with the Army stretched between the Afghanistan and Iraq requirements at the time, Air Force and Navy personnel who had relatively little expertise training foreign armies would arrive and be required to "speak Army" with little or no training, slowing down staff processes and taking time and resources away from the training and equipping mission.

Adviser and Training Missions Are Key to Success

Certainly, adviser and training missions are context-dependent. However, the United States needed to recognize the need for the training and adviser missions earlier in the campaign. While the adviser mission did improve from 2004 through 2007, it was delinquent on certain fronts. Many personnel interviewed noted the less-than-satisfactory performance of contractors who were hired to train the adviser team members prior to deployment. The training site also changed several times—from Fort Carson, to Fort Hood, to Fort Riley, and finally ending in Fort Polk—which led to a disunity of effort, duplication of training, and overall uncoordinated endeavor. When adviser teams arrived in Kuwait and Iraq, it was not MNSTC-I that took over admin-

---

[148] Former senior military commander, interview with the authors, July 31, 2015.

istrative command of the teams, but rather the IAG. For its part, the IAG lacked a coherent message to impart to incoming team members, could not provide replacements, had issues supporting the teams operationally, and generally let the teams figure things out on their own. Simply put, the training and advise-and-assist missions lacked urgency in their early days.

The position as a leader of an adviser team was also not a key developmental position. One former military commander we spoke with qualified this, noting, "Within the unit, being on an adviser team was not viewed as a great assignment or key for officer development. It wasn't viewed in the same light as an S3 [operations and training officer] or BN XO [battalion executive officer] position."[149] The institutional Army needs to appropriately address the importance of these missions.

Finally, all of the expertise that was gained from being on an adviser team has not been successfully captured by the Army. There is no Additional Skill Identifier, such as the parachutist badge or air assault badge, which identifies soldiers with particular experience. This experience should have been captured and used for future training missions.

Setting Up a Foreign Military Requires an Understanding of the Cultural Influences in Play

The Iraqi Army chain of command was set up in a manner that was unfamiliar to the U.S. forces, which led to a misjudgment of command and control. Advancement in Iraqi society was often not based on merit, but instead on personal relationships. At times, these intertribal and ethnic relationships convoluted the chain of command. An example of this can be found in the way that Prime Minister Maliki controlled the Iraqi Army. During an operation, Maliki would have direct contact with brigade commanders, and if he did not want to incur any Iraqi casualties, he made that clear.[150] Therefore, the Iraqi military leadership was risk-averse and effectively constrained by the Iraqi political leadership. The United States should try to identify such cultural influences at the outset of operations to better understand the dynamics that may influence how to build and advise a foreign military.

---

[149] Former military commander, interview with the authors, July 10, 2015.

[150] Former military commander, interview with the authors, May 18, 2015.

CHAPTER FIVE
The Surge

This chapter describes one of the most critical periods of the Iraq War. It begins by laying out the opposing poles of the debate over Iraq: Up the ante or get out. It examines how the decision to implement the Surge was reached and what it meant for the U.S. military in Iraq, particularly its actions to secure Baghdad and stop the civil war. It then turns to the military situation, detailing the views of the different parties involved in the debate. It also explores the civilian decision to support the surge of U.S. military forces and how that decision came to pass. It then describes the first seven months of the Surge, a period of intense fighting resulting in a spike of casualties, but essentially laying the groundwork for a more stable Baghdad. The chapter then discusses counterinsurgency efforts in the Surge and in practice. Next, it discusses two aspects pertaining to the Shia population. One is the Shia militias and their efforts to undermine U.S. efforts, and the second is the battle for Sadr City, a Shia stronghold within Baghdad. It then describes civilian perspectives on the Surge, which was controversial in many quarters. Many viewed the situation in Iraq as irretrievable and thought that additional troops would simply cost lives and only delay the inevitable. The chapter then turns to the efforts to create the ISF and describes some of the barriers complicating that process. It also provides some perspectives on the Surge. To this day, opinion divides over its success and its effects on the situation in Baghdad. The chapter concludes with lessons learned from this period of the war.

Key Debates: The Surge Versus the Iraq Study Group Report

Throughout 2005 and 2006, the situation in Iraq continued to deteriorate. The formation of a consensus government in Iraq after the 2005 elections eluded Iraqi politicians and revealed sectarian divides within Iraqi governing circles. Sectarian violence was on the rise and spiked after the al-Askari Mosque bombing in Samarra in February 2006.[1] Voices in Washington increasingly called for the turnover of responsibility for security to the ISF, even as those forces demonstrated their inability or unwillingness to secure

---
[1] Ellen Knickmeyer and K. I. Ibrahim, "Bomb Shatters Mosque in Iraq," *Washington Post*, February 23, 2006.

the population during Operations Together Forward I and II. Meanwhile, the U.S. military had been rotating troops into Iraq for more than four years and was starting to show signs of strain.[2] The U.S. military was nearing its 3,000th American casualty in Iraq. The requirement for high levels of troops had not abated, even as the calls for transition and the withdrawal of U.S. forces intensified.[3]

In 2006, former Secretary of State James Baker and former U.S. Congressman Lee Hamilton headed what became known as the Iraq Study Group. This bipartisan panel appointed by Congress and organized by the United States Institute of Peace carried out a nine-month initiative. Its remit was to assess the U.S.-led war in Iraq and to make policy recommendations based on these assessments. The report, released on December 6, 2006, included 79 recommendations and described the situation in Iraq as "grave and deteriorating."[4] The report ultimately endorsed a drawdown of American troops in Iraq and called for all combat brigades not essential for force protection to be removed by the first quarter of 2008.

Just 35 days after the release of the Baker-Hamilton report, President Bush formally announced what came to be known as the Surge strategy—a five-brigade increase in American force levels deployed to Iraq. That the President would arrive at a strategy to increase, rather than decrease, troop levels in Iraq was not a foregone conclusion. By this time, many voices were urging changes to the U.S. strategy and presence in Iraq—and they were all pushing in different directions.[5] Rather than adopting the Baker-Hamilton report's suggestions and alleviating the strain that repeated tours in Iraq were putting on the U.S. military, particularly the Army and Marine Corps, the Surge required in April 2007 that the Army extend tours in Iraq to 15 months to boost troop strength.[6] In Washington, the Surge required the Bush administration to sell the unpopular policy to a skeptical Congress and American public. In Baghdad, the Surge required an apparent shift in strategy from the previous four years of the war. As journalist Thomas Ricks claimed, the Surge was a grand "gamble" at all levels.[7]

The primary debate concerned a continuation of the strategy of "standing down to stand up the Iraqis" versus an option to pursue the Surge strategy.

---

[2] For an exploration of this topic, see James Hosek, *How Is Deployment to Iraq and Afghanistan Affecting U.S. Service Members and Their Families? An Overview of Early RAND Research on the Topic*, Santa Monica, Calif.: RAND Corporation, OP-316-OSD, 2011.

[3] B. Linwood Carter, *Iraq: Summary of U.S. Forces*, Washington, D.C.: Congressional Research Service, RL31763, November 28, 2005.

[4] Baker et al., 2006, p. xiii.

[5] Other voices called for various forms of partition or federalism in Iraq. See, for example, Joseph R. Biden and Leslie H. Gelb, "Unity Through Autonomy in Iraq," *New York Times*, May 1, 2006.

[6] Ann Scott Tyson and Josh White, "Strained Army Extends Tours to 15 Months," *Washington Post*, April 12, 2007.

[7] Ricks, 2009.

Military Situation and Operations

By the end of 2006, President Bush and many other Americans thought that the war was either stalemated or lost. The President eventually decided on the need for a new strategy in Iraq and arrived at the Surge of troops. Along with the Surge and arrival of GEN David Petraeus came the new American counterinsurgency manual, FM 3-24, that Petraeus and a group of retired and active Army and Marine Corps officers had written at Fort Leavenworth the year before. Writing in his memoirs four years after the Surge, President Bush recalled Petraeus's very different operational and strategic framework:

> After overseeing training of the Iraqi Security Forces, General Petraeus was assigned to Fort Leavenworth, Kansas, to rewrite the Army's counterinsurgency manual. The premise of counterinsurgency is that basic security is required before political gains can follow. That was the reverse of our existing strategy.[8]

Certainly the additional five brigades provided more firepower and presence on the ground to show an enlarged American presence. But whether the Surge actually brought with it changed counterinsurgency tactics and a new strategy, as President Bush remembered, was a question that analysts and scholars would debate in the years after its completion.

By the end of 2006, one former senior military commander we spoke with believed that the operations used to try to secure Baghdad in summer 2006—Operations Together Forward I and II—had failed. Part of the reason, in his view, was because the U.S. military did not have enough combat troops in Baghdad to leave behind in cleared areas to ensure that those areas did not revert to insurgent control. But another reason was that the Americans in Baghdad and around the country still did not know how to conduct counterinsurgency operations correctly. The former commander's assessment was that after troops entered Iraq, the U.S. Army never formed a military strategy designed to defeat the insurgency because the military strategy was to train the ISF so that the ISF could fight the insurgency. He also noted the importance of protecting the population by separating the population from the insurgents through patrolling in urban areas on foot and establishing a presence at platoon and company levels in neighborhoods in Baghdad. This was classic urban counterinsurgency designed to protect the people.[9]

That some senior military commanders—such as GEN Jack Keane, a former Army Vice Chief of Staff—would also see the fight in Iraq in this manner is perhaps unsurprising. As a young Army infantry officer in Vietnam, Keane had fought against another insurgency. After the war, he and many other Army officers came to believe that the reason that the U.S. Army had lost was because under its first commander, General William Westmoreland, it did not understand how to execute a counter-

---

[8] Bush, 2010, p. 365.

[9] Former senior military commander, interview with the authors, April 17, 2015.

insurgency campaign. Once Westmoreland was replaced with General Creighton Abrams, argued Keane, the Army eventually and belatedly discovered how to implement counterinsurgency correctly. Reflecting on Baghdad at the end of 2006, Keane feared that the U.S. Army was repeating the mistakes it made in Vietnam and was bleak in his assessment of the depth of the crisis. "A lot of people truly did not understand how far the war in Iraq had gone in terms of our failure," he stated, going on to say that "Iraq was clearly a fractured state and about to go off the cliff; we were in the throes of suffering a humiliating defeat."[10]

A Tough Seven Months

The first seven months of the Surge from February to August 2007 were hellish. American combat casualties rose to some of their highest levels since the start of the war, and the numbers of civilian casualties from the ongoing sectarian civil war were high: By some accounts, there were around 1,500 civilian deaths per month for the first half of 2007.[11] So when the numbers of American military and Iraqi civilian casualties started to drop precipitously by September 2007, only eight months after the Surge of troops began, soldiers and media reporters began to ask themselves what brought it about. Many observers and analysts attributed the drop to Petraeus's change in strategy and adoption of the new tactics embodied in FM 3-24. One American soldier remembered the early days of the Surge as a time when his battalion initially got "off on the wrong foot" but then started to "get back to the [counterinsurgency] basics that we had read about. Once we began to apply these lessons, things changed in our favor, and we never turned back."[12]

Tied inextricably to the operational framework that came with the Surge were a set of conditions on the ground in Iraq, and Baghdad specifically, that worked together with the increase of troops during the Surge to lower violence. One cannot understand the success of the Surge and concomitant lowering of violence by the end of 2007 without understanding these circumstances and the critical role that they played. First, probably the most significant condition in Iraq that had been developing for at least two years before the Surge began was what became known as the "Awakening" of Sunni tribes in Iraq's western Anbar Province (Figure 5.1). By the end of 2006, many Sunnis had become fed up with al Qaeda in Iraq. The slaughter of civilians, marrying off of local women, and takeover of the lucrative smuggling trade became onerous and fed resistance to al Qaeda's presence in the country. As early as 2004, the U.S.

---

[10] Mark Thompson, "The Rise and Fall of 'General Peaches,'" *Time*, November 14, 2012.

[11] This number is based on civilian deaths from violence in 2007, per an analysis of the year's toll, from Iraq Body Count, 2008.

[12] Nir Rosen, *Aftermath: Following America's Wars in the Muslim World*, New York: Nation Books, 2010, p. 241.

Figure 5.1
Anbar Province, Iraq

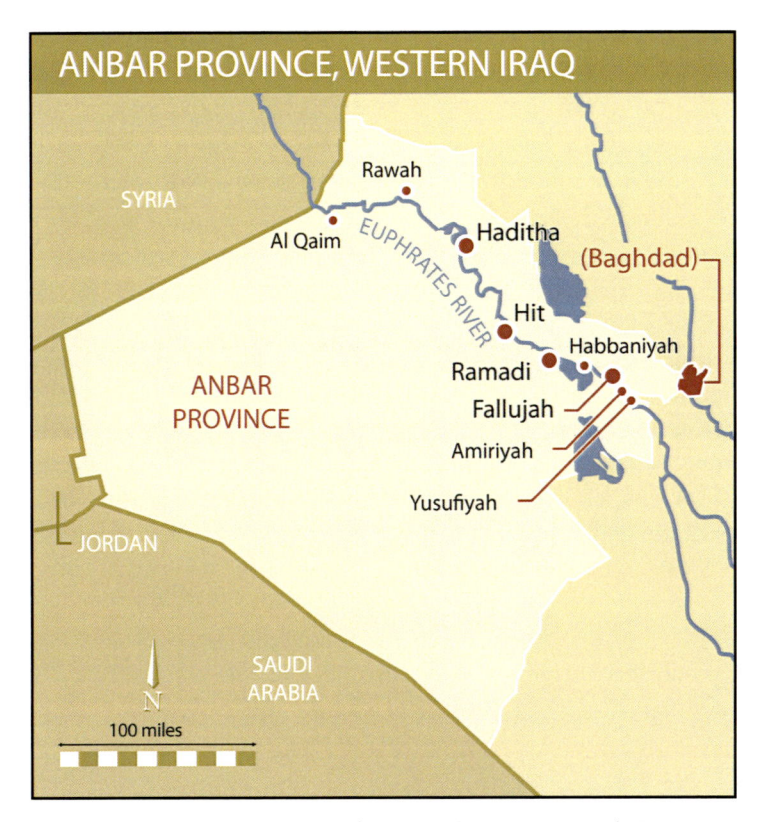

[Map: Anbar Province, Western Iraq, showing Syria, Jordan, Saudi Arabia borders; Euphrates River; cities: Rawah, Al Qaim, Haditha, Hit, Ramadi, Habbaniyah, Fallujah, Amiriyah, Yusufiyah, (Baghdad)]

SOURCE: Institute for the Study of War, "Anbar Province and Cities," November 13, 2008. Used with permission.

military enjoyed some important successes in different parts of Anbar in working with the Sunni tribes against al Qaeda. These more limited successes, combined with the mounting frustration on the part of other Anbar tribes, came to a head in the middle of 2006, prompting a large number of Sunni groups to make arrangements with the American military to fight al Qaeda. Very quickly, the idea of the Anbar Awakening—Sunni resistance to the extremes of al Qaeda—spread to other Sunni areas of Iraq and produced similar movements in the remaining Sunni areas in Baghdad, such as Dora and Amriya.[13]

---

[13] For more on the Anbar Awakening and firsthand accounts from its members, see the various interviews in Gary W. Montgomery and Timothy S. McWilliams, eds., *Al-Anbar Awakening*, Vol. II: *Iraqi Perspectives: From Insurgency to Counterinsurgency in Iraq, 2004–2009*, Quantico, Va.: Marine Corps University Press, 2009; Khalid al-Ansary and Ali Adeeb, "Most Tribes in Anbar Agree to Unite Against Insurgents," *New York Times*, September 18, 2006; Peter Beaumont, "Iraqi Tribes Launch Battle to Drive al Qaeda Out of Troubled Province, *The Guardian*, October 3, 2006; and Dexter Filkins, "US and Iraq Retake Ramadi One Neighborhood at a Time," *New York Times*, June 27, 2006.

These various Sunni groups assessed that they were losing the civil war with the Shia-dominated government led by Nouri al-Maliki. Caught between the closing vice of al Qaeda and the Shia-dominated government and its militias, many Sunni tribes determined that their best course of action was to ally with the Americans. In this relationship, the U.S. military acted as a balancing mechanism. It provided legitimacy through a formal alliance, and in turn, at least in public view, it also offered the tribes seeming credibility with the Iraqi government.[14] And according to a former senior military adviser to Iraqi forces in Baghdad, the Awakening was not so much an entity as it was *entities*, whereby individual Army and Marine Corps units in the several respective areas of operation managed their relationships with individuals and tribes that decided to turn against al Qaeda. This process transpired somewhat autonomously is numerous places:

> Every regiment and Marine battalion had a group of people they were paying out of Commander's Emergency Response Program funds,[15] that when you put it together in one document, it was a lot of people, . . . so this thing, the Awakening . . . , was not . . . a force in being, it was *forces* in being by a virtual nature of timing and by just sheer luck. . . . It grew because of the money; initially what started it was [the realization on the part of Anbaris that] "hey, we gotta take a different way ahead or we're gonna get slaughtered."[16]

U.S. casualties began to decline as increasing numbers of Sunni groups ceased attacks against coalition targets and focused their attention on al Qaeda. This willingness to confront rather than harbor al Qaeda operatives also came at a time of increased numbers of American combat brigades during the Surge. This combination allowed for effective information flows by former Sunni insurgents regarding location details and the identities of al Qaeda fighters. Armed with this information, American tactical firepower was much more capable of targeting and destroying the al Qaeda enemy. And with the reduction of al Qaeda came a lowering in the number of al

---

[14] Aymenn Jawad al-Tamimi, "Assessing the Surge in Iraq," *Middle East Review of International Affairs*, Vol. 15, No. 4, December 2011, p. 31; Bing West, *The Strongest Tribe: War, Politics, and the Endgame in Iraq*, New York: Random House, 2008, pp. 130–134; Rosen, 2010, pp. 230–234; Dale Andrade, *Surging South of Baghdad: The Third Infantry Division and Task Force Marne in Iraq, 2007–2008*, Washington, D.C.: Center of Military History, 2010, pp. 209–241; Carter Malkasian, "Counterinsurgency in Iraq, May 2003–January 2007," in Daniel Marston, ed., *Counterinsurgency in Modern Warfare*, New York: Osprey Publishing, 2008, p. 257; and David Kilcullen, "Anatomy of a Tribal Revolt," *Small Wars Journal*, August 29, 2007.

[15] Commander's Emergency Response Program funds used in Iraq were essentially large amounts of cash that American military commanders were authorized to spend on projects that would help the Iraqi people reconstruct their country. They could be used for such things as paying for Iraqi workers to repair holes in streets and remove garbage, for repairing school or hospital facilities, or for purchasing large generators for populated areas to produce additional electrical power. Initially, these funds were generated from the seizure of Iraqi funds after the invasion, but the money later became a congressional appropriation for DoD to distribute to commanders on the ground in Iraq.

[16] Former military adviser to Iraqi forces, interview with the authors, June 12, 2015.

Qaeda–directed bombing attacks against Iraqi civilians, mostly Shia.[17] This sustained success in almost completely dismantling and destroying al Qaeda in Iraq was one of the greatest accomplishments of the Surge.

Along with the important effect of the Sunni Awakening, the second condition on the ground that contributed to the success of the Surge period was a cessation of acts of violence by various Shia militia groups. As with the Sunnis, many Shia in Iraq had grown weary of the amount of slaughter that militias were carrying out against Iraqi civilians. Frustration with various militia groups came to a head in August 2007 when the Shia leader Moqtada al-Sadr's forces attacked an Iraqi Police brigade in the southern city of Karbala. In the fallout following the encounter, Sadr made the decision to freeze his militia's attacks against rival militias and civilians. The combination of these domestic Iraqi political factors (the cessation of intra-Shia violence and the Sunni Awakening) thus contributed to the decline in violence toward the end of 2007.[18]

The third contributing condition was the fact that Baghdad had become separated into discrete sectarian districts during the civil war in 2005 and 2006. As demographics shifted during campaigns of religious violence, Baghdad had become dominated by Shia areas, with a few small enclaves of Sunni districts. Other parts of Iraq, such as the Sunni Triangle north and west of Baghdad, experienced this same kind of sectarian separation. Beginning in early 2006, the division was reinforced as the U.S. military began to build large concrete walls to separate neighborhoods physically along sectarian lines. The walls reinforced this sectarian separation by essentially sealing off entire districts to either vehicular or foot movement and thus limiting access into a given district through one entrance and exit point usually controlled by the ISF. The concrete walls thus provided a strong measure of protection from Sunni mass casualty–producing individual suicide bombers or vehicular bombs moving into Shia areas or Shia militia squads moving into Sunni districts to take captives for torture, killing, and ransom.[19] Concurrent with these three aspects of the Surge—the Sunni Awakening,

---

[17] On the tactical action of American combat units working with the various Sunni groups, see Andrade, 2010; Sean MacFarland and Niel Smith, "Anbar Awakens: The Tipping Point," *Military Review*, March–April 2008; Andrew W. Koloski and John S. Kolasheski, "Thickening the Lines: Sons of Iraq, a Combat Multiplier," *Military Review*, January–February 2009; and Michael R. Gordon, "The Former Insurgent Counterinsurgency," *New York Times*, September 2, 2007.

[18] Alissa J. Rubin, "Shiite Rivalries Slash at a Once Calm Iraqi City," *New York Times*, June 21, 2007. See also the answers by Juan Cole, Shawn Brimley, Marina Ottaway, and Matthew Duss in Matthews, 2008; and Stephen Farrell, "50 Die in Fight Between Shia Groups in Karballa," *New York Times*, August 29, 2007.

[19] Agnew et al., 2008; Lawrence Korb, Brian Katulis, Sean Duggan, and Peter Juul, *How Does This End? Strategic Failures Overshadow Tactical Gains in Iraq*, Washington, D.C.: Center for American Progress, 2008; and Patrick Cockburn, "Who Is Whose Enemy?" *London Review of Books*, Vol. 30, No. 5, March 2008. For a useful essay that attempts to use various databases to analyze the role that the Surge played in the lowering of violence, see Stephen Biddle, Jeffrey A. Friedman, and Jacob N. Shapiro, "Testing the Surge: Why Did Violence Decline in Iraq in 2007?" *International Security*, Vol. 37, No. 1, Summer 2012.

the relative freeze in Shia attacks, and the de facto sectarian partition of Baghdad—was the U.S. military's approach to counterinsurgency. We turn to this issue next.

Counterinsurgency and the Surge

As the Surge began in February 2007, the interpretation of counterinsurgency doctrine noticeably shifted toward "providing protection" to the Iraqi population. Before this, an NSC study noted that the primary emphasis was on "transitioning responsibility to Iraqis." Now under this so-called new approach, the main focus would be on "population security."[20] Speaking in early January 2007 to newly appointed Secretary of Defense Robert Gates, Petraeus stated that if he took the job as commander in Iraq, he wanted the main operational emphasis to be on securing the Iraqi people.[21] Petraeus was also adamant that the Surge forces should consist of all five available combat brigades and the two Marine Corps battalions, and was very frank with CJCS GEN Peter Pace on this point.[22]

Although the launch of Petraeus's new strategy was a source of great expectation and reflection, his assessment of his predecessor is sympathetic, saying in 2015 that "Casey, to be fair, had a decent strategy, but kept getting squeezed by Rumsfeld to draw down, keep the numbers down, and transition faster." Petraeus further noted that "until the Samarra mosque bombing" in February 2006, the United States "had a reasonable strategy in Iraq." That bombing, however, "invalidated the strategy and rather than adopting a new one, the U.S. accelerated what was, increasingly, a losing strategy." Therefore, General Petraeus intended to turn a losing strategy into a winning one by implementing the Surge and making a "180 degree change" from what was being done before. U.S. Army combat units in Baghdad would move off the big bases and back into the neighborhoods. Petraeus surmised that gains made in neighborhoods during the day were quickly reversed at night by insurgents after troops had returned to their bases; the only way to secure the people was to live among them.[23]

The actual operational plan to secure Baghdad that Petraeus would put into effect came to be known by the Arabic name Fardh al Qanoon ("enforcing the law"). Petraeus's new MNC-I commander, LTG Raymond T. Odierno, would concentrate three of five new Surge brigades in Baghdad proper. He directed that they continue the practice of walling off certain districts in Baghdad to separate the warring Shia and Sunni factions. Odierno also emphasized the continuation of what had started in 2006 in Baghdad under General Casey: the setting up of Joint Security Stations that would

---

[20] National Security Council, "Highlights of the Iraq Strategy Review," briefing slides, January 2007.

[21] Ricks, 2009, p. 128.

[22] Former senior military commander, interview with the authors, July 31, 2015.

[23] Former senior military commander, interview with the authors, July 31, 2015.

be manned by the U.S. Army, Iraqi Army, and Iraqi Police. The idea behind the continued dispersion of combat forces throughout Joint Security Stations and in combat outposts was the belief that they would help to protect the Iraqi population and quell sectarian violence through the reduction of al Qaeda and marauding Shia militias. The increase in American troop strength in Baghdad allowed Odierno essentially to split the city into a southern and northern half. In the northern half, he had the 1st Cavalry Division under MG Joseph Fil, which had replaced the 4th Infantry Division in early December 2006. But in the southern half, by April, General Odierno created a new division-level command with the 3rd Infantry Division under MG Rick Lynch, titling it Multi-National Division, Baghdad–Center. Over the next six months, these two divisions would carry out the operations to secure Baghdad.[24]

But the Surge was not only about an increase in American brigades, it also was complemented by a significant refinement in the Iraqi Army chain of command in Baghdad. With the Surge came a unified Iraqi command that had one Iraqi Army officer in charge of all ISF troops in the capital. The Surge also included a component to drastically increase the numbers of trained ISF.[25]

Counterinsurgency Operations in Practice

Reflecting on the first eight months of the Surge from his headquarters in Baghdad in October 2007, General Odierno reflected on the significant lowering of violence he was observing and credited it to the idea that the troops under his command had

> made a significant amount of improvement in being able to protect the population over the last several months. Civilian casualties are down . . . and they have gone down now for four consecutive months. We are seeing that casualties to Coalition Forces are now going down. The number of improvised explosive devices is going down. Why does that show improved protection of the population? It shows that the population is really helping us to defeat the threat, which is making it easier for us to hunt down IED makers and stop IEDs from being exploded to help with the civilian casualties. What has clearly been evident is that the Iraqi people have rejected Al Qaeda.[26]

As operations to secure Baghdad progressed into spring and early summer 2007, the growing importance of the Anbar Awakening became more and more apparent to the success of U.S. Army combat units in Baghdad destroying al Qaeda fighters. For example, in the Baghdad Sunni district of Ameriyah, the commanding officer of

---

[24] Andrade, 2010.

[25] Frederik Pleitgen, "Colonel: Iraqi Forces Still Need Help from U.S. Troops," CNN, July 2, 2007.

[26] Raymond T. Odierno, interview, October 19, 2007, transcript provided to RAND by the OIF Study Group.

1-5 Cavalry (1st Cavalry Division), LTC Dale Kuehl, established his first combat outpost in the district on May 19, 2007. Highlighting the importance of the spread of the Anbar Awakening into Baghdad, Kuehl acknowledged that just a few days after the establishment of his first combat outpost on the outskirts of the district, he was able to cut a deal in the district with a former Sunni nationalist insurgent fighter named Abu Abed to ally with Kuehl's battalion to fight against al Qaeda. Kuehl confirmed that had the Ameriyah Sunnis led by Abu Abed not "come forward, we would have never been able to secure the population. They were essential in giving us the vital information we needed to effectively target [al Qaeda in Iraq]." The agreement cut with Sunni fighters proved to be an important catalyst that led to the lowering of violence in Ameriyah and ultimately the securing of its population.[27]

Kuehl's brigade commander, COL J. B. Burton, encouraged Kuehl to work out a deal with the Sunni fighters in Ameriyah under Abu Abed. Burton was interviewed in November 2007 when he was still in Baghdad as part of the Surge and in command of his brigade. In this interview, Burton gave a very detailed description not only of the cooperation between his troops and the Sunni fighters in Ameriyah against al Qaeda, but also of the way in which his BCT, and specifically Kuehl's battalion, conducted operations to take advantage of this new relationship. It is worth quoting at length what Burton had to say only four months after the operations he describes:

> That next day, a gentleman by the name of Abu Abed came forward and went to find Lieutenant Colonel Dale Kuehl and he said, "My name is Abu Abed. I have 17 fighters and I am going to kill the al-Qaeda in Ameriyah." So, Dale Kuehl called me and said, "Sir, what do we do?" and I said, "Let's put them to work," and he said, "How do we do this?" and I said, "I don't know. Let's just go ask them if they want any help." Well, they didn't want any help. They just wanted to do it. . . . These guys knew the area, they were from the area, and they knew who the bad guys were; so, let's put them to work. . . . They agreed to give us full transparency of their operations and I said, "Okay. Let's go." The next day, they got into a pretty robust fight and they killed six to eight al-Qaeda guys and two or three of the Baghdad Patriots, which was what they called themselves at that time, under Abu Abed . . . they lost two or three, lots of kids were wounded, and they got on the phone and said, "We need two things. We need medical support and we need ammunition." Well, the rules didn't allow me to give them ammunition; but . . . I called Brigadier General Ghassan [Burton's Iraqi Army counterpart] and I said . . . these guys need ammo. Can you get them ammo?" and he said, "I can get them ammo." So, he got authority and he gave them 30,000 rounds of AK-47 ammuni-

---

[27] Daniel Davis, *Dereliction of Duty II: Senior Military Leaders' Loss of Integrity Wounds Afghan War Effort*, January 27, 2012, p. 69; Dale Kuehl, interview with Steven Clay, Combat Studies Institute, January 18, 2010, transcript provided to RAND by the OIF Study Group; also see Julian E. Barnes, "Baghdad Outpost Plan Flawed, Some Troops Say," *Los Angeles Times*, July 8, 2007; and Dale Kuehl, "Testing Galula in Ameriyah: The People Are the Key," *Military Review*, March–April 2009.

tion and they went to work. . . . Then, the next day, we started into a formal dialogue and that formal dialogue was facilitated by something magical happening. On the grounds of the Abbas Mosque in Ameriyah, the Baghdad Patriots, under Abu Abed; the commander of the 2d Battalion, 1st Brigade, 6th Iraqi Army, at that time Lieutenant Colonel Sabah; and [Captain] Dustin Mitchell, my Brigade Reconnaissance Troop Commander, established a combined command post on the grounds of the Abbas Mosque to fight al-Qaeda. Now you have indigenous forces with Iraqi Security Forces with Coalition forces and they are fighting al-Qaeda and from that we started getting more and more momentum. From that came . . . the first real glimpse of what we could do with indigenous forces.[28]

Colonel Kuehl similarly reported how this initially "tentative" partnership "grew increasingly effective" as U.S. and Awakening forces began to work more closely together and eventually "trust" each other. He also noted that the growing success of the groups and charisma of some leaders meant that they soon began to compete with al Qaeda for the local youth, which was critical in reducing violence.[29] Burton's detailed description gives a telescopic view of the huge role that the spread of the Sunni Awakening was having in positively affecting tactical operations in Baghdad in spring and summer 2007. It also shows how American military operations in Baghdad at the time worked with these Sunni fighters and the complementary role each played with the other in reducing the levels of violence significantly in Baghdad by the end of 2007.

Burton's BCT was also involved in operations to secure what became known as "the Baghdad belts." The belts refer to residential, agricultural, and industrial zones surrounding Baghdad proper, as well as the roadways, rivers, and communication infrastructure within these areas. An important piece of intelligence revealed that maintaining control of the belts, as a means to transport weapons and fighters, was a key component in al Qaeda's strategy to make gains within the capital.[30] In 2006, coalition forces seized a hand-drawn map by al Qaeda leader Abu Musab al-Zarqawi depicting the strategic importance of the belts encircling Baghdad (Figure 5.2).

Burton referred to operations to try to control what he called the "rat lines" coming out of the belts from the northwest and directly into his area of operations in Baghdad. These "rat lines" were actually roads, trails, and waterways that insurgent groups used to move supplies and people into and out of Baghdad. The belts also included the provinces of Salah Din, Diyala, Babil, Wasit, and Anbar around the city, offering critical layers of access and control. They were often fought over by both

---

[28] J. B. Burton, interview with Jerry England, Combat Studies Institute, November 29, 2007, transcript provided to RAND by the OIF Study Group.

[29] Dale Kuehl, interview with Steven Clay, Combat Studies Institute, January 18, 2010, transcript provided to RAND by the OIF Study Group.

[30] Institute for the Study of War, "Baghdad Belts," webpage, undated.

Figure 5.2
Baghdad Belts

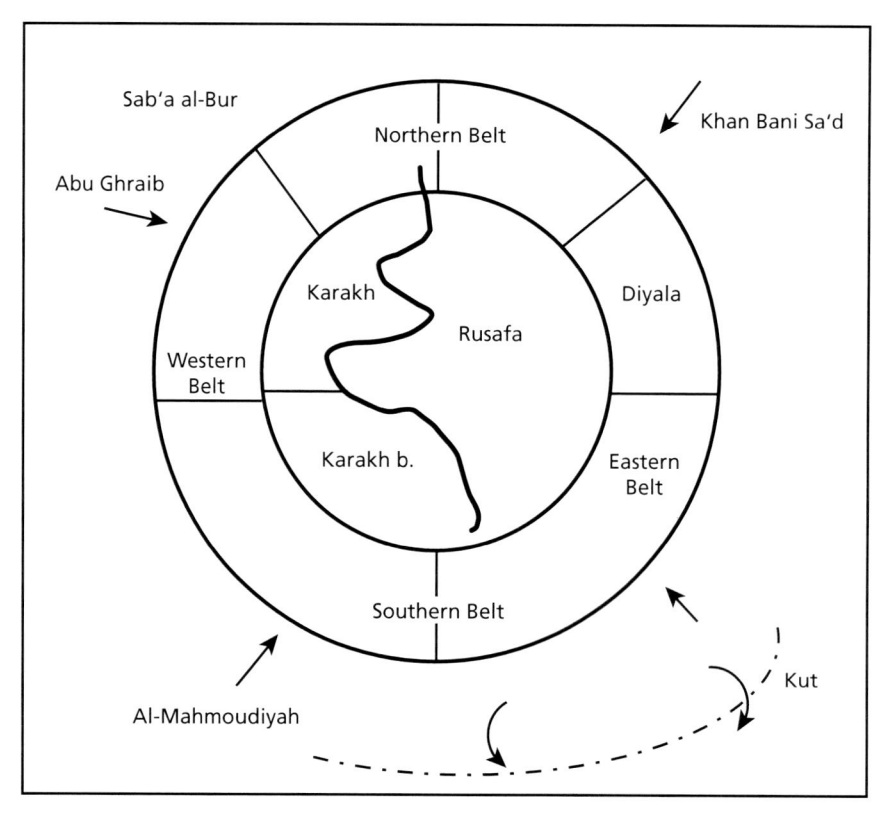

[Diagram: Concentric circle diagram showing Baghdad divided into inner sections (Karakh, Rusafa, Karakh b.) and outer belts (Northern Belt, Western Belt, Eastern Belt, Southern Belt), with surrounding areas labeled Sab'a al-Bur, Khan Bani Sa'd, Abu Ghraib, Diyala, Al-Mahmoudiyah, and Kut.]

SOURCE: Derived and translated from a map found on Musab al-Zarqawi in 2006, published in Bill Roggio, "Analysis: ISIS, Allies Reviving 'Baghdad Belts' Battle Plan," *Long War Journal*, June 14, 2014.

Sunni and Shia groups because controlling the belts allowed groups to restrict what went into and out of Baghdad.[31]

Before the Surge, General Casey had his subordinate tactical forces conduct operations in the belts, but during the Surge, General Odierno used combinations of all five Surge brigades to carry out new and more-forceful operations in these important areas. Combat operations in the belts targeted key roads and rivers to interdict the "accelerants" of the sectarian war by preventing the flow of fighters, weapons, and money into Baghdad.[32]

---

[31] Kimberly Kagan, *The Surge: A Military History*, New York: Encounter Books, 2009, pp. 116–147.

[32] Raymond T. Odierno, interview, October 19, 2007, transcript provided to RAND by the OIF Study Group; and Kagan, 2009.

In the first months of the Surge, General Odierno directed Generals Fil and Lynch to conduct reconnaissance into the belts to feel out enemy response and gain a better sense of the important terrain and the transportation networks. But the actual combat operations by Surge forces in the belts would begin in May 2007 and run well into July and August. North of Baghdad in Diyala province, the 3rd Stryker Brigade of the 2nd Infantry Division carried out operations Phantom Thunder and Phantom Strike. Important Diyala cities, such as Baqubah, were cleared of al Qaeda fighters largely because former Sunni insurgent groups, such as the 1920s Brigade, were now cooperating with American outfits and providing accurate intelligence on the locations of al Qaeda fighters so that American firepower could then more easily destroy them.[33]

In the belt south of Baghdad, Lynch's 3rd Infantry Division drew on the adaptations and improvisations of small-unit leaders, such as company and battalion commanders, to conduct similar types of operations that combined American combat capabilities with the newly forming group called the Sons of Iraq. A former military commander we spoke with had responsibility for the large rural areas immediately south of Baghdad, sometimes referred to as the "triangle of death" or the "Shakariyah Triangle" by U.S. soldiers. When the commander first arrived in late summer of 2006, he noticed that the limited American combat presence in the belt south of Baghdad was able only to "contain" insurgent activities but "not to sustain combat power in this known sanctuary" of the enemy. This limited presence left critical arteries uncontrolled and uncontested by either American or ISF forces. He recalled that when he took over his area of operations, he was told that this region was one of the "sanctuaries" for al Qaeda in Iraq attacks into the capital. Al Qaeda in Iraq would use the area and the canals of the Euphrates to run supplies and fighters into and out of the capital. The former commander recalled that the geography of the triangle "conspired to make both access and sustainability of U.S. and ISF combat forces problematic." To overcome these problems and contest and interdict this flow of enemy fighters and supplies, he used raids by special operations forces and his own combat units, eventually gaining control of the area. Equally important to his own combat operations was the new partnership the BCT was developing with former Sunni insurgent fighters now being swept up by the spread of the Anbar Awakening. In combining his own operations with these new Sunni allies and with additional ISF troops, rather than relying primarily on Military Transition Teams to train and coordinate with the ISF, he had his own combat companies work "directly with each Iraqi Army battalion" in his sector. This cooperation was in place when the initial movements of the Anbar Awakening began to appear, thus involving, as the commander recalled, the "Iraqi Army" in the Sunni "volunteer" movement. It was in this way that his BCT exerted considerable control over the area and significantly reduced the overall levels of violence in

---

[33] Gordon and Trainor, 2012, pp. 389–409; Mansoor, 2013.

Baghdad.³⁴ In agreement with the commander, General Odierno believed that the belt operations produced a "tipping point" by "getting into the Baghdad periphery":

> Our ability to secure the south and Yusufiyah, Mahmoudiyah, Iskandariya, Al-Salam, in the north and Talmiyah, and then going in and having the forces to really liberate Baqubah from Al Qaeda. That made a huge difference in those areas, but a huge difference and effect in Baghdad itself in reducing the level of violence.³⁵

Special Operations Command Ramps Up

Another key element of the Surge occurred in the shadows—in the form of targeted special operations raids, conducted by U.S. Special Operations Command (SOCOM). Indeed, while the authors of FM 3-24 (the counterinsurgency manual) often emphasized the nonkinetic parts of counterinsurgency, Petraeus recognized that counterinsurgency also required a harder edge. Writing in *Foreign Policy* in 2013, Petraeus recounted,

> Although I publicly acknowledged from the outset that we would not be able to kill or capture our way to victory (hence the need to support the Awakening), killing or capturing the most important of the "irreconcilables" was an inescapable and hugely important element of our strategy. Indeed, we sought to pursue key irreconcilables even more aggressively than was the case before the surge.³⁶

To hunt down these "irreconcilables," Petraeus turned to special operations forces and to their commander, then-LTG Stanley McChrystal.

The command had been operating in Iraq from the beginning of the conflict, but under McChrystal's leadership, SOCOM became a well-oiled machine, combining intelligence assets, mobility assets, and special operators to systematically target al-Qaeda in Iraq and other insurgent networks. During the Surge, SOCOM personnel routinely conducted as many as ten to 15 raids per night, many of them in Baghdad.³⁷ While much of the special operations side of the Battle for Baghdad remains classified, President Bush gave perhaps the best verdict on their impact. When asked in an interview about how the United States achieved intelligence and targeting breakthroughs in Iraq, he simply replied that the special operations forces are "awesome."³⁸

---

³⁴ Former military commander, interview with the authors, May 26, 2015.

³⁵ J. B. Burton, interview with Jerry England, Combat Studies Institute, November 29, 2007, transcript provided to RAND by the OIF Study Group.

³⁶ David Petraeus, "How We Won in Iraq," *Foreign Policy*, October 29, 2013.

³⁷ Petraeus, 2013.

³⁸ Woodward, 2008b.

Countering the Shia Element

In addition to counterinsurgency operations in the Baghdad neighborhoods and the combat operations in the Baghdad belts, there was another component to the overall operational framework for the Surge: the effort to capture or kill the active Shia militia cells and individual fighters who were continuing to attack Sunni civilians and U.S. forces. The Awakening gave the Americans a secure flank so that coalition forces could turn their attention to Sadr and the long-standing Shia problem. In 2006, and even into part of 2007, repeated requests by senior U.S. leaders to target various Shia militia groups were denied by Prime Minister Maliki, who even went so far as to purge Iraqi military officers for their willingness to target the groups.[39] With levels of sectarian violence so high, Malaki, still a relatively new prime minister, withheld his approval for American combat action against the Shia militias.

However, things had changed by 2007 with the Surge, and Maliki acquiesced to Petraeus's request, if not insistence, for permission to go after the militias. The situation in Baghdad was by then so grim that, in the words of one former senior military commander, "Maliki didn't have a choice."[40] The sense of Shia relief and boost in Maliki's standing after the death of Saddam may have also made the prime minister more willing to bend to American pressure.[41]

A former military adviser to Iraqi forces was even more frank in his assessment of Maliki's acquiescence and political calculus. According to him, the Awakening was fundamental in that it helped the prime minister solve his Sunni problem. With the Awakening, the Sunnis had partnered with the U.S. forces and were at least ostensibly committed to some form of political arrangement in Baghdad and the secession of attacks against Shia. The Americans were "guarantors," and Maliki decided that the time was finally ripe in late 2007 and early 2008 to "move against Sadr and Basra." The prime minster had made up his mind to "to put to bed forever [his problem with the Shia militia]."[42] Military efforts against the Shia militias now had Maliki's blessing.

In the Shia-dominated Khadamiya district in northeast Baghdad, the primary mission of LTC Michael Richardson's infantry battalion from the 82nd Airborne Division was "to conduct combined, full-spectrum operations . . . to defeat extremist actors, increase the Iraqi Security Force capability and capacity, and to improve local government's efforts to deliver essential services." In Richardson's view, the main threats to U.S. forces and the ISF in his area of operations were "Shia extremists consisting of

---

[39] Joshua Partlow, "Maliki's Office Is Seen Behind Purge in Forces," *Washington Post*, April 30, 2007.

[40] Former senior military commander, interview with the authors, July 31, 2015.

[41] See also "Taking on the Shia Militias," *The Economist*, January 24, 2007.

[42] Former military adviser to Iraqi forces, interview with the authors, June 12, 2015.

Jaysh al-Mahdi forces and other Shia criminals."[43] Richardson's battalion arrived in January 2007 and very quickly began to establish multiple combat outposts and Joint Security Stations in the area. He believed that over the course of the year, having this kind of presence in the area and a close relationship with the ISF gave him a much better sense of the different Shia militia groups that he was fighting. By working closely with the ISF, Richardson came to the important realization that active Shia militiamen dominated many of the Iraqi Police and, to a lesser extent, Iraqi Army units in his area. As a response to these threats, his battalion carried out Operation "Seventh Veil," which, as Richardson recalled, "targeted corrupt government officials" and aimed to rid various ISF units of Shia militiamen who were using their ISF units to capture and either kill or torture any Sunnis left in the area.[44]

The Battle of Sadr City

By the time Richardson's battalion departed Baghdad in January 2008, there was a growing problem with Jaysh al-Mahdi, the Shia militia under the leadership of Sadr.[45] The son of a famous Shia religious leader during Saddam's reign, Moqtada al-Sadr formed Jaysh al-Mahdi soon after major combat operations began. By early 2008, Sadr's militant Shia militia had established firm control over the Shia population in Sadr City, an area of well more than 2 million people. In March, Jaysh al-Mahdi forces overran a series of security checkpoints and fired an onslaught of rockets and mortars into the International Zone (formerly the Green Zone), home to national government offices and foreign embassies. The assault was a direct challenge to the authority of the national government and undermined its ability to establish and maintain a secure and stable environment for the Iraqi people.[46]

On March 25, 2008, the Maliki government authorized U.S. and Iraqi forces to stop the rocket attacks and defeat the militants in Sadr City. COL John Hort, commander of the 3rd Brigade Combat Team, 4th Infantry Division, developed a course of action that aimed to clear and hold enemy launch sites. The original operational concept envisioned a combined arms maneuver campaign employing Stryker light infantry forces supported by an employment of technological assets. Operation Striker

---

[43] Michael Richardson, interview with Laurence Lessard, Combat Studies Institute, December 11, 2009, transcript provided to RAND by the OIF Study Group.

[44] Michael Richardson, interview with Laurence Lessard, Combat Studies Institute, December 11, 2009, transcript provided to RAND by the OIF Study Group.

[45] Much of the text in this description of the Battle of Sadr City comes directly from David E. Johnson, M. Wade Markel, and Brian Shannon, *The 2008 Battle of Sadr City: Reimagining Urban Combat*, Santa Monica, Calif.: RAND Corporation, RR-160-A, 2013.

[46] Gordon and Trainor, 2012, pp. 484–504; Mansoor, 2013; and Michael Knights, "No Go No More: The Battle for Sadr City," *Jane's Intelligence Review*, Vol. 20, No. 7, July 2008.

Denial was to stop mortar and rocket fire into the International Zone further south. The International Zone was at the maximum range of Jaysh al-Mahdi's weapons. Thus, pushing back the group's area of operations would significantly reduce the effectiveness of its attacks. U.S. forces had to consider the enemy's capabilities (automatic weapons, .50-caliber sniper rifles, IEDs, rocket-propelled grenades, and SA-7 portable air defense systems) and how the city's urban terrain facilitated the group's operations. While armored combat platforms afforded significant lethality, survivability, and mobility, the urban terrain proved formidable. Hort's BCT carried out initial engagements in Stryker vehicles (light armored forces). But Stryker vehicles, lacking significant armored protection, fell victim to rocket-propelled grenade attacks launched from the city's low-rise buildings and IEDs frequently hidden under trash-piled streets. The city's small cluttered alleys also significantly restricted Stryker movements, given the vehicle's wide and large turning radius. The 1st Squadron, 2nd Stryker Cavalry Regiment, lost six Stryker vehicles within the first week of the fight. U.S. forces brought in M1 Abrams tanks and M2 Bradley fighting vehicles that could survive the IED and grenade assaults.

The operations against the Jaysh al-Mahdi militia in Sadr City further spurred Maliki's distress over rocket attacks into the International Zone. Therefore, in conjunction with the ground operations against Jaysh al-Mahdi, Hort's BCT, along with other elements of Multi-National Division–Baghdad, developed a tightly integrated air-ground intelligence, surveillance, and reconnaissance system to defeat the rocket launchers that was unprecedented in the capabilities that were given to a BCT. Figure 5.3, a slide from a briefing that a senior military commander used to discuss the battle of Sadr City, shows these resources.

To maintain the ability to continue to fire rockets into the International Zone, it soon became apparent that Jaysh al-Mahdi militants were determined to infiltrate market areas that they viewed as critical terrain. Unable to restrict them solely with maneuver forces, U.S. troops began constructing a 12-foot wall along what was called Route Gold. Heavy armor provided fire protection for soldiers and large construction equipment as the project "became a magnet for every bad guy in Sadr City." Thus, a secondary consequence of the wall's construction was that it drew out the enemy, allowing U.S. forces already in place to fight from a position of advantage. Forcing the enemy to come out and fight a newly tailored American combat force that had mobile, protected firepower essentially shrank the problem to manageable proportions. Bringing in armored forces once it was realized that Strykers and light infantry were taking too many casualties allowed the American task force to survive the enemy's attacks while applying lethal firepower.[47]

Another indication that the wall was having its intended effect of safeguarding populations and limiting enemy movements was the flood of reliable information

---

[47] Former military commander, interview with the authors, July 27, 2015; and Johnson et al., 2013, p. xvii.

Figure 5.3
Intelligence, Surveillance, and Reconnaissance and Strike Assets Employed in the Battle of Sadr City

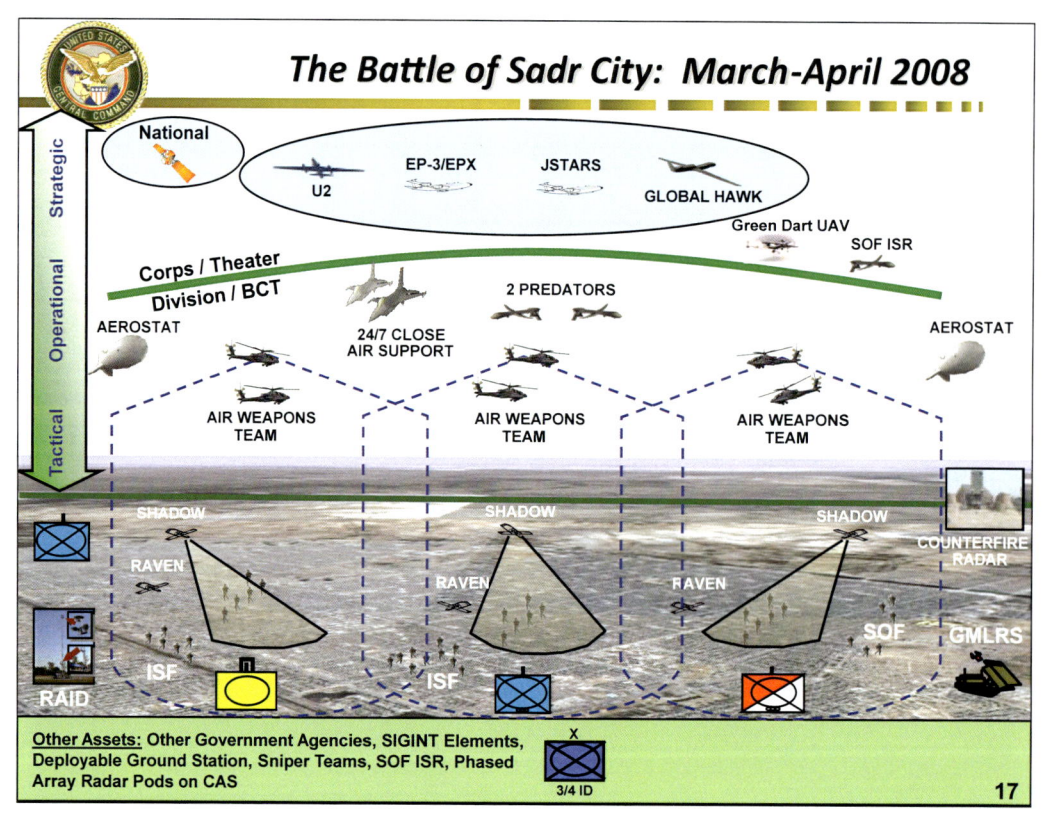

SOURCE: "CENTCOM Update, Center for a New American Security," briefing slides, 2009, provided to RAND by a former senior military commander.
NOTES: CAS = close air support; GMLRS = Guided Multiple Launch Rocket System; ISR = intelligence, surveillance, and reconnaissance; JSTARS = Joint Surveillance Target Attack Radar System; RAID = Rapid Aerostat Initial Deployment; SIGINT = signals intelligence; SOF = special operations forces; UAV = unmanned aerial vehicle.

about the enemy from the local population, seemingly more confident that U.S. and Iraqi forces were shifting momentum in their favor. The information proved essential for locating IED emplacements and identifying and locating remaining insurgent leaders. By mid-May 2008, the threat from Sadr's militant arm had largely been neutralized. Relentless pressure from U.S. and Iraqi forces had taken its toll on Jaysh al-Mahdi fighters in Sadr City who were showing up in ever-decreasing numbers. On May 11, 2008, Sadr requested a cease-fire, but not before an estimated 1,000 fighters lost their lives and much of the group's leadership fled the country. While pockets of resistance remained, the halt in large-scale violence enabled the government in Baghdad to focus on reconstruction efforts and winning the hearts and minds of its own population.[48]

The Battle for Sadr City was the last major combat operation of the Surge. Over the course of 2007, violence in Iraq dropped significantly. By the end of the year, the "tide had turned," according to COL Peter Mansoor (who had commanded a BCT in Baghdad in 2004 and was Petraeus's executive officer during the Surge), and, thanks in large part to the Surge, Iraq was finally on the path to peace.[49]

General Petraeus changed command of MNF-I in September 2008, passing it to General Odierno and thus giving a formal ending date to the Surge. There is much to learn from the Battle of Sadr City. The ability of Colonel Hort to conduct the counter-rocket fight was contingent on the elaborate network of sensors and networks that had been established over time in Baghdad, as well as extensive walling throughout much of the city.[50] Absent these preconditions, Colonel Hort's brigade would not have been able to operate the way it did. Thus, a major lesson from the Battle for Baghdad and the Battle of Sadr City is that what won the day was highly contingent on setting conditions over time against an irregular adversary with limited means. Whether an expeditionary army can conduct similar operations in the future against a more competent urban adversary remains to be seen.[51]

Subsequent years saw much debate over the role and significance of military operations during the Surge. One school of thought that emerged even while the Surge was ongoing was that violence dropped because General Petraeus fundamentally changed the strategy from his predecessor, George W. Casey, Jr., and that Petraeus's troops changed their operational approach to a new form of counterinsurgency operations.[52] This school of thought acknowledged that other conditions on the ground (described later) were certainly important for the lowering of violence; however, without the new and enlightened generalship of Petraeus and the change in operations and strategy that he brought about, those conditions would have never led to the drop in violence that occurred.

Yet the cause for the lowering of violence became a fiercely debated topic in the years following the Surge. In countering this school of thought, another emerged arguing that there really was no significant difference in strategy and operations between

---

[48] Mohammed Tawfeeq and Jomana Karadsheh, "Cease-Fire Reached in Baghdad's Sadr City," CNN, May 11, 2008.

[49] See, for example, Mansoor, 2013.

[50] Johnson et al., 2013, p. 55.

[51] For recent RAND work on the future of urban operations, see Gian Gentile, David E. Johnson, Lisa Saum-Manning, Raphael S. Cohen, Shara Williams, Carrie Lee, Michael Shurkin, Brenna Allen, and Sarah Soliman, *Reimagining the Character of Urban Operations for the United States Army Past, Present, and Future*, Santa Monica, Calif.: RAND Corporation, RR-1602-A, 2017.

[52] Mansoor, 2008b; see also Manea, 2011.

the Casey years and the Surge under Petraeus. While acknowledging that the additional Surge brigades were instrumental in success, their contribution is seen more in the extent to which they simply increased the amount of fighting power brought to bear against various insurgent groups. The Surge capitalized on the change in momentum brought about by the Awakening, rather than itself being the catalyst for change. Certainly, however, the increased combat action enabled by the Surge broke down insurgent resistance and brought an increased measure of security and protection to the population of Baghdad.

Civilians and the Surge: One Surge, Many Stories

As described in Chapter Four, by midway through 2006, civilian policymakers were increasingly convinced that the situation in Iraq was deteriorating and the Casey strategy of standing down U.S. forces so the Iraqis could stand up was not working. Indeed, throughout the time frame, the CIA reported that Iraq was descending into civil war. Unlike other civil wars, however, the CIA concluded that the Iraqi civil war was not characterized as a few major factions fighting to divide the state. Rather, Iraq was descending into chaos with "smaller and smaller groups fighting over smaller and smaller chunks."[53] And while the CIA's assessments were often bleaker than the military's assessment of the situation, even the military assessments were growing darker.[54] If these trends were to be reversed—civilian policymakers believed—something more dramatic needed to be done, and from this thought process was born the so-called Surge. Just how the Surge became American policy, however, is a matter of debate.

The Outsider Narrative: Jack Keane and the American Enterprise Institute

Thanks to a series of popular journalist and think tank accounts of the Iraq War, the perhaps dominant narrative traces the origin of the Surge to a small group of outside advisers in the Bush administration.[55] This group was led by former Army Vice Chief of Staff General Keane and aided by a small group of think tank analysts, including Fred Kagan from the American Enterprise Institute (AEI) and Kimberly Kagan from the Institute of the Study of War. Acting in concert with a handful of internal advocates within the Bush administration and the up-and-coming former Keane subordinate, then–Lieutenant General Petraeus, the group sketched out and eventually sold President Bush on the Surge.

---

[53] Former senior national security official, interview with the authors, April 13, 2015.

[54] Former senior national security official, interview with the authors, April 13, 2015.

[55] Fred Kaplan, *The Insurgents: David Petraeus and the Plot to Change the American Way of War*, New York: Simon and Schuster, 2013; Linda Robinson, *Tell Me How This Ends: General David Petraeus and the Search for a Way out of Iraq*, New York: Public Affairs, 2008; and Ricks, 2009.

The starting point for this narrative occurred sometime in the summer of 2006 in a house in McLean, Virginia. After listening to Rumsfeld and CENTCOM commander General Abizaid testify to the Senate Armed Services Committee, Keane—a Vietnam veteran—surmised that the United States was repeating its mistake of Vietnam and was on the verge of defeat. The following morning, he sketched out the reasons he thought that the United States was failing in Iraq and what the remaining options were for the United States to reverse course. The plan centered on a substantial addition of American troops, some eight to ten BCTs, largely to stabilize Baghdad and the surrounding region.

Unlike some of his peers in the general officer corps, Keane had a good working relationship with Secretary Rumsfeld and Deputy Secretary of Defense Paul Wolfowitz before retiring from active duty. As a member of the Defense Policy Board, he also had access to the senior defense leadership. And so, after developing his ideas, he shared them with Wolfowitz and CJCS General Pace, and later Rumsfeld. In the briefing, Keane argued that the United States did not have and had never had a strategy to deal with Iraq's insurgency. Rather, it had a plan to transition the war to the ISF, assuming that they could win a war that the United States so far could not. The point hit home with Rumsfeld, but he was noncommittal about changing the strategy, removing the generals, and increasing the number of troops.[56]

Before Keane could brief the White House, however, he got a call from Christopher Demuth, then the president of the AEI, a conservative-leaning Washington, D.C., think tank. Demuth informed Keane that one of his scholars, Fred Kagan, along with several other think tank scholars and some active-duty military officers, had developed an alternative strategy for Iraq and asked whether the team could brief Keane. Keane accepted the invitation and was amazed by its specificity, despite working from unclassified materials. AEI's plan, like Keane's, also called for a surge in American troops, and from its analysis, Kagan and his colleagues concluded that only five BCTs were available to go. Keane was impressed by the work and, because the ideas largely coincided with his own, offered to help sell it to the White House.

On December 8, 2006, with LTG Dave Barno and General Keane in attendance, Kagan rolled out an AEI report recommending a troop surge of five BCTs plus two Marine Corps regiments.[57] That same month, Bush made the decision to support the Surge at a meeting at his ranch in Crawford, Texas, and selected Petraeus as the new MNF-I commander. On January 4, 2007, Bush formally announced Petraeus as the new commander,[58] and a week later, on January 10, he announced the Surge as the new strategy.[59] For his part, Keane did not see the plan from then–Lieutenant General

---

[56] Former senior military commander, interview with the authors, April 17, 2015.
[57] Kaplan, 2013, p. 237.
[58] Kaplan, 2013, p. 243.
[59] Gordon and Trainor, 2012, p. 313.

Odierno, Multi-National Corps–Iraq commander, to employ the Surge troops until after the plan was beginning to be implemented. Still, Keane and AEI claim credit for advocating the Surge and, with it, shifting the course of the Iraq War.

The pivotal meeting occurred December 11, 2006, when Keane was invited to the White House to discuss alternative Iraq strategies with the President.[60] In addition to Keane, former Special Operations Command commander GEN Wayne Downing, former Southern Command commander GEN Barry McCaffrey, Johns Hopkins Professor Eliot Cohen, and Council on Foreign Relations Senior Fellow Stephen Biddle also attended. Bush asked each participant about the future of Iraq strategy. Keane advocated a major strategy shift, the so-called Surge; Downing pushed for more special operations forces; McCaffrey wanted more advisers; and Cohen encouraged the President to be more willing to hold Casey accountable for the military's performance in Iraq. For their part, and much to Keane's surprise, both Biddle and Cohen backed Keane's plan (indeed, Keane was surprised that he got more support from the two civilians than his own fellow former general officers). Shortly afterward, Keane and Kagan briefed Vice President Dick Cheney on the AEI plan as well.[61]

After the meeting, National Security Adviser Stephen Hadley and Cheney asked Keane to take over as commander in Iraq, or at least to direct the war from the White House. Although conflicted about the decision, Keane declined on the grounds that he needed to support his ailing wife. He also argued that if the White House recalled a retired general to lead the war, it would be seen as a sign of desperation, which was unnecessary. Instead, Keane recommended one of his protégés—the then–commander of Combined Arms Center in Fort Leavenworth, Kansas, Lieutenant General Petraeus.[62]

Importantly, the outside narrative provoked the ire of other key participants—both inside the administration and in Baghdad. They contend that Keane was *not* in Baghdad in either a military or civilian capacity during this time and therefore lacked firsthand knowledge of events on the ground,[63] nor was Keane on the NSC and thus lacked insight into how the policy actually was made.[64] Other general officers mostly accept that Keane had influence on the strategy but bristle about the fact that he did not address them about it directly. One former senior military commander recounted to us, "I did not and do not accept Keane's role as an 'adviser.' Whatever he recommended, it was outside of the chain of command and not discussed with either George Casey or me."[65] Ultimately, only Bush knows how much these meetings with Keane

---

[60] Woodward, 2008a, p. 279.

[61] Former senior military commander, interview with the authors, April 17, 2015.

[62] Former senior military commander, interview with the authors, April 17, 2015.

[63] Former official at the U.S. embassy in Baghdad, interview with the authors, May 26, 2015.

[64] Former senior national security official, interview with the authors, September 25, 2015.

[65] Former senior military commander, email correspondence with the authors on Jack Keane's influence on the Surge strategy, January 11, 2016.

and AEI influenced his decisionmaking. If the narrative is largely true, however, it teaches a clear lesson: After a prolonged period of groupthink and isolated decisionmaking, the White House finally reached outside its own self-created box, injected fresh ideas into the mix, and turned the war around.

The Partial Outside Narrative: The CIA and the U.S. Embassy

A second narrative about the Surge suggests that the policy shift did not originate from outside the government per se, but that it came from outside the White House.

For its part, the CIA reporting on Iraq became progressively darker. As a former senior national security official recounted, the reporting concluded that Iraq had turned into a civil war. Therefore, the Casey strategy of building up the ISF could not succeed, because it functionally was arming one side of the conflict. Instead, the agency argued, Iraq needed American troops to play the "honest broker" in the simmering sectarian civil war. The CIA also believed that sending the additional five BCTs would tamp down violence in Iraq and, more importantly, create the conditions for the Iraqi government to make political progress.[66]

The U.S. embassy in Iraq also promotes a narrative about its role in the Surge. According to a former senior State Department official, the joint embassy–MNF-I red team produced a strategic review that advocated a shift toward a more population-centric effort that would later be the basis of Petraeus's approach in Iraq. Indeed, the former official argued that some of the former participants in this red cell went on to help write FM 3-24.[67] Another former senior State Department official, who served at the U.S. embassy in Iraq during this period, agreed. He recounted how the embassy pushed hard to favor a focus on population security as the central element to changing the political and security dynamic in the country. He felt that a key to success was changing how the military patrolled and engaged the community. In particular, the military needed to remain in the communities alongside the ISF 24 hours a day rather than retiring at dusk to more-remote bases to ensure that communities felt protected around the clock.[68]

Other actors also toyed with the idea of the Surge. For example, in August 2006, on a plane ride to Baghdad, former Secretary of Defense under Bill Clinton and member of the Iraq Study Group William Perry developed the idea of a yearlong Surge in force levels as a means to tamp down violence. Once in Baghdad, he floated the idea with General Casey, the MNF-I commander who rejected the idea, citing the antibody thesis—that more American troops would only spark a larger backlash.[69] Seemingly, Perry dropped the idea after that.

---

[66] Former senior national security official, interview with the authors, April 13, 2015.

[67] Former senior State Department official, interview with the authors, May 18, 2015.

[68] Former senior State Department official, interview with the authors, June 12, 2015.

[69] Kaplan, 2013, pp. 205–208.

Importantly, it is difficult to trace a direct line between any one of these government reports and the actual decision to increase forces and change strategy in Iraq. At a minimum, however, they added to the general drumbeat of the calls for a change and likely helped contribute indirectly to the shift in policy.

The Insider Narrative: Bush and the National Security Council

A third narrative suggests that the decision to surge came not from the outside, but from within the bowels of the White House. This story of the Surge starts with a conversation between Bush and White House Chief of Staff Josh Bolten in 2006 about civil-military relations. Bolten argued that Bush needed to be more assertive and less deferential to his military leaders. Bolten cited Cohen's book on wartime heads of state with their senior military officials, *Supreme Command*, as evidence.[70] Although initially hesitant, Bush agreed about being more assertive and from then on became decisively engaged in the matter.[71]

With Bush personally engaged and now more skeptical of some of his military advisers, Hadley wanted to give the President options. As early as September and October 2006, Hadley authorized two lower-level reviews. One review, chaired by Meghan O'Sullivan and mostly comprising White House staff, was tasked with coming up with various policy options for the way forward in Iraq; a second review, led by William Luti, the senior director for Defense Policy and Strategy on the NSC, looked at what additional military resources could be brought to bear on Iraq.[72] In November 2006, a small group—including State Department Counselor Philip Zelikow; State Department Coordinator for Iraq David Satterfield; Secretary of State Condoleezza Rice; the Vice President's National Security Adviser John Hannah; NSC members Meghan O'Sullivan, Brett McGurk, and Peter Feaver; and military members—met to discuss Iraq strategy. The group asked the military whether it could surge forces in Iraq, only to be told by LTG Douglas Lute, then still the operations officer on the JCS, that it was impossible—"we're out of Schlitz."[73]

Nonetheless, Hadley directed Luti to analyze whether the United States, in fact, could surge extra forces into Iraq. Luti concluded that the United States had sufficient surge capacity to increase substantially the number of U.S. boots on the ground by about six brigades.[74] Beyond troop numbers, the NSC also identified Baghdad as the linchpin for the operation, as well as strategic, operational, and tactical shifts that needed to occur for a new military approach to succeed, although specific plans for

---

[70] Eliot A. Cohen, *Supreme Command: Soldiers, Statesmen, and Leadership in Wartime*, New York: Simon and Schuster, September 9, 2003.

[71] Former senior national security official, interview with the authors, September 25, 2015.

[72] Former senior national security official, email correspondence with the authors, December 28, 2015.

[73] Former senior State Department official, interview with the authors, March 23, 2015.

[74] Former senior national security official, interview with the authors, May 21, 2015.

how to achieve these shifts were left to military leaders. As one former senior national security official recalled, "We knew if you lost in Baghdad, you couldn't win anywhere else."[75] At the same time, he admitted, "We didn't get anywhere near the level of detail that Odierno and Petraeus wanted. I don't think anyone had that. The strategy had to be tailored to the local level, instead of the one size fits all."[76] Other civilians shared this Baghdad-centric view at the time. For example, a former senior State Department official recounted, "Historically in Iraq, he who ruled in Baghdad ruled the country. It was apparent that the control of Baghdad was essential to stability and security elsewhere. That said, there were significant differences between Basra, Mosul, and so forth. It was also important to work regional peculiarities in their own terms. It was a combination of both, but Baghdad was the key."[77] Beyond this, however, the NSC left the majority of the details to the military.

The NSC explored other strategic options as well—such as forming a protective ring around Baghdad or withdrawing from the city altogether. From there, according to a former senior State Department official, the options narrowed to two basic choices: "Very rapidly it became Surge or no Surge, or to put it in blunt terms, whether to stand by and watch Baghdad burn or to intervene to reset the advance of al Qaeda and sectarian violence."[78]

For most of the civilians on the NSC, the decision between "let it burn" and the Surge was clear: the Surge option was favored.[79] More importantly, Bush himself became increasingly convinced about the need to surge in Iraq. A former senior DoD official recalled talking to Bush before the November 2006 election and recounted how, thanks to Bush's own observations and reading of intelligence and policy reports, the President had become convinced that Iraq would require a change in strategy and in U.S. military leadership in Iraq.[80] A former senior State Department official at the U.S. embassy in Baghdad agreed. Hadley shaped the NSC's policy review structure to make certain that a Surge option was included.[81]

Outside the NSC, however, the Surge was deeply unpopular. As already discussed, with coalition casualties remaining high in the controversial war, there was little appetite for putting yet more troops in harm's way. On December 31, 2006, the U.S. government announced the loss of its 3,000th American service member in

---

[75] Former senior national security official, interview with the authors, May 8, 2015.

[76] Former senior national security official, interview with the authors, May 8, 2015.

[77] Former senior State Department official, interview with the authors, April 16, 2015.

[78] Former senior State Department official, interview with the authors, June 24, 2015.

[79] Former senior national security official, interview with the authors, September 25, 2015.

[80] Former senior DoD official, interview with the authors, June 4, 2015.

[81] Former senior State Department official, interview with the authors, June 24, 2015.

Iraq since major combat operations began in 2003.[82] According to those in the White House at the time, internal polling showed that support for a troop surge in Iraq hovered at about 18 percent, and one poll even showed that more Americans believed in alien aircraft than believed that a surge would work.[83] Within the military, while a handful of general officers—such as then–Lieutenant General Odierno—supported the Surge, many in the military hierarchy opposed it for various reasons.[84] On the civilian side, there was equally little appetite for doubling down on Iraq. According to a former senior State Department official, the State Department and much of the intelligence community also were largely opposed, either because they thought it would not work or because it restricted the United States' ability to respond to other contingencies outside Iraq, if they arose.[85] To overcome the internal opposition to the Surge, the NSC turned to outside experts to help bolster the case for the policy shift.

In this respect, the insider narrative intersects with the outsider narrative, while the narrative from some others focuses on what they said to President Bush when they were in the room with him, the NSC-centric narrative focuses on the NSC's role in controlling which outside experts had face time with the President. Peter Feaver, who served on the NSC as Special Adviser for Strategic Planning and Institutional Reform from 2005 to 2007, recalled how the NSC stacked the deck in a June 2006 meeting with the President on Iraq strategy.[86] Knowing that the future of Iraq strategy would be discussed during the meeting, Feaver invited Kagan of AEI to begin discussing the Surge with Bush and Michael Vickers from the Center for Budgetary and Strategic Assessments to lay out the opposing view, which focused more on special operations than conventional troops. To help tilt the balance in favor of the Surge, Feaver also invited Cohen, who also was leaning in the direction of the Surge.[87]

Ultimately, this narrative portrays the decision to surge as primarily an insiders' game and a testament to a combination of analysis by the NSC backed by political courage on the part of President Bush. A former senior national security official who served on the NSC argued:

> Khalilzad opposed the Surge. Zelikow, Satterfield, and everyone in the system opposed the Surge. No one at DoD supported the Surge except for Odierno, but that was late in the game. Petraeus also joined the conversation late. The Keane stuff was useful, but it was outside-in. The NSC wrote Bush a memo every night outlining the flaws in the strategy. This became the nucleus of the Surge. These

---

[82] "U.S. Death Toll in Iraq Passes 3,000," *USA Today*, January 1, 2007.

[83] Former senior national security official, interview with the authors, September 25, 2015.

[84] Former senior DoD official, interview with the authors, June 4, 2015.

[85] Former senior State Department official, interview with the authors, June 24, 2015.

[86] Kaplan, 2013, p. 200.

[87] Former senior national security official, interview with the authors, May 8, 2015.

memos questioned the force ratios needed, whether those ratios were available, the underlying assumptions, and, given all this, why this could work. The NSC could show analytically that any time the military had applied force and staying power, the situation had improved.[88]

Secretary of State Rice, who initially opposed the Surge, agreed and emphasized that if people are worried about their security, political development will not be a priority for them.[89] On the one hand, Rice's point about security before politics seems basic, but it marks a break from the strategic thinking that dominated Iraq policy during an earlier period—where solving Iraq's political schisms was seen as the key to stabilizing its security problems. Ultimately, the White House—and Bush himself—needed to reverse the causality inherent in the strategy.

Civilians and the Surge

Although the decision to implement the Surge was dominated largely by civilians, the responsibility to do so fell largely to the military. While Bush closely monitored the situation in Iraq, he mostly stayed out of the tactical discussions. As Secretary of Defense Gates recounted,

> I would say that 98% of those calls were either the Commander giving the President the situation report or me, or having some dialogue about some political problem in Baghdad or Washington that the Commander, the President or I were discussing with each other. I don't think I ever heard either Bush or Obama give a tactical direction or question a tactical decision that had been made in the field.[90]

For the most part, the same was true with lower-level members of the administration. Civilians did play a role in implementing the Surge, but they mainly played around the edges.

Implementing the Surge in Washington

There were at least two areas in which Washington played some role in implementing the Surge. First, as mentioned before, Bush and other senior members of the cabinet directly interfaced with their Iraqi counterparts. From accounts of those who were in the White House at the time, Bush's increasing focus on Iraq was readily apparent, especially in the latter two years of his presidency. Lieutenant General Lute, who

---

[88] Former senior national security official, interview with the authors, September 25, 2015.

[89] Condoleezza Rice, interview with Jason Awadi and Jeanne Godfroy, U.S. Department of State, Office of the Historian, July 12, 2014, p. 12, transcript provided to RAND by the OIF Study Group.

[90] Robert Gates, interview, July 21, 2014, p. 5, transcript provided to RAND by the OIF Study Group.

served as the Deputy National Security Adviser for Iraq and Afghanistan, recounted, "For the last 19 months of that I was in the Bush Administration every weekday morning at 7:00, I was to be sitting outside President Bush's Office, he would come in, throw his hat on the coat rack and say, 'Lute,' and I would go in there and update him on the last 24 hours."[91] Every Monday morning, Bush chaired a full NSC meeting on Iraq at 9 a.m., with all the principals present and Ambassador Ryan Crocker and General Petraeus attending via video or teleconference. Afterward, he talked directly to Prime Minister Maliki. As Lute recounted, "Every Monday it is also the first topic he addresses for that week. He is sending a very clear signal about the primacy of this issue for his Administration."[92]

According to a former senior State Department official, these relationships were "helpful and absolutely critical for Iraqi leaders to feel they had a direct connection to American leaders. It was vital for the political progress that was made."[93] In particular, Bush's own interaction with Maliki, according to the official we spoke with, helped give Maliki the confidence to lead, which he otherwise would not have had.[94]

Second and equally important, civilians in Washington provided political top cover to allow the Surge to work. The Republicans lost the November 2006 elections, thanks partially, if not primarily, to mounting opposition to the Iraq War. With mounting congressional opposition, the Bush administration needed to retain enough votes to keep the wars funded. The effort consumed key cabinet members. A former senior DoD official said that he spent his days during the Surge preoccupied with the "Washington battle," trying to prevent congressional opponents from "kill[ing] this baby in the cradle."[95] Indeed, many of Robert Gates's calls with senior field commanders—Generals Petraeus, Odierno, and, later, Lloyd Austin—were less about Gates giving tactical direction and more about Gates gaining situational awareness to communicate effectively with Capitol Hill.[96] The effort consumed even lower-profile administration officials. As one former senior national security official recalled, after the Surge decision, "my focus shifted primarily to the political side of the Surge, holding together the [Republican] votes on the hill to keep the Surge alive."[97] Even so, Congress came close to defunding the war during the summer of 2007 and barely was convinced to hold off

---

[91] Douglas Lute, interview with Mathew Wharton, undated, p. 11, transcript provided to RAND by the OIF Study Group.

[92] Douglas Lute, interview with Mathew Wharton, undated, p. 12, transcript provided to RAND by the OIF Study Group.

[93] Former senior State Department official, interview with the authors, April 16, 2015.

[94] Former senior State Department official, interview with the authors, April 16, 2015.

[95] Former senior DoD official, interview with the authors, June 4, 2015.

[96] Robert Gates, interview, July 21, 2014, p. 2, transcript provided to RAND by the OIF Study Group.

[97] Former senior national security official, interview with the authors, May 8, 2015.

a decision until September, when Crocker and Petraeus could return to Washington to testify on the effect of the Surge.[98]

Implementing the Surge in the Field

Civilians also played a modest role in implementing the Surge in Baghdad. Much to the anger of some in the military, there was no equivalent civilian surge, for many reasons—starting with a lack of capacity. Condoleezza Rice acknowledged that the State Department was limited in the number of Foreign Service officers it could send to Iraq.[99] A similar story plays out in the intelligence world as well. Although the exact number of officers in Iraq remains classified, a former senior national security official noted that he did not push operatives into Iraq during the Surge, because the agency had already maxed out its commitment, given its other demands at the time.[100]

Moreover, there is an active debate about the utility of a civilian surge. Unlike the military—in which an increase in soldiers can readily translate into direct improvements over the control of larger areas—more diplomats do not necessarily yield more agreements, and more operatives do not necessarily yield better intelligence. According to some senior diplomats, the military logic that the quantity of personnel and funds committed to a task equated to the quality of outcomes was challenged by many in the civilian government. For example, a former senior State Department official remarked, "Secretary Rice felt pressure to effect a 'civilian surge,' aware that everything possible needed to be done to avoid the charge that 'the military won the war; then civilians lost it.'"[101]

Even if the civilians did not surge along with their military counterparts, they still played an important role in the operations. Crocker led political efforts in Baghdad, while PRTs—teams established in 2006 and led by Foreign Service officers—focused on political and economic development in the field.[102] On the direct action front, the close integration of CIA and other intelligence officers with the special operations community began to pay dividends, with special operations raids increasing dramatically throughout the Surge.[103] At the end of the day, though, the Surge was predominantly a military-led effort. As Rice concluded, "When you are at war, the Pentagon or the Defense Department or the Ministry of Defense in any country has the lead. That's just the nature of the business."[104]

---

[98] Robert Gates, interview, July 21, 2014, p. 2, transcript provided to RAND by the OIF Study Group.

[99] Condoleezza Rice, interview with Jason Awadi and Jeanne Godfroy, U.S. Department of State, Office of the Historian, July 12, 2014, p. 10, transcript provided to RAND by the OIF Study Group.

[100] Former senior national security official, interview with the authors, April 13, 2015.

[101] Former senior State Department official, interview with the authors, June 24, 2015.

[102] Former senior national security official, interview with the authors, May 21, 2015.

[103] Former senior national security official, interview with the authors, April 13, 2015.

[104] Condoleezza Rice, interview with Jason Awadi and Jeanne Godfroy, U.S. Department of State, Office of the Historian, July 12, 2014, p. 9, transcript provided to RAND by the OIF Study Group.

Iraqi Security Forces Through 2008

By the time Petraeus took command of MNF-I in February 2007, MNSTC-I had grown exponentially in size and scope. From its humble beginnings with one two-star general and five officers on loan from CENTCOM, MNSTC-I had evolved to an organization of considerable size, with 13 general officers and ten directorates responsible for training more than a dozen units of the ISF.[105] As with all headquarters, the command had developed to meet the demands of the mission, subsequently growing in scale and scope.

The ISF training mission underwent substantial changes during the war's early years, with responsibility for the mission moving from CPA to military control. The creation of MNSTC-I in 2004, under then–Major General Petraeus, ushered in additional changes to the mission and elevated the organization to a multinational command that was staffed with U.S. personnel from all U.S. services, NATO countries, and other coalition partners. The programs had expanded from primarily training Iraqi MOD and MOI forces to include additional Iraqi forces in the intelligence community, Joint Headquarters, Air Force and Navy teams, special counterterrorism units, and a directorate of security assistance responsible for helping the ministries and Joint Headquarters use the U.S. Foreign Military Sales program.[106] The commander of MNSTC-I also commanded the NATO Training Mission–Iraq and was responsible for its efforts to train ISF as well.

Additionally, new U.S. institutions were created to address gaps in the training and preparation of U.S. forces deploying to Iraq. As noted earlier, the counterinsurgency academy was fashioned at Camp Taji to teach an advanced course to the leadership of units rotating into Iraq. The Phoenix Academy was also created to augment the training of U.S. adviser forces, intended to provide specific training for adviser teams before they partnered with their ISF units. Concurrently, the U.S. institutions in the United States were morphing to cope with increased demand for adviser teams in Iraq. The U.S. Army's training location had changed multiple times, landing at Fort Riley by 2006; the Army had given the training adviser mission to the 1st Infantry Division, which modified an entire BCT to train advisers for Iraq more effectively.

During the summer and fall of 2006, as the debate raged in Washington about the benefits and drawbacks of a new Surge strategy, the American military continued to shoulder the responsibility for security in Iraq. The mounting violence and increasing death toll clearly signaled the inability of the ISF to secure Baghdad and the surrounding areas. By 2007, as the first of the new Surge brigades began to filter into Iraq,

---

[105] Former senior military commander, interview with the authors, April 4, 2015; and former senior military commander, interview with the authors, April 7, 2015.

[106] James M. Dubik, *Building Security Forces and Ministerial Capacity: Iraq as a Primer*, Washington, D.C.: Institute for the Study of War, August 2009, p. 17.

new plans were being formed to pacify Baghdad and the surrounding belts. To augment the new U.S. brigades rotating into Iraq, MNSTC-I had to increase the training of the ISF to create additional forces for the coming offensive.

However, the total number of ISF soldiers, police, and other personnel needed to support the Surge was unknown. LTG James M. Dubik, commander of MNSTC-I from June 2007 to July 2008, began to reexamine the end-strength numbers by using a set of planning factors received from MNF-I. He asked for inputs from senior U.S. and Iraqi officials, including Lieutenant General Odierno (the MNC-I commander), the Minister of Interior, the Minister of Defense, and the Chairman of the Iraqi Joint Forces. Dubik received several estimates, including one from the Center for Army Analysis, which all said that between 600,000 and 650,000 ISF personnel would be needed to maintain security.

As he began to prepare for his mission as commanding general, Dubik thought deeply about the Surge strategy; how it would affect the ISF; and, more generally, security operations in Iraq. Ultimately, the Surge was not just about an increase in U.S. and Iraqi forces but a combination of things: "The Surge was first an intellectual Surge. Second, it was physical, with on-the-ground soldiers. Third, it was a Surge of Iraqi Army forces. Fourth, it was a diplomatic and political Surge, stopping the foreign fighters and working to improve the quality of Iraqi political decisions. Fifth, it was economic and development."[107] The Surge would therefore entail an increase in the raw numbers of ISF fighters and a renewed focus of effort in the diplomatic, political, and economic realms.

The training of the ISF during this period was to be one of the contributing elements to the success of the Surge, and many overlook the huge growth in personnel trained. Most of these new forces were assigned to newly created Iraqi security units in an effort to complement the additional five coalition Surge brigades. However, the creation of these forces was fraught with challenges and complexities. While MNSTC-I did ramp up its efforts to raise the number of ready personnel during this period, many of the additional security elements were hastily trained, sometimes were without proper equipment, and suffered from a continual lack of leadership. Additionally, some of the forces that made the largest contributions to security came from outside the Iraqi government's control. By 2008, the Sons of Iraq program had more than 98,000 volunteers, coming largely from Sunni tribes, which were securing areas and actively operating with coalition forces. As additional combat forces were put into action against al Qaeda in Iraq, the dynamic between the U.S. forces and the ISF continued to morph. But what remained was the long-term question about security: Was it to last?

---

[107] Former senior military commander, interview with the authors, April 7, 2015.

Creating an Enterprise in Security Force Assistance—Changing MNSTC-I

When General Petraeus arrived to take command of MNF-I, GEN Martin Dempsey was in the final few months of his tenure as the commander of MNSTC-I. During his time at the command, Dempsey viewed his primary remit as standing up indigenous forces to enable the United States to leave Iraq. This strategy was premised on the realization that the U.S. exit plan was principally built on developing the ISF. Toward this effort, he oversaw a number of new institutional initiatives and reorganizations. One of these included working to develop Iraqi military leadership. General Dempsey was particularly concerned that even if the ISF were well trained at the lower level, the success of the entire operation would be at risk if there was no companion leadership development at higher echelons. He therefore moved to begin a leadership development pillar as a central component to the training command. According to Dempsey, this line of operation

> was kind of ministerial reform, which I suppose we would call security sector reform in doctrinal terms. That was trying to develop the leaders in the Ministry of Defense to be able to provide the functions that a ministry has to provide, whether that is pay and allowances, promotions or retirements, the life cycle of human capital, or how to prepare and execute a budget.[108]

This initiative notwithstanding, leadership remained a constant issue for the ISF.

Dempsey also oversaw the implementation of a new education and training system. The education system that MNSTC-I set up during this period largely mirrored the systems in the United States. This pursuit included the construction of a training center near Baghdad for the continued use and rotation of Iraqi units. There was also a military academy, basic training, and an officer candidate school. A command and general staff college and war college were erected as well. While these institutions were rudimentary, they were established with the intention of laying the foundations for further development of credible, identifiable military and police forces.[109] However, the supporting structures of intelligence, logistics, and planning were still largely lacking at this time because basic fighting teams could be trained much faster than logistical and support units. This was primarily because the majority of the infantry units deployed for training purposes were more capable at teaching basic soldier skills than such skills as all-source analysis, targeting, planning, and logistics.

---

[108] Martin Dempsey, interview with Lynne Chandler Garcia, Contemporary Operations Study Team, Combat Studies Institute, June 10, 2008, p. 4, transcript provided to RAND by the OIF Study Group.

[109] Martin Dempsey, interview with Lynne Chandler Garcia, Contemporary Operations Study Team, Combat Studies Institute, June 10, 2008, p. 5, transcript provided to RAND by the OIF Study Group.

As emphasized, the Surge period represented not only an increase in U.S. military personnel but also a surge in Iraqi forces. Consequently, MNSTC-I expanded its training efforts away from the centralized system it had employed up to that time. Prior to the Surge, all of the training of Iraqi forces occurred in or around Baghdad. Subsequent to the Surge, Dempsey's command established a training center in the north, south, east, and west of Iraq. The aim was strictly to increase throughput. As General Dempsey reflected in 2008,

> Now, I will tell you that [it] worked, meaning we got more soldiers through quicker; but, one of the lessons of this conflict and in the building of security forces is you can't grow leaders on that pace. You can't crank leaders out the way you crank out riflemen. So, I would suggest that it succeeded; but, there was risk and there were instances where the leadership failures that accrued later were a direct result of us pushing these units through on that pace. There is a fine balance to be struck there.[110]

The initiative to raise output levels continued under MNSTC-I's next commander, Lieutenant General Dubik, who pushed to raise the total end strength of trained Iraqi Army, Iraqi Police, MOI, MOD, and other ISF personnel from 390,000—which was the stated number to be trained by the coalition at the time—to 600,000. Fortunately, the commander was able to rework the budget to accommodate the increase in numbers without requesting additional funds.[111] But this dramatic uptick in raw numbers was not the only alteration Dubik pushed for and oversaw. Under his leadership, MNSTC-I again underwent immense organizational changes.

Having six months to prepare for the MNSTC-I commanding general position, Dubik hand-picked individuals to form the core elements of his team. He brought with him to Iraq his chief of staff and command sergeant major from his prior command at 1st Corps.[112] The lieutenant general's new command was ad hoc in nature and had a mix of foreign and U.S. personnel from various services. This composition of personnel brought with it challenges different from a fixed headquarters (whose personnel train and deploy together) and led to idiosyncrasies within the command.

Additional issues with contractors and personnel caused even more headaches. The organization had changed and improved significantly from the CMATT days of General Eaton, but new problems with the proper placement and use of people had emerged. Lieutenant General Dubik constantly fielded replacements for positions that were no longer needed or were even obsolete. Time and energy were therefore spent reorienting individuals rotating into the command toward jobs that required filling.

---

[110] Martin Dempsey, interview with Lynne Chandler Garcia, Contemporary Operations Study Team, Combat Studies Institute, June 10, 2008, p. 8, transcript provided to RAND by the OIF Study Group.

[111] Former senior military commander, interview with the authors, April 7, 2015.

[112] Former senior military commander, interview with the authors, April 7, 2015.

Contractors, however, presented no easy fix to this problem because they could not shift as the mission shifted in the same way that military personnel did. At one point, it took Dubik eight months to change a Dyncorp contract that was inhibiting progress.[113] Volunteers from foreign nations also presented a staffing problem because they primarily sought adviser positions to MOD or MOI, but some felt that the command suffered from a surplus of MOD and MOI advisers. Lieutenant General Dubik ultimately cut MNSTC-I staff by about 10 or 15 percent and refocused the effort with the ministries to include only specific functional areas in MOD and MOI that required the most assistance.[114]

It would be difficult to overstate the organizational changes taking place in MNSTC-I during this period, and the organization ultimately received a complete overhaul. A March 2008 DoD report to Congress offers a sense of the vast scope and reach of the restructuring:

> In order to align its structure more effectively to support building MoD and MoI capacity in these key institutional functions, MNSTC-I reorganized—effective January 1, 2008—into the following directorates and teams: a Directorate of Defense Affairs (DDA), a Directorate of Interior Affairs (DoIA), an Intelligence Transition Team, an Iraqi National Counter Terror Force (INCTF) Transition Team and a Functional Capabilities Directorate. The DDA is led by a U.S. Air Force Brigadier General and advises the MoD and the Joint Headquarters (JHQ) through the MoD and JHQ Advisory Teams (formerly known as transition teams). It also advises the military services through the Coalition Army Advisory Training Team (CAATT, formerly CMATT), the Coalition Air Force Transition Team (CAFTT) and the Maritime Strategic Transition Team (MaSTT). The DoIA is commanded by a U.S. Army Major General who advises the MoI and its associated police forces. The Intelligence Transition Team (INT-TT) is led by a Senior Executive Service-level DoD civilian intelligence professional. It advises the key intelligence organizations within the security ministries—the MoD Directorate General for Intelligence and Security (DGIS) and the JHQ Intelligence Directorate (JHQ M2)—as well as the MoI National Information and Investigation Agency (NIIA). The INCTF-TT is led by a U.S. Navy Rear Admiral who advises the Counter-Terrorism Bureau (CTB) and Command (CTC), as well as Iraqi special operations forces. The DDA, the DoIA, the INT-TT and the INCTF-TT focus on building valued relationships with key security ministry personnel, and on-site training and advisory support to their Iraqi counterparts. The new Functional Capabilities Directorate focuses on developing Iraqi capacity and providing subject-matter expertise to both security ministries in the developing areas of

---

[113] Former senior military commander, interview with the authors, April 7, 2015.

[114] Former senior military commander, interview with the authors, April 7, 2015.

force management, personnel acquisition and management, materiel acquisition, resource management, sustainment, training and development.[115]

DoD was apparently impressed with the changes. On account of these initiatives, MNSTC-I would win DoD managers' Internal Control Program's "Most Improved Process Award," sponsored by the Deputy Secretary of Defense.[116]

By the time that LTG Frank Helmick took over the command in July 2008, even with all of the improved processes, MNSTC-I was still large and unwieldy. And its mandate was similarly expansive: to train 600,000 ISF personnel. By this time, MNSTC-I had evolved into a fully joint and NATO command comprising individuals from several countries, as well as civilians from various U.S. departments and agencies. A former senior military commander noted that there were so many different people within the organization that he relied on colonels to manage things. And yet 25 percent of MNSTC-I staff was turning over each month.[117] The constant and steady loss of staff was a problem. Since its relatively unambitious beginning in mid-2003 as CMATT, MNSTC-I grew into a military structure of giant proportion.

Increased Training Efforts

Concurrent with the organizational restructuring at MNSTC-I during the Surge period, efforts to significantly step up ISF capacity and training efforts were under way. The focus was in the following four major areas:

- Develop ministerial capacity.
- Improve the proficiency of military and police forces through the assistance of embedded advisers and partnered relationships.
- Build logistic, sustainment, and training capacity for MOD and MOI.
- Support the Iraqi Army and the creation of a National Police brigade at Samarra through the Prime Minister's Initiative.[118]

Unfortunately, efforts to build Iraqi institutional capacity across these four areas continued to lag. On the ministerial front, little in the way of guidance flowed from MOD, and individual service plans, contingency plans, a National Military Strategy, or the development of integrated capability lists for force development were all absent.

---

[115] DoD, 2008a, p. 33.

[116] DoD, 2008a, p. 33.

[117] Former senior military commander, interview with the authors, August 7, 2015.

[118] DoD, *Measuring Stability and Security in Iraq*, Washington, D.C., September 2007b, pp. 29–30. The prime minister created a special initiative designed to provide additional security to the al-Askari Mosque in Samarra that was bombed in 2006.

Regarding logistics, even with the focus on building ISF logistical capability, the sustainment, procurement, and delivery of military material remained extremely limited throughout this period. Often, items needed at battalions and brigades would be stored at nearby Iraqi Army depots, but the Iraqi units had no way of accessing them.

Efforts to support the Iraqi Army during this period were also changing. MNF-I made a decision that more ISF troops would be necessary to secure Iraq. As a result, by late 2006, the Iraqi Army had grown to approximately 138,000 soldiers, amounting to an end-strength growth of 30 percent from the previous year.[119] The effort was continued into 2007 when trained Iraqi Army personnel reached 194,233 soldiers.[120] Training continued to be streamlined across installations, and the training cycle from new recruitment to the field was 12 weeks. This condensed timeline—implemented to meet the growing demand for operational forces—stressed the rapid development of Iraqi forces. Consequently, units that were barely capable of the most rudimentary tasks were being placed in the operational force, suffered from discipline and leadership issues, and often lacked proper equipment.

These issues often confronted the advisory teams that were paired up with newly trained units. At the tactical level, ISF leadership continued to develop through close personal relationships with coalition forces. A former military commander who stood up a Military Transition Team noted that by this time, the ISF leadership was out in the population engaging locals.[121] Although additional capabilities were growing—such as additional police academies and military training centers—there was still a significant shortfall in the numbers of officers and NCOs needed. In 2008, a Special Inspector General for Iraq Reconstruction report found that the shortfall in officers would take more than a decade to eliminate because officers had to be promoted from within.[122] While leaders in the ISF continued to develop at the tactical level, there was still a lack of strategic guidance emanating from MOD and MOI.

As additional ISF battalions and brigades were generated, additional command structures were needed to control their movements and actions. The Baghdad Operations Center was one entity created to manage these new units. Although many of these newly created commands were ineffective, the Baghdad Operations Center had some achievements, successfully coordinating operations and conducting joint rehearsals with U.S. forces. The United States was limited in the intelligence that it could share with the Iraqis about targets, but the planning and operations that were jointly conducted with the ISF greatly helped the Iraqi forces to grow and become more con-

---

[119] DoD, *Measuring Stability and Security in Iraq*, Washington, D.C., November 2006b, p. 31.

[120] DoD, 2006b, p. 31.

[121] Former military commander, interview with the authors, May 18, 2015.

[122] DoD, 2008a, p. 32. See also DoD, 2007b, p. 31; and Anthony H. Cordesman and Adam Mansner, *Iraqi Force Development: Conditions for Success, Consequences of Failure*, Washington, D.C.: Center for Strategic and International Studies, September 2007.

fident.[123] While success was being observed at the Baghdad Operations Center, other operational commands were viewed with suspicion because their mandate and reporting chain was through MOD directly to the prime minister's office. For Sunnis in particular, this caused concern because the commands were seen as pro-Shiite rather than as serving the national interest and falling in normal military channels.[124]

The lack of institutional capacity for informed decisionmaking continued to be problematic and remained a focus of MNSTC-I throughout this period.[125] Advisers with the headquarters elements of the ISF, including teams embedded with the Iraqi Ground Forces Command and the Iraqi Joint Forces Command, often had different challenges than advisers at lower echelons of command. At these levels, there were more bureaucratic hurdles to overcome after the creation of advanced administrative processes, something common in most militaries but particularly difficult to implement in Iraq.

By the time that all five U.S. Surge BCTs, two Marine battalions, the Marine Expeditionary Unit, an Australian battle group, the Georgian brigade, and the Polish contingent left Iraq in October 2008, the numbers of Iraqi forces trained had grown significantly.[126] The coalition had trained more than 531,000 Iraqi MOD, MOI, and Counter Terrorism Bureau security personnel, and the total assigned strength of the ISF numbered nearly 600,000.[127] The quantity of ISF personnel employed had grown dramatically, although quality remained uncertain, especially considering the speed with which most of the forces were put through their training.

Problems with MOI—Police, Corruption, and Security

In addition to training MOD forces, MNSTC-I spearheaded efforts to bring the oversight and training of Iraqi Police into its remit. Alarmed by the rate at which Iraqi Police stations and officers were targets of violence, General Dempsey sought to bring them under MNSTC-I early in his tenure. And over time, the responsibility for training the Iraqi Police eventually shifted to MNSTC-I and away from the Bureau of International Narcotics and Law Enforcement in the State Department. According to a former senior military commander, the intent was to train the Iraqi Police first to survive, and then to do their job. The aim also was to deal with the widespread problem of corruption. A 2008 report by the United States Institute of Peace sums up this process: In April 2006, MNSTC-I persuaded MOI to combine all of the police

---

[123] Former military commander, interview with the authors, May 18, 2015.

[124] Cordesman and Mansner, 2007, p. 20.

[125] DoD, 2007a, p. 29.

[126] DoD, 2008b.

[127] DoD, 2008b.

commando units into a single organization—the Iraq National Police. In October, the U.S. military began a purge of National Police units that were involved in sectarian violence, arresting their leaders and subjecting the rank and file to vetting and training ("re-bluing") in civilian police skills.[128]

But oversight of the police eventually entailed bringing MOI into the fold of MNSTC-I. In fact, it was General Dempsey who, in October 2005, asked for responsibility for developing MOI capabilities. Similar to its relationship with MOD, MNSTC-I assumed responsibility for building up the new institution from individual policemen on the ground through the Minister of Interior. And if MOD was a large and cumbersome institution, MOI was larger still. Iraq's MOI was intended to provide policy guidance, training, and administrative support for Iraq's four civilian security services: the Iraqi Police service at the provincial level; the Iraq National Police in Baghdad and other cities; the Iraqi Border Enforcement Service along Iraq's long borders with Iran, Syria, and Turkey; and the Facilities Protection Services used for guarding government ministries. It would be difficult to overstate the expanse of MOI's responsibility. In support of its vast functional areas, MOI was extensively staffed; in 2008, it included a force of nearly half a million people. This was roughly triple the size of the combined Iraqi armed forces. It also subsumed responsibility for various civil functions, including passport control, immigration, and regulation of the private sector.[129]

In December 2006, MNSTC-I announced that it met the target of training and equipping 187,800 police and border patrol personnel. But problems persisted. For instance, there was little accountability—on the part of the U.S. military or MOI—for the actual number of trainees entering the police force or the number of police officers serving in various cities. There was similarly little to no tracking of uniforms, weapons, and equipment issued from training centers. Many of these items are purported to have ended up on the black market. Worse still, MOI exercised little oversight of hiring practices by the police chiefs it hired. Shia militia exerted undue influence over all aspects of MOI's operations. The ministry was also marred by widespread corruption and, according to the U.S. Institute of Peace, suffered severe shortfalls in planning, program management, personnel, procurement, logistics, communication, and maintenance.[130]

The coalition forces were mostly, if not wholly, incapable of preventing the increased politicization of MOI. At the end of 2006, on direct orders from Maliki, MOI took control over an estimated 150,000 members of the Facilities Protection Services responsible for guarding ministries, public buildings, and essential infrastructure

---

[128] Robert M. Perito, "Iraq's Interior Ministry: Frustrating Reform," USIPeace Briefing, Washington, D.C.: United States Institute of Peace, May 2008, p. 3.

[129] Perito, 2008.

[130] These issues are all presented in Perito, 2008.

in Iraq. Prime Minister Maliki's aim may have been to reign in the influence of local political elements, but MOI's ability to discharge this order was questionable:

> The political parties that controlled the various government ministries had been allowed to recruit security units that were armed and issued badges and police-style uniforms. These private armies were a source of patronage jobs and a means of funding militia groups. The prime minister ordered MOI to supervise, downsize and retrain the [Facilities Protection Services]. This task was clearly beyond the capacity of an institution that already was overwhelmed by its existing responsibilities for nearly 200,000 employees and police personnel.[131]

Relations between the Iraqi Army and Iraqi Police were also tense. Cooperation and coordination between units was spotty, tending to vary by locale. By 2008, the operational commands that were in control of Iraqi Army units were given the additional responsibility to coordinate with MOI security forces. While intended to facilitate coordination between the Iraqi Army and National Police, a report by the Center for Strategic and International Studies found that cooperation remained poor and that the commands themselves were seen as very sectarian and not in service of the Iraqi national interest.[132] The Iraqi Army tended to view the Iraqi Police as unprofessional and corrupt. This was a further source of division. According to a former senior military commander, the Iraqi Army sought to avoid being tainted and corrupted by MOI and saw itself as the "savior of Iraq"; the police represented a necessary inconvenience on the street.[133] The Iraqi Police, on the other hand, often viewed the Iraqi Army as ungrateful and arrogant. "They do not respect us. They think they know everything," a young Iraqi Police officer from Rawah stated.[134] There were even reported disconnects within the Iraqi Police forces between those officers active in the counterinsurgency fight and those operating in a more secure setting.[135]

But a former senior military commander we spoke with came to appreciate that the U.S. military could not root out the vice and graft that was endemic to such a large bureaucratic and traditionally authoritarian institution with a history of patronage. In fact, he came to rue the day that he asked to be in charge of Iraqi police forces: "Police live at the point of corruption. . . . When you take a policeman and station him at a particular street corner in Ramadi or Tikrit, that's the point of corruption. Iraqi society has always been corrupt and it didn't take long to restore old habits."[136]

---

[131] Perito, 2008, p. 4.

[132] Cordesman and Mansner, 2007.

[133] Former senior military commander, interview with the authors, May 13, 2015.

[134] Cordesman and Mansner, 2007.

[135] Former senior military commander, interview with the authors, April 7, 2015.

[136] Former senior military commander, interview with the authors, May 13, 2015.

Adviser Teams—Did the United States Get It Right?

With the training centers operating at full capacity to achieve the desired end-strength goals, the adviser teams were hard pressed to partner with every unit that needed an adviser. Of the adviser teams that were partnered with the ISF, most were unprepared for the influx of relatively poorly trained Iraqi soldiers. Many of the Iraqi units were not ready for combat and could function effectively only when partnered with U.S. forces. By September 2007, there were more than 6,000 advisers in Iraq organized across more than 500 adviser teams, embedded across multiple levels of command.[137] Even with this supply of advisers, the demand was greater still. Additional advisers had to be found, and several options were considered, including using private contractors.[138]

Ultimately, the decision was made to augment the advisory capability from units already in theater. These units would have to form more teams from within their existing organizational structure. There was a twofold reason for this. First, finding personnel to go through the advisory training at Fort Riley and, later, Fort Polk was becoming increasingly difficult. The military was severely short of company-level officers and mid- to senior-level NCOs, who filled the majority of adviser team positions. Second, as the effort shifted away from direct combat operations to training the ISF to take the security lead, U.S. brigades could afford to dedicate more personnel to the advisory effort. This had an added benefit of increasing U.S. unity of command. When the adviser teams came from a brigade, there was an increased feeling of ownership by the brigade, which, in turn, facilitated communication and support to those teams.[139] Therefore, by 2007 and 2008, as more adviser teams were established, the ISF was receiving increased levels of training and support.[140]

However, this was not the first effort to increase the operational effectiveness of the ISF, nor was it the first time that U.S. commanders had tried to delineate the convoluted chain of command for adviser teams. In the summer of 2006, the IAG, which was assigned administrative control of all externally sourced adviser teams in Iraq, was established. The IAG was a one-star command with a joint support staff under MNC-I, and its primary mission was to provide administrative and logistical support to the adviser teams. Previously, adviser teams assigned to work with ISF elements were assigned to MNSTC-I, which created difficulties for the adviser teams to procure weapons, ammunition, vehicles, and other items necessary to operate effectively as an embedded team with the ISF.[141]

---

[137] DoD, 2007b, p. 30.

[138] Walter Pincus, "U.S. Seeks Contractors to Train Iraqi Military," *Washington Post*, May 4, 2008.

[139] Former military commander, interview with the authors, July 27, 2015.

[140] Former military commander, interview with the authors, July 10, 2015.

[141] Patrick Colloton and Tommy Stoner, "Transition Teams and Operational Integration," *Infantry*, Vol. 95, No. 6, November–December 2006, p. 32.

Throughout this period, the adviser capacity continued to grow, bringing with it additional capabilities for its ISF partners, and much of the success of the Surge should be attributed to the ISF and their embedded advisers. However, with the removal of the advisers, many of the capabilities that U.S. forces brought to operations were lost. And an over-reliance on those U.S. capabilities, combined with an underdevelopment of the quality of the ISF, is often attributed to their performance in the face of a resurgent al Qaeda in Iraq in subsequent years.

Did the Surge Work?

Reviewing Civilian Perspectives

Ultimately, civilian policymakers are divided about whether the Surge worked, and if so, why it did. For some, the Surge worked less because of a new strategy or the additional U.S. forces and more because of the Sunni Awakening.[142] As a former senior State Department official explained, he, Rice, and others who were skeptical of the Surge decision were "wrong but for the right reasons," whereas Bush and the NSC were "right but for the wrong reasons." When the Surge policy was being debated, Washington did not know about the extent of the Sunni "flip" against al Qaeda and the extent to which both Sunni tribes and Shia militias were moving away from attacks on coalition and Iraqi forces. As it happened, "the Surge came at the right time to solidify and sustain what the tribes were doing. The Surge was a critical element of the success that took place in 2007."[143] The former official argued that, had it not been for the shift in position toward al Qaeda and coalition and Iraqi forces, however, the Surge alone would not have been successful.

This same former senior State Department official also offered another, grimmer reason for the Surge's success in reducing levels of sectarian violence in Baghdad—sectarian cleansing. As a result of the large-scale sectarian fighting of 2006, heterogeneous neighborhoods segregated into Sunni and Shia enclaves. As the official explained,

> Baghdad quieted because the mixed neighborhoods had largely been separated under violence and force. Baghdad didn't pose the same challenges of comingling because there was ethnic separation and cleansing. This stabilized—tragically—the city. Because of this separation, Baghdad hasn't returned to sectarian violence to the extent that other parts of Iraq have.[144]

The concrete barriers that U.S. forces laid to cordon off various districts also contributed to this effect.

---

[142] Former official at the U.S. embassy in Baghdad, interview with the authors, May 26, 2015.

[143] Former senior State Department official, interview with the authors, June 24, 2015.

[144] Former senior State Department official, interview with the authors, June 24, 2015.

Others give the Surge a little more credit. One influential foreign expert on Iraq argued that the Surge worked because of a new strategy, although not the kinder, gentler form outlined in the Army's counterinsurgency manual (FM 3-24). To the contrary, he stated that, if anything, Petraeus was more kinetic than his predecessors: "Petraeus was behaving more coercively than a common-view FM 3-24 presupposes, and he was using much more firepower. There is an assumption that 3-24 is about hearts and minds and getting people to like you. The manual doesn't say that, and that's not how Petraeus was operating."[145] One former senior DoD official largely agreed. For him, the change in strategy was more about "getting more aggressive with T-walls [large concrete barriers], going into Sadr City, and stabilizing the areas that were previously Sunni."[146] By controlling access to the city and physically separating the factions, the coalition managed to stop the large-scale killing of civilians and restore some semblance of order to Baghdad.

Still others emphasized the role of American forces. A notable military historian we spoke with argued that prior operations "failed because [Iraqi] Security Forces were not neutral in the fight. Many Iraqi forces were more responsive to Shia militias than they were to the U.S. They used force that accelerated violence. Operations to clear neighborhoods weren't followed by operations to hold them. When they did, they were through sectarian violence." According to this military historian, one of the reasons that the Surge worked was precisely because it acknowledged the limitations of the ISF and injected more "impartial" forces in the simmering ethnic conflict.[147]

Ultimately, the different views on why the Surge worked and the effect it had may depend partially on where one stood at the time. A former senior State Department official perhaps summed it up best:

> We were lucky it came together nicely. One was the progress with the Sunnis and changes in political participation. They had already started ceasefires in Anbar before the Surge. Two, the investment in ISF began to pay off around this time. Three, Maliki was a decisive prime minister and his decisiveness in Basra was important. Four, al Qaeda's overreach and brutality were helpful. The Surge helped bring all this together. We tend to focus on the impact of the Surge because that was how we were most involved. Awakening people would probably say they won the war for Iraq. ISF would say the same.[148]

Given the controversy over the policy at the time, as well as Iraq's complexity, multiple actors can claim credit for the Surge's development and can explain the Surge's success.

---

[145] Foreign policy expert on Iraq, interview with the authors, March 24, 2015.

[146] Former senior DoD official, interview with the authors, June 4, 2015.

[147] Military historian, interview with the authors, May 14, 2015.

[148] Former senior State Department official, interview with the authors, May 18, 2015.

In some ways, the more important question than who deserves credit for the Surge's success is what to learn from it all. Perhaps this is best understood through the lens of the principals involved. For Gates, he understood the Surge to be largely about a change in strategy—away from transitioning to the Iraqis as soon as possible to deploying troops throughout violent areas—but particularly in Baghdad—to stabilize the region and allowing political reconciliation to take hold.[149] Rice learned a similar lesson from the Surge: "I think the Surge of 2007 just demonstrated that, actually, as Steve Hadley said, sometimes a security problem is just a security problem. There was this conceit that if we just solve the political problem, the security problem would solve itself."[150] After years of arguing that political reconciliation was needed to ensure security, the Surge reversed the causality to dramatic effect.

Building Security in Iraq
There can be no denying the effort that went into training the ISF for operations against al Qaeda and the Shia militias. Although the sheer number of ISF trained was astonishing, the lasting effect was dubious. Throughout 2007 and 2008, the ISF was fielding new units every 12 weeks; once they became operational, problems quickly arose. Without continued assistance by adviser teams, many of these new units added to an already overtaxed and underdeveloped logistics and supply system. Many of them were incapable of self-sustainment, movement, or other basic functions without months of additional training and support. All of this raises the question: Would it not have been better to have a smaller, better-trained force?

The training, equipping, and fielding of the ISF during this period included exponential growth of MNSTC-I. That command accomplished many objectives during this period, including expanding institutional training and adviser capacity, downsizing its workforce, and streamlining its focus; it fundamentally shifted its outlook and took on an enterprise approach to building capacity in the security sector. These tasks were addressed while pressure from Washington simultaneously demanded improvements to ISF abilities. The artificial timelines set in Washington did not recognize the complexity of building foreign security forces or reforming the security sector. The realities on the ground in Iraq were that MNSTC-I could train and field small units faster than larger ones, MNSTC-I could produce fighting units faster than logistics units, junior sergeants could be developed faster than senior officers, and Iraqi units could be built faster than ministerial processes could be formed.[151]

At the point when the U.S. Surge culminated and violence in Iraq—particularly in Baghdad and the surrounding areas—significantly decreased, there were more ISF

---

[149] Robert Gates, interview, July 21, 2014, p. 6, transcript provided to RAND by the OIF Study Group.

[150] Condoleezza Rice, interview with Jason Awadi and Jeanne Godfroy, U.S. Department of State, Office of the Historian, July 12, 2014, p. 12, transcript provided to RAND by the OIF Study Group.

[151] Dubik, 2009, p. 8.

personnel in uniform than at any other postinvasion period. This seemed to have established a false sense of confidence in the ISF, incorrectly based on the stand-alone capabilities of the ISF, when considerable recognition should have been given to American soldiers. Not many American commanders, at any level, thought that the ISF could stand on their own without direct supervision.[152]

When it came to training, the ISF did not possess the capability to effectively run individual and collective training at the battalion level and below without direct U.S. oversight and support; and without additional force augmentation, the adviser teams had limited manpower to run this training effort for the ISF. Multi-echelon training could be effectively executed only with the assistance of additional U.S. forces.[153] However, other training opportunities were available for the ISF—including MOD- and MOI-run schools—that were mirrored after the U.S. military education system. These Iraqi institutions included a military academy, basic training facilities, an officer candidate school, and Iraqi equivalents to the U.S. Army Command and General Staff College and various services' war colleges.[154] However, many ISF commanders were reluctant to send their forces to these institutions because there was a pervasive belief that the ministries did not care about the individual ISF personnel. Sustaining forces once they were operational was a point of particular concern because much of the infrastructure to support the new forces was not in place. Summing up the sentiment he heard as he traveled around Iraq as the commander of MNSTC-I in the fall of 2005, General Dempsey stated, "You would hear American counterparts [to the ISF] say, 'Yeah. They fight well; but, their government doesn't care about them. They are not paying them, they are not feeding them, they are not transporting them, they are not providing for them.'"[155]

In addition to these issues, questions emerged about the creation of all these new schools and institutions in such a short, if not forced, period of time. Can such an immature force as the ISF actually require and properly benefit from these training schools? The limited evidence suggests that ambition possibly exceeded the capacity to absorb and instill lessons in a limited time frame. Institutional knowledge—the kind of which these schools are intended to impart—may take years or even decades to develop. The hasty manner in which these schools were erected likely worked against this process of development. This calls into question the wisdom of such an exacting endeavor in so short a time frame.

---

[152] Former military commander, interview with the authors, May 18, 2015.

[153] Colloton and Stoner, 2006, p. 32.

[154] Martin Dempsey, interview with the Contemporary Operations Study Team, Combat Studies Institute, June 10, 2008, p. 5, transcript provided to RAND by the OIF Study Group.

[155] Martin Dempsey, interview with the Contemporary Operations Study Team, Combat Studies Institute, June 10, 2008, p. 10, transcript provided to RAND by the OIF Study Group.

Assessing the Surge—An Endless Debate?

What did the Surge accomplish? Was it the primary factor that led to the significant lowering of violence in Baghdad and in other parts of Iraq by the end of 2007? What role did the new counterinsurgency doctrine, FM 3-24, play? How important was the shift in generalship between Casey and Petraeus? Did strategy and tactics change fundamentally with the Surge from what came before?

The Surge spawned a wide body of literature dedicated to answering these questions.[156] From this collection of literature emerged two primary schools of thought that come down very differently in their interpretive answers to these questions about the Surge. The first school of thought—in this report, the *Surge success school*—argues that there was a fundamental shift in tactics and strategy brought about under the leadership of General Petraeus. Although other conditions on the ground—such as the Anbar Awakening and the Shia militias' decision to stand down attacks—were important, it was ultimately the changes in tactics and operations during the Surge that were the primary cause responsible for lowering violence. According to this line of thought, without the Surge and the new leadership of Petraeus, these other conditions would not have independently effected a significant change in the operational situation. Violence would have remained at high levels, keeping Iraq in a state of chaos. For supporters of the Surge success school, the Surge and Petraeus were fundamentally game-changing factors that put Iraq on the path to peace.

Others, however, questioned the purported direct causative linkage between the Surge and the lowering of violence. This report calls supporters of this idea the *Surge skeptic school*. This school posits that there was not a radical change in tactics and strategy between the Surge and what came before it. Instead, the Surge skeptic school argues that the Surge success school allows for much more continuity than discontinuity and that the levels of ethnic cleansing and separation transpiring within Baghdad had eventually run their course by late 2007. Moreover, in explaining the lower levels of violence attained by the end of 2007, the Surge skeptic school emphasizes the critical importance of the Anbar Awakening and the Shia militias' decision to stand down attacks. While the Surge was certainly an important factor in reducing violence, the Surge skeptic school believes that it was not *the* decisive factor, but rather an interactive component to a broader process. The Surge skeptic school maintains that because of other, more-important conditions on the ground, the absence of General Petraeus and FM 3-24 would not have brought about a different outcome from the one observed with the Surge. In this regard, the new commanding general therefore did not represent a change. Accompanied by the Anbar Awakening and the standing down of the Shia militias, the increase of troops requested by General Casey would have precipitated a similar drop in violence.

---

[156] See, for example, Biddle, Friedman, and Shapiro, 2012; and Feaver, 2011.

From the arguments of these two schools of thought, it is clear that the Surge achieved the following two important effects:

1. Additional BCTs added combat power that used the intelligence provided by the Sunni Awakening to employ kinetic tactical action to reduce and destroy al Qaeda in Iraq.
2. As a result of the reduction of al Qaeda in Iraq, combined with the Shia decision to stand down attacks, the overall levels of violence dropped and the Iraqi people, as a result of this lowered violence, were protected.

Lessons from This Era

This section identifies and describes the lessons learned from the U.S. experience in Baghdad during the Surge.

Both Quantity and Quality Are Necessary When Training Indigenous Forces

There was a dramatic change in the scale and scope of MNSTC-I during this period. Scaling up the effort led to increased output but not necessarily increased capability. MNSTC-I had so many efforts going on that it needed to reorganize, refocus on the mission, and streamline processes.

Furthermore, adviser capacity requires institutional dedication to build and maintain a training force. The institutional U.S. Army dedicated more effort to the adviser mission, subsequently placing more resources, manpower, and effort into the mission.

The Surge Worked Because of Many Factors, Not Simply an Increase in Troops

Many factors contributed to the success of the Surge. Success was likely the result of a confluence of events and changing circumstances. The groundwork had been laid by previous U.S. commanders, ethnic separation had already taken place in many Baghdad neighborhoods, efforts to segregate Sunni and Shia enclaves continued, the Sunnis were revolting against al Qaeda in Iraq, and the additional five U.S. brigades began to arrive.

Sufficient Manpower Is Essential for Effective Counterinsurgency Operations

As the additional five brigades came online, more U.S. forces were on the street providing security, partnering with the ISF, and building relationships. Counterinsurgency cannot be accomplished cheaply. In this case, the successful counterinsurgency came at the cost of straining an already stretched Army by extending deployments to 15 months. Still, sufficient forces are needed to secure the population.

Coupled with the Sunni rejection of al Qaeda in Iraq, more information about al Qaeda's activities began to emerge, increasing successful U.S. targeting efforts.

Consistent Guidance and Support for a "Clear, Hold, Build" Approach Is Necessary

Fardh al Qanoon (the operational plan Petraeus implemented to enforce the law and secure Iraq) was a departure from Operations Together Forward I and II in the degree to which U.S. and Iraqi forces were able to apply maximum amounts of kinetic action against various enemy elements in their respective areas of responsibility. Before this, the consistency and amount of kinetic action with which units executed combat operations against insurgent forces tended to be sporadic and inconsistent. Thus, the additional manpower and firepower applied in innovative ways were an important factor in creating the conditions in Baghdad in which the population was protected.

At the same time, joint U.S. and Iraqi operations were not seamless, but they were more coordinated with the Joint Operations Centers (such as the Baghdad Operations Center).

Without Security, Nation-Building Will Not Succeed

Solving political impasses is not a precursor to delivering security or ceasing hostilities. Based on the Surge experience, the opposite appears more likely the case.

CHAPTER SIX
Withdrawal

On Friday, October 21, 2011, President Obama announced that all American forces would leave Iraq by the year's end. Only 160 soldiers and Marines would remain, mostly to help guard the embassy and manage the American-Iraqi military relationship.[1] The announcement marked an end to years of Status of Forces Agreement (SOFA) negotiations. While some Americans and Iraqis praised the end to the controversial war—in the Shia-dominated Baghdad neighborhood of Sadr City, there was a public celebration of 1,000 people—many on both sides had not predicted this outcome.[2] Indeed, as the *New York Times* summed it up, "Despite difficult talks, the United States and Iraq had expected some American troops to stay."[3] The exact size of the enduring commitment proved fiercely controversial, but most expected that at least 3,000 to 5,000 U.S. soldiers would remain in Iraq for a few years after the war.[4] Interestingly, less than two months before, on August 25, 2011, Iraqi Ambassador to the United States Samir Sumaida'ie remarked, "The principle that there will be some military presence to help train Iraqi military and police has been largely agreed upon," and he suggested that the force would be sizable—between 8,000 and 20,000 American troops largely in a training capacity.[5] Surprising as it was, the President's October 2011 withdrawal announcement laid groundwork for the end—or at least what many thought would be the end—of the Iraq War.

This chapter tells the story of the aftermath of the Surge, how MNF-I transitioned into USF-I, and how the United States withdrew forces from Iraq. The chapter is divided into four sections. The first section focuses on the military story—that is, how American military presence withdrew from the Iraqi cities and then from Iraq

---

[1] Mark Landler, "U.S. Troops to Leave Iraq by Year's End, Obama Says," *New York Times*, October 21, 2011.

[2] Landler, 2011.

[3] Tim Argano and Michael S. Schmidt, "Despite Difficult Talks, U.S. and Iraq Had Expected Some American Troops to Stay," *New York Times*, October 21, 2011.

[4] Argano and Schmidt, 2011.

[5] Josh Rogin, "Iraqi Ambassador: We Will Request U.S. Troop Extension 'in Our Own Sweet Time,'" *Foreign Policy*, August 25, 2011a.

itself between 2009 and the end of 2011. Second, the chapter recounts the frenzied negotiations conducted by civilians to try to keep an American presence in Iraq after 2011. Third, it charts the U.S. withdrawal's effect on the ISF and how those forces grew increasingly politicized after their American advisers left. Lastly, this discussion touches on Iraq's collapse in 2014 and why after eight years of American investments of blood and treasure into Iraq, the Islamic State still managed to capture large swathes of the northern half of the country a mere two years after American forces withdrew.

The Military Story

On June 30, 2009, U.S. combat troops withdrew from Iraq's cities, as stipulated in the 2008 "Agreement Between the United States of America and the Republic of Iraq on the Withdrawal of United States Forces from Iraq and the Organization of Their Activities During Their Temporary Presence in Iraq," which had taken effect at the beginning of 2009, just before Obama was inaugurated.[6] Early in his term, President Obama had laid out his vision for the United States' eventual exit, tracing a two-stage process beginning with the withdrawal of "combat brigades" from Baghdad to bases on the outskirts of the city and ending completely the combat mission in Baghdad by September 2010.[7]

As Iraqis celebrated the withdrawal of American combat troops from Baghdad with parades, fireworks, and a national holiday,[8] U.S. troops took up positions at forward operating bases on the outskirts of Baghdad, having formally transferred responsibility for Baghdad to the ISF.[9] Months before, GEN Raymond T. Odierno had insisted that the new arrangement amounted to a change only in operating environment, rather than a change of mission, and added that in many ways, the agreement only reflected

---

[6] Alissa J. Rubin, "Iraq Marks Withdrawal of U.S. Troops from Cities," *New York Times*, June 30, 2009. To view the agreement, see United States of America and Republic of Iraq, "Agreement Between the United States of America and the Republic of Iraq on the Withdrawal of United States Forces from Iraq and the Organization of Their Activities During Their Temporary Presence in Iraq," status of forces agreement, November 17, 2008.

[7] Barack Obama, "Responsibly Ending the War in Iraq," remarks as prepared for delivery, Camp Lejeune, N.C., February 27, 2009.

[8] Tim Cocks and Muhanad Mohammed, "Iraq Regains Control of Cities as U.S. Pulls Back," Reuters, June 30, 2009.

[9] Rick Brennan, Jr., Charles P. Reis, Larry Hanauer, Ben Connable, Terrence K. Kelly, Michael McNerney, Stephanie Young, Jason Campbell, and K. Scott McMahon, *Ending the U.S. War in Iraq: The Final Transition, Operational Maneuver, and Disestablishment of United States Forces-Iraq*, Santa Monica, Calif: RAND Corporation, RR-232-USFI, 2013, p. 68.

realities that were already in place at the time.[10] Iraq expert Richard Brennan explained the operational implications of the change, noting,

> General Odierno emphasized that the "out of cities" order would require a new mind-set if U.S. forces were to succeed. This meant that military forces could not interpret the order as meaning they should just do less; they needed to do things differently. In discussions with the MNF-I leaders and staff, General Odierno likened the order to the surge in that it was not just a change in number but a change in tactics, techniques, and procedures that had been the key to success. The CG [Commanding General] emphasized that the "out of cities" order would require a similar degree of innovation and would require the collective attention of leaders at all levels of command to implement properly.[11]

One immediate effect of this withdrawal of American combat troops who had been positioned throughout Baghdad in small combat outposts was a decline in the quality and quantity of intelligence that U.S. forces received, because their presence among the Iraqi population diminished. It also soon became clear that approvals by senior Iraqi political leaders for American special operations forces raids against high-value targets were becoming restricted and onerous and added another layer of complexity to the American military's prosecution of its goals.[12]

The withdrawal of American forces from cities also affected the military advising effort. Although some American soldiers remained in limited "joint security stations" to train ISF personnel within the city, the U.S. forces were also limited in what they could do and what help they could provide.[13] American transition teams focused more on "inside-the-wire" tasks (such as intelligence-sharing and staffing of joint operations centers) with fewer "outside-the-wire" missions (such as joint patrolling).[14]

On January 1, 2010, the remaining U.S. forces observed the consolidation of five commands into a single headquarters command—USF-I. Speaking at the ceremony, General Petraeus, then in command of CENTCOM, reflected on the evolution of the tactics and concepts of the conflict and the "important milestone" that the transition represented in the ongoing drawdown of U.S. forces. General Odierno, assuming the new role of commander of USF-I, reiterated America's ongoing commitment to Iraq

---

[10] Fred W. Baker III, "Odierno: Troops Out of Iraqi Cities by Summer," Armed Forces Press Service, U.S. Central Command, December 14, 2008.

[11] Brennan et al., 2013, p. 68.

[12] Brennan et al., 2013, pp. 68–69.

[13] Jane Arraf, "US Troops to Exit Iraq's Cities but New Role Still Evolving," *Christian Science Monitor*, June 29, 2009.

[14] Heath Druzin, "U.S. Forces Introducing Iraqis to High-Tech Tools," *Stars and Stripes*, August 4, 2009.

and praised the contributions of MNF-I, MNC-I, MNSTC-I, and Task Force 134 (Special Operations Command) before their colors were retired.[15]

A major planning effort that the new USF-I had to undertake was the operational plan to move the remaining U.S. forces out of the country over the following year.[16] In conjunction with moving U.S. personnel and equipment out of Iraq, the sequence of transitioning scores of bases across Iraq to the ISF and other Iraqi government agencies had to be planned carefully and in detail. Considering the resulting complexity of nearly seven years of the American occupation during which the United States had established its own institutions alongside the developing Iraqi institutions, the execution of the transition plan was quite challenging indeed.

The wrinkle in this planning effort, of course, was that even though the bulk of U.S. materiel and troops would be withdrawn by the end of 2011, the decision had not been made on whether to keep a small contingent of American troops (around 10,000) on the ground in Baghdad to continue the formal training and advising of the ISF and relatively robust ongoing U.S. special operations raids. So for American military leaders in Iraq, it was a tricky planning and execution problem: Plan either for drawing down to virtually no remaining U.S. troops in place or for keeping 10,000 U.S. troops in place. The leaders handled this uncertainty by coming up with a plan that was "conditions-based" and tied to key presidential decisions. For example, if a political decision to retain the 10,000 American troops had not been made by a certain point, that would trigger further operational actions to remove those troops.[17]

At the same time that USF-I was planning and executing the transition of U.S. materiel and personnel out of Iraq, American special operations forces were still in contact operationally with the enemy in Iraq. Although most of SOCOM had refocused efforts to Afghanistan by 2010, a limited force remained, continuing to have marked tactical success targeting al Qaeda networks throughout the country.[18] Building on the intelligence exploited from the successful cross-border raid against Abu Ghadiya in 2008, the command eventually facilitated the capture of the emir of Baghdad, Manaf Abd al-Rahim al-Rawi, as well as his twin brother. Patient tracking of couriers then

---

[15] Luke Koladish and Kat Briere, "New Command Marks Milestone in Iraq," U.S. Army, January 2, 2010.

[16] For examples of this planning effort, see Walter L. Perry, Stuart E. Johnson, Keith Crane, David C. Gompert, John Gordon IV, Robert E. Hunter, Dalia Dassa Kaye, Terrence K. Kelly, Eric Peltz, and Howard J. Shatz, *Withdrawing from Iraq: Alternative Schedules, Associated Risks, and Mitigating Strategies*, Santa Monica, Calif.: RAND, MG-882-OSD, 2009.

[17] Brennan et al., 2013, pp. 66–67.

[18] Gordon and Trainor, 2012, pp. 620, 621. For a useful discussion of U.S. special operations in Iraq between 2003 and 2008, see Stanley McChrystal, *My Share of the Task: A Memoir*, London: Penguin Books, 2013.

led the forces to Abu Ayyub al-Masri (al Qaeda in Iraq's top country leader), as well as Abu Omar al-Baghdadi (the leader of the Islamic State of Iraq).[19]

Despite this tactical success against Sunni extremist groups, the ability of U.S. forces to target Shia militants effectively was repeatedly undercut by the political constraint put in place by Prime Minister Maliki. Militants from Kataib Hezbollah detained by U.S. and Iraqi forces following raids near the Iranian border on February 11, 2010, were swiftly released upon handover to Iraqi officials, after Maliki threatened to end all high-level special operations forces collaboration if the militants remained in U.S. custody.[20]

By July 2011, there was another upsurge in the use of improvised rocket assisted munitions by Shia fighters operating from Sadr City. First introduced in 2008,[21] this signature weapon of Iran-supported Shia groups had become less prevalent, only to reappear during the withdrawal with enough lethality to make June 2011 the deadliest month for U.S. troops since 2009.[22] The increase in attacks came as Iran sought to dial up pressure ahead of the U.S. drawdown, and Iraqis prepared for an impending shift in the domestic balance of power following full U.S. departure. Maliki's political reliance on Shia leader Muqtada al-Sadr also likely contributed to his reluctance to deal with rising attacks from Shia groups more forcefully.[23]

In the last years before the complete U.S. withdrawal in 2011, Brennan observed a gradually "widening gap between established strategic goals and the means and resources available to achieve them."[24] In addition to being "woefully" underresourced, the new Office of Security Cooperation–Iraq also lacked the requisite authorities to accomplish its mission.[25]

USF-I began the last retrograde of forces from Baghdad in July 2011. At this point, more than 50 bases, nearly 1.8 million pieces of equipment, and more than 100,000 troops and contractors remained in Iraq.[26] Baghdad, of course, had a significant por-

---

[19] Bill Roggio, "Al Qaeda Leader Abu Omar al Baghdadi Confirmed Captured: Prime Minister Maliki," *Long War Journal*, April 27, 2009.

[20] Kataib Hezbollah is an Iraqi Shia extremist group that works at the direction of Tehran and, specifically, Islamic Revolutionary Guards Corps—Quds Force; see Brennan et al., 2013, p. 125. For the Iranian connection, see Gordon and Trainor, 2012, pp. 621–622; and Aref Mohammed, Jack Kimball, and Waleed Ibrahim, "Five Killed as U.S., Iraqi Troops Raid Border Village," Reuters, February 12, 2010. See also Bill Roggio, "Iraqi, US Forces Kill 10 During Clash with Hezbollah Brigades Near the Iranian Border," *Long War Journal*, February 12, 2010.

[21] Bill Roggio, "Mahdi Army Uses 'Flying IEDs' in Baghdad," *Long War Journal*, June 5, 2008.

[22] Spencer Ackerman, "Iraq's Flying Bombs Return," *Wired*, July 5, 2011.

[23] Jane Arraf, "US Military Officials in Iraq Warn of Growing Iranian Threat," *Christian Science Monitor*, July 27, 2011.

[24] Brennan et al., 2013, p. xxxiv.

[25] Brennan et al., 2013, p. xxxiv.

[26] Brennan et al., 2013, p. xxvi.

tion of those numbers. Under cover of intelligence, surveillance, and reconnaissance and air escort, this withdrawal of the U.S. force was led by route-clearing engineers; the northwestern-most units withdrew first, assuming a "strategic reserve mission" upon their safe and orderly crossing into Kuwait.[27] The success of this immensely complex logistical and operational maneuver was particularly impressive given the compressed five-month time frame in which it took place.

On December 18, 2011, the last American convoy of tractor-trucks with Bradley fighting vehicles and their crews mounted on the back crossed the border into Kuwait. In more than a decade of U.S. military operations in Iraq, with a good part of those occurring in Baghdad, 4,475 U.S. service members had died and another 32,227 had been wounded in operations in Iraq. The loss of Iraqi civilian life in Baghdad had been considerably higher. After leaving, many in the military breathed a sigh of relief. Soon after crossing into Kuwait, one of the American soldiers told an American newspaper reporter that he just couldn't "wait to tell his wife and kids that he was safe."[28] Thus, the American occupation of Baghdad had ended with the exit of an American combat soldier.

SOFA: Tried and Failed

While the military withdrew in 2011, civilians in the Department of State and other agencies engaged in a frenzied series of talks to maintain an American military presence in Iraq by negotiating a new SOFA to replace the one signed by President Bush at the end of 2008. Agreements of this type—negotiated between the United States and the host country—provide a legal basis for the continuing presence of American troops in a sovereign foreign country. In the waning days of the Bush administration, the United States concluded an agreement that allowed for continued American presence in Iraq until 2011. In the years that followed, the Obama administration tried but ultimately could not conclude a successor agreement, and as a result, in December 2011, U.S. forces largely left Iraq, keeping a small contingent based out of the American embassy.

Because of the rise of the Islamic State, its occupation of large portions of northern and western Iraq in 2013 and 2014, and the collapse of the Iraqi Army, the SOFA negotiations have become the subject of intense scrutiny and controversy,[29] spawning three major questions: How were the SOFA negotiations conducted? Could the United States have achieved a different outcome had negotiations been conducted differently?

---

[27] Brennan et al., 2013, p. xxvii.

[28] Joseph Logan, "Last U.S. Troops Leave Iraq, Ending War," Reuters, December 18, 2011.

[29] BBC, "What Is 'Islamic State'?" October 8, 2015.

Could a small "stay-behind" force in Baghdad and in the rest of Iraq have prevented what occurred in 2013 and 2014? These three questions are addressed next.

How Were the SOFA Negotiations Conducted?

The 2011 SOFA negotiations have their roots in the 2008 SOFA agreement. On December 14, 2008, President Bush made his fourth and final visit to Iraq as commander-in-chief. While much of the substance of the trip was overshadowed by a press conference during which an Iraqi journalist, protesting the war, threw his shoe at Bush, the focus was supposed to be on Bush and Maliki signing a Strategic Framework Agreement.[30] The 2008 SOFA agreement was also signed the same day. The agreements—forged after almost a year of intense negotiations led by U.S. Ambassador Ryan Crocker in Washington and GEN David Petraeus in Baghdad—set a June 30, 2009, deadline for American troops to withdraw from Iraqi cities and towns and authorized American troops to operate in the country through December 2011.[31]

According to Bush administration officials, the December 2011 date, however, was not supposed to be a hard-and-fast deadline for American forces to leave Iraq.[32] A former senior national security official recalls that when the original 2008 SOFA was being negotiated, then–Iraqi Defense Minister Abdul Qadir told him that Iraq would need a follow-on agreement past 2011 because, among other things, he could not provide adequate capability to preserve Iraq's air sovereignty.[33] For her part, Secretary of State Condoleezza Rice expressed similar sentiments in a November 2011 interview.[34] Indeed, the official transcript of Bush's comments on the "Strategic Framework Agreement for a Relationship of Friendship and Cooperation Between the United States of America and the Republic of Iraq" hints at this truth. While Bush stated that the Strategic Framework Agreement would mark the beginning of an American withdrawal from Iraq, he concluded, "There is still more work to be done. The war is not yet over—but with the conclusion of these agreements and the courage of the Iraqi people

---

[30] Jomana Karadsheh and Octavia Nasr, "Iraqi Journalist Throws Shoes at Bush in Baghdad," CNN, December 15, 2008.

[31] Karadsheh and Nasr, 2008; and Campbell Robertson and Stephen Farrell, "Pact, Approved in Iraq, Sets Time for U.S. Pullout," *New York Times*, November 16, 2008.

[32] In fact, as a means of forcing the withdrawal question, Sen. Edward Kennedy amended the 2008 Consolidated Security, Disaster Assistance, and Continuing Appropriations bill to fund a RAND Corporation study on various withdrawal options for the next administration, with a window of 12 to 18 months. See Perry, Johnson, et al., 2009, p. 121.

[33] Former senior national security official, interview with the authors, May 21, 2015.

[34] Josh Rogin, "Condoleezza Rice: We Never Expected to Leave Iraq in 2011," *Foreign Policy*, November 2, 2011b.

and the Iraqi troops and American troops and civilian personnel, it is decisively on its way to being won."[35]

A few months later, most of the American civilians who negotiated the Strategic Framework Agreement were no longer working in government. On January 20, 2009, Obama assumed the presidency and most of the politically appointed foreign policy leadership in Washington—with a few notable exceptions, such as Secretary of Defense Robert Gates—changed over, as is the case with every incoming administration, particularly when there is a change in party. In April 2009, Christopher Hill, the longtime Asia expert and former Assistant Secretary for Asian-Pacific Affairs, took over as the new U.S. ambassador to Iraq. The principal remaining point of continuity was General Odierno, who took over from his erstwhile boss General Petraeus as MNF-I commander in September 2008 and held this post—and its successor position as commander of USF-I—until September 2010.

The faces on the Iraqi side nearly all changed too. On March 7, 2010, Iraq held a parliamentary election. With a 62-percent voter turnout, the election was a triumph of Iraqi democracy.[36] However, no party won a majority in Iraq's 325-seat parliament, and Iraq plunged into political gridlock. Former prime minister and secular Shiite Ayad Allawi's Iraqiya party narrowly edged out sitting Prime Minister Maliki's State of Law Coalition to capture a slim plurality of the seats, some 91 to 89.[37] But Allawi was unable to form a coalition, and after months of internal wrangling, Maliki ultimately became prime minister for a second term in November 2010.[38]

The new set of actors on the American side created new tensions for civil-military relations in Baghdad and Washington. In Baghdad, General Odierno clashed with Ambassador Hill about how to handle Maliki. While relations with the heads of state normally lie in the provenance of the U.S. embassy, this was not the case in Iraq. In a postwar interview, Hill remarked that despite all the public rhetoric, "I do not think it was a Department of State lead until the military actually got out."[39] Hill and Odierno also disagreed sharply over policy. Hill believed that the United States should treat Iraq the same as other sovereign countries with sovereign leaders. Odierno believed that although Iraq was relatively secure, it still required a more hands-on approach, particularly to help its political leaders—who learned about the exercise of political

---

[35] White House, "President Bush and Iraq Prime Minister Maliki Sign the Strategic Framework Agreement and Security Agreement," December 14, 2008.

[36] "The 2010 Iraqi Parliamentary Elections," *New York Times*, March 26, 2010.

[37] "The 2010 Iraqi Parliamentary Elections," 2010.

[38] CNN, "Nuri al-Maliki Fast Facts," July 3, 2015e.

[39] Christopher R. Hill, interview with Lynne Chandler Garcia, May 14, 2012, p. 10, transcript provided to RAND by the OIF Study Group.

power under the Saddam Hussein regime; they still needed to be carefully monitored and mentored.[40]

Multiple explanations account for this friction. Some of the tension between Odierno and Hill can be chalked up to bureaucratic politics. As Deputy Assistant Secretary of State Greta Holtz asserted, "Civil-military friction is often overstated. In any whole of government operation, including our stability efforts in Iraq, there will most certainly be interagency friction as well-intentioned leaders try to reconcile different and often competing missions."[41] Still others in the U.S. embassy attributed the tension to a cultural clash. Minister Counselor for Political Affairs Gary Grappo noted that while a handful of diplomats had military backgrounds, the military rarely had former diplomats, and as a result, "I do not think they entirely understood the role of diplomacy."[42] Either way, the close relationship between the embassy and MNF-I that characterized the Crocker-Petraeus period began to unravel.

Civil-military tensions boiled over into the debate about the SOFA. According to newspaper accounts, Odierno's successor at USF-I, GEN Lloyd Austin, originally developed plans for a residual force of between 23,000 and 24,000 troops.[43] The Obama administration dismissed these figures on political grounds. When Obama was elected in early November 2008, a Gallup poll found that 58 percent of Americans thought the Iraq War was a mistake.[44] Obama had won the presidency at least partially for his steadfast opposition to the war and his promise to redeploy all combat brigades by the summer of 2010.[45] According to Colin Kahl, former Obama administration Deputy Assistant Secretary of Defense for the Middle East and later National Security Adviser to Vice President Joe Biden, "The White House looked at the 20,000 number and was like, you've got to be kidding. This looks like a permanent Korea-style presence in Iraq, which nobody supported."[46] The administration also noted that Iraq, at least on the surface, looked stable. As a former senior DoD official recounted, "The security situation by late 2006 deteriorated to the point where Iraqis couldn't handle it on their own. So the [American] military came in and helped them, trained them, and

---

[40] Former senior military commander, interview with the authors, April 17, 2015.

[41] Greta Holtz, interview with Lynne Chandler Garcia, July 20, 2012, p. 7, transcript provided to RAND by the OIF Study Group.

[42] Greta Holtz, interview with Lynne Chandler Garcia, July 20, 2012, p. 7, transcript provided to RAND by the OIF Study Group.

[43] Peter Baker, "Relief over U.S. Exit from Iraq Fades as Reality Overtakes Hope," *New York Times*, June 22, 2014.

[44] Gallup, "Iraq," webpage, undated.

[45] See Barack Obama, "My Plan for Iraq," *New York Times*, July 14, 2008.

[46] Baker, 2014.

then began that transition. As of the end of 2010, there was an Iraq that was reasonably stable, democratic, and secure."[47]

General Austin and the U.S. military then developed plans for 19,000, 16,000, and 10,000 remaining troops, laying out what American forces could and could not do at each force level.[48] As Gates recounted, "I give Lloyd and [Ambassador James] Jeffrey credit, they laid out at these levels . . . here is what we can and can't do. At 10,000, monitoring the green line with the Kurds became problematic. We would still have the ability to provide helicopter support and security for the State Department."[49] Inside the Obama administration, Biden and many White House aides pushed for a smaller presence.[50] For their part, Gates, CJCS ADM Michael Mullen, and CENTCOM commander GEN James N. Mattis pushed for the 16,000-troop option.[51]

In an April 29, 2011, principals' meeting, the NSC discussed three options for troop levels—16,000, 10,000, and 8,000.[52] Gates eventually agreed to accept 10,000 troops.[53] The military, however, was split. Mullen wrote a memorandum to then–National Security Adviser Thomas Donilon expressing concern about the 10,000-troop limit and expressed support for the 16,000-man option.[54] His deputy, Vice CJCS Gen. James Cartwright, dissented and said that 8,000 to 10,000 would be sufficient, a number that he later revised down to 3,000.[55] In a May 19 NSC meeting, Obama backed the 10,000-troop level as well.[56] A few weeks later, on June 10, Donilon issued formal guidance to Jeffrey and Austin that specified the 10,000-troop number, but he instructed them not to tell Maliki about it, fearing that Maliki would prefer an even lower number.[57] The administration also set a target of August 1, 2011, to conclude the SOFA negotiations.[58]

Maliki, as Donilon feared, did not agree to a stay-behind force, nor was he committed to the White House's timeline. When Obama officially started the SOFA negotiations in a June 2, 2011, video teleconference, Maliki was, at best, lukewarm to the

---

[47] Former senior DoD official, interview with the authors, June 4, 2015.

[48] Baker, 2014.

[49] Robert Gates, interview, July 21, 2014, p. 9, transcript provided to RAND by the OIF Study Group.

[50] Baker, 2014.

[51] Michael R. Gordon, "In U.S. Exit from Iraq, Failed Efforts and Challenges," *New York Times*, September 22, 2012.

[52] Gordon and Trainor, 2013, p. 658.

[53] Baker, 2014; Gordon and Trainor, 2013, p. 658.

[54] Gordon and Trainor, 2013, p. 659.

[55] Gordon and Trainor, 2013, p. 662.

[56] Baker, 2014; Gordon and Trainor, 2013, p. 666.

[57] Gordon and Trainor, 2013, p. 667.

[58] Gordon and Trainor, 2013, p. 668.

idea. He doubted whether a SOFA could pass the Iraqi parliament.[59] Indeed, Maliki's political concerns were justified. On August 2, 2011, he received the backing of his coalition for only a memorandum of understanding with the United States and even then, he could ask only for American trainers and the agreement would need parliamentary approval.[60] The principal sticking point for the new SOFA became whether American forces would be granted immunity from prosecution under Iraqi law. Maliki supposedly offered to grant immunity by an "exchange of notes" or executive order, but DoD insisted that these protections be passed by the Iraqi parliament.[61]

Over the next several months, as heated negotiations continued, several new developments occurred in Washington. On the personnel front, Leon Panetta, the former director of the CIA, replaced Gates as Secretary of Defense. Although Panetta backed the 10,000-troop number, this change removed one of the last remaining cabinet officials who was responsible for the Surge.[62] Obama was also caught in a bitter budget battle with congressional Republicans, increasing the focus on the cost of sustaining a larger footprint in Iraq.[63] Additionally, Deputy National Security Advisers Denis McDonough and Tony Blinken visited Iraq over the summer and concluded that American forces did not need to monitor the Kurdish-Arab fault line in northern Iraq, further decreasing the troop numbers.[64] Other observers, such as Ambassador Jeffrey, suggested that the White House inner circle simply lost its appetite to continue an American presence in Iraq, "and every time we were running into trouble trying to get the Iraqis to go along, they wanted to pull the plug."[65]

Whatever the true reason, the NSC began to lower the size of the stay-behind force. In late July 2011, Vice President Biden chaired a principals' meeting and asked DoD for a new set of troop levels—from 10,000 on down to 1,600.[66] For his part, in a follow-on August 10, 2011, principals' meeting, Panetta advocated the 10,000-troop level but deferred to the negotiators to make the final decision.[67] Ultimately, in an August 13 meeting with Panetta, Mullen, and then–Secretary of State Hillary Clinton, Obama reduced the size of the forces to stay behind—first to 7,000 troops and then to

---

[59] Baker, 2014.

[60] Gordon and Trainor, 2013, p. 670.

[61] Baker, 2014; and former senior national security official, interview with the authors, September 25, 2015.

[62] Gordon, 2012.

[63] Baker, 2014.

[64] Gordon and Trainor, 2013, p. 671.

[65] Baker, 2014.

[66] Gordon and Trainor, 2013, p. 671.

[67] Gordon and Trainor, 2013, p. 672.

3,500 on longer-term assignment, with an additional 1,500 on shorter-term rotations, plus six F-16 fighter aircraft.[68]

Despite the shift in the United States' bargaining terms, negotiations with Iraq stalled. On their end, the Iraqis made little progress at passing a SOFA. In August 2011, Iraqi Ambassador Sumaida'ie told *Foreign Policy*, "You'll see it [the formal SOFA] when you see it. Americans want everything now or yesterday. We don't do it like this. We do it in our own sweet time."[69] And yet, in early October 2011, Iraqi leaders approved only a small American training presence, and only the Kurdish political leadership approved granting American troops immunity.[70] Even more concerning, Washington believed that Maliki was not committed to pushing the immunity through parliament.[71] Eventually, the White House had enough. On October 21, 2011, Obama held another videoconference with Maliki (his first since beginning the talks in June), ending the negotiations and announcing the withdrawal of American forces.[72]

Could the United States Have Achieved a Different Outcome Had Negotiations Been Conducted Differently?

There is open debate about whether the SOFA negotiations were doomed to fail. On the one hand, the U.S. team negotiating the SOFA was one of the most experienced that the State Department could put together. As Ambassador Grappo recounted,

> We felt very confident in how we were doing this because we were all pretty senior diplomats, 20 plus years. [Ambassador] Chris Hill, [Ambassador] Cameron Munter, [Ambassador] Pat Haslach and other senior diplomats; we all had 20-plus years in the Foreign Service and Senior Foreign Service. In the political section, I had 30-plus officers, 15 of whom were Arabic Speakers, the most we ever had.[73]

As Grappo admitted, however, the composition of the negotiating team may have unintentionally given the embassy a pro-Sunni slant because most of the Middle Eastern countries—except Iran (where the United States currently does not have diplomatic relations) and Lebanon—are Sunni-dominated, and, as a result, most Foreign Service officers spend their careers working with Sunni leaders.[74] Nonetheless, the embassy

---

[68] Gordon, 2012; Gordon and Trainor, 2013, p. 672.

[69] Rogin, 2011a.

[70] Gordon and Trainor, 2013, p. 673.

[71] Gordon and Trainor, 2013, p. 670.

[72] Gordon, 2012.

[73] Gary Grappo, interview with Lynne Chandler Garcia, July 30, 2012, p. 4, transcript provided to RAND by the OIF Study Group.

[74] Gary Grappo, interview with Lynne Chandler Garcia, July 30, 2012, p. 10, transcript provided to RAND by the OIF Study Group.

had an experienced team. With a democracy and human rights program exceeding $200 million, it also had ample financial resources at its disposal.[75] If the embassy still could not successfully negotiate a deal despite all such experience and resources—the argument went—no one could.

At the same time, those who believed that the SOFA was doomed to fail noted that, over his time in office, Maliki had become increasingly sectarian and hostile to an enduring American presence. As a former senior State Department official remarked, Maliki's default "mindset was that Sunnis equate to Ba'athists equate to Saddamists. Effectively, although he himself argued against the accusation, Maliki was, in fact, sectarian because of this core, exaggerated variant of the Shia narrative of Sunni suppression."[76] The longer that Maliki was in power, the more inclined he was to act on these sectarian impulses. As early as 2008, Maliki purged the Sunni and nonsectarian Shia leadership from the Iraqi intelligence services, replacing them with his own political supporters.[77] Maliki became increasingly hostile to Sunni Vice President Tariq al-Hashimi and later tried to arrest him for conspiracy to murder, all while actively protecting Shia accused of similar crimes.[78] According to this reasoning, Maliki opposed a continued American presence because the United States would prevent him from executing his sectarian agenda.

Moreover, the "doomed to fail" proponents argued that, by the end, the United States had little leverage over Maliki to coerce him to play nicely. As Hill noted,

> Many people who did not like Maliki—in fact nobody likes Maliki—and did not understand the dynamic that by 2009 the United States was not in a position to fire Iraqi Prime Ministers and replace them with people we liked. Those people thought, 'Well, why are we supporting Maliki?' We were never supporting Maliki. We were dealing with the reality that this gentleman was not about to go quietly into the night.[79]

And there is some truth to this narrative. Indeed, Gates recounted that he had to personally intervene—one of the only times he did so during the course of the war—to

---

[75] Gary Grappo, interview with Lynne Chandler Garcia, July 30, 2012, 2012, p. 9, transcript provided to RAND by the OIF Study Group.

[76] Former senior State Department official, interview with the authors, June 24, 2015.

[77] Former senior national security official, interview with the authors, April 13, 2015; and Rob Alberts, interview with Steve Gripshaw, September 9, 2014, p. 11, 15, transcript provided to RAND by the OIF Study Group.

[78] Former senior State Department official, interview with the authors, June 12, 2015; and Rob Alberts, interview with Steve Gripshaw, September 9, 2014, p. 19, transcript provided to RAND by the OIF Study Group.

[79] Christopher R. Hill, interview with Lynne Chandler Garcia, May 14, 2012, p. 5, transcript provided to RAND by the OIF Study Group.

push Maliki to do something to curb Shia attacks with improvised rocket-assisted munitions on American forces in Baghdad in 2010.[80]

Finally, "doomed to fail" proponents noted that, in general, the Iraqi political scene was not favorably disposed to the enduring political presence. In 2007 and 2008, Iraq needed the United States to help stabilize the country, and its leaders recognized this. Condoleezza Rice recounted that, in 2007, Maliki still feared that the United States would try to overthrow him, and she could use that fear as leverage.[81] Even so, as former Deputy National Security Adviser Douglas Lute recalled, it took "a herculean effort by Ryan Crocker" to get the SOFA passed by the Iraqi parliament in 2008.[82] A former senior State Department official agreed and believed that without direct engagement by Bush and MNF-I commander Odierno to approve critical portions of the SOFA text to meet Iraqi requirements, he did not think the SOFA would have passed.[83]

By 2011, however, the situation was different. A 2007 incident in which private Blackwater security guards killed 14 Iraqi civilians while shooting into a crowded public square inflamed Iraqi public opinion against not only Blackwater but also the American presence as a whole.[84] Moreover, as another former senior State Department official argued, as soon as the 2008 SOFA was concluded, the United States lost its leverage to negotiate a successor agreement. The 2008 SOFA specified a deadline—intentional or not—for an American withdrawal by December 2011, and as a result, the United States was functionally a lame duck.[85] More broadly, others pointed to a rising tide of Iraqi nationalism in the aftermath of the Surge that left the Iraqi government and public disinclined to "continue the occupation."[86] As a result, even if Maliki wanted to, he would have been unable to get a SOFA through the Iraqi parliament. As Lute summarized, "I never understood how folks believed that Maliki in 2011 could do what he barely did in 2008."[87]

On the other hand, many critics—often outside the Obama administration—argue that a SOFA—or at least something very similar—was possible for a variety of

---

[80] Robert Gates, interview, July 21, 2014, p. 3, transcript provided to RAND by the OIF Study Group.

[81] Condoleezza Rice, interview with Jason Awadi and Jeanne Godfroy, U.S. Department of State, Office of the Historian, July 12, 2014, p. 15, transcript provided to RAND by the OIF Study Group.

[82] Douglas Lute, interview with Mathew Wharton, undated, p. 9, transcript provided to RAND by the OIF Study Group.

[83] Former senior State Department official, interview with the authors, June 24, 2015.

[84] Associated Press, "Iraq: Blackwater Shootings Killed 17," *USA Today*, October 7, 2007.

[85] Former senior State Department official, interview with the authors, March 23, 2015. The SOFA is fairly explicit. In Article 24, paragraph 1, it states, "the United States Forces shall withdraw from all Iraqi territory no later than December 31, 2011" (United States of America and Republic of Iraq, 2008).

[86] Former senior State Department official, interview with the authors, June 24, 2015.

[87] Douglas Lute, interview with Mathew Wharton, undated, p. 10, transcript provided to RAND by the OIF Study Group.

reasons. First, they contend that Maliki was not as bad as he seemed. A former senior State Department official claimed, "There are two Malikis—Maliki in the first term and Maliki in the second term."[88] The first Maliki was cooperative with American forces and worked well with Khalilzad and other American diplomats.[89] The second Maliki was more sectarian, but partially as a result of his own growing sense of insecurity as American forces drew down, which in turn forced him to look for alternative outside backers.[90] As a former senior national security official recounted, "When it was clear the U.S. was leaving, Maliki's relationship with the Iranians got stronger."[91]

As a result, Iraqi opposition to a new SOFA may not have run as deeply as commonly portrayed. As Gates explained, on the one hand, the Iraqis viewed American forces as occupiers, "but they realized they needed us. The problem in 2008 was that all the Iraqi leaders supported the SOFA and the strategic agreement but none wanted to be the first one to say so publicly."[92] Ambassador Lawrence Butler, political adviser to General Austin, agreed: "The Iraqis have come to value us more as partners, mentors, and enablers. They see us as helping them succeed. That's a change. They still see us through the prism of occupiers. We're foreigners, we're always going to be outsiders but less so. The tone of the conversations has just changed."[93] Even Hill admitted that most Iraqis had conflicting opinions, stating, "The problem was the Iraqis were of two minds of having a strong U.S. military component. They liked some of the security it provided, but they did not like being occupied. Iraqis are quite capable of saying two different things to you and, in fact, they are quite capable of holding two different opinions simultaneously."[94] As a result, if the United States played its cards differently, critics claim, it likely would have been able to extract concessions from the Iraqi leadership.

Critics point to at least four things that the United States could have done to secure Iraqi support for the 2011 SOFA. First, some fault the Obama administration for whittling down the number of troops it was willing to leave in Iraq. According to a former senior military commander we spoke with, Maliki knew he needed about 23,000 American troops to stabilize Iraq, which was the recommendation of General Austin, the new commander in Iraq. Once the Obama administration offered fewer

---

[88] Former senior State Department official, interview with the authors, May 18, 2015.

[89] Zalmay Khalilzad, interview with Peter Connors, Combat Studies Institute, April 30, 2008, p. 14, transcript provided to RAND by the OIF Study Group.

[90] Former senior State Department official, interview with the authors, May 18, 2015.

[91] Former senior national security official, interview with the authors, September 25, 2015.

[92] Robert Gates, interview, July 21, 2014, p. 7, transcript provided to RAND by the OIF Study Group.

[93] Lawrence Butler, interview with Jerry Brooks, August 20, 2011, p. 16, transcript provided to RAND by the OIF Study Group.

[94] Christopher R. Hill, interview with Lynne Chandler Garcia, May 14, 2012, p. 9, transcript provided to RAND by the OIF Study Group.

than half that number, Maliki knew that the United States was not serious.[95] A former senior national security official echoed this narrative. In his opinion as an informed outsider, Maliki saw Generals Odierno and Austin's request for forces as being cut for American political reasons. Eventually, it reached a point where Maliki was not willing to take the political risk for a force that would be a fraction of what was needed to get the job done.[96]

Second, the United States could have tried to influence the Iraqi elections. For the most part, the United States remained neutral during the 2010 Iraqi government impasse, if not moderately supportive of Maliki's continued hold on the premiership.[97] Iran was backing Maliki. Ironically, one of the driving motivations for keeping Maliki was that he was both a strong leader and likely to extend the SOFA past 2011. According to journalistic accounts, Vice President Joe Biden said, "Maliki wants us to stick around because he does not see a future in Iraq otherwise. I'll bet you my vice presidency Maliki will extend the SOFA."[98] Instead, the United States should have backed Ayaad Allawi, who was generally considered to be more pro-American, or at least forced the Iraqis to form more of a unity government.[99] According to a former senior military commander, this lack of direct engagement was due to Hill and the Obama administration's desire to "normalize" relations with Iraq and treat the Iraqi elections just as the United States would respond to the political processes of any of its allies.[100]

A third perspective focuses on the lack of presidential emphasis on the SOFA. According to Gates, President Obama wanted to reduce American force presence largely for political considerations: "I believe saying that we are going to be at zero by the end of 2016 is so that the President can say that I ended both of these wars, and as I leave the presidency there isn't a single American combat soldier in either theater."[101] This, in turn, shaped what kind of effort the President put into Iraq policy. Where Bush staked his presidency on Iraq and engaged in Iraq policy on a weekly basis, particularly in the last two years of his presidency, Obama focused on other priorities.[102] And there was some logic to this prioritization. As one former senior military commander remarked,

---

[95] Former senior military commander, interview with the authors, April 17, 2015.

[96] Former senior national security official, interview with the authors, May 21, 2015.

[97] Gordon, 2012.

[98] Gordon, 2012. See also Ali Khedery, "Why We Stuck with Maliki—and Lost Iraq," *Washington Post*, July 3, 2014.

[99] Foreign policy expert on Iraq, interview with the authors, March 24, 2015; and former senior military commander, interview with the authors, April 17, 2015.

[100] Former senior military commander, interview with the authors, April 17, 2015.

[101] Robert Gates, interview, July 21, 2014, p. 8, transcript provided to RAND by the OIF Study Group.

[102] Christopher R. Hill, "How the Obama Administration Ignored Iraq: One Ambassador's Story of an Exit Strategy Gone Wrong," *Politico*, October 2, 2014. See also Jeff Zeleny, "Obama Calls for U.S. to Shift Focus on Terrorism," *New York Times*, August 1, 2007; Caren Bohan, "Obama: U.S. Must End 'Single-Minded' Focus on

"By 2009, the level of violence is down 90 percent from 2006. Hill's orders were to distance the administration from Maliki and Iraq. The administration didn't see that Iraq could be a force for stability in the region as a democratic and capitalist country."[103]

Finally, some argue that, by dropping some of its demands, the United States could have negotiated a stay-behind presence. According to a former senior national security official, Maliki feared that he would not have enough votes to pass a SOFA through the Iraqi parliament, but, as mentioned before, offered the United States an "exchange of notes" that would have allowed for up to 5,000 American soldiers to remain in Iraq. The United States—specifically, lawyers at DoD—insisted that any proposition go through the parliament, which in turn caused the talks to collapse.[104]

In the end, it is impossible to prove which, if any, of these measures would have changed the calculus sufficiently to let the United States maintain forces in Iraq. Even if the United States were allowed to maintain a residual presence, there remains a heated debate over how much good such a force would have done and whether it would have affected Iraq's long-term trajectory.

Could a Small Stay-Behind Force in Baghdad and in the Rest of Iraq Have Prevented What Occurred in 2013 and 2014?

Even if the United States had successfully negotiated a SOFA, some doubt whether a small American stay-behind force would have mattered that much for Iraq's future. Thinkers in this camp argue that the force would have been too small to do much good. As Gates recounted, most of the effort would have been to provide security and transportation for the State Department officials at the embassy.[105] And if the United States had left a force comprising only a few thousand, much of the force would have been focused on protecting themselves and could not have effectively prevented the disintegration of the ISF and the fall of the northern half of the country to the Islamic State. Even if there were sufficient forces in country, it is not clear that the Iraqis would have allowed them to operate: Since the end of June 2009, forces were mostly confined to bases outside Iraq's cities.

On the other hand, others suggest that even a small continued American presence could have had a disproportionate influence on Iraq's future for at least three reasons. First, some claim that even a small presence would have had military utility. One former senior national security official noted that even in September 2015, the United States had 3,400 troops in Iraq, and the United States could still conduct counterterrorism operations and limited training of the ISF. So, the 5,000-troop limit—which

---

Iraq," *Reuters*, July 15, 2008; and "Obama Shifts US Focus from Iraq to Afghanistan Early in Presidency," *Voice of America*, January 14, 2014.

[103] Former senior military commander, interview with the authors, April 17, 2015.

[104] Former senior national security official, interview with the authors, September 25, 2015.

[105] Robert Gates, interview, July 21, 2014, p. 9, transcript provided to RAND by the OIF Study Group.

the official thought was a plausible troop limit for a new SOFA under an exchange of notes—would have provided significant combat power.[106] At the very least, even a small force could provide the United States with early warning about Mosul's impending fall to the Islamic State and the collapse of the Iraqi military resistance in northern Iraqi. It would also enable the State Department to move about the country. As Gates remarked, "My thinking was that if you didn't have the troops, the State Department would be in way over its head, and that basically they would sit in that new castle and pull up the draw bridge."[107]

Second, a small American force might have saved Maliki from himself. According to Gates, Edelman, and others, an American military presence might have been able to prevent some of the corruption and politicization of the military, and may have leaned on Maliki to avoid provocative actions, such as arresting the Sunni Vice President.[108] One foreign policy expert on Iraq claimed that an American presence might have prevented Maliki from eliminating the Sons of Iraq program—the Sunni militia that proved so essential during the Surge—and upsetting the sectarian balance of power.[109] Moreover, American forces could have functioned as an honest broker in Iraq's civil war. Gates remarked, "I think what they [the Obama administration] didn't appreciate in 2011 was the political role our Commanders had played in buffering the sectarian conflicts with the government. I mean Petraeus or Ray [Odierno] or Lloyd Austin had the ability to evoke those guys around a dinner table or in a meeting and make those guys talk to each other and work together."[110]

Finally, an American presence would have symbolic value. It would signal an enduring American commitment to Iraq. As Gates claimed, "I think that [the complete withdrawal argument] is oblivious to the importance played by the continuing presence of our troops in Europe 65 years after WWII and our continuing presence in Korea. I think it just had a continuous stabilizing effect on people that manifests that we are not going to walk away."[111] In Iraq, this was not the case.

Politicization of the Iraqi Security Forces

The drawdown and ultimate withdrawal would have profound ramifications for the ISF as well. As Surge brigades departed in 2008, the adviser teams that were part of

---

[106] Former senior national security official, interview with the authors, September 25, 2015.

[107] Robert Gates, interview, July 21, 2014, p. 10, transcript provided to RAND by the OIF Study Group.

[108] Robert Gates, interview, July 21, 2014, p. 8, transcript provided to RAND by the OIF Study Group; and former senior national security official, interview with the authors, May 21, 2015.

[109] Foreign policy expert on Iraq, interview with the authors, March 24, 2015.

[110] Robert Gates, interview, July 21, 2014, p. 8, transcript provided to RAND by the OIF Study Group.

[111] Robert Gates, interview, July 21, 2014, p. 8, transcript provided to RAND by the OIF Study Group.

them also departed. The adviser mission continued—albeit with a reduced capacity—even as the Strategic Framework Agreement was implemented, and most U.S. forces were required to move to large bases outside Iraqi urban areas. By 2009, "the focus of U.S. forces [had] almost completely shifted to advising, training, assisting, and equipping the ISF and away from taking a direct role in security operations."[112] With the responsibility for security firmly in the hands of the ISF, advisers continued to embed with Iraqi units at the tactical level, although in increasingly smaller numbers until the total withdrawal of U.S. forces from Iraq in December 2011.

The post-2009 mission, however, slowly began to change from hands-on training of the ISF to military equipment sales. In fact, a former senior military commander described a chief aspect of his responsibilities in 2008 as ensuring that the Iraqis had sufficient U.S. equipment: "My major job was pushing for a military sales program . . . using Iraqi money to sell U.S. equipment to the Iraqis."[113] He pronounced this effort a success and noted that the United States in fact sold Iraq a significant amount of hardware and equipment. His team even primed discussions for the sale of F-16 aircraft, which were finally delivered in 2015.[114] And this was not because the ISF were already fully trained: Even with the herculean efforts that U.S. forces had put into training and equipping the ISF, they still lacked many of the enabler forces that make the United States effective at combat operations.

After the American withdrawal in 2011, the ISF's situation went from bad to worse. Not only did the ISF no longer have the benefit of American advisers, but ISF leadership became increasingly politicized; competent Sunni and Kurdish officers were systematically purged and replaced with Shia friendly to the Maliki regime.[115] In 2003, the United States was explicit in the ethnic makeup of the Iraqi Army it intended to create: It was to be roughly 60 percent Arab Shia, 20 percent Arab Sunni, and 20 percent Kurdish.[116] This construction was an approximate reflection of the broader Iraqi population. The Iraqi Army would, therefore, be representative of the nation it served. After 2011, this carefully woven demographic fabric—particularly at the senior leadership level—began to unravel.[117] By 2014, MG Paul Eaton, former CMATT command-

---

[112] DoD, *Measuring Stability and Security in Iraq*, Washington, D.C., June 2010a, p. 40.

[113] Former senior military commander, interview with the authors, August 7, 2015.

[114] Dan Lamothe, "Iraq Has Finally Started Using the F-16 Fighter Jet in Combat Operations," *Washington Post*, September 6, 2015.

[115] Partlow, 2007; and Tom Bowman, "U.S. Faces Challenges in Shoring Up Iraq's Crumbling Military," NPR, June 24, 2014.

[116] Former senior military commander, interview with the authors, April 23, 2015.

[117] "Why Iraq's Army Crumbled," *The Economist*, June 21, 2014.

ing officer, estimated that the Iraqi Army comprised 90 percent Shia and, worse yet, now incorporated former Shia militias accused of attacking and torturing Sunnis.[118]

LTG James M. Dubik, commanding general of MNSTC-I, characterized the years between 2011 and 2014 as critical for the growth of the Islamic State in an environment in which Iraqi politicians intentionally meddled with the Iraqi defense institution. During this time, Maliki turned to "his dark side," instituting policies that created more enemies, particularly among the Sunni population; marginalized the people; and eroded the capacity of his own security forces. Moreover, the Iraqi prime minister never trusted the Iraqi Army—the less proficient it was, the safer he was. Aggregating most power into the position of the Office of the Commander in Chief, Maliki "started to sell command positions and politicized the target list."[119]

Although the politicization of the ISF picked up after American forces (and the American military advisers to the ISF) left Iraq, the genesis of the problem can be traced to the creation of the Office of the Commander in Chief in 2006. Ostensibly, this office was established as a means to coordinate national security policy, but it quickly evolved into a security and intelligence apparatus that targeted enemies of the prime minister.[120] With the transfer of several Iraqi special operations forces units and the creation of an intelligence service that reported directly to the prime minister, the groundwork was laid for a Ba'athist-like organization that had no oversight and little transparency and that consistently operated above the law.

Beyond the politicization of the Iraqi defense forces, a larger issue also stands out: the confidence and esprit de corps of a fighting force. LTG Joseph Peterson, former commander of the Coalition Police Assistance Training Team, spoke about the difficulties of instilling this spirit:

> In the context of transitions, the real issue is that you have to get to a point where your policemen or your security force organizations are confident and competent. Well, confidence comes not only from knowing your job. It also comes from the belief that if you are in trouble that somebody is going to help you. In Iraq, that is critical, and it leads to the concept of partnership. . . . [T]he guys that have to come to their aid should be either the National Police or the Army. Confidence of that level of direct support is critical.[121]

---

[118] See David Zucchino, "Why Iraqi Army Can't Fight, Despite $25 Billion in U.S. Aid, Training," *Los Angeles Times*, November 3, 2014.

[119] Former senior military commander, interview with the authors, April 7, 2015. This possibility for the politicization of the ISF was anticipated prior to the withdrawal of American forces; indeed, analysts were already working possible mitigation measures (see Perry, Johnson, et al., 2009, pp. 63–65, 99–103).

[120] See Arwa Damon, "Shadowy Iraq Office Accused of Sectarian Agenda," CNN, May 1, 2007.

[121] Joseph Peterson, interview with Lynne Chandler Garcia, June 11, 2008, transcript provided to RAND by the OIF Study Group.

Although that was the concept in theory, in practice, the level of distrust and the disunity of command often left the forces operating independently.

It is not clear that the kind of confidence Peterson described was ever evident in Iraq or even something that U.S. forces could instill in the soldiers and policemen they trained. Superior weaponry is a meager substitute for belief in a cause. A former senior military commander also emphasized this point, noting that in the U.S. Army, such a belief system is practically taken for granted by the young men and women who serve.[122] These beliefs are not inherently part of the Iraqi military, an institution with its own unique history.

Postmortem

Only two years after Operation New Dawn ended, the Islamic State—the successor to al Qaeda in Iraq—launched an offensive that captured much of northern Iraq. By January 2014, the Islamic State had seized Fallujah, the Sunni-dominated city west of Baghdad.[123] In June 2014, the Iraqi Army capitulated in the face of a lightning campaign by the Islamic State to seize control of four Iraqi townships, including Mosul, a city of more than 1.7 million people. The dramatic collapse of the forces in northern Iraq trained mostly by U.S. forces received extensive media coverage. One account described two divisions of Iraqi soldiers—some 30,000 men—turning and running from an assault by an insurgent force of just 800 fighters.[124] The U.S.-trained Iraqi Army troops and Iraqi Police discarded their equipment, abandoned their posts, donned civilian clothing, and melted into the population. Their retreat left prisons, police stations, military facilities, and provincial government headquarters open for capture by insurgents.[125] A war that was supposed to end with Iraq becoming a vibrant democracy seems to have resulted in a divided state, a sizable area of which was under the control of violent Islamic fundamentalists just a short time after U.S. troops officially departed.

The staggering and swift collapse of the Iraqi forces in the face of an attack from inferior forces raises the question of how it all went so wrong. After eight years of continuous American military involvement, with more than 1 million troop years invested, the collapse did not occur for lack of effort. The collapse was also not for want of equipment or resources. Over the course of a ten-year occupation of Iraq, the

---

[122] Former senior military commander, interview with the authors, April 23, 2015.

[123] BBC, 2015.

[124] Martin Chulov, Fazel Hawramy, and Spencer Ackerman, "Iraq Army Capitulates to ISIS Militants in Four Cities," *The Guardian*, June 11, 2014.

[125] Liz Sly and Ahmed Ramadan, "Insurgents Seize Iraqi City of Mosul as Security Forces Flee," *Washington Post*, June 10, 2014.

United States spent more than $60 billion in Iraqi reconstruction, $20 billion of which was dedicated specifically to the ISF.[126] Iraqi forces were equipped with high-quality American equipment, including M1A1 Abrams tanks, C-130 transport aircraft, patrol boats, M109A6 howitzers, armored personnel carriers, surveillance and intelligence systems, and all manner of personal protection equipment, small arms, and munitions.[127] In the wake of this disaster, possible explanations for what went wrong abound.

For some, the failure of the Iraq War lay in the operational planning and tactics: not planning for the occupation ahead of time, not adopting a population-centric counterinsurgency strategy early on, or poor negotiating of the SOFA. For example, a former military commander we spoke with, who advised Iraqi Ground Forces Command, argued that the United States was too ambitious and historically ill-informed when it came to standing up the ISF:

> When the [former] Iraqi army was dismantled, a conscious decision was to build a joint force that was modeled after the U.S. military, though there was never a consideration of what the Iraqis wanted. It took the U.S. 180 years to form a joint force, and we were going to try and do that overnight. At the same time, you had 30 percent of the ISF force wearing ski masks to go to and from work because of the security threat.[128]

Ambassador Hill echoed these claims and argued that the Iraqi military's sudden collapse was partially the result of the United States never preparing the Iraqis to stand and fight on their own: "So, the advantages were, of course, the military was able to keep the place in order and, when there was a counterterrorism operation to be done, [the U.S.] military was pretty brilliant at it. The disadvantages were they were pretty brilliant at it and the Iraqis were not prepared to stand up until the U.S. military left."[129] In some sense then, by claiming that the United States is a victim of its own success, Hill's argument is an extension of General Casey's position about standing up the ISF. The United States' fatal mistake in Iraq was doing too much and not having the Iraqis do enough.

For Hill and others, the Iraq problem was larger than a training failure. As Hill argued, "Americans never understood Iraq any better when they left [than] when they arrived. That is, they never understood the yawning gap between Shia political power and Sunni political power. Many Americans—pundits, journalists, whoever—to this

---

[126] Luis Martinez, "US May Have Wasted $8 Billion in Effort to Rebuild Iraq," ABC News, March 6, 2013.

[127] DoD, 2010a, pp. 48–51.

[128] Former military commander, interview with the authors, August 6, 2015.

[129] Christopher R. Hill, interview with Lynne Chandler Garcia, May 14, 2012, p. 9, transcript provided to RAND by the OIF Study Group.

day do not understand what drives Iraq's political scene."[130] For Hill, Iraq was a giant intelligence failure, a far greater problem than whether Iraq had WMDs. The United States, Hill claimed, has never understood what makes Iraq tick.

Beyond the intelligence failure, however, Hill and others believed that the United States blundered into a civilizational clash that extends far beyond anything that the United States could hope to control. Hill, for example, argued that the "Sunni-Shia divide is something that has been around for over 1,000 years and is not going to go away with a few years of American presence."[131] A former senior State Department official agreed: "In the end, there was no way to turn this place into a shining vessel of democracy. There was no Eastern Europe solution for Iraq, Syria, or the Middle East. We're stuck with this thing."[132] A former senior national security official also gives a very stark view:

> It's not Iraq, it's the whole Middle East. I think you've got to have a fundamental, underlying assumption of what's happening in the Middle East. . . . The Roman Empire falls; it took about 1,500 years for Europe to settle out into the border that we know now, including two world wars in the last century. . . . We're less than 100 years out from the fall of the Ottoman Empire. . . . The first-principle assumption is being called into question—borders, identity. This is going to be chaotic in my view for many decades to come. We need to be pretty humble about our ability to direct the course of events, but that doesn't mean be paralyzed. That means defining our interests and protecting and advancing our interests.[133]

In this former official's estimation, Iraq likely could have stumbled along—even without a SOFA or an enduring American presence—had it not been for Syria. Once conflict in Syria began and the United States gave tacit approval to aiding groups opposing Syrian President Bashaar al-Assad, the entire region became a magnet for Sunni fundamentalists worldwide, further destabilizing Syria and Iraq in the process.[134] After that happened, there was little the United States could do in response.

Whatever the actual reason for the collapse of the SOFA negotiations, one thing remains clear. Neither the war in Iraq—nor the war in Baghdad—ended with the withdrawal of American troops. Indeed, the December 2011 withdrawal of American forces did not even signal the end of American participation in the Iraq War. As the Islamic State captured Mosul in June 2014 and then pressed closer to the outskirts of

---

[130] Christopher R. Hill, interview with Lynne Chandler Garcia, May 14, 2012, p. 9, transcript provided to RAND by the OIF Study Group.

[131] Christopher R. Hill, interview with Lynne Chandler Garcia, May 14, 2012, p. 10, transcript provided to RAND by the OIF Study Group.

[132] Former senior State Department official, interview with the authors, April 9, 2015.

[133] Former senior national security official, interview with the authors, September 25, 2015.

[134] Former senior national security official, interview with the authors, September 25, 2015.

Baghdad, President Obama ordered gradually increasing numbers of American troops back to Iraq—some to Baghdad to serve as advisers to the ISF. As of January 2017, some 5,000 U.S. military personnel remained engaged in combat in the country, and the United States planned to double the number of advisers in the country.[135] And so, although in a different form, the Battle for Baghdad continues.

Lessons from This Era

This section identifies and describes the lessons learned from the U.S. experience in Baghdad leading up to and just after the 2011 withdrawal of U.S. troops from Iraq.

Presence Matters

With the withdrawal from Iraq's cities in June 2009, the military lost more than the ability to act against insurgent and terrorist threats. The quality of intelligence also declined because forces were no longer interacting with the local population. Being away from the urban centers also limited the kind of training that teams could provide the ISF. Moreover, the withdrawal provided Maliki an opportunity to begin purging the ISF of officers whom he felt could be potential threats to him. In sum, American military presence matters.

Plan Early for a Status of Forces Agreement

SOFAs are time-consuming affairs in general, but particularly in places like Iraq, where their approval gets caught up in larger debates about American presence in the region and general government dysfunction. In this case, the clock on negotiations ran out before an agreement could be reached. As a result, it is important to begin planning early for a SOFA.

Understand the Interaction Between Troops and Politics

Carl von Clausewitz famously noted that war is the extension of politics, but the reverse is also true. Having troops on the ground in places like Iraq does not simply affect military capabilities; it also shapes local actors' political behavior. As the United States decreased the numbers of troops it proposed to leave in Iraq, Maliki proved less inclined to fight for the SOFA in the Iraqi parliament and more inclined to seek alternative guarantors for his power, particularly from such actors as Iran.

---

[135] Richard Sisk, "U.S. Doubles Number of Advisers in Iraq as Forces Push into Mosul," Military.com, January 4, 2017.

Military Forces Are Needed to Support Diplomatic Efforts

One of the ways to hedge the risks incurred by an American military withdrawal was to build up the American embassy. Ultimately, this buildup did not produce many of the results that the United States had hoped. Maliki still grew increasingly sectarian, the Islamic State still rose, and there was little the embassy in Baghdad could do in response. Ultimately, diplomats do not substitute for military forces.

Expect Policy to Be Uncertain and Even Confused, So the Military Must Have Multiple Operational Options for Withdrawal

The final year for U.S. forces in Baghdad presented a confused and uncertain policy situation for Army strategists trying to plan for the military withdrawal from Iraq. The U.S. forces therefore had to have multiple options for various policy outcomes, such as complete withdrawal or varying levels of forces remaining in place. As a result, if the U.S. military ever finds itself under similar circumstances in the future, it should be prepared for multiple operational options for withdrawal.

CHAPTER SEVEN

Overarching Lessons for the U.S. Army

The U.S. Army's adaptations in Iraq were remarkable, particularly in the areas of doctrine, organization, training, materiel, personnel, and leader development and education. Doctrine became dynamic, with a process to incorporate lessons learned in theater into tactics, techniques, and procedures and capture those adjustments in field manual revisions. In the realm of organization, the Army implemented modularity, going from a division-based to a brigade-based Army, to facilitate deployments and readiness over a protracted conflict. Many said that the Army would crumble under the stress of the war, but it did not. Training at the combat training centers began to emulate the conditions that soldiers would face in Iraq and Afghanistan. The Army also developed and deployed a host of materiel developments, including improved body armor, mine-resistant ambush-protected vehicles, and sophisticated networks. These materiel developments, coupled with enhancements in military medicine, saved soldiers' lives and increased operational effectiveness. In addition, though under enormous stress, the Army was able to keep up with the troop commitments required in Iraq despite the predictions of many that it would not. Finally, Army leaders and soldiers proved their competence in combat, often over multiple tours.[1]

During its years in Iraq, the Army adapted in many areas—and institutionalized those adaptations; however, other important lessons have not yet been institutionalized. In an article about the lessons of Vietnam originally published in 1986, then-Major David Petraeus used the following quotation from Harvard political scientist Stanley Hoffman: "Of all the disasters of Vietnam the worst could be our unwillingness to learn enough from them."[2] The same can be said about Iraq.

---

[1] See, for example, Sandra Erwin, "An Army Under Stress: A Tale of Two Green Lines," *National Defense*, April 2006. According to former Secretary of Defense William Perry, the nation had reason to fear that the Army eventually would break:

> We believe that the Bush administration has broken faith with the American soldier and Marine—by failing to plan adequately for post-conflict operations in Iraq, by failing to send enough forces to accomplish that mission at an acceptable level of risk, and by failing to adequately equip and protect the young Americans they sent into harm's way. (Erwin, 2006)

[2] David H. Petraeus, "Lessons of History and Lessons of Vietnam," *Parameters*, Winter 2010–2011, p. 48.

A willingness to learn from the war in Iraq (and Afghanistan) should not be a problem, given that instability is on the rise in many places in the world and the U.S. Army is likely to be called on to serve the nation in this type of environment in the future. As noted in Chapter Three, one of the Army's primary functions is to "develop concepts, doctrine, tactics, techniques, and procedures, and organize, train, equip, and provide forces with expeditionary and campaign qualities" to "occupy territories abroad and provide for the initial establishment of a military government pending transfer of this responsibility to other authority."[3] It is the only service charged with this function; absent Army capacity and capabilities, no other service or government agency is capable of executing this function, as shown in Iraq. In the aftermath of the Vietnam War, the Army largely turned its attention to conventional combat in NATO and, as Operation Desert Storm and Operation Iraqi Freedom demonstrated, became formidable in combined arms maneuver warfare.[4] It did not, however, prepare itself adequately for postconflict security operations, as demonstrated in the period after removing Saddam Hussein from power. The overarching lessons discussed in this chapter are ones that the Army must institutionalize to prepare itself for a future in which it may again be left to solve (or, ideally, prevent) problems caused by erroneous policy or strategy assumptions. However, if the Army is to sustain and advance its capabilities and capacity for occupation and military governance, this must be made a priority in U.S. defense strategy, and Congress must authorize and appropriate the necessary resources.

Ironically, the discussion of any lessons from Iraq would have been far different without the calamity caused by the rise of the Islamic State. This reality reframes whether several U.S. policies and adaptations were strategic and enduring or tactical, operational, and ephemeral. What follows is not an attempt to rationalize what happened in Iraq after the U.S. withdrawal in 2011. Rather, this chapter examines the learning that occurred between major combat operations and the stabilization of Baghdad. It also looks at whether that learning has been institutionalized and, in several cases, offers historical examples of options that did work for the Army.

The Nature of the Lessons from Iraq—and the Constraints on Learning

An important first step in assessing what the U.S. Army should do about a lesson is understanding which lessons the Army has the authority to institutionalize. Thus, the lessons from the previous chapters fall into three broad categories: lessons the Army can institutionalize through its own internal processes, lessons the Army does not have the authority to institutionalize, and lessons the Army must institutionalize through a combined effort with other actors (e.g., developing joint doctrine).

---

[3] DoD, 2010b, p. 30. See also Crane and Terrill, 2003, pp. 11–18.

[4] See also David E. Johnson, "Failure to Learn: Reflections on a Career in the Post-Vietnam Army," *War on the Rocks*, January 24, 2014.

Lessons the Army Has the Authority to Institutionalize

In the cases in which the Army does have the authority to institutionalize a lesson, the constraints likely will be budgetary, and in the face of downsizing and shortfalls, actions to institutionalize a lesson could be neglected for more-pressing priorities. Furthermore, there is a strong desire inside and outside the Army to move beyond the war in Iraq. The Army is reshaping itself for the missions that it believes it will confront in the future while the bureaucratic environment is characterized by little appetite to engage in large-scale counterinsurgency or stability operations or to resource capabilities to execute them. The 2012 DoD strategic guidance was explicit in this regard:

> **Conduct Stability and Counterinsurgency Operations.** In the aftermath of the wars in Iraq and Afghanistan, the United States will emphasize non-military means and military-to-military cooperation to address instability and reduce the demand for significant U.S. force commitments to stability operations. U.S. forces will nevertheless be ready to conduct limited counterinsurgency and other stability operations if required, operating alongside coalition forces wherever possible. Accordingly, U.S. forces will retain and continue to refine the lessons learned, expertise, and specialized capabilities that have been developed over the past ten years of counterinsurgency and stability operations in Iraq and Afghanistan. *However, U.S. forces will no longer be sized to conduct large-scale, prolonged stability operations.*[5]

The report of the 2014 Quadrennial Defense Review repeated the language of the 2012 defense guidance—"our forces will no longer be sized to conduct large-scale prolonged stability operations"—but also promised to "preserve the expertise gained during the past ten years of counterinsurgency and stability operations in Iraq and Afghanistan" and to "protect the ability to regenerate capabilities that might be needed to meet future demands."[6] In a letter to Congress requesting the authorization to use military force against the Islamic State, President Obama further reinforced this message, saying that he "would not authorize long-term, large-scale ground combat operations like those our Nation conducted in Iraq and Afghanistan."[7] Thus, the message is clear across the government: no more Iraqs.

This is the difficult environment within which the Army finds itself: facing reductions in end strength (forced by budget cuts) below levels that it believes advisable to meet worldwide demands against more-capable adversaries than those in Iraq and Afghanistan, and no bureaucratic incentive to retain stability or counterinsurgency capabilities and capacities. In such an environment, the July 2014 deactivation of the

---

[5] DoD, *Sustaining U.S. Global Leadership: Priorities for 21st Century Defense*, Washington, D.C., January 2012, p. 6.

[6] DoD, *Quadrennial Defense Review 2014*, Washington, D.C., March 2014, p. viii.

[7] Barack Obama, "Letter from the President—Authorization for the Use of United States Armed Forces in Connection with the Islamic State of Iraq and the Levant," White House, February 11, 2015.

162nd Infantry Brigade, which was responsible for training military transition teams, should not be surprising.[8] Thus, for many of the lessons in this report, the focus may be on "not forgetting" by institutionalizing the hard-earned lessons in ways that can be expanded rapidly. Congressional resourcing and DoD leadership also remain critical ingredients.

Lessons the Army Does Not Have the Authority to Institutionalize—but for Which It Does Have an Advisory Role

This report has described many lessons that the Army cannot independently institutionalize. Prime examples include the need to establish intergovernmental unity of command and to resolve interdepartmental disputes (discussed in Chapter Two). Clearly, the Army can do little to force these types of bureaucratic changes. Nevertheless, Army leaders need to provide expert military advice and attempt to influence decisions beyond their authority because those decisions have direct and indirect effects on the Army. How the Army can prepare strategic leaders to provide this advice is discussed later in this chapter.

Lessons the Army Must Institutionalize Through a Combined Effort with Other Actors

There are some lessons for which the Army does not have independent authority to act but does have a direct interest in the outcome and a role in developing solutions; for these, the Army must be involved in a collaborative role to institutionalize the lessons from Iraq. At the strategic level, these opportunities include, for example, analyzing the overall end strength of the Army within the joint force to accomplish missions specified in national strategies and assessing what capabilities the Army must have to deter or defeat the potential range of adversaries that the nation may face in the future.[9] At

---

[8] These cuts to organizations that were developed in response to the wars in Iraq and Afghanistan are not unique to the Army. The Marine Corps shuttered its Advisor Training Group Marine Corps Air Ground Combat Center in Twentynine Palms, California, in June 2014 (see Gina Harkins, "Shuttering of Elite Unit Spells End of 7-Year Mission for Marines," *Marine Corps Times*, July 4, 2014). In addition, the State Department dissolved its Civilian Response Corps program (see USAID, "The Office of Crisis Surge Support Staff," webpage, May 12, 2014), but USAID maintained some capability after that dissolution. According to its website,

> The Office of Crisis Surge Support Staff (CS3) rapidly deploys highly qualified technical experts providing critical development skill sets in support of USAID operations worldwide. CS3 aims to meet Mission-specific staffing needs by deploying personnel knowledgeable about USAID systems and processes, helping Missions to better adjust to the rapidly changing conditions in which USAID regularly finds itself. To this end, CS3 recruits, hires, and trains staff with an array of skills and experiences to immediately deploy when needed. (USAID, 2014)

[9] For an analysis of the sufficiency of Army end strength to meet projected missions, see Timothy M. Bonds, Michael Johnson, and Paul S. Steinberg, *Limiting Regret: Building the Army We Will Need*, Santa Monica, Calif.: RAND Corporation, RR-1320-RC, 2015. On needed Army capabilities to address the full range of adversaries, see David E. Johnson, *The Challenges of the "Now" and Their Implications for the U.S. Army*, Santa Monica, Calif.: RAND Corporation, PE-184-A, 2016.

the operational level, the Army must anticipate what will happen in an operation when assumptions are not fully addressed and plan for alternatives. This did not happen in Iraq, and the Army was largely left holding the bag.

What capabilities and capacities does the Army need to be able to respond to changing conditions and subsequent combatant commander demands? How do Army senior leaders advise civilian leaders and other military leaders about the potential consequences of courses of action before they are taken? Answers to these questions are discussed in the remainder of this chapter. Importantly, these answers can now be framed with the authority of the realities of what did and did not work in Iraq and what changes must be made to institutionalize these lessons and prepare for the future. Table 7.1 outlines lessons from this report's individual chapters and the Army's role in addressing them.

Table 7.1
Specific Lessons for the U.S. Army, by Chapter

Lesson	Army Can Institutionalize[a]	Army Has Advisory Role[b]	Army Is Direct Contributor[c]
Chapter Two			
Start planning early, remain focused, and expect policy to cause friction.			◆
Establish unity of command.			◆
Resolve disputes among principals.		◆	
Question assumptions and plan for contingencies.	◆		
Combined arms training and mobile protected firepower are the essential ingredients of combat operations.	◆		
Chapter Three			
Plan early for an occupation and for a full range of contingencies.	◆		
Stabilize a situation as quickly as possible after combat operations are complete.			◆
Embrace the training of security forces and tailor the approach to the society.	◆		
Promote unity of the chain of command and positive civil-military relations.			◆
Focus on nonmilitary intelligence.	◆		
Embrace the military's role in an occupational government.			◆
Anticipate abnormality.			◆
Balance justice and pragmatism.		◆	

Table 7.1—Continued

Lesson	Army Can Institutionalize[a]	Army Has Advisory Role[b]	Army Is Direct Contributor[c]
Chapter Four			
In complex urban environments, the factors causing an insurgency will have a powerful effect on whether military operations succeed or fail.			◆
Tactical adaptation and creativity are important.	◆		
Strong civil-military cooperation requires a concerted effort from all parties.			◆
The State Department has limited resources.		◆	
Outcome-based metrics need to be precisely tailored to the conflict.			◆
Build institutions around existing organizations rather than in an ad hoc fashion.	◆		◆
Adviser and training missions are key to success.	◆		
Setting up a foreign military requires an understanding of cultural influences in play.	◆		
Chapter Five			
Both quantity and quality are necessary when training indigenous forces.			◆
The Surge worked because of many factors, not simply an increase in troops.			◆
Sufficient manpower is essential for effective counterinsurgency operations.			◆
Consistent guidance and support for a "clear, hold, build" approach is necessary.	◆		
Without security, nation-building will not succeed.		◆	
Chapter Six			
Presence matters.		◆	
Plan early for a SOFA.			◆
Understand the interaction between troops and politics.			◆
Military forces are needed to support diplomatic efforts.			◆
Expect policy to be uncertain and even confused, so the military must have multiple operational options for withdrawal.		◆	

[a] The Army has the authority to make the necessary changes to learn the lesson.

[b] The Army has a vested interest in the lesson being learned but does not have the authority to institutionalize the lesson.

[c] The Army has a role to play in developing joint and interagency solutions.

Overarching Lessons from the Iraq War and Recommendations for the Army

In addition to the specific lessons in this report's individual chapters, some overarching, cross-cutting lessons are important for the Army to learn. The lessons and recommendations that follow all fall within the Army's authority to institutionalize, and in some cases, the Army is already acting to do so.

The Center for Army Lessons Learned describes such lessons as a methodology to approach how to understand what should be drawn from an experience as part of the Army's institutional toolkit for future conflicts. The center defines *lessons learned* as

> validated knowledge and experience derived from observations and the historical study of military training, exercises, and combat operations that lead to a change in behavior at either the tactical (standing operating procedures, TTP [tactics, techniques, and procedures], etc.), operational, or strategic level or in one or more of the Army's DOTMLPF (doctrine, organization, training, materiel, leadership and education, personnel, and facilities) domains.[10]

The focus in this report remains principally on identifying the strategic and operational lessons from the war in Iraq, assessing the observations, and offering recommendations for the Army to institutionalize the lesson.

Lesson 1: DoD War Plans Need to Include Actions to Ensure Long-Term Stability
Observation: U.S. Forces Did Not Immediately Establish Security in Iraq and Had to Spend Years Countering Insurgency

The major combat operations in Iraq in March 2003 accomplished their goal of toppling the Saddam regime with a minimum number of forces. The history of that part of the Iraq War is covered in the earlier chapters of this report. However, as discussed in detail in Chapter Three, two key unstated assumptions that drove force planning for the war proved highly problematic. The first assumption was that coalition forces would be greeted as liberators instead of occupiers, and the second was that the Iraqi government would continue to function once Saddam was removed from power. These assumptions were not challenged by CENTCOM planners. At the same time, there was no alternative plan if these assumptions proved wrong, and when they did, there were insufficient troops and capabilities to stop the slide of Iraq into chaos.

Indeed, as noted in Chapter Two, GEN Tommy Franks essentially avoided the question of Phase IV operations and, though recognizing the importance of security,

---

[10] Department of the Army, *Commander's Guide to Operational Records and Data Collection*, Handbook No. 09-22, Fort Leavenworth, Kan.: Center for Army Lessons Learned, 2012, p. 14.

believed such operations were contingent on "reconstruction and civic action."[11] A 2005 Council on Foreign Relations report summed up the situation as follows:

> In Iraq, pre-war inattention to post-war requirements—or simply misjudgments about them—left the United States ill-equipped to address public security, governance, and economic demands in the immediate aftermath of the conflict, seriously undermining key U.S. foreign policy goals and giving early impetus to the insurgency.[12]

A key takeaway from the Iraq War is that the Army is responsible for providing forces to the combatant commanders with the necessary capabilities and capacities to ensure long-term stability in the wake of initial combat success. This was—and remains—a primary function of the Army as specified in the August 1, 2002, DoD Directive 5100.1, *Functions of the Department of Defense and Its Major Components*, which stated that the Army is "to provide forces for the occupation of territories abroad, including initial establishment of military government pending transfer of this responsibility to other authority."[13] It is important to note that no other service has occupation and military government as primary functions. The closest is the Marine Corps' mission to "conduct security and stability operations and *assist* with the initial establishment of a military government pending transfer of this responsibility to other authority."[14] Thus, in the early days of Iraq, because of many factors—including OSD interruptions of the alert of forces, the request-for-forces process, and insufficient capacity and capabilities—CENTCOM was unable to secure and stabilize postwar Iraq. CFLCC's Cobra II and Eclipse II planned for Phase IV operations. However, without sufficient capacity and capabilities, these plans were inadequate for complete success, and little, if any, interest or support was given from levels above the planning staff to raise, much less address, these key shortfalls.

As this report notes, there were no plans for the occupation of Iraq, and there was enormous pressure on military leaders to adhere to civilian assumptions about the outcome of the war. This is a U.S. government failure. Nevertheless, the Army had and continues to have the responsibility to be prepared to provide the capacity and capabilities to ensure a successful occupation in the aftermath of successful combat operations, and argue the consequences if its best military advice is ignored. Civilian leaders and Congress must also provide the Army with the resources to carry out such missions.

---

[11] Franks and McConnell, 2004, p. 422.

[12] Berger and Scowcroft, 2005, p. 4.

[13] DoD, *Functions of the Department of Defense and Its Major Components*, DoD Directive 5100.1, Washington, D.C., August 1, 2002. See also the December 21, 2010, revision of this directive, which made a minor change to the language, stating that the Army is to provided forces to "occupy territories abroad and provide for the initial establishment of a military government pending transfer of this responsibility to other authority" (DoD, 2010b).

[14] DoD, 2010b, emphasis added.

This was an exceptionally difficult argument to make in the political environment leading up to the war, particularly after GEN Eric Shinseki's treatment subsequent to his testimony that suggested the occupation of Iraq would require several hundred thousand soldiers. Even given the tasks outlined in Cobra II and Eclipse II, which addressed the CENTCOM plans for Phase IV in Iraq, the Army did not have the requisite capacities or capabilities to provide forces trained, organized, and equipped for major combat operations and military governance functions. In short, the United States could not prevent an insurgency and spent until 2008 countering the insurgency that erupted from the postwar chaos.

Even if the number of troops had been much higher in Iraq at the end of the war, there were significant Army capability issues, as an Army War College report presciently noted in February 2003:

> Recent American experiences with post-conflict operations have generally featured poor planning, problems with relevant military force structure, and difficulties with a handover from military to civilian responsibility.
>
> To conduct their share of the essential tasks that must be accomplished to reconstruct an Iraqi state, military forces will be severely taxed in military police, civil affairs, engineer, and transportation units, in addition to possible severe security difficulties.[15]

Recommendation: Resource and Prepare the Army to Provide Forces to the Combatant Commanders to Ensure Long-Term Stability

The Army needs to be prepared for postconflict scenarios in which it will be thrown into the breach to prevent or mitigate chaos, instability, and humanitarian disaster. This is not the type of operation that civilian leaders are interested in, given recent experiences. Secretary of Defense Robert Gates's comments in a July 2008 speech typify the views of senior political leaders in the aftermath of the Iraq War and the ongoing operations in Afghanistan:

> Repeating an Afghanistan or an Iraq—forced regime change followed by nation-building under fire—probably is unlikely in the foreseeable future. What is likely though, even a certainty, is the need to work with and through local governments to avoid the next insurgency, to rescue the next failing state, or to head off the next humanitarian disaster.[16]

---

[15] Crane and Terrill, 2003, p. 1.

[16] Robert M. Gates, "Remarks by Secretary of Defense Robert M. Gates at USGLC Tribute Dinner," U.S. Global Leadership Campaign, July 15, 2008.

Gates's statement seemingly lets DoD off the hook for in-depth assessment of the lessons learned in Iraq and Afghanistan. And, as noted earlier, the Obama administration shared the view that U.S. forces should not repeat the mistakes from Iraq and Afghanistan.

This perspective has persisted even in the wake of the rise of the Islamic State, the Syrian civil war, and the disintegration of Libya after Operation Odyssey Dawn in 2011. It will persist in the political realm until policy risks change strategy. Regardless of whether the United States will ever want to repeat operations like Iraq or Afghanistan, the Army must be resourced and prepared to provide and sustain forces that are trained, organized, and equipped for such operations if required.

As *The Army Operating Concept: Win in a Complex World* recognizes, "Compelling sustainable outcomes in war requires land forces to defeat enemy organizations, establish security, and consolidate gains."[17] It also notes, "Wide area security includes the essential stability tasks including: establish civil security; [establish] security force assistance; establish civil control; restore essential services; support governance; and support economic and infrastructure development."[18] These are key tasks that the Army was not resourced or prepared to conduct in the aftermath of regime change in Iraq in 2003. Nevertheless, the operating concept recognizes the difficult challenges facing the Army "to strike the right balance between current readiness and investment of future capabilities."[19]

It is essential that the Army retain and continue to develop the capabilities it will need to provide postconflict security and initial military governance. This is in keeping with DoD guidance that while its "forces will no longer be sized to conduct large-scale prolonged stability operations," the services will "preserve the expertise gained during the past ten years of counterinsurgency and stability operations in Iraq and Afghanistan" and "protect the ability to regenerate capabilities that might be needed to meet future demands."[20]

Thus, an understanding of what happened in Iraq is central to preparing the Army for the eventuality that it might again have to deal with a post–regime change operation. This is particularly true because the Army will be the service responsible for providing the capacity and capabilities in the aftermath of a regime change to prevent the slide into chaos that happened in Iraq in 2003. Congress and DoD have the responsibility to ensure that the Army is adequately resourced to preserve these capabilities and provide the necessary capacity when so directed.

---

[17] Department of the Army, *The U.S. Army Operating Concept: Win in a Complex World*, TRADOC Pamphlet 525-3-1, Washington, D.C.: Headquarters, Department of the Army, October 31, 2014b, p. 16.

[18] Department of the Army, 2014b, p. 23.

[19] Department of the Army, 2014b, p. 24.

[20] DoD, 2014, p. viii.

Lesson 2: Capacity and Capability Matter, and the "Whole of Government" Beyond the Military Could Not Provide Them in Iraq
Observation: CENTCOM Did Not Have the Capacity to Secure Iraq at the End of Major Combat Operations

Simply stated, *capacity* is the sufficiency of the Army "to help execute the nation's defense strategy in terms of three dimensions: (1) the number of Army soldiers, which is referred to as end strength; (2) how well prepared the Army's units are to operate, which is called their readiness; and (3) how good modern Army equipment is."[21] There were clearly times since the terrorist attacks of September 11, 2001, when the Army did not have the end strength, readiness, or appropriate equipment for the war in Iraq.

The debate that surrounded the number of forces that went into Iraq had been contentious since before the war. It came to a head, as noted in Chapter Two, when then–Army Chief of Staff Shinseki testified on February 25, 2003, before the Senate Armed Services Committee about the number of forces that would be required to stabilize Iraq.[22]

As discussed in this report, policies, desired end states, and capabilities evolved over time to stabilize Iraq. Capacity, however, remained fundamental to providing security, particularly in the crucial city of Baghdad. In his speech announcing the Surge on January 10, 2007, President Bush made it clear that his administration understood the shortfall: "Our past efforts to secure Baghdad failed for two principal reasons: There were not enough Iraqi and American troops to secure neighborhoods that had been cleared of terrorists and insurgents, and there were too many restrictions on the troops we did have."[23]

What also became clear during the early years of the war was the reality that demands for capacity would fall largely on the U.S. military, for two key reasons. First, military service members are required to deploy. This was not so with other government agencies, as CJCS Richard B. Myers recalled:

> Either our U.S. government departments and agencies didn't have the manpower, or people just weren't that interested in serving in a dangerous assignment (people still tended to covet the assignments that historically had been beneficial to career advancement). Over time, the CPA's chronic personnel shortage became emblematic of our country's inability to focus *all* instruments of national power on a critical security problem. And there was no mechanism to require them to go. Many who did come served on short temporary duty assignments.[24]

---

[21] Bonds, Johnson, and Steinberg, 2015, p. 2.

[22] Shanker, 2007.

[23] CQ Transcriptions, 2007.

[24] Myers, 2009, pp. 254–255.

Second, other agencies of the U.S. government have never had the excess capacity or resources inherent in U.S. Armed Forces, which are maintained as a hedge against existential uncertainty. There have never been battalions of ambassadors-in-training preparing for future threats. The reality is that the State Department "has fewer officers than positions, a shortage compounded by the personnel demands of Iraq and Afghanistan." In April 2009, this resulted in "1,650 vacant Foreign Service positions in total." Quite simply, the assignment of foreign service officers . . . is a zero sum game—other positions will go vacant to meet this demand . . . other U.S. government agencies face similar issues.[25]

To provide personnel, the Department of State and other agencies had to rely on volunteers. Given the hardships inherent in these assignments, the department created incentives for volunteering, including increased pay, the opportunity to serve in "up-stretch jobs" (jobs above current experience level), student loan repayments, one-year tours of duty, promotion consideration, and follow-on assignment priority.[26] The Army and the other military services provided the vast majority of the capacity on the ground in Iraq. Thus, a key lesson from Iraq is that the "whole of government" cannot compensate for sufficient boots on the ground, nor does it have the capabilities to provide what the military can.

This realization that U.S. forces were required to restore security in Iraq, especially Baghdad, caused a shift in strategy that provided sufficient troops to secure Baghdad, as discussed in Chapters Four and Five. GEN George W. Casey, Jr.'s, approach of growing the ISF to take over the fight by 2007—an "accelerated transition"—aided by the addition of two Army brigades and two Marine Corps battalions, was rejected. President Bush decided to send five more Army BCTs and to replace General Casey with General Petraeus.[27] The five BCTs were essentially all the forces available in an Army already heavily committed in Afghanistan and Iraq, and Army deployments temporarily changed from 12 months to 15 to squeeze more capacity from the force.[28] But not until the Surge were there sufficient coalition forces in Baghdad to do the job. Then, for the first time in the war, the doctrinal rule of thumb (which had historical antecedents

---

[25] David E. Johnson, "What Are You Prepared to Do? NATO and the Strategic Mismatch Between Ends, Ways, and Means in Afghanistan—and in the Future," *Studies in Conflict and Terrorism*, Vol. 34, No. 5, May 2011b, p. 394. For a discussion of the issues in the State Department, see Kori N. Shake, *State of Disrepair: Fixing the Culture and Practices of the State Department*, Stanford, Calif.: Hoover Institution Press, 2012.

[26] Johnson, 2011b, p. 395.

[27] Casey, 2012, pp. 136–146. Casey recalled, "I had provided the President my military advice on what I felt was the best approach to accomplish our strategic objectives in Iraq as rapidly as possible. He chose a different course of action. His decision was disappointing to me, to say the least, but I immediately set out to make it successful."

[28] Former senior military commander, interview with the authors, April 17, 2015. Part of the issue with the availability of Army forces was the result of how the Army Force Generation created capacity for rotational readiness.

during insurgencies in Malaya and Northern Ireland and stability operations in Bosnia and Kosovo) of 20 counterinsurgents for every 1,000 residents was finally met.[29]

Nevertheless, the Surge exacerbated a situation in the Army in which "the current operational demand for Army forces exceed[ed] the sustainable supply." In January 2007, the Army received approval of its plan to begin addressing the personnel shortfall with an increase in Army end strength of 74,200 troops and the authority to expand the force to 76 BCTs.[30] This growth would take time. In the interim, the Army had to exceed its goal of having soldiers spend two years out of theater for each year spent in theater, a ratio of boots on the ground in theater to dwell time out of theater from 1:2 to 1:1 or less, with Surge units spending 15 months in Iraq.[31] The increased demand on the Army also affected its ability to execute other missions. In 2007, the 82nd Airborne Division relinquished the mission of maintaining a brigade ready to begin deploying anywhere in the world in 18 hours.[32]

Recommendation: Build More Capacity for the Challenges the Army Will Likely Face in the Future

The Army needs more capacity to do the missions it currently faces.[33] Indeed, some stability operations and counterinsurgencies may be beyond the capacity of the U.S. military to execute once disorder breaks out.[34] Again, the imperative is to ensure that the

---

[29] See James T. Quinlivan, "Force Requirements in Stability Operations," *Parameters*, Winter 1995–1996. Quinlivan's analysis informed Army and Marine Corps doctrine on this topic in FM 3-24, 2006, which notes, "Twenty counterinsurgents per 1000 residents is often considered the minimum troop density required for effective [counterinsurgency] operations; however as with any fixed ratio, such calculations remain very dependent upon the situation. . . . As in any conflict, the size of the force needed to defeat an insurgency depends on the situation" (pp. 1–13). See also David E. Johnson, "Fighting the 'Islamic State': The Case for US Ground Forces," *Parameters*, Vol. 45, No. 2, Summer 2015, which notes,

> One could argue that they were not met across Iraq during the surge, but within Baghdad, considered by many to be the center of gravity of the war, there were approximately 131,000 US-Iraqi security forces in a city with a population of some 7,000,000, which came close to the doctrinal ratio. Interestingly, these ratios do not appear in the 2014 version of the US Army-Marine Corps FM 3-24/MCWP 3-33.5: Insurgencies and Countering Insurgencies. (p. 14)

Indeed, the ratio may have been even higher. Per U.N. estimates, Baghdad had a population of 5,054,000 in 2008 (see United Nations, *World Statistics Pocketbook 2009*, Series V, No. 34, New York, 2010, p. 96.

[30] Department of the Army, *2008 Army Posture Statement Information Papers: Accelerate Army Growth*, 2008. For historical data on the strength of the U.S. Armed Forces, see Defense Manpower Data Center, "DoD Personnel, Workforce Reports & Publications," webpage, undated.

[31] Timothy M. Bonds, Dave Baiocchi, and Laurie L. McDonald, *Can the Army Deploy More Soldiers to Iraq and Afghanistan?* Santa Monica, Calif.: RAND Corporation, RB-9618-A, 2011.

[32] Jay Price, "War Leads to Changes in the 'Division Ready Brigade,'" *Knoxville News Sentinel*, March 21, 2007.

[33] See Richard Lardner, "Army Secretary Nominee Worried About Cuts to Army's Size," Associated Press, January 21, 2016.

[34] Quinlivan, 1995–1996. Quinlivan noted that in heavily populated countries, the ratio of 20 counterinsurgents per 1,000 residents may be unattainable and surmised that "we must finally acknowledge that many countries

country in which the United States changes a regime does not erupt in chaos because of insufficient preparation that would quickly outstrip the capacity to establish order. During an April 2007 interview, David Samuels of *The Atlantic* remarked to former Secretary of State Colin Powell,

> You were famously quoted as saying "if you break it, you own it" about the consequences of an American invasion of Iraq. So do we own it? And, as a practical matter, is it possible for the United States to declare at this late date that we don't take part in other people's Civil Wars, and to withdraw our troops?

Powell responded,

> The famous expression, if you break it you own it—which is not a Pottery Barn expression, by the way—was a simple statement of the fact that when you take out a regime and you bring down a government, you become the government. On the day that the statue came down and Saddam Hussein's regime ended, the United States was the occupying power. We might also have been the liberating power, and we were initially seen as liberators. But we were essentially the new government until a government could be put in place. And in the second phase of this conflict, which was beginning after the statue fell, we made serious mistakes in not acting like a government. One, maintaining order. Two, keeping people from destroying their own property. Three, not having in place security forces—either ours or theirs or a combination of the two to keep order. And in the absence of order, chaos ensues.[35]

Regardless of whether it is prepared to do so, the U.S. Army will be responsible for providing the majority of security forces to ensure the "order" that Powell described, as well as the bulk of the CA and military government capabilities, until the transition to civil authority occurs. And that transition will not occur until there is at least a modicum of order. This point is driven home further in a later recommendation on how the Army might create a surge capacity.

Observation: The Army Lacked Key Capabilities Needed to Occupy, Secure, and Provide Transitional Military Government in Iraq

The absence of capacity beyond the services exacerbated the lack of capability in the military. Aside from serious capacity issues, gaps in capabilities soon manifested themselves in Iraq. The approach became one of adapting and developing capabilities to deal with the challenges in the war. Initially, operations were ad hoc, particularly given

---

are simply too big to be plausible candidates for stabilization by external forces." Quinlivan's work is updated in James T. Quinlivan, "Burden of Victory: The Painful Arithmetic of Stability Operations," *RAND Review*, Vol. 27, No. 2, Summer 2003. Increasing the size of the U.S. military and modernizing its forces were key issues raised by Donald Trump during the 2016 U.S. presidential campaign.

[35] David Samuels, "A Conversation with Colin Powell," *The Atlantic*, April 2007.

the shortage of personnel in DoD or elsewhere who understood counterinsurgency and nation-building, which became the objectives of the coalition effort after Iraq fell apart. Exacerbating the absence of expertise were the tour lengths of civilians: "Stays in Baghdad were short, from three to six months, so turnover was much more rapid than in other post-conflict situations. Because most staff did not return to departments that continued to be engaged in Iraq, much of what they learned was lost. Institutional memory was short."[36]

Even if CENTCOM plans for Phase IV had been comprehensive, the U.S. government and the military did not have the capabilities or capacity to arrest the descent of Iraq into chaos or to adjust rapidly to the postinvasion security environment. Planning alone could not have made up this inherent capability deficit.

A prime example of this capability deficit was the 800th Military Police Brigade, which was responsible for running Abu Ghraib prison. MG Antonio M. Taguba, then deputy commanding general in support of CFLCC, investigated the allegations of abusive treatment of prisoners at Abu Ghraib in late 2003 and found that the 800th Military Police Brigade was not prepared for the conditions it encountered in Iraq. Not only was this reserve-component unit understaffed, but it was also trained, organized, and equipped to "conduct standard EPW [enemy prisoner of war] operations in the [communications zone] (Kuwait)."[37] The underlying premise of EPW operations is predicated "on a compliant, self-disciplining EPW population, and not criminals or high-risk security internees."[38] The prisoner population at Abu Ghraib was fraught with a lack of adequate Iraqi facilities. As Taguba explained, "Iraqi criminals (generally Iraqi-on-Iraqi crimes) are detained with security internees (generally Iraqi-on-Coalition offenses) and EPWs in the same facilities, though [they are] segregated in different cells/compounds."[39] Furthermore, the brigade's 320th Military Police Battalion found itself in charge of a detainee population that was different in character from what the battalion was trained to manage. It was also much larger, at 6,000–7,000 detainees rather than the Army doctrinal norm of 4,000 detainees under the control of a battalion. In short, Taguba found that the 800th Military Police Brigade

---

[36] Bensahel et al., 2008, p. 111. For a description of the early period of CPA, see Chandrasekaran, 2006a.

[37] Antonio M. Taguba, *Article 15-6 Investigation of the 800th Military Police Brigade*, Department of the Army, May 27, 2004, p. 10. Taguba found that "between October and December 2003, at the Abu Ghraib Confinement Facility (BCCF), numerous incidents of sadistic, blatant, and wanton criminal abuses were inflicted on several detainees. This systemic and illegal abuse of detainees was intentionally perpetrated by several members of the military police guard force" (p. 16).

[38] Taguba, 2004, p. 10.

[39] Taguba, 2004, pp. 11, 16; see also Independent Panel to Review Department of Defense Detention Operations, *The Schlesinger Report: An Investigation of Abu Ghraib*, New York: Cosimo, 2005.

"was not adequately trained" and "relied heavily on individuals within the Brigade who had civilian corrections expertise."[40]

The absence of civilian capacity and capabilities meant that the Army and the other services had to fill gaps for which they were not adequately prepared. This is reminiscent of the remark by retired GEN William Knowlton to an Army War College class in 1984: "Remember one lesson from the Vietnam era: Those who ordered the meal were not there when the waiter brought the check."[41] As in Vietnam, the military once again bore the heaviest burden in Iraq and Afghanistan. The Army gradually adapted and shifted its force structure to attain the capabilities needed in the wars, "decreasing the number of field artillery, air defense, engineer, armor and ordnance battalions while increasing military police, transportation, petroleum and water distribution, civil affairs, psychological operations and biological detection units."[42]

Nevertheless, shortages in capabilities persisted and were explicitly acknowledged in the 2006 counterinsurgency manual, FM 3-24. The manual notes that successful counterinsurgency required a whole-of-government approach but recognized that "[p]articipants best qualified and able to accomplish nonmilitary tasks are not always available. . . . In those cases, military forces perform those tasks. Sometimes forces have the skills required; other times they learn them during execution." The list of "useful skill sets" is daunting:

- Knowledge, cultural understanding, and appreciation of the host nation and region.
- Functional skills needed for interagency and [host-nation] coordination (for example, liaison, negotiation, and appropriate social or political relationships).
- Language skills needed for coordination with the host nation, [nongovernmental organizations], and multinational partners.
- Knowledge of basic civic functions such as governance, infrastructure, public works, economics, and emergency services.[43]

The Army did not have a ready supply of individuals with these skills and would endeavor to train them. In the interim, FM 3-24 advised commanders to "identify people in their units with regional and interagency expertise, civil-military competence, and other critical skills needed to support a local populace and [host-nation]

---

[40] Taguba, 2004, p. 37. Taguba also found that the mismatch between unit capacity and prisoner population could have been ameliorated within the brigade, given that one facility containing 100 high-value detainees "was run by an entire battalion" (p. 37).

[41] William A. Knowlton, "Ethics and Decision-Making," address delivered at the U.S. Army War College, Carlisle Barracks, Pa., October 22, 1984, p. 28.

[42] Anne Plummer, "Army Chief Tells President Restructuring Force Could Cost $20 Billion," *Inside the Army*, February 9, 2004, p. 2.

[43] FM 3-24, 2006, p. 2-9.

government."[44] This approach was necessary, given the absence of preparation for these roles before the Iraq War.

Recommendation: Continue Efforts to Provide Sufficient Military Government Capabilities

U.S. Army CA and military government capabilities should form the core of U.S. government efforts to transition after a regime change. As noted, the December 21, 2010, DoD Directive 5100.01 outlines the Army's responsibilities for providing capabilities to "occupy territories abroad and provide for the initial establishment of a military government pending transfer of this responsibility to other authority."[45] Historically, the Army has had to perform this function after many of the wars it has fought, with mixed results.[46]

World War II was the exception to the norm. Learning from its experiences in World War I, the U.S. Army manned, organized, trained, and equipped units for military government and CA functions under the direction of the Civil Affairs Division in the War Department. The division was also responsible for "making certain that all plans to occupy enemy or enemy-controlled territory included detailed planning for civil affairs."[47] The capabilities for these functions were largely drawn from the civil sector through a recruitment and selection process that provided direct commissions to those qualified because they were "well established in civilian jobs."[48]

---

[44] FM 3-24, 2006, p. 2-9. See also M. L. R. Smith and David Martin Jones, *The Political Impossibility of Modern Counterinsurgency: Strategic Problems, Puzzles, and Paradoxes*, New York: Columbia University Press, 2015. Smith and Jones argue that the "construction of the doctrine [in FM 3-24] served the Machiavellian purpose of providing ethical cover to sell the continuation of a controversial war to an increasingly skeptical public" (p. 54). The authors also believe that the British examples of counterinsurgency success were incomplete, if not inaccurate: "far from a flair for minimum force and hearts and minds, it was a talent for escalation into the dark arts of intelligence-led Special Forces Operations and the penetration of rebel networks—from Malaya to Northern Ireland to the back streets of Baghdad—where Britain's capacities really lay and continue to reside" (p. 183).

[45] DoD, 2010b, p. 30. See also Crane and Terrill, 2003, pp. 11–18.

[46] See Erwin F. Ziemke, *The U.S. Army in the Occupation of Germany 1944–1946*, Washington, D.C.: U.S. Army Center of Military History, 2003, p. 3. Ziemke noted,

> Military government, the administration by military officers of civil government in occupied enemy territory, is a virtually inevitable concomitant of modern warfare. The US Army conducted military government in Mexico in 1847 and 1848; in the Confederate states during and after the Civil War; in the Philippines, Porto [Puerto] Rico, and Cuba after the Spanish American War; and in the German Rhineland after World War I. In each instance, neither the Army nor the government accepted it as a legitimate military function. Consequently, its imposition invariably came as a somewhat disquieting experience for both, and the means devised for accomplishing it ranged from inadequate to near disastrous. (p. 3)

For a discussion of the World War II U.S. Army Civil Affairs program, see Harry L. Coles and Albert K. Weinberg, *Civil Affairs: Soldiers Become Governors*, Washington, D.C.: U.S. Army Center of Military History, 1992.

[47] Ziemke, 2003, p. 17.

[48] Ziemke, 2003, p. 18.

The Civil Affairs Training Program that prepared officers for their duties was a joint effort between the Army and contracted civilian institutions. The Army's Provost Marshall General's School provided "military and basic military government training." Universities offered language training and foreign-area studies for officers who would be assigned as specialists and technicians in occupied areas. Another school at the University of Virginia prepared officers for higher-level duties on staffs.[49] The overall requirement was established in September 1942 as "6,000 trained officers would be needed worldwide, [with] another 6,000 being recruited from tactical units as areas were occupied."[50] Doctrine, promulgated in the December 1943 *United States Army and Navy Manual of Military Government and Civil Affairs*, specified that "the chief function of the civil affairs officers during hostilities is to further the mission of the combat forces in every way possible." The manual further noted that during an extended occupation, the duties of CA officers "may range all the way from controlling a few simple functions of government in a small isolated rural region or a primitive island or group of islands, to controlling the many and complex functions of government in a large, densely populated, industrialized, continental area."[51]

When the United States, mainly U.S. Army forces, occupied its zone in Germany, it faced a defeated nation and a devastated country. Nevertheless, security was a principal focus, given the concerns "about creating a security vacuum in the country." Additionally, the German military "needed to be disarmed and demobilized promptly and efficiently . . . [and] Nazi war criminals needed to be identified and brought to trial." Finally, "the Allies feared that renegade guerrilla groups of German military forces would re-form into small units and launch attacks against Allied forces."[52] Consequently, the initial occupation force in the American sector had 1,622,000 soldiers for a German population of 16 million, which rapidly shrank

---

[49] Ziemke, 2003, pp. 18–19.

[50] Ziemke, 2003, p. 17.

[51] FM 27-5/OpNav 50E-3, *United States Army and Navy Manual of Military Government and Civil Affairs*, Washington, D.C.: U.S. War Department and Navy Department, 1943, pp. 15–20. This manual also detailed the "Functions of Civil Affairs Officers": political government and administration; maintenance of law and order; courts and law; civilian defense; civilian supply; public health and sanitation; censorship; communications; transportation; port duties; public utilities; money and banking; public finance; commodity control, prices, rationing; agriculture; industry and manufacture; commerce and trade; labor; custody and administration of property; information; disposition, repatriation, or relocation of displaced persons and enemy nationals; education; public welfare; records; and miscellaneous. Under the miscellaneous category, it notes,

> In addition, the civil affairs officer will be concerned with other civilian activities as may in any way affect the occupying forces or the war effort of the United States and its allies. Cutting across all of the foregoing activities will be problems common to most or all of them, such as the selection and use of local officials and personnel, matters of coordination and priority and the obtaining of information and intelligence. (p. 20)

[52] James Dobbins, John G. McGinn, Keith Crane, Seth G. Jones, Rollie Lal, Andrew Rathmell, Rachel Swanger, and Anga Timilsina, *America's Role in Nation-Building: From Germany to Iraq*, Santa Monica, Calif.: RAND Corporation, MR-1753-RC, 2003, p. 4.

to a constabulary force of 31,000 troops within an overall troop strength of some "200,000 by the end of 1946."[53]

This is not to say that all went smoothly in the occupation of Germany or other countries. In particular, there were issues with denazification efforts. As the Army's history of the occupation of Germany noted:

> Denazification gave the Army the mission of carrying out as radical an experiment in removing a source of international conflict as had been undertaken in modern times. Worthy as denazification was in principle, it was not, as military government was painfully aware, realistically conceived. Conducted as a full-scale social revolution, it imposed dangerous strains on the structure of occupation without necessarily promising any future returns other than more trouble.[54]

This experience with denazification parallels the decision for de-Ba'athification during Ambassador L. Paul Bremer III's tenure at CPA, although the results in Iraq were much worse given the absence of security.

In the aftermath of World War II, "the capabilities required to carry out military government were shunned and neglected by DoD and the Army at large until the conflicts in Afghanistan and Iraq made it terribly clear that history was repeating itself: the United States was quite unprepared for the responsibilities of administering Iraq and supporting the government of Afghanistan, and the ad hoc means we devised once again 'ranged from inadequate to near disastrous.'"[55] Issued in February 2000, Army FM 41-10, *Civil Affairs Operations*, reflected an approach in which the vast majority of actual CA technical expertise in 16 functional skills would reside in the reserve components, given the difficulty in developing and maintaining these skills in active-component CA units. Such units were designed to be composed mainly of CA generalists, whose function involved "support[ing] the commander's immediate needs by planning and coordinating CA activities that support the mission." Furthermore, for CA generalists, a premium was placed on "the ability to negotiate with local civilians and a thorough knowledge of the military decision-making process."[56]

---

[53] Dobbins, McGinn, et al., 2003, p. 10.

[54] Ziemke, 2003, p. 446. See also James J. Carafano, *Waltzing into the Cold War: The Struggle for Occupied Austria*, College Station, Tex.: Texas A&M University Press, 2002.

[55] David Stott Gordon, "Military Governance: The Essential Mission of Civil Affairs," in Christopher Holshek and John C. Church, Jr., eds., *2014–2015 Civil Affairs Issue Papers: The Future of Civil Affairs*, Carlisle Barracks, Pa.: U.S. Army War College Press, 2015, p. 90.

[56] FM 41-10, *Civil Affairs Operations*, Washington, D.C.: Headquarters, Department of the Army, 2000, pp. 3-1–3-2. The manual emphasizes the importance of the reserve-component CA units as a source of technical expertise:

> [Reserve-component] CA units are organized to provide expertise in 16 functional skills. Although the [active component] has the capability to execute missions in some of these functional specialty areas, it cannot maintain the high-level skills required for specialized CA activities. CA activities requiring specific civilian skills are,

This situation persisted throughout the wars in Iraq and Afghanistan:

> Current doctrine calls for functional specialists that are "Soldiers, both officer and enlisted, with technical expertise (normally acquired by civilian education and career experience) in those civilian sectors [Rule of Law, Economic Stability, Infrastructure, Governance, Public Health and Welfare, Public Education and Information] most likely to affect [civil military operations]."[57] With the exception of the Special Functions Teams of the active duty 85th CA Brigade that are based on military rather than civilian skills, U.S. Army CA functional specialist positions are exclusively assigned in the U.S. Army Reserve (USAR). The functional specialties currently include 14 areas of civil sector expertise intended to support governance across the range of military operations.[58]

The results of a March 2013 survey identified 559 positions in reserve CA units coded with skill identifiers (SIs). According to Hugh C. Van Roosen, who was the director of the IMSG at the time, "Only one officer assigned to these positions had the appropriate SI."[59] Moreover,

> The problem is further aggravated by the low standards that current SIs require. Current SIs also lack a measure with which to determine a specialist's capability to provide advice at the national or theater level versus the subnational level. For example, an elementary school teacher with a master's degree in education and one year of experience can hold the same SI as a state Secretary of Education with 20 years of experience. Neither may be knowledgeable about applying their skill to a foreign educational system. The unreliable accreditation and certification of [military government officer] functional specialists led to reliance on other Army

---

therefore, maintained in the [reserve component]. Within each specialty, technically qualified and experienced individuals advise and assist the commander and can assist or direct their civilian counterparts. (p. 3-2)

The 16 functional specialties are public administration, public education, public safety, international law, public health, public transportation, public works and utilities, public communications, food and agriculture, economic development, civilian supply, emergency services, environmental management, cultural relations, civil information, and dislocated civilians (pp. 3-9–3-17).

[57] FM 3-57, *Civil Affairs Operations*, Washington, D.C.: Headquarters, Department of the Army, 2011, p. 2-17.

[58] Hugh C. Van Roosen, *Military Support to Governance*, Version 7-Draft, white paper, January 12, 2015, p. 2.

[59] Van Roosen, 2015, p. 3. In the paper, Van Roosen recommended expanding the SIs from 11 (5Y–Civil Defense Officer, 6C–Economist, 6D–Public Education Officer, 6E–Civil Supply Officer, 6F–Public Transportation Officer, 6G–Public Facilities Officer, 6H–Public Safety Officer, 6R–Public Communications Officer, 6U–Agricultural Officer, 6V–Cultural Affairs Officer, 6W–Archivist) to 19 in five categories, reminiscent of the categories in the 1943 FM 27-5/OpNav 50E-3 (Economy and Infrastructure [Agri-Business and Food, Commerce and Trade, Finance and Economics, Industry and Production, Transportation, Energy, Water and Sanitation, Technology and Telecommunications]; Government and Administration [Civil Administration; Laws, Regulations, and Policies; Environment and Natural Resources; Emergency Management]; Rule of Law and Civil Security [Judiciary and Legal System, Law and Border Enforcement, Corrections]; Public and Social Services [Education, Public Health, Cultural Heritage Preservation]; External Security [Defense]).

branches functioning in mission areas for which they are not trained, organized, or equipped. As a result, [Army reserve] CA units lack the capability needed to fulfill these assigned roles and responsibilities.[60]

In August 2013, the commanding general of the U.S. Army Special Operations Command and the chief of the Army reserve partnered to establish the Institute for Military Support to Governance (IMSG) at the U.S. Army John F. Kennedy Special Warfare Center and School to correct the functional specialty capability gap in reserve-component CA units.[61] While recognizing that effective execution of the CA mission requires "civil sector expertise with education and experience developed through accomplished professional careers," Van Roosen also noted that "those civilian skills have been happenstance and lacked predictably to dependably aid military commanders in their responsibility to establish stability during the wars in Iraq and Afghanistan."[62]

The IMSG's mission statement shows that the CA and military government lessons for Iraq and Afghanistan are being partially institutionalized by the Army: "The IMSG organizes, trains, and coordinates Governance Advisory Teams, integrates with U.S. Government and community of interest partners, and provides ongoing research and analysis to meet theater requirements across all operational phases in support of Unified Action." The IMSG is a worthwhile investment to ensure that the capability gaps that the U.S. Army encountered in Iraq and Afghanistan are understood and ameliorated in the future.[63] The IMSG concept, in many ways, emulates the strategy deployed in World War II to use civil-sector expertise to create military government and CA units,[64] and it establishes a new area of concentration—military government officer. These officers are

> organized into Governance Advisory Teams . . . . [Military government] officers will be sourced from within the [Army reserve] (where available), other Services, and the civilian sector. Direct commissioning of civil sector experts in the ranks of captain or major through colonel is expected for some percentage of the [military government officer] positions (along the same concept as medical).[65]

In other words, the Army can use direct commissions for specially qualified civilians to acquire expertise that the Army needs from the civil sector.

---

[60] Van Roosen, 2015, p. 3.

[61] Van Roosen, 2015, p. 3.

[62] Van Roosen, 2015, p. 1.

[63] Van Roosen, 2015, p. 5.

[64] Van Roosen, 2015, p. 9.

[65] Van Roosen, 2015, p. 4. Medical Corps officers can receive direct commissions into the Army.

The Army should continue to support the IMSG and begin assessing several areas against plausible postconflict scenarios to ensure that it has the needed capacity and capabilities to meet its occupation and military government functions. For example, the Army should assess the following:

- Is the capacity of the Governance Advisory Teams sufficient against the scenarios?
- How are Governance Advisory Teams and other Army forces integrated to provide security and stabilization?
- Absent World War II conscription, how will sufficient military government officers be obtained to satisfy mission demands?
- What is the role of contractors?

Lesson 3: Robust and High-Quality Headquarters Are Critical
Observation: The Joint Task Force Organized Around the V Corps Headquarters Was Not Capable of Executing the Mission It Was Given

Chapters Two and Three of this report examined the transition from LTG David McKiernan's Joint Force Land Component Command headquarters to LTG Ricardo Sanchez's V Corps headquarters. McKiernan had a robust, hand-picked senior staff, including general officers, capable of operating at the nexus of operations and strategy.[66] Sanchez's headquarters were operational and designed by Army doctrine to control the actions of subordinate divisions, as stated in the then-authoritative 1996 FM 100-15, *Corps Operations*: "Corps are the largest tactical units in the U.S. Army. They are the instruments by which higher echelons of command conduct operations at the operational level."[67] Current Army doctrine similarly defines the corps as an operational headquarters:

> The corps headquarters is organized, trained, and equipped to serve as the [senior Army headquarters] in campaigns and major operations, with command of two or more Army divisions, together with supporting theater-level organizations, across the range of military operations. As the [senior Army headquarters] for the [joint force commander], the corps serves as an operational-level headquarters, conducting land operations as the Service component.[68]

Quite simply, neither General Sanchez's headquarters nor Ambassador Bremer's CPA was up to the challenges it faced. Succeeding as an operational headquarters is not about personalities. Instead, it is about providing adequate headquarters with the necessary capabilities to cope with the challenges at hand. Not until the creation of

---

[66] Former senior military commander, interview with the authors, April 17, 2015.

[67] FM 100-15, *Corps Operations*, Washington, D.C.: Headquarters, Department of the Army, 1996, p. 1-1.

[68] FM 3-94, *Theater Army, Corps, and Division Operations*, Washington, D.C.: Headquarters, Department of the Army, 2014, p. 4-1.

MNF-I, under General Casey, combined with the creation of MNC-I, did the headquarters on the ground have the talent and the horsepower to link tactics and operations effectively to strategy and policy. That said, it took some time for MNF-I to become fully capable. As General Casey recalled:

> The MNF-I headquarters was established on May 15, 2004, with personnel authorizations for individual officers and noncommissioned officers from across the U.S. Services and coalition countries. These personnel were slow to arrive, and the headquarters was still forming when I arrived at the end of June.[69]

This was more than a year into the war, and much time had been lost.

Finally, many Army headquarters in Iraq were ad hoc by nature and experienced high levels of turnover. For example, as noted in Chapter Five, MNSTC-I turnover was 25 percent per month in 2008. This personnel turbulence was deleterious both to continuity of operations and to effectiveness.

In the aftermath of the war in Iraq, DoD began reducing its end strength in response to the 2011 Budget Control Act. Facing significant directed budget cuts, particularly under sequestration, the Army saw its authorized end strength drop from 563,600 Regular Army, 358,200 National Guard, and 205,000 reserves in 2010 to a potential end strength in 2019 of 420,000 Regular Army, 315,200 National Guard, and 185,000 reserves.[70] Headquarters at the two-star-general level and above, both institutional and operational, were targeted for a 25-percent aggregate reduction by the Secretary of the Army and Chief of Staff of the Army.[71] For division headquarters, the cuts amounted to some 225 soldiers, and for corps-sized headquarters, around 222 soldiers.[72]

The 2016 National Defense Authorization Act continued to pressure DoD to reduce the size of its headquarters, requiring a 25-percent reduction against a baseline amount.[73] Anticipating these congressionally mandated cuts, Deputy Secretary of Defense Robert Work issued guidance that "the department needs the savings [25 percent] that will be achieved through this reduction to fund higher priority requirements in support of the warfighter and to address underfunded strategic needs."[74]

---

[69] See Casey, 2012, p. 22.

[70] National Commission on the Future of the U.S. Army, *Report to the President and the Congress of the United States, January 28, 2016*, Arlington, Va., 2016

[71] Department of the Army, "2013 Focus Areas," memorandum, August 14, 2015.

[72] C. Todd Lopez, "Army to Realign Brigades, Cut 40,000 Soldiers, 17,000 Civilians," U.S. Army, July 9, 2015.

[73] U.S. Congress, 114th Congress, 1st Sess., National Defense Authorization Act for Fiscal Year 2016, Washington, D.C., S. 1356, January 6, 2015, p. 72. The "baseline amount" is defined in the Act as "the amount authorized to be appropriated by this Act for fiscal year 2016 for major Department of Defense headquarters activities, adjusted by a credit for reductions in such headquarters activities that are documented, as of the date that is 90 days after the date of the enactment of this Act, as having been accomplished in earlier fiscal years in accordance with the December 2013 directive of the Secretary of Defense on headquarters reductions" (p. 72).

[74] Charles S. Clark, "Pentagon Moves Ahead With HQ Staff Cuts," *Government Executive*, September 8, 2015.

Recommendation: Provide Robust Division, Corps, and Theater Army Headquarters

Operational headquarters from the Army have served as the core of joint task forces in Afghanistan and Iraq since the beginning of both wars. Elements of III Corps deployed to Kuwait in September 2015 to serve as the CJTF headquarters for Operation Inherent Resolve,[75] and the 101st Airborne Division headquarters replaced the 82nd Airborne Division headquarters as the Combined Joint Force Land Component Command in Iraq and Kuwait in December 2015.[76] These headquarters deploy while leaving many of their subordinate units at their home stations.

As the Army has transitioned to a brigade-centric force, it has spent considerable effort ensuring that these units are cohesive. It should do the same for its higher operational headquarters. Rather than seeing headquarters as sources for manpower reductions, the Army should assess the need for more-robust division and corps headquarters that can operate simultaneously as deployed headquarters.[77]

Lesson 4: As the U.S. Military Continues to Perform the Training and Advising Missions, Developing Competent Advisors and Understanding Sustainable Outcomes Are Key

Observation: The Army Did Not Adequately Prepare or Incentivize Advisers to Create Sustainable Iraqi Security Forces

Building partner capacity remains a stated objective for DoD, and the Army provides trainers and advisers to the combatant commands to execute this mission.[78] The Army Operating Concept states this explicitly:

> To promote regional security, Army special operations forces and regionally aligned conventional forces engage in a broad range of theater security cooperation activities including security force assistance. These activities are special operations forces-specific, special operations forces-centric, or conventional force-centric depending on the nature of the mission. When needed, Army forces reinforce or bolster the efforts of partners. Army units tailored to the mission provide advice as well as access to combined joint and Army capabilities.[79]

Again, given current force-structure trends, the Army is deciding what is absolutely necessary and what is not. The trend is understandably toward preparing for

---

[75] "450 Fort Hood Soldiers Headed to Kuwait," *Army Times*, August 5, 2015.

[76] Michelle Tan, "101st Airborne to Deploy to Iraq, Kuwait," *Army Times*, November 16, 2015.

[77] For specific recommendations on improving JTF headquarters, see Timothy M. Bonds, Myron Hura, and Thomas-Durell Young, *Enhancing Army Joint Force Headquarters Capabilities*, Santa Monica, Calif.: RAND Corporation, MG-675-1-A, 2010.

[78] See DoD, 2014, p. 61; and Department of the Army, *2014 Army Strategic Planning Guidance*, Washington, D.C., 2014a, pp. 5–6.

[79] Department of the Army, 2014b, p. 17.

the most-consequential missions with a focus on decisive action and combined arms maneuver. Retired Army LTG James M. Dubik, a former commander of MNSTC-I, neatly summed up the dilemma: "The United States cannot hope to build the capacity of potential partners by overly shrinking its general purpose forces and then asking its special operations forces to do what they cannot."[80]

Proposals about how to prepare the Army for conventional combat, stability operations, and advisers have come and gone. They range from Andrew Krepinevich's call for the Army to focus more on constabulary and expeditionary operations to John Nagl's proposal for a "Permanent Army Advisory Corps."[81]

In several wars in its history, the Army's objective was to create and train an indigenous force that could provide for its own security. This was the case in the Philippines, Korea, and Vietnam. It was also a key objective in Afghanistan and Iraq. The collapse of the Iraqi military to the Islamic State provides lessons for the future in several areas, including determining what kind of Army the host nation requires and providing advisers and trainers for the effort in order to create sustainable outcomes. Additionally, U.S. military forces may be tasked to train and reform national police forces, as they did in Iraq and Afghanistan, because other U.S. government departments or agencies do not have the capacity to execute this mission.[82] This requirement should be addressed in military planning, and the U.S. Army military police community should be tasked to develop such plans.

Recommendation: Continue to Institutionalize Efforts to Prepare Trainers and Advisers

Proposals like those of Krepinevich and Nagl for how to advise and assist foreign armies are solutions frequently posed for a specific problem within a larger problem set. They do not consider the totality of the demands on the Army in the current war or the wars in which it may find itself in the future. Nevertheless, the Army should understand the problems that spawned the call for these solutions, understand how to learn from these experiences, and then institutionalize the relevant capabilities that were created for Iraq. The Army should be resourced to provide adequate capacity to prepare trainers and advisers, particularly for advising on combined arms operations at battalion and higher echelons.

---

[80] James M. Dubik, "A Closer Look at the 'Build Partner Capacity' Mission," *Army Magazine*, January 2012, p. 16.

[81] See Andrew F. Krepinevich, *Transforming the Legions: The Army and the Future of Land Warfare*, Washington, D.C.: Center for Strategic and Budgetary Analysis, January 14, 2004; and John A. Nagl, *Institutionalizing Adaptation: It's Time for a Permanent Army Advisor Corps*, Washington, D.C.: Center for a New American Security, June 2007.

[82] Robert M. Perito, *The Iraq Federal Police: U.S. Police Building Under Fire*, Washington, D.C.: United States Institute of Peace, Special Report No. 291, 2011, p. 1. Perito notes, "Transferring responsibility for civilian police training to the U.S. military was unprecedented. In all previous peace operations, State and the [Department of Justice] had led police assistance programs" (p. 3).

The Army should also reestablish an entity with the specific mission of preparing trainers and advisers. And it should look to foreign militaries for different approaches to preparing trainers and advisers.

In February 2017, the Army announced that it is establishing six Security Force Assistance Brigades and a Military Advisor Training Academy, beginning in October 2017. These initiatives have the potential to institutionalize the train, advise, and assist lessons from the Iraq War and ongoing efforts to bolster the ISF in the war against the Islamic State.

Lesson 5: The Goal of Building and Advising Foreign Military and Police Forces Should Be to Make Them Self-Sufficient
Observation: The ISF Could Not Operate Effectively Without Continued Access to U.S. Enablers
U.S. efforts to train and advise the ISF—a key mission in enabling a viable Iraqi state after the withdrawal of U.S. forces—are detailed in earlier chapters. On the eve of the U.S. departure from Iraq, a June 2010 quarterly report to Congress gave an optimistic, if somewhat caveated, account on the state of the ISF:

> The ISF have executed their security responsibilities extremely well, maintaining historically low levels of security incidents. . . . USF-I is on track to complete the transition to stability operations by September 1, 2010. The ongoing implementation of the [Strategic Framework Agreement] this reporting period sets the stage for long-term cooperative efforts as Iraq develops into a sovereign, stable, self-reliant partner in the region and as the United States transitions roles and responsibilities from U.S. Forces to the [Government of Iraq], the U.S. Embassy Baghdad, and other non-USF-I entities.[83]

This assessment likely would have been unchallenged if not for the collapse of the ISF to the Islamic State in many areas of northern Iraq, particularly Mosul. In reality, the ISF that fled in the face of the Islamic State's offensive in 2014 bolted because they were designed largely as an internal security force that "did little more than staff checkpoints."[84] The ISF could operate effectively only with significant U.S. assistance when facing anything other than moderate-scale internal threats. The ISF were incapable of the combined arms maneuver required to defeat the Islamic State. The tough urban fights in Iraq—Fallujah in 2004 and Sadr City in 2008—were dominated by U.S. forces with modest ISF participation. Although the Iraqis conceived and led the

---

[83] DoD, 2010a, p. x. The optimistic, but inaccurate, assessment of the state of the ISF on the eve of U.S. withdrawal from Iraq should also bring into question the ability of DoD or other U.S. government agencies to accurately assess and honestly provide feedback on the results of large-scale training and military assistance programs.

[84] Rod Nordland, "U.S. Soldiers, Back in Iraq, Find Security Forces in Disrepair," *New York Times*, April 14, 2015.

battle for Basra in 2008, the effort required massive U.S. assistance to succeed. The U.S. ground formations in these key battles were not just "boots on the ground." They were skilled, professional forces capable of something that the ISF are not: the expert execution of highly synchronized joint combined arms operations.[85] Finally, the motivation of the Shia-dominated ISF to fight to the death for Sunnis was also an issue.

Indeed, the causes for the failure of Iraq's army against the Islamic State were numerous. Perhaps most significant was the rampant corruption within the ISF, which worsened after U.S. forces departed and Prime Minister Maliki staffed the ISF with officers personally loyal to him, creating a force dominated by Shia and not trusted by Sunnis. Furthermore, the United States did not create sustainable Iraqi institutions that could continue the training programs put in place during the U.S. presence.[86]

Ironically, the ISF suffered from many of the same deficiencies as those of South Vietnam after the U.S. withdrawal there. The ISF were organized on a U.S. model, and absent U.S. support in the form of trainers, advisers, combat enablers (particularly air power), and logistics, they collapsed in the face of the Islamic State.[87] The training systems the United States had put in place prior to its withdrawal suffered an almost complete collapse. LTC John Schwemmer, a U.S. Army officer training Iraqis at Camp Taji in Iraq in April 2015, was stunned by the poor state of the ISF upon his return: "It's pretty incredible. . . . I was kind of surprised. What training did they have after we left?"[88]

Thus, the ultimate lesson from this experience should be to question whether the U.S. Army can advise another army to be something that does not resemble the U.S. Army in a conflict environment in which there is political pressure to leave. That pressure is greatest when there are continuing U.S. casualties. In a more benign situation, such as the Republic of Korea after the Korean War, evolving to a U.S. model is viable. This also pertains to other indigenous government functions. It borders on trite, but the platitude that "Rome wasn't built in a day" serves as reasonable caution when attempting to achieve wholesale nation-building under fire. Is there another model? As the Army prepares and provides forces to support combatant command efforts in building partner capacity around the world in support of U.S. policy, it is worth questioning whether a U.S. Army adviser can train another army to be something that is outside the experience of the U.S. adviser.

---

[85] Johnson, 2015, p. 11.

[86] David D. Kirkpatrick, "Graft Hobbles Iraq's Military in Fighting ISIS," *New York Times*, November 23, 2013.

[87] There were obviously other factors at work, such as the sectarian nature of the Maliki government, his use of the Army as a patronage system, and rampant corruption. That said, even if those other factors had not been in play, the question remains: Could an Iraqi Army designed largely for internal stability operations have stood up to the Islamic State?

[88] Nordland, 2015.

Recommendation: When Designing Efforts to Build Indigenous Security Forces, Account for Their Ability to Operate Absent Large-Scale U.S. Support

U.S. military objectives and approaches for building institutions and security forces must work within the culture and situation at hand and not necessarily be designed to emulate U.S. approaches. Proposed solutions must be politically and economically feasible to the indigenous state. Achieving this objective requires a deep understanding of the capabilities of the host nation, which should help shape the type of adviser and foreign military sales strategies employed. Again, adviser and trainer preparation is a key ingredient for success.

Lesson 6: Military Transition Teams and Advisers Are Key to Developing Forces That Provide Sustainable Security

Observation: Training and Advising the ISF Was a Key Mission That the U.S. Military Was Not Initially Resourced or Prepared to Execute

As documented in this report, U.S. efforts to prepare advisers for what was the top priority in Iraq for much of the war—build and train a competent Iraqi security force—were slow to get started and reminiscent of Vietnam, when advisory duty was not seen as career-enhancing.[89] As COL Kevin P. Reynolds noted, "As with Vietnam, the priority of quality officer fill in Iraq goes to U.S. combat units. Most officers view their chances for school selection, promotion, and command assignment as directly tied to their performance in U.S. units leading and commanding U.S. soldiers."[90]

Reflecting on the observations by GEN Donn Starry on advisers in Vietnam and noting the similarities between advisers in Vietnam and Iraq, Jason Fritz also wrote about how the Army eventually adapted in Iraq:

> The first lesson I will highlight here is best summed by Starry's succinct observation, "It is . . . plain that the American advisers to the South Vietnamese Army were important but that their preparation for the tasks that confronted them was poor." Until the advent of the Advise-and-Assist Brigades of the late-2000s, the selection and training of military advisers was relatively unchanged since 1962. Officers and NCOs were chosen because they were available and for no other reason. The Army launched an adviser training course at Fort Bragg in 1962 that lasted 6 weeks and focused on infantry tasks, not the other combined arms tasks with which advisers would be dealing. No language or cultural training was included.

---

[89] On perceptions of advisory duty during the Vietnam War, see Andrew J. Birtle, *U.S. Army Counterinsurgency and Contingency Operations Doctrine, 1942–1975*, Washington, D.C.: U.S. Army Center of Military History, 2006, p. 451. Birtle writes,

> Many soldiers were also convinced, rightly or otherwise, that advisory duty was detrimental to their careers. Sincere and repeated efforts by the Army to dispel this belief, as well as to improve the quality of the advisory effort through career incentives and increased education, never succeeded in overcoming the officer corps' innate aversion for this key component of American policy.

[90] Kevin P. Reynolds, "Insurgency/Counterinsurgency: Does the Army 'Get It?'" paper presented at the International Studies Association Annual Convention, Carlisle, Pa., February 28–March 3, 2007.

Now, as then, there were and are a number of problems with how the United States has grown, trained, and advised Iraqi and Afghan forces, but high among these has been our consistent failure to provide properly trained advisers. As an example, Owen West stated that his training to lead an adviser team in 2006 lasted only 42 days and was of poor quality—hardly the level of quality we should expect for the key element of the U.S. withdrawal plans. It took until 2009 and the fielding of Advise-and-Assist Brigades for the Army to institutionalize advising at a minimal level, although this unit was chosen because it was available and not for its superior ability to advise indigenous forces. In short, we were just as good at advising, institutionally, in Iraq and Afghanistan as we were in Vietnam.[91]

Recommendation: Consider Institutionalizing Advisory Capabilities in Army Training, Culture, and Leader Development

A first step in ensuring that advisory capabilities survive within the U.S. Army as it continues to downsize is to incorporate and institutionalize those capabilities into Army training, culture, and leader development.[92] This could include prioritizing advisory capabilities in leader development criteria and training. Currently, the Army selects brigade and battalion commanders through boards, rightly picking its best to lead soldiers. Prioritizing and recognizing advising as a skill that can enhance success in command has the potential to change a culture that views advising as a second-tier position.

As this report was being prepared, the Army began studying how to prepare battalions and brigades for the training and advising mission.[93] In essence, as explained by Army Chief of Staff Mark Milley,

> The train-and-advise units would have all the officers and NCOs of a regular battalion or even an entire brigade . . . but not the rank-and-file. That's because advisors and trainers are advising and training some other country's combat troops, not holding the line on their own. They need lots of experienced military professionals to mentor the host nation's leadership in conducting operations and/or training. They don't need regular riflemen, truck drivers, mechanics, and the like.[94]

---

[91] Jason Fritz, "Lessons Observed on Lessons Observed: IEDs, Advising, and Armor," *War on the Rocks*, February 3, 2014.

[92] See Remi Hajjar, "What Lessons Did We Learn (or Re-Learn) About Military Advising after 9/11?" *Military Review*, November–December 2014. As Hajjar recommends, "Institutionalizing a concentration on military advising, including an effectual advisor training center, while preserving relevant soft-skill programs (such as culture centers, culture education and training, and other helpful culture-based initiatives) will help the military to remain balanced and well prepared for multifaceted future contingencies" (p. 74).

[93] Sydney J. Freedburg, Jr., "Army Mulls Train and Advise Brigades: Gen. Milley," *Breaking Defense*, December 14, 2015.

[94] Freedburg, 2015.

Additionally, General Milley explained,

> During [peacetime] Phase 0 type operations, they can be used for train, advise, and assist.... Then in time of national emergency, you have a coherent chain of command that I can bring soldiers in, put them through Basic [Training] and [Advanced Individual Training], and match them up with those leaders, put them through a few months of pretty significant training, and then I'd have a reasonably decent capability that could backstop the regular Army forces and the Guard.[95]

Thus, the approach described by Milley would provide the United States with an Army better prepared to build partner capacity in friendly nations. Additionally, it would provide the basis for rapid Army expansion in the event of a crisis or a need to surge forces while living within end-strength constraints.

In February 2017, the Army announced that it would create six security force assistance brigades (SFABs), with the first brigade set to activate at Fort Benning, Georgia, in October 2017. These brigades will "contribute to the train, advise, and assist partnership the U.S. has with security forces of partner nations and will have teams tailored to each echelon of partner forces from company to division or corps." The SFABs are a recognition that the train, advise, and assist missions are "likely to grow." When the first SFAB activation was announced, there were some 4,500 trainers in Iraq alone.[96] The brigades also reduce the current practice for providing advisers from BCTs, as General Milley explained:

> We've taken brigades apart, active-duty, full-up infantry and armor brigades, and ripped them apart, ripped the leadership up, so what is the effect? ... The effect is several thousand soldiers left at home station with very little—if any—inherent organic chain of command, so then you have discipline, cohesion problems, and so forth, training problems.[97]

Thus, the SFABs, with 500 officers and noncommissioned officers, not only provide focused capability for the train, advise, and assist mission but they "will enhance the Army's readiness by reducing demand for existing brigade combat teams, which will allow BCTs to perform full-spectrum operations instead."[98]

Importantly, on October 1, 2017, the Army was set to establish the Military Advisor Training Academy at Fort Benning, housed within the Maneuver Center of Excel-

---

[95] Freedburg, 2015.

[96] Charlsy Panzino, "Fort Benning to Stand Up Security Force Brigades, Training Academy," *Army Times*, February 16, 2017.

[97] Panzino, 2017.

[98] Panzino, 2017.

lence.[99] This provides the Army with an institutional entity charged with preparing the soldiers and leaders for the train, advise, and assist mission.

These initiatives are big steps forward in learning and institutionalizing key lessons from the Iraq War. Importantly, the future competitiveness for promotion and key assignments for those who serve in SFABs will also be key as a validation to the officers and noncommissioned officers in the Army that SFAB duty is a valuable, career-enhancing assignment. Thus, the SFABs have the potential to change the culture of the Army in a useful way.

Lesson 7: The Battle for Baghdad Offers Insights About How to Prepare for Future Urban Combat

Observation: The Army Used Urban Combat Operations in the Battle for Baghdad and Can Draw on Those Experiences

There is increased awareness that future military operations will almost certainly have to contend with the challenges presented by large urban areas, including megacities with populations greater than 10 million people.[100] Though not a megacity, Baghdad did have some 5–7 million residents. The final part of that battle—the Battle of Sadr City—centered on a dense urban area containing about 2 million residents. The Army gradually "shrank the problem" in Baghdad by using walls, presence, integrated operations with conventional and special operations forces, highly integrated cross-agency intelligence, and a host of other innovative methods to secure the city and protect its population.

In Sadr City, brigade commanders had resources at their disposal never imagined at that level before the Battle for Baghdad. They also created a condition whereby the Jaysh al-Mahdi militia left Sadr City, giving the coalition an enormous advantage. However, the Army has yet to fully institutionalize the lessons from Sadr City.

The Army recognizes the challenges of urban warfare, particularly in megacities, as seen in General Milley's comments at the October 2016 Association of the U.S. Army. He noted,

> The Army has been designed, manned, trained and equipped for the last 241 years to operate primarily in rural areas. . . . In the future, I can say with very high degrees of confidence, the American Army is probably going to be fighting in urban areas. . . . We need to man, organize, train and equip the force for operations

---

[99] Panzino, 2017.

[100] See, for example, Kevin M. Felix and Frederick D. Wong, "The Case for Megacities," *Parameters*, Vol. 45, No. 1, Spring 2015, which discusses megacity challenges, Army efforts to understand them, and several operational approaches. See also Michael Bailey, Robert Dixon, Marc Harris, Daniel Hendrex, Nicholas Melin, and Richard Russo, "A Proposed Framework for Appreciating Megacities: A U.S. Army Perspective," *Small Wars Journal*, April 21, 2014; Richard Russo, "The Gotham Division and Staff Sergeant Parker: Imagining the Future of Urban Warfare," *Small Wars Journal*, June 11, 2014; and Michael A. Bailey and John D. Via, "Military Medical Implications of Future Megacity Operations," *Small Wars Journal*, February 13, 2015.

in urban areas, highly dense urban areas, and that's a different construct. We're not organized like that right now.[101]

Recommendation: Understand and Institutionalize Lessons from the Army's Recent Urban Warfare Experiences

The Battles of Baghdad and Sadr City are detailed in Chapter Five.[102] They—as well as the Battle of Fallujah and the fights against the Islamic State in Mosul and against Russian operations in Grozny—have many insights and lessons that should be helpful as the Army prepares for this difficult operational environment.

The Army has undertaken studies, both internally (within the Chief of Staff of the Army Strategic Studies Group and the U.S. Army Training and Doctrine Command) and externally (with the RAND Corporation) on the broader question of urban operations and megacities.[103] The Army should continue this work but also understand that each city is an independent and distinct (even unique) entity. Thus, the doctrine, organization, training, materiel, leadership and education, personnel, and facilities process should focus on specific cases where the Army might be engaged in urban combat and what types of adversaries it will face in those cities. Additionally, many of the solutions employed in Baghdad relied on infrastructure established over years that would not be available immediately during expeditionary operations and perhaps would leave U.S. forces vulnerable if they were to encounter adversaries with greater capabilities than the insurgents in Baghdad.

Lesson 8: Professional Military Education Is Critical in Preparing Army Leaders for the Future

Observation: The U.S. Professional Military Education System Did Not Adequately Prepare Leaders for Post-Saddam Iraq

The U.S. professional military education (PME) system did not prepare officers for the war in which they found themselves following major combat operations in 2003. This was most apparent at the senior levels, where operations had to be designed to achieve policy and strategic goals. Indeed, an Army study on its training and leader development noted in 2002 that "officers are concerned that the officer education system does not provide them with the skills for success in full spectrum operations."[104] The report

---

[101] Michelle Tan, "Army Chief: Soldiers Must Be Ready to Fight in 'Megacities'," *Defense News*, October 5, 2016.

[102] See Johnson, Markel, and Shannon, 2013.

[103] See, for example, Johnson, Markel, and Shannon, 2013; Gentile et al., 2017.

[104] Department of the Army, *The Army Training and Leader Development Panel Officer Study Report to the Army*, Arlington, Va., 2003, p. 6.

also noted that the officer education system has been "largely untouched since the end of the Cold War" and that it "is out of synch with Army needs."[105]

A 2002 RAND report prepared for the Army confirmed the Army report's finding:

> What appears to be missing from both the [Command and General Staff Officer Course] and Army War College core curricula are any in-depth examinations of actual post–Cold War other-than-[major theater war] experiences to provide students an understanding of the nondoctrinal realities these operations imposed on Army senior leaders. The emphasis seems to be on doctrinal solutions. Furthermore, the [military operations other than war] sections of the curricula appear to be focused principally on understanding the role of Army forces in these operations, with consideration of jointness, other services and agencies, allies, and [nongovernmental organizations] being a secondary issue.[106]

In that same report, the perspectives of several general officers on their readiness for command in ongoing operations in Bosnia were both candid and concerning. GEN William C. Crouch, U.S. Army Europe commander at the beginning of the Implementation Force Bosnia deployment and the eventual commander of Implementation Force and the successor Stabilization Force, stated "I was on my own. I'd certainly never trained for something like this."[107] MG Kevin Byrnes developed his own senior-level training program for the 1st Cavalry Division and "flew many of the senior leaders to Europe for on-the-ground training; that was very useful. It was too short, but it was the best we could get at the time."[108] Generals Shinseki and Montgomery Meigs also served as Stabilization Force commanders after General Crouch. Shinseki "believed that in the absence of a coherent Army doctrine for large-scale stability operations, commanders found themselves in a 'roll-your-own situation.'" Meigs agreed, stating, "I got nothing . . . for this mission. I visited a lot of folks, but the [A]rmy didn't sit me down and say, 'Listen, here is what you need to know.'"[109]

In Bosnia, senior U.S. commanders were unprepared, and they found themselves in a similar state in the aftermath of major combat operations in Iraq, but operating in a much more lethal and complex environment. Their PME experiences had focused

---

[105] Department of the Army, 2003, p. 22. See also Henry A. Leonard, J. Michael Polich, Jeffrey D. Peterson, Ronald E. Sortor, and S. Craig Moore, *Something Old, Something New: Army Leader Development in a Dynamic Environment*, Santa Monica, Calif.: RAND Corporation, MG-281-A, 2006.

[106] David E. Johnson, "Preparing Potential Senior Army Leaders for the Future: An Assessment of Leader Development Efforts in the Post–Cold War Era," Santa Monica, Calif.: RAND Corporation, IP-224-A, 2002, p. 19.

[107] Howard Olsen and John Davis, *Training U.S. Army Officers for Peace Operations: Lessons from Bosnia*, Special Report, Washington, D.C.: United States Institute of Peace, October 29, 1999, p. 4.

[108] Olsen and Davis, 1999, p. 4.

[109] Olsen and Davis, 1999, p. 2.

on preparing for operations against the same adversary encountered during Operation Desert Storm—the conventional military of Saddam—that had been so handily defeated by AirLand Battle doctrine. Neither the Army, nor the other services and joint PME systems, had done much to prepare for anything else, as documented in the early chapters of this report.

Another pattern emerged similar to what had happened in Bosnia. General Crouch started a program to pass on lessons learned from Bosnia, but it was not an Army-wide initiative and the learning was local.[110] This is not dissimilar to General Casey starting the Phoenix Academy to "train the trainers" to work with the Iraqi Army and the counterinsurgency academy to prepare incoming leaders for the fight in Iraq. Both of these initiatives were needed because the Army education and doctrine systems had not caught up to the problem the Army was facing.[111] It took until December 2006 for the Army and the Marine Corps to publish doctrine (FM 3-24) and adopt institution-wide approaches to the challenges of Iraq and Afghanistan.

The Army prepares the majority of its senior leaders at the U.S. Army War College, whose students are selected for attendance based on their potential for future service at the colonel and general officer levels.[112] A review of Army War College course directives shows that the institution eventually caught up to what was happening in the wars. It shifted from a focus on major theater war and military operations other than war in 2002 to a curriculum in 2005 that included counterinsurgency and counterterrorism.[113] The key question that still remains is: What needs to happen to Army PME to ensure that senior leaders are prepared for an environment like the one in Iraq following major combat operations?

Recommendation: Prepare Senior Leaders for the Full Range of Operations in Which They Will Operate

Studies on the need for PME and how it should be reformed are exhaustive, as can be seen in an 87-page bibliography (as of October 2007) compiled by the Naval Postgraduate School.[114] The most recent Army effort was the *2013 Chief of Staff of the Army*

---

[110] Johnson, 2002, pp. 12–13.

[111] Casey, 2012, pp. 61, 73–74.

[112] The majority of Army officers attend the U.S. Army War College, although many attend joint PME programs at the National Defense University, attend other service war colleges, or participate in a variety of fellowship opportunities. However, at the Army War College, the Army largely shapes the curriculum.

[113] See U.S. Army War College, "Directive Academic Year 2002: Core Curriculum Course 4: Implementing National Military Strategy," Carlisle Barracks, Pa., 2001; and U.S. Army War College, "Directive Academic Year 2002: Core Curriculum Course 4: Implementing National Military Strategy," Carlisle Barracks, Pa., 2005.

[114] Greta E. Marlatt, *A Bibliography of Professional Military Education (PME)*, Monterey, Calif.: Naval Postgraduate School, October 2007.

Leader Development Task Force Final Report, which contains a "Historical Review of Leader Development Studies" conducted by the Army since 1970.[115]

Thus, it is difficult to make a recommendation on what to do in PME, given that it has long been recognized and advertised that one of PME's central missions is to create critical thinkers. David A. Fastabend and Robert H. Simpson commented on this in 2004, stating, "Most Army schools open with the standard bromide: We are not going to teach you what to think . . . we are going to teach you how to think. They rarely do."[116] It is beyond the scope of this report to do much more than echo the observations made by James Carafano of the Heritage Foundation in his May 2009 testimony before the House Armed Services Committee's Subcommittee on Oversight and Investigations:

> The services and the Defense Department continue to adjust to the realities of the post–Cold War world in an ad hoc manner. This committee has asked an appropriate question—whether such incremental adjustments make sense. I don't think they do.
>
> In part, my recommendation was a reflection of watching the officer corps struggle with the challenges of adapting to military operations in Iraq and Afghanistan, but more deeply it stemmed from the observation that military schools had changed only modestly since the end of the Cold War. Preparing to fight a known enemy required certain skills and knowledge, and professional education focused on those narrow areas. As a result, officer schools and development programs continued to train and promote leaders with skills and attributes to meet the needs of the 20th century, not future challenges.[117]

PME should use case studies and war games to teach officers vicariously about the U.S. Army's role across the range of operations. Since 2003, the focus has necessarily been on the irregular wars in which the Army was deeply engaged. Broadening the curricula is particularly important as the Army broadens its focus to preparing for high-end adversaries (for instance, Russia and China) while retaining the hard-won lessons of the past 15 years. For many officers, major combat operations against competent, well-armed adversaries are as unfamiliar as irregular warfare was in 2003. PME can provide future senior Army leaders with the intellectual underpinnings to be able

---

[115] Department of the Army, *2013 Chief of Staff of the Army Leader Development Task Force Final Report*, Washington, D.C., June 14, 2013.

[116] David A. Fastabend and Robert H. Simpson, "'Adapt or Die': The Imperative for a Culture of Innovation in the United States Army," *Army Magazine*, February 2004, p. 20.

[117] James J. Carafano, "20 Years Later: Professional Military Education," testimony before the Subcommittee on Oversight and Investigations, House Armed Services Committee, Washington, D.C., May 20, 2009.

to understand the tactical, operational, and strategic implications of a range of operational environments.[118]

This broader approach to PME should also improve the ability of senior Army leaders to advise civilian appointees and senior officers about whether a strategy will achieve policy objectives. Again, this is a perennial question and has been given exhaustive treatment in the literature on civil-military relations ever since Samuel Huntington's 1959 classic, *The Soldier and the State: The Theory and the Politics of Civil-Military Relations*.[119]

As already noted, the treatment of General Shinseki seemingly silenced the rest of the uniformed military leadership. The key question is, why was General Shinseki's advice on force levels not sufficient to change the minds of U.S. policymakers? Possibly, the answer lies in the inability of most to imagine what Iraq would look like after the regime was toppled, and dealing with the chaos required more than additional soldiers. As a former senior military commander we spoke with recalled, his troops were largely without instructions about what to do in what was a de facto occupation.[120]

PME should teach officers to understand the dynamics of what has happened in the past as a way to think about the future, Furthermore, PME should prepare officers to provide better military advice and plans to civilian policymakers based on empirical analysis, which enables policymakers to make better decisions or at least understand the potential consequences of those decisions. In short, PME can help future Army leaders avoid the surprise experienced by General Wallace (described in Chapter Two): "But what in fact happened, which was unanticipated at least in [my mind], is that when [we] decapitated the regime, everything below it fell apart.[121] This lack of anticipation explains why there was little demand in CENTCOM for a comprehensive Phase IV plan or the capacity and capabilities to execute such a plan. Not until the Surge did the United States have a plan *and* the requisite number of forces that could solve the security problem in Baghdad. It is also telling that the initial plan for the Surge was broached to President Bush by those outside the active-duty military ranks. By that point, the strategic end state of the policy had shifted from Iraq as a beacon of democracy for the Middle East to getting security strong enough for the United States to hand over the future of Iraq to its own leaders. The results of that end state are playing out today in Iraq, Libya, Syria, and Yemen.

---

[118] For a discussion of the implications of operating against a range of adversaries, see David E. Johnson, *Hard Fighting: Israel in Lebanon and Gaza*, Santa Monica, Calif.: RAND Corporation, MG-1085-A/AF, 2011, pp. 148–181.

[119] Samuel P. Huntington, *The Soldier and the State: The Theory and Politics of Civil-Military Relations*, Cambridge, Mass.: Harvard University Press, 1957.

[120] Former senior military commander, interview with the authors, July 21, 2015.

[121] Bensahel et al., 2008, p. 18.

Final Thoughts

Over the past several years of conflict in Iraq, the U.S. Army—largely trained, organized, and equipped in 2003 to "dominate land warfare," with the expectation that an army so prepared "also provides the ability to dominate any situation in military operations other than war"—has adapted in combat to meet the demands it faced on the ground after the collapse of the Saddam regime.[122] Tactical units generally adapted quickly, but they did not have a strategic or doctrinal framework to give that adaptation coherence and any linkage to policy objectives, which were initially unrealistic. Eventually, the Army as an institution caught up to practice in theater and provided the forces and capabilities needed to win the Battle for Baghdad but not adequate to build an Iraqi army with the will to defend against the ISIS threat.

These adaptations, detailed in the earlier chapters of this report, were extraordinarily broad-ranging, including building and advising the ISF, advising Iraqi ministries, staffing provisional reconstruction teams, and accomplishing a host of other missions that DoD and other U.S. government agencies had not sufficiently prepared for before Operation Iraqi Freedom. The challenge now is to shape the Army for the future detailed in the *Army Operating Concept*, while institutionalizing the hard-learned lessons of the Iraq War. Instability and insurgency are almost certainly part of that future, and if history is any guide, the United States will look to the Army to deal with these challenges. More than the other services, the Army is charged with the mission of providing security and transitional military governance in the aftermath of successful major combat operations. Thus, the ultimate goal of this report is to help the Army continue to institutionalize the lessons from the Iraq War and the Battle for Baghdad as it prepares for an uncertain future.

---

[122] FM 3-0, *Operations*, Washington, D.C.: Headquarters, Department of the Army, 2001, p. vii.

APPENDIX

Timeline of Major Events in the Battle for Baghdad

Date	Key U.S. Political Actions and Events	Key U.S. Military Actions and Events	Other Key Actions and Events
June 2001	6/22: National Security Council deputies meet to discuss Iraq.[1]		
July 2001	7/26: Feith and Wolfowitz propose switching from an Iraq airstrike policy of going tit for tat to "breaking the logjam" and giving wholesale support to the opposition; the policy is endorsed by Rumsfeld and sent to Powell, Cheney, and Rice.[2]		
September 2001	9/26: Bush asks Rumsfeld to look at the condition of military plans for Iraq.[3] 9/29: Rumsfeld asks Myers to begin developing military options for Iraq.[4]		9/11: Terrorists successfully perpetrate attacks in New York, Pennsylvania, and Washington, D.C.
October 2001	Operation Enduring Freedom in Afghanistan begins.		
November 2001	Wolfowitz, Myers, Pace, and Feith begin to review war plans.[5]		
December 2001		12/28: Franks meets with Bush to discuss revised Iraq war plans. Rumsfeld and Myers join by video teleconference.[6]	

---

[1] Feith, 2008, p. 206.

[2] Feith, 2008, pp. 209–210.

[3] Rumsfeld, 2011, p. 425.

[4] Feith, 2008, p. 218.

[5] Feith, 2008, p. 219.

[6] Rumsfeld, 2011, p. 429.

Date	Key U.S. Political Actions and Events	Key U.S. Military Actions and Events	Other Key Actions and Events
May 2002	5/22: Peter Rodman, Assistant Secretary of Defense for International Security Affairs, proposes organizing "democratic opposition groups" to "avoid a political vacuum" in Iraq.[7]		
June 2002	6/1: At West Point's graduation, President Bush announces his doctrine of "preemptive action" to destroy threats before they materialize.[8] Feith meets Christina Shelton, Defense Intelligence Agency officer on loan to the Under Secretary of Defense for Policy, who critiques the CIA's Iraq intelligence—specifically its connection with al Qaeda.[9]		
July 2002	7/1: Rumsfeld sends Rodman's idea to organize democratic opposition groups to the principals.[10] 7/25: Armitage distributes a paper, "Diplomatic Plan for the Day After," at the deputies' lunch.[11]	7/9: CJCS issues a planning order for possible military operations against Iraq.[12] Casey, then the chief of strategic plans and policy (J5) on the Joint Staff, sets up an interagency working group to assist CENTCOM in planning for the war.[13]	
August 2002	8/6: Rice circulates a "Liberation Strategy for Iraq," reflecting democracy promotion, at a National Security Council Principals Committee meeting.[14]	General Franks (CENTCOM commander) meets with the UK Chief of Joint Operations to request an analysis of capability requirements by 9/25. The plan calls for UK forces to assemble and deploy from Turkey.[15]	

---

[7] Feith, 2008, p. 252.

[8] Wright and Reese, 2008, p. 621.

[9] Feith, 2008, p. 266.

[10] Feith, 2008, p. 252.

[11] Feith, 2008, p. 277.

[12] JCS, "Operation Iraqi Freedom (OIF) History Brief," briefing slides, May 14, 2003.

[13] Feith, 2008, p. 276.

[14] Feith, 2008, p. 283.

[15] JCS, 2003.

Date	Key U.S. Political Actions and Events	Key U.S. Military Actions and Events	Other Key Actions and Events
August 2002 (cont.)	8/9–8/10: Mark Grossman and Feith meet with Iraqi politicians Allawi, Chalabi, Jalal Talabani, Hoshyar Zebari, and Abdulaziz el-Hakim at the Department of State for the first time. Powell, Rumsfeld, and Cheney speak to them as well.[16] 8/12: Frank Miller, NSC staffer, forms the Executive Steering Committee with the Department of State, DoD, CIA, and White House to direct Iraq political-military policy.[17] 8/15: Former National Security Adviser Brent Scowcroft writes an op-ed warning of consequences of war in Iraq.[18] 8/27: Rumsfeld visits Saudi Arabia to ask for greater cooperation for Operation Southern Watch, including expanded air operations, sharing of intel, unrestricted overflight, and hot pursuit of terrorists from Yemen. But the Saudi king is informed that no decision on Iraq has been made.[19] Shelton briefs Rumsfeld, George Tenet (director of the CIA), and CIA analysts critiquing their Iraq assessment and highlighting Iraq's role in terrorism.[20] President Bush signs a classified document outlining the "freedom agenda," which proclaimed that the United States would support the development of a democratic Iraq.[21]	8/22: CJCS General Myers presents a briefing, "Iraq: Political-Military Strategic Plan," that describes Northern Front and Turkish air base operability as critical. The CENTCOM war plan calls for near-simultaneous employment of both North and South forces.[22]	

---

[16] Feith, 2008, p. 281.

[17] Feith, 2008, p. 276; JCS, 2003.

[18] Feith, 2008, pp. 307–308.

[19] JCS, 2003.

[20] Feith, 2008, p. 266.

[21] Gordon and Trainor, 2012, p. 8.

[22] JCS, 2003.

Date	Key U.S. Political Actions and Events	Key U.S. Military Actions and Events	Other Key Actions and Events
September 2002	9/12: Bush travels to the U.N. to make the case for military action against Iraq.[23] 9/17: Bush issues the 2002 National Security Strategy.[24]	9/12: CJCS Myers issues a planning order for training the FIF.[25]	
October 2002	10/15: Feith completes the "Parade of the Horribles" memo, detailing everything that could go wrong in an American intervention in Iraq.[26] 10/15: In a principals committee meeting, Tenet claims to have located a site that will produce a smoking gun on Iraq's WMDs.[27] 10/16: Bush signs the "Authorization for the use of Military Force Against Iraq Resolution of 2002."[28] 10/18: Rumsfeld requests an information plan for Iraq and asks about follow-on Iraqi governance.[29]	10/4–10/5: CENTCOM holds a war game for the overthrow of the Iraqi regime.[30] 10/7: CJCS Myers issues a planning order for air and ground operations from Turkey, which is an integral part of the war plan.[31]	10/19: Saddam Hussein announces amnesty for all those held in Iraqi prisons.[32]

---

[23] Wright and Reese, 2008, p. 621.

[24] White House, *National Security Strategy of the United States of America*, Washington, D.C., September 17, 2002.

[25] JCS, 2003.

[26] Feith, 2008, pp. 333–334.

[27] Feith, 2008, p. 314.

[28] Wright and Reese, 2008, p. 621.

[29] Feith, 2008, p. 317.

[30] JCS, 2003.

[31] JCS, 2003.

[32] Wright and Reese, 2008, p. 621.

Timeline of Major Events in the Battle for Baghdad 239

Date	Key U.S. Political Actions and Events	Key U.S. Military Actions and Events	Other Key Actions and Events
October 2002 (cont.)	10/28: Rumsfeld tasks Feith to develop the end state for Iraq (short of Rice's pluralistic democracy vision).[33]	10/29: CJCS Myers issues the "National Military Strategic Plan for the War on Terrorism."[35]	
	LtGen. Gregory Newbold, the Joint Staff Director of Operations (J-3), retires in silent protest of Iraq War planning.[34]	10/31: CENTCOM commander publishes the OPLAN 1003V war plan.[36]	
November 2002	11/15: The Department of State sends cables to 52 countries seeking support for potential U.S. combat operations in Iraq.[37]		11/7: The U.N. Security Council adopts Resolution 1441 demanding that Iraq declare all of its WMD stockpiles within 30 days.[38]
			11/27: Saddam allows U.N. weapons inspectors back into Iraq.[39]
December 2002	12/18: At an NSC meeting, Bush and his cabinet agree that Saddam is not cooperating with U.N. Security Council Resolution 1441.[40]	12/19: CJCS Myers reviews postwar planning, then directs Franks to refine the Phase IV plan.[41]	
		CFLCC finalizes Operation Cobra II, the plan for ground forces to invade Iraq.[42]	
		The 3rd Infantry Division begins deployment to Kuwait.[43]	

---

[33] Feith, 2008, p. 319.

[34] Margolick, 2007.

[35] JCS, 2003.

[36] JCS, 2003.

[37] JCS, 2003.

[38] Feith, 2008, pp. 335–336.

[39] Feith, 2008, p. 345.

[40] Feith, 2008, p. 339.

[41] Feith, 2008, p. 292.

[42] Wright and Reese, 2008, p. 622.

[43] Wright and Reese, 2008, p. 622.

Date	Key U.S. Political Actions and Events	Key U.S. Military Actions and Events	Other Key Actions and Events
January 2003	1/9: Feith calls Garner to ask him to help run postwar planning.[44] 1/20: NSPD-24 gives DoD lead responsibility for postwar Iraq.[45] 1/21: The NSC's Luti outlines a plan for rebuilding the Iraqi Army, eliminating secret police and elite units but keeping the bulk of nonsecret units in place.[46] 1/20: NSPD-24 directs DoD to coordinate postwar planning and take the lead for postwar reconstruction.[47]	1/22: The 4th Infantry Division receives an order to begin deployment to Southwest Asia.[48] 1/27: V Corps begins exercise VICTORY SCRIMMAGE in Germany. The exercise closely resembles major combat operations in Iraq.[49]	U.N. Chief Weapons Inspector Hans Blix tells U.N. Security Council that Iraq's disarmament initiatives do not appear to be genuine.[50]
February 2003	2/5: Powell briefs the U.N. Security Council on Iraq WMD intelligence.[51] 2/11: Feith testifies to the Senate Foreign Relations Committee on how Iraqis could better administer their country.[52] 2/14: Feith briefs Bush on the FIF program, which had 5,000 nominees, of whom 625 were vetted and 1,809 partially vetted, and only 55 were in training in Hungary on February 1.[53]	2/1: U.S. military begins training FIF in Hungary.[54] 2/6: 101st Airborne Division begins deployment to Kuwait.[55]	2/12: Saudi Arabia agrees to the United States' basing request at Prince Sultan Air Base in Al Kharj.[56] 2/14: U.N. Chief Weapons Inspector Blix reports to the U.N. Security Council that his team has found no WMDs in Iraq.[57]

---

[44] Frontline, 2006a.

[45] Ali A. Allawi, *The Occupation of Iraq: Winning the War, Losing the Peace*, New Haven, Conn.: Yale University Press, 2007, p. 3.

[46] Feith, 2008, p. 366.

[47] Rumsfeld, 2011, p. 487.

[48] Wright and Reese, 2008, p. 622.

[49] Wright and Reese, 2008, p. 622.

[50] Feith, 2008, p. 352.

[51] Feith, 2008, p. 253.

[52] Feith, 2008, p. 369.

[53] Feith, 2008, p. 385.

[54] JCS, 2003.

[55] Wright and Reese, 2008, p. 622.

[56] JCS, 2003.

[57] CNN, "Operation Iraqi Freedom and Operation New Dawn Fast Facts," April 21, 2015d.

Timeline of Major Events in the Battle for Baghdad   241

Date	Key U.S. Political Actions and Events	Key U.S. Military Actions and Events	Other Key Actions and Events
March 2003	3/1: The principals committee takes up the idea of an Iraqi Interim Authority—a group of Iraqi leaders to manage parts of the Iraqi government and pave the way to return to sovereignty.[58] 3/10: Bush approves the Iraqi Interim Authority, which will include both expats and current Iraqis and will transition to elected officials as possible.[59] 3/10: NSC briefs the war council on de-Ba'athification.[60] 3/12: Bush and the war cabinet approve a plan to disband the Republican Guard.[61] 3/12: Bush expresses support for Garner's plan to remove only senior Ba'ath party members, administer government by assigning advisers to ministries, and recall the Iraqi Army.[62] 3/17: Bush issues Saddam an ultimatum to leave Iraq in 48 hours or risk war.[63]	3/19: Bush announces that the war against Iraq has begun and the air campaign commences.[64] 3/20: Operation Iraqi Freedom begins.[65] 3/21: The 3rd Infantry Division advances almost 100 miles into Iraq.[66] 3/22: Due to Turkish opposition, the 4th Infantry Division is redirected to Kuwait.[67] 3/23: The 101st Airborne Division conducts air assault into Iraq.[68] 3/26: The 173rd Airborne Division conducts air assault into northern Iraq.[69] 3/31: FIF training is suspended after producing 76 graduates.[70]	3/23: Members of the U.S. Army's 507th Maintenance Company are ambushed and captured outside Nasiriyah.[71]

---

[58] Feith, 2008, p. 403.

[59] Feith, 2008, p. 408.

[60] Chandrasekaran, 2006a, p. 69.

[61] Chandrasekaran, 2006a, p. 74.

[62] Gordon and Trainor, 2012, p. 11.

[63] Feith, 2008, p. 391.

[64] CNN, "Bush Declares War: Mar. 19 2003," March 19, 2003a.

[65] Gordon and Trainor, 2006, p. 192.

[66] Gordon and Trainor, 2006, p. 247.

[67] Wright and Reese, 2008, p. 622.

[68] Fontenot, Degen, and Tohn, 2004, p. 89.

[69] Gordon and Trainor, 2006, p. 388.

[70] JCS, 2003.

[71] Gordon and Trainor, 2006, p. 274.

Date	Key U.S. Political Actions and Events	Key U.S. Military Actions and Events	Other Key Actions and Events
April 2003	4/11: Garner visits Iraq for the first time.[72] 4/16: Franks visits Iraq and outlaws the Ba'athist Party.[73] 4/28: Garner holds a second political conference with Iraqis in Baghdad, attended by 250.[74]	4/2: The 3rd Infantry Division seizes Baghdad International Airport.[75] 4/5: The 3rd Infantry Division launches the first Thunder Run.[76] 4/7: The 3rd Infantry Division launches the second Thunder Run.[77] 4/9: U.S. forces topple Saddam statue in Baghdad.[78] 4/9: Cordon around Baghdad is completed.[79] 4/22: The 4th Infantry Division arrives in Tikrit and begins combat operations.[80] U.S. troop levels are at 93,900.[81]	4/1: PFC Jessica Lynch is rescued by U.S. forces.[82]

---

[72] Allawi, 2007, p. 7.

[73] Allawi, 2007, p. 11.

[74] Feith, 2008, p. 42.

[75] "U.S. Captures, Renames Baghdad Airport," *USA Today*, April 3, 2003.

[76] Gordon and Trainor, 2006, p. 434.

[77] Gordon and Trainor, 2006, p. 452.

[78] Gordon and Trainor, 2006, p. 455.

[79] Fontenot, Degen, and Tohn, 2004, p. 321.

[80] Gordon and Trainor, 2006, p. 511.

[81] Amy Belasco, *The Cost of Iraq, Afghanistan, and Other Global War on Terror Operations Since 9/11*, Washington, D.C.: Congressional Research Service, RL33110, December 8, 2014.

[82] CNN, "Jessica Lynch Fast Facts," April 15, 2015c.

Date	Key U.S. Political Actions and Events	Key U.S. Military Actions and Events	Other Key Actions and Events
May 2003	5/1: From the USS *Abraham Lincoln*, Bush declares that "major combat operations" are over.[83] 5/3: Bush announces that Bremer will head CPA.[84] 5/8: At a principals meeting, Powell, Rice, and Bremer question the ability of the Iraqi Interim Authority, and the concept of such a group begins to lose steam.[85] 5/12: Bremer arrives in Baghdad.[86] 5/16: Bremer announces the de-Ba'athification policy.[87] 5/23: Bremer announces the disbanding of the entire Iraqi military and intelligence community.[88] 5/22: Bremer sends a memo to Bush saying that there will be no Iraqi sovereignty until after elections.[89] 5/22: At an NSC meeting, Bremer announces his intention to formally disband the military and security ministries.[90]	U.S. troop levels in Iraq are at 145,700.[91]	5/22: U.N. Security Council Resolution 1483 formally recognizes the United States and UK as occupying powers in Iraq.[92]

---

[83] Gordon and Trainor, 2006, p. 531.

[84] Allawi, 2007, p. 11.

[85] Feith, 2008, p. 440.

[86] Allawi, 2007, p. 11.

[87] Allawi, 2007.

[88] Allawi, 2007, p. 57.

[89] Feith, 2008, p. 446.

[90] Gordon and Trainor, 2012, p. 15.

[91] Belasco, 2014, p. 82.

[92] United Nations Security Council, 2003a; Allawi, 2007, p. 12.

Date	Key U.S. Political Actions and Events	Key U.S. Military Actions and Events	Other Key Actions and Events
June 2003	6/23: Bremer announces that former members of the Iraqi army will be paid a stipend.[93]	6/13: Major General Eaton arrives in Iraq in charge of CPA's CMATT to build the new Iraqi Army.[94] 6/14: CJTF-7 (led by LTG Sanchez) replaces CFLCC as the lead U.S. military command in Iraq.[95] U.S. troop levels in Iraq are at 147,400.[96]	
July 2003	7/4: General Keane visits Baghdad and meets with Bremer and Sanchez.[97] 7/13: Iraqi Governing Council is established.[98]	7/7: General Abizaid replaces Franks as commander of CENTCOM.[99] 7/22: U.S. forces kill Saddam's sons Uday and Qusay.[100] U.S. troop levels in Iraq are at 149,400.[101]	7/18: Shia leader Sadr announces a plan to form a militia separate from the Iraqi Army to challenge the United States and the Iraqi Governing Council.[102]

---

[93] Feith, 2008, p. 434.

[94] Former senior military commander, interview with the authors, April 23, 2015.

[95] Gordon and Trainor, 2006, p. 559.

[96] Belasco, 2014, p. 82.

[97] Kaplan, 2013, p. 229.

[98] Allawi, 2007, p. 46.

[99] Gerry J. Gilmore, "Abizaid Set to Supplant Franks as CENTCOM Commander," DoD News, July 2, 2003.

[100] CNN, "Pentagon: Saddam's Sons Killed in Raid," July 22, 2003b.

[101] Belasco, 2014, p. 82.

[102] Wright and Reese, 2008, p. 624.

Date	Key U.S. Political Actions and Events	Key U.S. Military Actions and Events	Other Key Actions and Events
August 2003	Feith visits Baghdad for the first time.[103]	8/21: Coalition officials announce that Ali Hassan al-Majid, also known as "Chemical Ali," has been captured.[104] U.S. troop levels in Iraq are at 146,000.[105]	8/7: The Jordanian embassy in Iraq is bombed.[106] 8/19: A car bomb explodes outside U.N. headquarters in Baghdad, killing Sergio Vieira de Mello, head of the U.N. mission to Iraq.[107] 8/29: An explosion at Najaf mosque kills Ayatollah Muhammed Bakr al-Hakim, leader of the Supreme Council for the Islamic Revolution in Iraq.[108]
September 2003	9/8: Bush asks Congress for $87 billion in supplemental funds to continue the wars in Iraq and Afghanistan.[109] 9/24: Bremer testifies to Congress after releasing his seven-step plan to achieve Iraqi sovereignty in an op-ed on 9/8.[110]	U.S. troop levels in Iraq are at 130,300.[111]	

---

[103] Feith, 2008, p. 449.

[104] Bill Brink, "Former Iraqi Official Known as 'Chemical Ali' Is Captured," *New York Times*, August 21, 2003.

[105] Belasco, 2014, p. 82.

[106] Allawi, 2007, p. 170.

[107] Allawi, 2007, p. 170.

[108] Wright and Reese, 2008, p. 624.

[109] CNN, "Bush to Ask Billions More for Iraq," September 8, 2003c.

[110] Gordon and Trainor, 2012, p. 28.

[111] Belasco, 2014, p. 82.

Date	Key U.S. Political Actions and Events	Key U.S. Military Actions and Events	Other Key Actions and Events
October 2003	10/2: David Kay of the Iraq Survey Group issues an initial report to Congress about not finding WMDs, although finding plenty of evidence of Iraqis covering up a program.[112] 10/22: Rumsfeld leads an Iraq Strategic Review ahead of a meeting with Bremer.[113] 10/26: Rumsfeld meets with Bremer to discuss shutting down CPA.[114] 10/29: Bush approves a plan to build an interim Iraqi government even without a full-fledged constitution.[115] Rice establishes the Iraqi Stabilization Group to coordinate reconstruction and stabilization activities.[116]	U.S. troop levels in Iraq are at 136,900.[117]	10/9: Sadr's militia attacks the 2nd Cavalry Regiment in Sadr City, effectively ending the truce between Sadr's militia and the coalition.[118] 10/16: U.N. Security Council 1511 passes, which envisions a multinational force and preserves the U.S. control of Iraq.[119] 10/30: The U.N. withdraws all of its non-Iraqi personnel from Baghdad.[120] The first battalion of the new Iraqi Army completes a coalition training program.[121]

---

[112] Feith, 2008, p. 471.

[113] Feith, 2008, p. 461.

[114] Feith, 2008, p. 463.

[115] Feith, 2008, p. 465.

[116] Wright and Reese, 2008, p. 624.

[117] Belasco, 2014, p. 82.

[118] Wright and Reese, 2008, p. 624.

[119] United Nations Security Council, Resolution 1511 (2003) [on Authorizing a Multinational Force Under Unified Command to Take All Necessary Measures to Contribute to the Maintenance of Security and Stability in Iraq], New York, October 16, 2003b.

[120] Wright and Reese, 2008, p. 624.

[121] Wright and Reese, 2008, p. 624.

Date	Key U.S. Political Actions and Events	Key U.S. Military Actions and Events	Other Key Actions and Events
November 2003		11/2: In the heaviest single loss for the coalition troops to this point, one U.S. Army Chinook is shot down near Fallujah. The attack kills 16 soldiers and wounds 20.[122] U.S. troop levels in Iraq are at 131,300.[123]	11/1: The Associated Press publishes a report on Abu Ghraib prison abuse.[124] 11/15: The November 15 Agreement determines that a caucus system will be used to select members of the new national assembly, which will officially transfer sovereignty back to Iraqis.[125]
December 2003		12/13: Coalition forces capture Saddam near Tikrit.[126] U.S. troop levels in Iraq are at 123,700.[127]	
January 2004	1/20: Bush outlines the "freedom agenda" in his first State of the Union since major combat operations began in Iraq.[128] 1/28: Kay testifies to the Senate Armed Services Committee that no WMDs have been found in Iraq.[129]	1/19: Sanchez requests an investigation into the U.S. Army 800th Military Police Brigade's treatment of Iraqi prisoners, including those at Abu Ghraib.[130] 1/31: CFLCC commander Lieutenant General McKiernan appoints Major General Taguba to conduct an investigation into the 800th Military Police Brigade, which was tactical control to CJTF-7 and operational control to CFLCC.[131] U.S. troop levels in Iraq are at 126,900.[132]	

---

[122] CNN, "U.S. Helicopter Shot Down in Iraq," November 2, 2003d.

[123] Belasco, 2014, p. 82.

[124] Charles J. Hanley, "AP Enterprise: Former Iraqi Detainees Tell of Riots, Punishment in the Sun, Good Americans and Pitiless Ones," *San Diego Union Tribune*, November 1, 2003.

[125] Gordon and Trainor, 2012, p. 34.

[126] Gordon and Trainor, 2012, p. 39.

[127] Belasco, 2014, p. 82.

[128] Gordon and Trainor, 2012, p. 46.

[129] Wright and Reese, 2008, p. 625.

[130] "Chronology of Abu Ghraib," *Washington Post*, February 17, 2006.

[131] "Chronology of Abu Ghraib," 2006.

[132] Belasco, 2014, p. 83.

Date	Key U.S. Political Actions and Events	Key U.S. Military Actions and Events	Other Key Actions and Events
February 2004	Wolfowitz visits Iraq for the first time.[133]	2/1: III Corps replaces much of V Corps personnel with CJTF-7.[134] U.S. troop levels in Iraq are at 108,400.[135]	
March 2004		3/3: Taguba completes his classified report on the 800th Military Police Brigade.[136] MG Karl Eikenberry submits a report to Wolfowitz that cites issues with unity of effort in the organizing, training, equipping, and employment of the ISF.[137] CMATT and the Civilian Police Assistance Training Team are transferred from CPA to CJTF-7.[138] U.S. troop levels in Iraq are at 119,600.[139]	3/2: Suicide bombers kill 140 in Baghdad and Karbala during Shia religious festivals.[140] 3/8: A provisional Iraqi Constitution is signed.[141] 3/31: Insurgents in Fallujah ambush, kill, and mutilate four U.S. contractors working for Blackwater.[142]

---

[133] Gordon and Trainor, 2012, p. 50.

[134] Wright and Reese, 2008.

[135] Belasco, 2014, p. 83.

[136] "Chronology of Abu Ghraib," 2006.

[137] Timothy Davis, *Building the Iraqi Army: Teaching a Nation to Fish*, thesis, Fort Leavenworth, Kan.: U.S. Army Command and General Staff College, 2005, p. 24.

[138] Wright and Reese, 2008, p. 450.

[139] Belasco, 2014, p. 83.

[140] Richard D. Hooker, Jr., and Joseph J. Collins, *Lessons Encountered: Learning from the Long War*, Washington, D.C.: National Defense University Press, September 2015, p. 460.

[141] Sharon Otterman, "Iraq: The Interim Constitution," *CFR Backgrounder*, March 8, 2004.

[142] Jeffrey Gettleman, "Enraged Mob in Fallujah Kills 4 American Contractors," *New York Times*, March 31, 2004.

Timeline of Major Events in the Battle for Baghdad   249

Date	Key U.S. Political Actions and Events	Key U.S. Military Actions and Events	Other Key Actions and Events
April 2004	4/9: Two members of the Iraqi Governing Council resign over U.S. military actions in Fallujah.[143] 4/22: Bremer announces reinstatement of thousands of teachers who had been removed from their jobs because of de-Ba'athification.[144] The media questions the credibility of intel provided by the Iraqi National Congress; Rumsfeld initially defends the Iraqi National Congress and Chalabi.[145]	4/4: Operation Vigilant Resolve begins in Fallujah. 4/6: CJTF-7 extends the 1st Armory Division's deployment by 120 days.[146] 4/9: Operation Vigilant Resolve is terminated.[147] 4/20: Coalition forces transfer command of ICDC to the Iraqi MOD.[148] 4/28: Photos of U.S. soldiers abusing Iraqi prisoners at Abu Ghraib emerge.[149] 4/30: Taguba's report of the 800th Military Police Brigade is publicly released.[150] U.S. troop levels in Iraq are at 131,700.[151]	4/27: CBS's *60 Minutes* airs an episode on the Abu Ghraib prison abuse scandal.[152]

---

[143] Wright and Reese, 2008, p. 626.

[144] Wright and Reese, 2008, p. 626.

[145] Feith, 2008, p. 488.

[146] Gordon and Trainor, 2012, p. 71.

[147] Wright and Reese, 2008, p. 346.

[148] Wright and Reese, 2008, p. 465.

[149] Hooker and Collins, 2015, p. 460.

[150] CNN, "Iraq Prison Abuse Scandal Fast Facts," March 27, 2015b.

[151] Belasco, 2014, p. 83.

[152] Rebecca Leung, "Abuse of Iraqi POWs by GIs Probed," CBS News, April 27, 2004.

Date	Key U.S. Political Actions and Events	Key U.S. Military Actions and Events	Other Key Actions and Events
May 2004	5/5: Bush convenes an NSC meeting to review the military strategy in Iraq in the wake of intense fighting in Sadr City and Anbar.[153] 5/11: Bush issues NSPD-36, which assigned CENTCOM the mission of organizing, training, and equipping the ISF.[154]	5/15: MNF-I and MNC-I are stood up to replace CJTF-7.[155] General Casey is assigned as commander of MNF-I.[156] LTG Thomas F. Metz is assigned as MNC-I commander.[157] U.S. troop levels are at 139,800.[158]	5/10: Seymour Hersh's "Torture at Abu Ghraib" is published in the New Yorker.[159] 5/11: A video depicting the beheading of U.S. contractor Nick Berg surfaces on a jihadi website.[160] 5/17: Abdel-Zahraa Othman, President of the Iraqi Governing Council, is assassinated.[161]
June 2004	Bremer issues CPA Order Number 96 declaring Iraq one voting district.[162] 6/28: Bremer signs sovereignty over to the Iraqis.[163] 6/30: U.S. Marines raise a flag for the U.S. embassy in Baghdad for the first time in 13 years.[164]	6/28: MNF-I stands up MNSTC-I, which assumed the duties of CMATT and the Civilian Police Assistance Training Team. Lieutenant General Petraeus becomes the first commander of MNSTC-I.[165]	6/1: The interim Iraqi government is created.[166] 6/8: U.N. Security Council Resolution 1546 mandates the political road map for the new sovereign state of Iraq.[167]

---

[153] Gordon and Trainor, 2012, p. 73.

[154] Catherine Dale, *Operation Iraqi Freedom: Strategies, Approaches, Results, and Issues for Congress*, Washington, D.C.: Congressional Research Service, RL34387, February 22, 2008, p. 62.

[155] Wright and Reese, 2008, p. 174.

[156] Former senior military commander, interview with the authors, September 30, 2015.

[157] Wright and Reese, 2008, p. 174.

[158] Belasco, 2014, p. 83.

[159] Seymour M. Hersh, "Torture at Abu Ghraib," *New Yorker*, May 10, 2004.

[160] Wright and Reese, 2008, p. 626.

[161] Wright and Reese, 2008, p. 626.

[162] Allawi, 2007, p. 324.

[163] Allawi, 2007, p. 325.

[164] Headquarters Marine Corps, "Marines Raise American Flag over New U.S. Embassy in Iraq," July 1, 2004.

[165] Former senior military commander, interview with the authors, July 31, 2015.

[166] George W. Bush, "The Iraqi Interim Government," Washington, D.C.: U.S. Department of State Archive, June 1, 2004.

[167] Wright and Reese, 2008, p. 626; and United Nations Security Council, Resolution 1546 (2004) [on Formation of a Sovereign Interim Government of Iraq], New York, June 8, 2004.

Timeline of Major Events in the Battle for Baghdad   251

Date	Key U.S. Political Actions and Events	Key U.S. Military Actions and Events	Other Key Actions and Events
June 2004 (cont.)		6/30: Legal control of Saddam is transferred to the interim Iraqi government, but Saddam remains physically under U.S. control.[168] U.S. troop levels are at 144,300.[169]	
July 2004		7/1: Casey officially assumes command in Iraq.[170] U.S. troop levels are at 140,600.[171]	7/1: Saddam goes on trial for war crimes.[172] 7/8: Ali Abbas Hasan, leader of the disbanded Ba'ath party, is killed in southern Baghdad.[173] 7/20: Insurgents assassinate the governor of Basra, Hazem al-Ainachi.[174]
August 2004		8/5: Coalition units begin operations in Najaf.[175] U.S. troop levels are at 126,800.[176]	
September 2004		U.S. troop levels are at 137,700.[177]	9/6: The number of U.S. troops killed in Iraq reaches 1,000.[178]

[168] CNN, "Saddam Hussein Trial Fast Facts," March 12, 2015a.

[169] Belasco, 2014, p. 83.

[170] Gordon and Trainor, 2012, p. 92.

[171] Belasco, 2014, p. 83.

[172] CNN, 2015a.

[173] United Nations High Commissioner for Refugees, "Chronology of Events in Iraq, July 2004," September 28, 2004.

[174] United Nations High Commissioner for Refugees, 2004.

[175] Wright and Reese, 2008, p. 626.

[176] Belasco, 2014, p. 83.

[177] Belasco, 2014, p. 83.

[178] CNN, 2015d.

Date	Key U.S. Political Actions and Events	Key U.S. Military Actions and Events	Other Key Actions and Events
October 2004		The 98th Infantry Division deploys to Iraq, fills MNSTC-I posts.[179] U.S. troop levels are at 134,600.[180]	
November 2004	11/4: Bush is elected for a second term.[181]	11/7: Between 10,000 and 15,000 U.S. soldiers and Marines—including the 2nd Battalion, 7th U.S. Cavalry Regiment, and the 2nd Battalion, 2nd Infantry Regiment (Mechanized)—begin combat operations in Fallujah in Operation Phantom Fury.[182] U.S. troop levels are at 132,837.[183]	11/14: Senior Iraqi officials declare Fallujah to be liberated.[184]
December 2004	Derek Harvey, a Middle East expert from the Defense Intelligence Agency, briefs Bush on the dire situation in Iraq.[185] 12/8: In response to a U.S. soldier's question about availability of armored vehicles, Rumsfeld issues infamous statement: "You go to war with the Army you have. They're not the Army you might want or wish to have at a later time."[186]	U.S. troop levels are at 142,600.[187]	

---

[179] Wright and Reese, 2008, p. 462.

[180] Belasco, 2014, p. 83.

[181] Dan Balz, "Bush Wins Second Term," *Washington Post*, November 4, 2004.

[182] Gordon and Trainor, 2012, p. 117.

[183] Belasco, 2014, p. 83.

[184] Jackie Spinner and Karl Vick, "Troops Battle for Last Parts of Fallujah," *Washington Post*, November 14, 2004.

[185] Woodward, 2008a, p. 24.

[186] Helmut Sonnenfeldt and Ron Nessen, "You Go to War with the Press You Have," Brookings Institution, December 30, 2004.

[187] Belasco, 2014, p. 83.

Timeline of Major Events in the Battle for Baghdad   253

Date	Key U.S. Political Actions and Events	Key U.S. Military Actions and Events	Other Key Actions and Events
January 2005		1/26: 37 U.S. military personnel are killed in Iraq in multiple incidents. This is the deadliest day of Operation Iraqi Freedom for the U.S. military.[188] U.S. troop levels are at 150,682.[189]	1/30: Iraq holds national elections. Voter turnout is higher than expected, but most Sunnis boycott the elections.[190]
February 2005		2/10: LTG John Vines replaces Metz as commander of MNC-I.[191] The IAG is established within MNC-I. IAG "owns" all of the transition teams that are embedded with Iraqi units. Later (mid-2007), transition teams are attached to BCTs, but IAG still serves as the executive agent.[192] U.S. troop levels are at 161,200.[193]	
March 2005		U.S. troop levels are at 144,875.[194]	3/16: Iraqi National Assembly holds its first meeting.[195]
April 2005		U.S. troop levels are at 144,776.[196]	4/6: Iraqi National Assembly elects Kurdish leader Jalal Talibani as president.[197]

---

[188] CNN, "Deadliest Day for the U.S. in Iraq War," January 27, 2005a.

[189] Belasco, 2014, p. 83.

[190] Perry, 2005.

[191] Casey, 2012, p. 194.

[192] Dale, 2008, p. 64.

[193] Belasco, 2014, p. 83.

[194] Belasco, 2014, p. 83.

[195] "Iraqi National Assembly Meeting," live coverage from Baghdad, C-SPAN, March 16, 2005.

[196] Belasco, 2014, p. 83.

[197] CNN, "Jalal Talabani Fast Facts," August 28, 2014.

Date	Key U.S. Political Actions and Events	Key U.S. Military Actions and Events	Other Key Actions and Events
May 2005		MNF-I establishes the Police Partnership Program to improve police capacity and ministerial development.[198] Operation Matador begins in Al Qaim to reduce the flow of foreign fighters crossing into Iraq.[199] U.S. troop levels are at 137,157.[200]	Monthly Iraqi civilian deaths from bombings and shootings increase to 672, up from 364 the previous month.[201]
June 2005	6/5: Zelikow and Jeffrey present Rice with a classified memo expressing frustrations with Maliki and outlining options to combat the insurgency.[202] 6/6–10: At an academic conference on the future of counterinsurgency, Odierno states, "We in the Army don't think much about [counterinsurgency]."[203] 6/21: During trip to Washington, D.C., Casey outlines plans to draw down U.S. force presence.[204]	MNSTC-I launches concept for embedding Military Transition Teams into Iraqi Army and Police units.[205] U.S. troop levels are at 141,100.[206]	
July 2005	7/19: O'Sullivan writes memo for Hadley recommending that the security situation be reevaluated before troops are withdrawn.[207]	U.S. troop levels are at 136,475.[208] A DoD report states that there are 171,300 trained and equipped ISF personnel (77,300 in MOD; 94,000 in MOI).[209]	

---

[198] Brennan et al., 2013, p. 42.

[199] Fox News, "U.S.: Operation Matador a Success," May 15, 2005.

[200] Belasco, 2014, p. 83.

[201] Hooker and Collins, 2015, p. 460.

[202] Woodward, 2008a, p. 54.

[203] Kaplan, 2013, pp. 108–115.

[204] Woodward, 2008a, p. 59.

[205] Brennan et al., 2013, p. 42.

[206] Belasco, 2014, p. 83.

[207] Woodward, 2008a, p. 68.

[208] Belasco, 2014, p. 83.

[209] DoD, *Measuring Stability and Security in Iraq*, Washington, D.C., July 2005.

Timeline of Major Events in the Battle for Baghdad   255

Date	Key U.S. Political Actions and Events	Key U.S. Military Actions and Events	Other Key Actions and Events
August 2005	8/2: Charles Robb, former governor of Virginia and U.S. senator, asks if a troop surge is possible (first time the word *surge* is used).[210]	U.S. troop levels are at 140,776.[211]	8/31: Al Aaimmah bridge stampede in Baghdad kills 953 Iraqis during 1-million-person pilgrimage toward the Al Kadhimiya Mosque.[212] A draft constitution is accepted by Shia and Kurdish negotiators, but Sunni representatives reject it.[213]
September 2005	9/19: In a meeting with Rumsfeld and CJCS Pace, Keane—now retired—says that the United States is on the verge of strategic failure in Iraq.[214] Zelikow returns to Iraq and reports back that changes are needed at the top leadership levels.[215]	An MNF-I assessment states that all Iraq ministries "lack effective senior leadership, a professional civil service, and suffer from patronage."[216] Dempsey replaces Petraeus as commander of MNSTC-I.[217] U.S. troop levels are at 145,078.[218]	McMaster's 3rd Armory Cavalry Regiment begins offensive to secure the city of Talafar.[219]

---

[210] Woodward, 2008a, p. 82.

[211] Belasco, 2014, p. 83.

[212] BBC, "Iraq Stampede Deaths Near 1,000," August 31, 2005.

[213] Hooker and Collins, 2015, p. 461.

[214] Kaplan, 2013, pp. 230–231.

[215] Kaplan, 2013, pp. 193–194.

[216] Brennan et al., 2013, p. 41.

[217] Casey, 2012, p. 185.

[218] Belasco, 2014, p. 83.

[219] Jay B. Baker, "Tal Afar 2005: Laying the Counterinsurgency Groundwork," *Army Magazine*, June 2009.

Date	Key U.S. Political Actions and Events	Key U.S. Military Actions and Events	Other Key Actions and Events
October 2005	Rice and Zelikow visit Iraq. With Odierno (now assistant to the JCS), they come up with the phrase "clear, hold, build."[220] 10/19: In a Senate Foreign Relations Committee meeting, Rice defines Iraq strategy as clear, hold, build.[221]	10/1: MNSTC-I is assigned the role of security ministry institutional development of MOD. The responsibility of building capacity for MOI is also transferred to MNSTC-I from the Department of State's Iraqi Reconstruction Management Office.[222] U.S. troop levels are at 149,379.[223]	10/15: Iraqi Constitution Referendum approves Iraq's new constitution.[224] 10/25: The number of U.S. troops killed in Iraq reaches 2,000.[225]
November 2005		11/25: DoD Directive 3000.05, "Military Support for Stability, Security, Transition and Reconstruction," outlines the interagency plan for reconstruction and puts the first counterinsurgency principles into formal DoD guidance.[226] U.S. troop levels are at 153,681.[227]	11/5: U.S. Marine Corps begins Operation Steel Curtain in Al Qaim to reduce the flow of foreign fighters crossing into Iraq. This operation is the first large-scale deployment of the new Iraqi Army.[228] 11/19: U.S. Marines kill at least 24 Iraqi civilians in Haditha.[229]
December 2005	U.S. leaders decide to block the return of Prime Minister Ibrahim al-Jaafari, thereby allowing Maliki to rise to power.[230]	U.S. troop levels are at 157,982.[231]	12/15: In the first national election under the new constitution, millions of Iraqis cast ballots to elect a parliament to a four-year term. Sunnis turn out in large numbers, but Shia parties win the largest bloc.[232]

---

[220] Kaplan, 2013, pp. 194–195.

[221] Woodward 2008a, p. 31.

[222] Dale, 2008, p. 63.

[223] Belasco, 2014, p. 83.

[224] CNN, "Iraqi Constitution Passes, Officials Say," October 25, 2005b.

[225] CNN, 2015d.

[226] Kaplan, 2013, p. 122.

[227] Belasco, 2014, p. 83.

[228] Bill Roggio, "Operation Steel Curtain in Husaybah," *Long War Journal*, November 5, 2005.

[229] Gordon and Trainor, 2012, p. 201.

[230] Joel Rayburn, *Iraq After America: Strongmen, Sectarians, Resistance*, Stanford, Calif.: Hoover Institution Press, 2014, p. 23.

[231] Belasco, 2014, p. 83.

[232] "Timeline of Major Events in the Iraq War," *New York Times*, October 21, 2011.

Date	Key U.S. Political Actions and Events	Key U.S. Military Actions and Events	Other Key Actions and Events
January 2006		Chiarelli replaces Vines as commander of MNC-I.[233] U.S. troop levels are at 153,239.[234]	
February 2006		2/23: A counterinsurgency manual drafting workshop held just outside Fort Leavenworth produces a *Military Review* article that contains a lot of the counterinsurgency material ultimately outlined in FM 3-24.[235] U.S. troop levels are at 137,365.[236]	2/22: The al-Askari Mosque in Samarra is destroyed, sparking waves of sectarian violence.[237]
March 2006	3/15: Congress appoints the Iraq Study Group.[238]	U.S. troop levels are at 129,713.[239]	3/16: Iraq's Council of Representatives holds its first session.[240]
April 2006	National Security Adviser O'Sullivan flies to Baghdad; she returns with the impression that the violence must be brought under control before a political settlement is reached.[241]	U.S. troop levels are at 129,467.[242]	4/22: Shia leaders select Maliki as their nominee for prime minister.[243]

---

[233] Casey, 2012.

[234] Belasco, 2014, p. 84.

[235] Kaplan, 2013, p. 153.

[236] Belasco, 2014, p. 84.

[237] Gordon and Trainor, 2012, p. 192.

[238] Ted Barrett, "Congress Forms Panel to Study Iraq War," CNN, March 15, 2006.

[239] Belasco, 2014, p. 84.

[240] Charles P. Trumbull IV and Julie B. Martin, "Elections and Government Formation in Iraq: An Analysis of the Judiciary's Role," *Vanderbilt Journal of Transnational Law*, Vol. 44, No. 331, 2011, p. 338.

[241] Kaplan, 2013, p. 195–196.

[242] Belasco, 2014, p. 84.

[243] "Timeline of Major Events in the Iraq War," 2011.

Date	Key U.S. Political Actions and Events	Key U.S. Military Actions and Events	Other Key Actions and Events
May 2006	5/26: At an NSC meeting, Rice announces that only 48 people from various departments and agencies are willing to go to Iraq.[244]	A DoD report states that there are 263,400 trained and equipped ISF personnel (117,900 in MOD; 145,500 in MOI).[245] U.S. troop levels are at 130,231.[246]	5/20: Maliki becomes Iraqi prime minister.[247] The Iraq Transitional Government is replaced by the new government.[248] The U.N. reports that at least 100 civilians are killed in Iraq each day.[249]
June 2006	6/12–13: Bush meets with Kagan, Kaplan, Cohen, and Vickers, who argue for a shift in strategy in Iraq, including replacing Casey.[250]	6/14: U.S. and Iraqi military forces begin Operation Together Forward in Baghdad to curb sectarian killings.[251] U.S. troop levels are at 128,789.[252]	6/7: Coalition forces kill al-Zarqawi, the leader of al Qaeda in Iraq.[253]
July 2006	7/22: At an NSC meeting, Casey and Abizaid face at least 50 questions.[254]	U.S. troop levels are at 124,876.[255]	

---

[244] Woodward, 2008a, p. 53.

[245] DoD, *Measuring Stability and Security in Iraq*, Washington, D.C., May 2006a, p. 46.

[246] Belasco, 2014, p. 84.

[247] CNN, 2015e.

[248] CNN, 2015e.

[249] Hooker and Collins, 2015, p. 461.

[250] Kaplan, 2013, p. 200.

[251] Gordon and Trainor, 2012, p. 212.

[252] Belasco, 2014, p. 84.

[253] John F. Burns, "Abu Masab al-Zarqawi, Leader of Al Qaeda in Iraq, Is Killed in U.S. Airstrike," *New York Times*, June 8, 2006.

[254] Woodward, 2008a, p. 73.

[255] Belasco, 2014, p. 84.

Timeline of Major Events in the Battle for Baghdad   259

Date	Key U.S. Political Actions and Events	Key U.S. Military Actions and Events	Other Key Actions and Events
August 2006	8/17: At a war council meeting, Bush indicates to Rumsfeld, Casey, and Abizaid that if the Iraq strategy is not working, they need to try something else.[256] 8/30: While on a plane to Baghdad, Perry develops the idea of a short-term (yearlong) surge in troops to enable withdrawal. 8/31: Perry proposes the troop surge idea to Casey in Baghdad, but Casey says that more troops will only spark more of a backlash.[257] 8/31: Several members of the Iraq Study Group arrive in Baghdad.[258]	8/3: Abizaid testifies to the Senate Armed Services Committee that it is possible Iraq could move into civil war, making national headlines.[259] The Army Vice Chief of Staff orders creation of Task Force ODIN (observe, detect, identify, and neutralize). The task force comprises the Army's newest aviation battalions, chartered specifically to conduct reconnaissance, surveillance, targeting, and acquisition operations in support of the counter-IED fight.[260] U.S. troop levels are at 131,057.[261]	
September 2006	9/3: Perry proposes the same idea (a troop surge) to Chiarelli in Baghdad, and Chiarelli also declines the forces, as long as Maliki is preventing a crackdown on the Shia militia.[262]	9/27: Council of Colonels begin to meet.[263] U.S. troop levels are at 140,264.[264]	Sheik Abdul Sattar Abu Rishawi forms the Anbar Salvation Council, which allies 40 Sunni tribes to the coalition against al Qaeda in Iraq.[265]

---

[256] Woodward, 2008a, p. 88.

[257] Kaplan, 2013, pp. 205–208.

[258] Woodward, 2008a, p. 110.

[259] Woodward, 2008a, p. 84.

[260] A. T. Ball and Berrien T. McCutchen, Jr., "Task Force ODIN Using Innovative Technology to Support Ground Forces," Tikrit, Iraq: Defense Video and Imagery Distribution System, September 20, 2007.

[261] Belasco, 2014, p. 84.

[262] Kaplan, 2013, pp. 205–208.

[263] Woodward, 2008a, p. 158. The Council of Colonels was a task force of senior officers created by the Joint Chiefs of Staff that reexamined the strategy for the war in Iraq.

[264] Belasco, 2014, p. 84.

[265] Todd Pitman, "Iraq's Sunni Sheiks Join Americans to Fight Insurgency," *San Diego Union Tribune*, March 25, 2007.

Date	Key U.S. Political Actions and Events	Key U.S. Military Actions and Events	Other Key Actions and Events
September 2006 (cont.)	9/5: The White House announces the National Strategy for Combating Terrorism, which describes successes in the global war on terror and warns of the evolving terrorist threat.[266] 9/19: Keane meets with Rumsfeld and emphasizes the need for more troops, a new strategy, and new military leadership.[267]		
October 2006	10/5: Rice arrives unannounced in Baghdad.[268] 10/29: Hadley, O'Sullivan, and Feaver leave for Iraq.[269]	U.S. troop levels are at 139,421.[270]	
November 2006	11/7: Democrats win majorities in the U.S. House of Representatives and U.S. Senate in midterm elections.[271] 11/8: Bush accepts Rumsfeld's resignation.[272] 11/8: Hadley reports on his firsthand look at Iraq in a classified memo later leaked to the media. Hadley recommends asking the Secretary of Defense and Casey if more troops are needed in Baghdad.[273] 11/10: Bush directs Cheney, Rice, Hadley, Pace, Negroponte, and Crouch to begin a formal review of the Iraq strategy.[274] 11/26: Crouch presents the Iraq strategy review to Bush.[275]	U.S. troop levels are at 147,796.[276]	11/5: An Iraqi court finds Saddam guilty of war crimes and sentences him to death.[277]

---

[266] Woodward, 2008a, p. 123.

[267] Woodward, 2008a, p. 129.

[268] Woodward, 2008a, p. 162.

[269] Woodward, 2008a, p. 184.

[270] Belasco, 2014, p. 84.

[271] CNN, "Bush, Dems Promise Cooperation as Senate Shifts," November 9, 2006.

[272] "Secretary Rumsfeld Stepping Down," NBC News, November 8, 2006.

[273] Woodward, 2008a, p. 206.

[274] Woodward, 2008a, p. 207.

[275] Woodward, 2008a, p. 244.

[276] Belasco, 2014, p. 84.

[277] CNN, "Saddam Hussein Fast Facts," October 17, 2013.

Date	Key U.S. Political Actions and Events	Key U.S. Military Actions and Events	Other Key Actions and Events
December 2006	12/6: Gates is confirmed as Secretary of Defense.[278] 12/6: The Iraq Study Group presents its findings to Bush.[279] 12/8: With Barno and Keane in attendance, Kagan rolls out an AEI report recommending a troop surge of five BCTs plus two Marine Corps regiments.[280] 12/11: Five outside experts, including Keane, meet with Bush to share their views of the military strategy in Iraq.[281] 12/13: Bush and Cheney visit the JCS.[282] 12/18: Gates is sworn in as Secretary of Defense.[283]	12/15: The Department of the Army publishes FM 3-24.[284] 12/14: Odierno replaces Chiarelli as commander of MNC-I.[285] A DoD report states that there are 322,600 trained and equipped ISF personnel (134,400 in MOD; 188,200 in MOI).[286] U.S. troop levels are at 133,718.[287]	12/30: Saddam is hanged.[288] 12/30: The number of U.S. troops killed in Iraq reaches 3,000.[289]

---

[278] Anne Plummer Flaherty, "Gates Confirmed as Secretary of Defense," *Washington Post*, December 7, 2006.

[279] Woodward, 2008a, p. 262.

[280] Kaplan, 2013, p. 237.

[281] Woodward, 2008a, p. 279.

[282] Gordon and Trainor, 2012, p. 304.

[283] Gordon and Trainor, 2012, p. 305.

[284] FM 3-24, 2006.

[285] Matt Millham, "Odierno Takes Command of Multi-National Corps-Iraq," *Stars and Stripes*, December 15, 2006.

[286] DoD, *Measuring Stability and Security in Iraq*, Washington, D.C., December 2006c.

[287] Belasco, 2014, p. 84.

[288] CNN, 2013.

[289] CNN, 2015d.

Date	Key U.S. Political Actions and Events	Key U.S. Military Actions and Events	Other Key Actions and Events
January 2007	1/4: Bush announces Petraeus as the new MNF-I commander.[290] 1/10: Bush announces the Surge in a 20-minute televised address.[291] 1/26: The Senate confirms Petraeus as the new commander in Iraq.[292] 1/30: The Senate confirms ADM William J. Fallon as CENTCOM commander.[293]	U.S. troop levels are at 128,569.[294]	1/16: The U.N. reports that 34,452 Iraqi civilians were killed in 2006, nearly three times more than the Iraqi government reported.[295]
February 2007		2/10: Petraeus officially replaces Casey as commander of MNF-I.[296] U.S. troop levels are at 134,754.[297]	
March 2007		3/16: Fallon officially replaces Abizaid as CENTCOM commander.[298] U.S. troop levels are at 137,976.[299] Nine U.S. Army BCTs are operating in Multi-National Division–Baghdad. A DoD report states that there are 328,700 trained and equipped ISF personnel (136,400 in MOD; 192,300 in MOI).[300]	

---

[290] Kaplan, 2013, p. 243.

[291] Gordon and Trainor, 2012, p. 313.

[292] Woodward, 2008a, pp. 327–328.

[293] Woodward, 2008a, pp. 327, 337.

[294] Belasco, 2014, p. 84.

[295] DoD and Associated Press, "OIF Timeline/Significant Events," March 21, 2008.

[296] Gordon and Trainor, 2012, p. 332.

[297] Belasco, 2014, p. 84.

[298] Woodward, 2008a, pp. 327, 337.

[299] Belasco, 2014, p. 84.

[300] DoD, *Measuring Stability and Security in Iraq*, Washington, D.C., March 2007a, p. 25.

Timeline of Major Events in the Battle for Baghdad 263

Date	Key U.S. Political Actions and Events	Key U.S. Military Actions and Events	Other Key Actions and Events
April 2007	Gates and Pace announce an extension of deployments to Iraq.[301]	U.S. troop levels are at 144,486.[302] The U.S. military force structure in Baghdad subdivides, creating the Multi-National Division, Baghdad–Center.[303]	
May 2007	Keane visits Baghdad for 11 days.[304]	U.S. troop levels are at 144,202.[305]	
June 2007	6/8: Gates announces that Pace will step down as CJCS.[306]	U.S. troop levels are at 150,336.[307]	
July 2007	7/12: A White House report says that Iraq has made satisfactory progress on eight of 18 political and security benchmarks.[308]	U.S. troop levels are at 156,247.[309]	
August 2007		U.S. troop levels are at 157,674.[310]	8/29: Sadr announces that, for six months, he will suspend his Jaysh al-Mahdi militia's operations, including attacks on U.S. troops.[311]

---

[301] Woodward, 2008a, p. 342.

[302] Belasco, 2014, p. 84.

[303] Andrade, 2010.

[304] Woodward, 2008a, p. 356.

[305] Belasco, 2014, p. 84.

[306] Woodward, 2008a, p. 364.

[307] Belasco, 2014, p. 84.

[308] DoD and Associated Press, 2008.

[309] Belasco, 2014, p. 84.

[310] Belasco, 2014, p. 84.

[311] "Timeline of Major Events in the Iraq War," 2011.

Date	Key U.S. Political Actions and Events	Key U.S. Military Actions and Events	Other Key Actions and Events
September 2007	9/10: Petraeus testifies before the U.S. House of Representatives and Senate.[312] 9/13: Bush gives a televised address in which he acknowledges that the war will last beyond his presidency.[313]	U.S. troop levels are at 165,607.[314]	Basra is turned over to local authorities after British troops withdraw to an airport outside the city. Blackwater security guards protecting a diplomatic convoy kill 17 Iraqis in Baghdad.[315]
October 2007		U.S. troop levels are at 164,353.[316]	10/23: The Office of the U.N. High Commissioner for Refugees states that nearly 2.3 million people are displaced inside Iraq and more than 2.2 million have fled to neighboring countries.[317]
November 2007		U.S. troop levels are at 164,424.[318]	
December 2007	During a visit to Baghdad, Rice decides not to support Iraqi Vice President Abd al-Mahdi's request for a vote of no confidence against Maliki.[319]	U.S. troop levels are at 161,783.[320] A DoD report states that there are 439,678 trained and equipped ISF personnel (194,233 in MOD; 241,960 in MOI; 3,485 in the Counterterrorism Bureau).[321]	

---

[312] Woodward, 2008a, p. 384.

[313] Woodward, 2008a, p. 388.

[314] Belasco, 2014, p. 84.

[315] "Timeline of Major Events in the Iraq War," 2011.

[316] Belasco, 2014, p. 84.

[317] DoD and Associated Press, 2008.

[318] Belasco, 2014, p. 84.

[319] Rayburn, 2014, p. 27.

[320] Belasco, 2014, p. 84.

[321] DoD, *Measuring Stability and Security in Iraq*, Washington, D.C., December 2007c.

Timeline of Major Events in the Battle for Baghdad   265

Date	Key U.S. Political Actions and Events	Key U.S. Military Actions and Events	Other Key Actions and Events
January 2008		U.S. troop levels are at 155,846.[322] 155 Military Transitions Teams are operating in Iraq.[323]	1/9: The World Health Organization estimates that 151,000 Iraqi civilians have died from violence since the U.S. intervention began.[324]
February 2008		2/14: Austin replaces Odierno as commander of MNC-I.[325] U.S. troop levels are at 158,400.[326]	
March 2008	3/11: Gates announces Fallon's resignation as CENTCOM commander.[327]	3/23: The 3rd Brigade, 4th Infantry Division begins combat operations in the battle for Sadr City.[328] 3/28: Dempsey replaces Fallon as acting commander of CENTCOM.[329] U.S. troop levels are at 159,700.[330]	3/2: Iranian President Mahmoud Ahmadinejad visits Iraq, marking the first time an Iranian president has visited Baghdad since the Iran-Iraq War ended in 1988.[331] 3/22: The number of U.S. troops killed in Iraq reaches 4,000.[332] 3/24: Maliki orders Iraqi forces to fight Sadr's Jaysh al-Mahdi in Basra.[333]
April 2008	4/23: Gates announces his recommendation of Petraeus for CENTCOM commander.[334]	U.S. troop levels are at 162,400.[335]	

---

[322] Belasco, 2014, p. 85.

[323] Dale, 2008, p. 66.

[324] DoD and Associated Press, 2008.

[325] Laura M. Bigenho, "Austin Assumes Control of MNC-I," U.S. Army, February 24, 2008.

[326] Belasco, 2014, p. 85.

[327] CNN, "Fallon Resigns as Chief of U.S. Forces in Middle East," March 12, 2008.

[328] Johnson, Markel, and Shannon, 2013, p. 1.

[329] CENTCOM, "USCENTCOM Bids Farewell to Commander," MacDill Air Force Base, Fla., March 28, 2008.

[330] Belasco, 2014, p. 85.

[331] Hooker and Collins, 2015, p. 462.

[332] CNN, 2015d.

[333] Hooker and Collins, 2015, p. 462.

[334] Woodward, 2008a, p. 415.

[335] Belasco, 2014, p. 85.

Date	Key U.S. Political Actions and Events	Key U.S. Military Actions and Events	Other Key Actions and Events
May 2008		U.S. troop levels are at 158,900.[336]	
June 2008		U.S. troop levels are at 153,300.[337]	
		The 3rd Brigade, 4th Infantry Division (within Multi-National Division–Baghdad) conducts combat operations in Sadr City.[338]	
July 2008		U.S. troop levels are at 147,400.[339]	7/16: The Surge officially ends.[340]
August 2008		U.S. troop levels are at 145,000.[341]	
September 2008		9/16: Odierno replaces Petraeus as commander of MNF-I.[342]	9/1: U.S. commanders formally return security responsibilities for Anbar Province over to the Iraqi Army and Iraqi Police.[344]
		U.S. troop levels are at 146,900.[343]	
October 2008		U.S. troop levels are at 147,700.[345]	
November 2008		U.S. troop levels are at 148,100.[346]	
December 2008	The Iraqi government approves the SOFA, which calls for a withdrawal of troops by the end of 2011.[347]	U.S. troop levels are at 148,500.[348]	

---

[336] Belasco, 2014, p. 85.

[337] Belasco, 2014, p. 85.

[338] Johnson, Markel, and Shannon, 2013, p. xvi.

[339] Belasco, 2014, p. 85.

[340] CNN, "The Iraq War: A Nine-Year Timeline," October 21, 2011.

[341] Belasco, 2014, p. 85.

[342] Thom Shanker and Stephen Farrell, "Odierno Replaces Petraeus as U.S. Commander in Iraq," *New York Times*, September 16, 2008.

[343] Belasco, 2014, p. 85.

[344] "Timeline of Major Events in the Iraq War," 2011.

[345] Belasco, 2014, p. 85.

[346] Belasco, 2014, p. 85.

[347] CNN, 2011.

[348] Belasco, 2014, p. 85.

Date	Key U.S. Political Actions and Events	Key U.S. Military Actions and Events	Other Key Actions and Events
January 2009	1/20: Obama is inaugurated.[349] Within a couple of weeks of Obama's inauguration, Odierno and Crocker submit a proposal to the White House for troop withdrawal and a residual force size.[350]	U.S. troop levels are at 147,700.[351]	The ISF take responsibility for the International Zone.[352]
February 2009	2/26: Obama and Gates brief their withdrawal plan to congressional leaders. The plan includes a residual force of no more than 50,000, which differs from Mullen's previous recommendations.[353] 2/27: Obama announces that he will gradually withdraw troops from Iraq, with most forces being brought home by August 2010.[354]	U.S. troop levels are at 146,400.[355]	
March 2009		U.S. troop levels are at 141,300.[356]	
April 2009		U.S. troop levels are at 139,400.[357]	
May 2009		U.S. troop levels are at 134,200.[358]	
June 2009		6/30: U.S. troops withdraw from Iraqi cities to forward operating bases.[359] U.S. troop levels are at 134,500.[360]	

---

[349] Macon Phillips, "President Barack Obama's Inaugural Address," White House, January 21, 2009.

[350] Gordon and Trainor, 2012, pp. 564–570.

[351] Belasco, 2014, p. 85.

[352] Hooker and Collins, 2015, p. 463.

[353] Gordon and Trainor, 2012, p. 574.

[354] CNN, "Obama: U.S. to Withdraw Most Iraq Troops by August 2010," February 27, 2009.

[355] Belasco, 2014, p. 85.

[356] Belasco, 2014, p. 85.

[357] Belasco, 2014, p. 85.

[358] Belasco, 2014, p. 85.

[359] Rubin, 2009.

[360] Belasco, 2014, p. 85.

References

"450 Fort Hood Soldiers Headed to Kuwait," *Army Times*, August 5, 2015. As of February 1, 2016:
http://www.armytimes.com/story/military/2015/08/05/450-fort-hood-soldiers-headed-kuwait/31165459/

"The 2010 Iraqi Parliamentary Elections," *New York Times*, March 26, 2010. As of November 4, 2015:
http://www.nytimes.com/interactive/2010/03/11/world/middleeast/20100311-iraq-election.html

ABC News, "ABC/BBC/ARD/NHK Poll—Iraq Five Years Later: Where Things Stand," March 17, 2008. As of August 12, 2016:
http://abcnews.go.com/images/PollingUnit/1060a1IraqWhereThingsStand.pdf

Ackerman, Spencer, "Iraq's Flying Bombs Return," *Wired*, July 5, 2011. As of December 17, 2015:
http://www.wired.com/2011/07/iraqs-flying-bombs-return-killing-6-g-i-s/

Agnew, John, Thomas W. Gillespie, Jorge Gonzalez, and Brian Min, "Baghdad Nights: Evaluating the U.S. Military Surge Using Nighttime Light Signatures," Los Angeles: California Center for Population Research, CCPR-064-08, December 2008.

Ahern, Colin, "Clear, Hold, Build: Modern Political Techniques in COIN," Fort Huachuca, Ariz.: University of Military Intelligence, 2008.

al-Ansary, Khalid, and Ali Adeeb, "Most Tribes in Anbar Agree to Unite Against Insurgents," *New York Times*, September 18, 2006.

Allawi, Ali A., *The Occupation of Iraq: Winning the War, Losing the Peace*, New Haven, Conn.: Yale University Press, 2007.

al-Tamimi, Aymenn Jawad, "Assessing the Surge in Iraq," *Middle East Review of International Affairs*, Vol. 15, No. 4, December 2011, p. 26–38.

Alter, Jonathan, *The Promise: President Obama, Year One*, New York: Simon and Schuster, 2010.

Andrade, Dale, *Surging South of Baghdad: The Third Infantry Division and Task Force Marne in Iraq, 2007–2008*, Washington, D.C.: Center of Military History, 2010.

Argano, Tim, and Michael S. Schmidt, "Despite Difficult Talks, U.S. and Iraq Had Expected Some American Troops to Stay," *New York Times*, October 21, 2011. As of November 4, 2015:
http://www.nytimes.com/2011/10/22/world/middleeast/united-states-and-iraq-had-not-expected-troops-would-have-to-leave.html

Arraf, Jane, "US Troops to Exit Iraq's Cities but New Role Still Evolving," *Christian Science Monitor*, June 29, 2009. As of December 1, 2015:
http://www.csmonitor.com/World/Middle-East/2009/0629/p06s04-wome.html

———, "US Military Officials in Iraq Warn of Growing Iranian Threat," *Christian Science Monitor*, July 27, 2011. As of August 12, 2016:
http://www.csmonitor.com/World/Middle-East/2011/0727/
US-military-officials-in-Iraq-warn-of-growing-Iranian-threat

Associated Press, "Iraq: Blackwater Shootings Killed 17," *USA Today*, October 7, 2007. As of January 14, 2016:
http://usatoday30.usatoday.com/news/world/iraq/2007-10-07-blackwater-investigation_N.htm

Bahry, Louay, "Baghdad," *Encyclopedia Britannica*, undated. As of November 13, 2015:
http://www.britannica.com/place/Baghdad

Bailey, Michael A., Robert Dixon, Marc Harris, Daniel Hendrex, Nicholas Melin, and Richard Russo, "A Proposed Framework for Appreciating Megacities: A U.S. Army Perspective," *Small Wars Journal*, April 21, 2014.

Bailey, Michael A., and John D. Via, "Military Medical Implications of Future Megacity Operations," *Small Wars Journal*, February 13, 2015.

Baker, Fred W., III, "Odierno: Troops Out of Iraqi Cities by Summer," Armed Forces Press Service, U.S. Central Command, December 14, 2008. As of August 12, 2016:
http://www.centcom.mil/news/news-article/odierno-troops-out-of-iraqi-cities-by-summer

Baker, James A., Lee H. Hamilton, Lawrence S. Eagleburger, Vernon E. Jordan, Jr., Edwin Meese III, Sandra Day O'Conner, Leon E. Panetta, William J. Perry, Charles S. Robb, and Alan K. Simpson, *The Iraq Study Group Report*, December 2006. As of January 29, 2016:
https://www.thepresidency.org/sites/default/files/pdf/iraq_study_group_report.pdf

Baker, Jay B., "Tal Afar 2005: Laying the Counterinsurgency Groundwork," *Army Magazine*, June 2009.

Baker, Peter, "Relief over U.S. Exit from Iraq Fades as Reality Overtakes Hope," *New York Times*, June 22, 2014. As of November 4, 2015:
http://www.nytimes.com/2014/06/23/world/middleeast/
relief-over-us-exit-from-iraq-fades-as-reality-overtakes-hope.html

Baker, Ralph O., "The Decisive Weapon: A Brigade Combat Team Commander's Perspective on Information Operations," *Military Review*, May–June 2006.

Ball, A. T., and Berrien T. McCutchen, Jr., "Task Force ODIN Using Innovative Technology to Support Ground Forces," Tikrit, Iraq: Defense Video and Imagery Distribution System, September 20, 2007.

Balz, Dan, "Bush Wins Second Term," *Washington Post*, November 4, 2004.

Barnes, Julian E., "Baghdad Outpost Plan Flawed, Some Troops Say," *Los Angeles Times*, July 8, 2007.

Barrett, Ted, "Congress Forms Panel to Study Iraq War," CNN, March 15, 2006.

BBC, "Iraq Stampede Deaths Near 1,000," August 31, 2005.

———, "What Is 'Islamic State'?" October 8, 2015. As of November 3, 2015:
http://www.bbc.com/news/world-middle-east-29052144

Beaumont, Peter, "Iraqi Tribes Launch Battle to Drive al Qaeda Out of Troubled Province," *The Guardian*, October 3, 2006.

Belasco, Amy, *Troop Levels in the Afghan and Iraq Wars, FY2001–FY2012: Cost and Other Potential Issues*, Washington, D.C.: Congressional Research Service, R40682, July 2, 2009. As of December 10, 2015:
https://www.fas.org/sgp/crs/natsec/R40682.pdf

———, *The Cost of Iraq, Afghanistan, and Other Global War on Terror Operations Since 9/11*, Washington, D.C.: Congressional Research Service, RL33110, December 8, 2014. As of August 12, 2016:
https://www.fas.org/sgp/crs/natsec/RL33110.pdf

Bennett, Brian, "Who Are the Insurgents?" *Time*, November 16, 2003. As of December 18, 2015:
http://content.time.com/time/magazine/article/0,9171,543740,00.html

Bensahel, Nora, "Mission Not Accomplished: What Went Wrong with Iraqi Reconstruction," *Journal of Strategic Studies*, Vol. 29, No. 3, June 2006, pp. 453–473.

Bensahel, Nora, Olga Oliker, Keith Crane, Richard R. Brennan, Jr., Heather S. Gregg, Thomas Sullivan, and Andrew Rathmell, *After Saddam: Prewar Planning and the Occupation of Iraq*, Santa Monica, Calif.: RAND Corporation, MG-642-A, 2008. As of August 12, 2016:
http://www.rand.org/pubs/monographs/MG642.html

Bensahel, Nora, Olga Oliker, Keith Crane, Heather S. Gregg, Richard R. Brennan, Jr., and Andrew Rathmell, "The Aftermath: Civilian Planning Efforts and the Occupation of Iraq," in Walter L. Perry, Richard E. Darilek, Laurinda L. Rohn, and Jerry M. Sollinger, eds., *Operation IRAQI FREEDOM: Decisive War, Elusive Peace*, Santa Monica, Calif.: RAND Corporation, RR-1214-A, 2015, pp. 319–340. As of August 12, 2016:
http://www.rand.org/pubs/research_reports/RR1214.html

Benson, Kevin C. M., unpublished personal war journal and files compiled while serving as the Director of Plans, C/J-5, Coalition Forces Land Component Command, 2002/2003.

Berger, Samuel R., and Brent Scowcroft, eds., *In the Wake of War: Improving U.S. Post-Conflict Capabilities*, Report of an Independent Task Force, Washington, D.C.: Council on Foreign Relations, 2005.

Biddle, Stephen, Jeffrey A. Friedman, and Jacob N. Shapiro. "Testing the Surge: Why Did Violence Decline in Iraq in 2007?" *International Security*, Vol. 37, No. 1, Summer 2012, pp. 7–40.

Biden, Joseph R., and Leslie H. Gelb, "Unity Through Autonomy in Iraq," *New York Times*, May 1, 2006. As of February 1, 2016:
http://www.nytimes.com/2006/05/01/opinion/01biden.html?pagewanted=all

Bigenho, Laura M., "Austin Assumes Control of MNC-I," U.S. Army, February 24, 2008.

"Biography: James F. Jeffrey," U.S. Department of State, November 21, 2006. As of October 26, 2015:
http://2001-2009.state.gov/r/pa/ei/biog/56704.htm

"Biography: Ronald E. Neumann," U.S. Department of State, August 1, 2005. As of October 26, 2015:
http://2001-2009.state.gov/outofdate/bios/n/50490.htm

Birtle, Andrew J., *U.S. Army Counterinsurgency and Contingency Operations Doctrine, 1942–1975*, Washington, D.C.: U.S. Army Center of Military History, 2006.

Blair, Tony, "A Battle for Global Values," *Foreign Affairs*, Vol. 86, No. 1, January–February 2007, pp. 79–90.

Bohan, Caren, "Obama: U.S. Must End 'Single-Minded' Focus on Iraq," Reuters, July 15, 2008. As of March 3, 2016:
http://www.reuters.com/article/us-usa-politics-obama-iraq-idUSN1332805020080715

Bonds, Timothy M., Dave Baiocchi, and Laurie L. McDonald, *Can the Army Deploy More Soldiers to Iraq and Afghanistan?* Santa Monica, Calif.: RAND Corporation, RB-9618-A, 2011. As of August 12, 2016:
http://www.rand.org/pubs/research_briefs/RB9618.html

Bonds, Timothy M., Myron Hura, and Thomas-Durell Young, *Enhancing Army Joint Force Headquarters Capabilities*, Santa Monica, Calif.: RAND Corporation, MG-675-1-A, 2010. As of August 12, 2016:
http://www.rand.org/pubs/monographs/MG675-1.html

Bonds, Timothy M., Michael Johnson, and Paul S. Steinberg, *Limiting Regret: Building the Army We Will Need*, Santa Monica, Calif.: RAND Corporation, RR-1320-RC, 2015. As of August 12, 2016:
http://www.rand.org/pubs/research_reports/RR1320.html

Bowman, Tom, "U.S. Faces Challenges in Shoring Up Iraq's Crumbling Military," NPR, June 24, 2014. As of February 10, 2017:
http://www.npr.org/2014/06/24/325229834/whats-behind-the-collapse-of-iraqs-military

Bremer, L. Paul, III, "Iraq Coalition Provisional Authority Order Number One: De-Ba'athification of Iraqi Society," May 16, 2003a.

———, "Coalition Provisional Authority Order Number 2: Dissolution of Entities," May 23, 2003b. As of October 26, 2003:
http://nsarchive.gwu.edu/NSAEBB/NSAEBB418/docs/
9b%20-%20Coalition%20Provisional%20Authority%20Order%20No%202%20-%208-23-03.pdf

———, *My Year in Iraq: The Struggle to Bring a Future of Hope*, New York: Simon and Schuster, 2006.

———, "How I Didn't Dismantle Iraq's Army," *New York Times*, September 6, 2007. As of November 24, 2015:
http://www.nytimes.com/2007/09/06/opinion/06bremer.html?_r=0

Brennan, Rick, Jr., Charles P. Reis, Larry Hanauer, Ben Connable, Terrence K. Kelly, Michael McNerney, Stephanie Young, Jason Campbell, and K. Scott McMahon, *Ending the U.S. War in Iraq: The Final Transition, Operational Maneuver, and Disestablishment of United States Forces-Iraq*, Santa Monica, Calif.: RAND Corporation, RR-232-USFI, 2013. As of August 12, 2016:
http://www.rand.org/pubs/research_reports/RR232.html

Brigham, Robert, *The United States and Iraq Since 1990: A Brief History with Documents*, Chichester, UK: Wiley-Blackwell, 2013.

Brink, Bill, "Former Iraqi Official Known as 'Chemical Ali' Is Captured," *New York Times*, August 21, 2003.

Bryan, Wright, and Douglas Hopper, "Iraq WMD Timeline: How the Mystery Unraveled," NPR, November 15, 2005. As of December 9, 2015:
http://www.npr.org/templates/story/story.php?storyId=4996218

Bull, Bartle, "Iraqi Elections: Looking for Purple Fingers in Sadr City," *New York Times*, January 31, 2005.

Burns, John F., "On Way to Baghdad Airport, Death Stalks Main Road," *New York Times*, May 29, 2005. As of December 1, 2015:
http://www.nytimes.com/2005/05/29/world/middleeast/on-way-to-baghdad-airport-death-stalks-main-road.html

———, "Abu Masab al-Zarqawi, Leader of Al Qaeda in Iraq, Is Killed in U.S. Airstrike," *New York Times*, June 8, 2006.

Burns, John F., and Dexter Filkins, "Shiite Alliance Adds to Leads as More Are Counted in Iraq," *New York Times*, February 4, 2005.

Bush, George W., speech delivered to the United Nations General Assembly, New York, September 12, 2002. As of October 29, 2015:
http://www.theguardian.com/world/2002/sep/12/iraq.usa3

———, "The Iraqi Interim Government," Washington, D.C.: U.S. Department of State Archive, June 1, 2004. As of April 28, 2017:
https://2001-2009.state.gov/p/nea/rls/rm/33042.htm

———, *Decision Points*, New York: Crown Publishers, 2010.

Byman, Daniel, "An Autopsy of the Iraq Debacle: Policy Failure or Bridge Too Far?" *Security Studies*, Vol. 17, October 2008, pp. 599–643.

Carafano, James J., *Waltzing into the Cold War: The Struggle for Occupied Austria*, College Station, Tex.: Texas A&M University Press, 2002.

———, "20 Years Later: Professional Military Education," testimony before the Subcommittee on Oversight and Investigations, House Armed Services Committee, Washington, D.C., May 20, 2009.

Carter, B. Linwood, *Iraq: Summary of U.S. Forces*, Washington, D.C.: Congressional Research Service, RL31763, November 28, 2005. As of August 12, 2016:
https://www.fas.org/sgp/crs/mideast/RL31763.pdf

Casey, George W., Jr., *Papers of George W. Casey*, National Defense University, various years.

———, *Command Report: Multi-National Force Iraq, July 2004–February 2007*, Washington, D.C.: National Defense University Press, undated, draft copy provided to RAND.

———, *Strategic Reflections: Operation Iraqi Freedom—July 2004–February 2007*, Washington, D.C.: National Defense University Press, October 2012.

Cavallaro, Gina, "War Zone Training Will Garner Command Credit," *Army Times*, June 19, 2008.

CENTCOM—*See* U.S. Central Command.

"CENTCOM Update, Center for a New American Security," briefing slides, 2009, provided to RAND by a former senior military commander.

Center for American Progress, "Questions for Paul Wolfowitz," April 20, 2004. As of January 26, 2016:
https://www.americanprogress.org/issues/security/news/2004/04/20/733/questions-for-paul-wolfowitz/

Center for Military History, "The April 2004 Battle of Sadr City," April 21, 2014. As of December 18, 2015:
http://www.history.army.mil/news/2014/140421a_sadrCity.html

Chandrasekaran, Rajiv, *Imperial Life in the Emerald City*, New York: Vintage Books, 2006a.

———, "Who Killed Iraq?" *Foreign Policy*, Vol. 156, September–October 2006b, pp. 36–43.

Chiarelli, Peter W., and Patrick R. Michaelis, "Winning the Peace: The Requirement for Full-Spectrum Operations," *Military Review*, July–August 2005.

"Chronology of Abu Ghraib," *Washington Post*, February 17, 2006.

Chulov, Martin, Fazel Hawramy, and Spencer Ackerman, "Iraq Army Capitulates to ISIS Militants in Four Cities," *The Guardian*, June 11, 2014. As of December 17, 2015: http://www.theguardian.com/world/2014/jun/11/mosul-isis-gunmen-middle-east-states

Clark, Charles S., "Pentagon Moves Ahead with HQ Staff Cuts," *Government Executive*, September 8, 2015. As of February 1, 2016: http://www.govexec.com/defense/2015/09/pentagon-moves-ahead-hq-staff-cuts-union-cries-fowl/120518/

CNN, "Journalists Given Tour of Huge Iraqi Palaces," December 19, 1997.

———, "Bush Declares War: Mar. 19 2003," March 19, 2003a.

———, "Pentagon: Saddam's Sons Killed in Raid," July 22, 2003b.

———, "Bush to Ask Billions More for Iraq," September 8, 2003c.

———, "U.S. Helicopter Shot Down in Iraq," November 2, 2003d.

———, "Time Reporter: Iraqi Resistance Getting Smarter," November 20, 2003e.

———, "Deadliest Day for the U.S. in Iraq War," January 27, 2005a.

———, "Iraqi Constitution Passes, Officials Say," October 25, 2005b.

———, "Bush, Dems Promise Cooperation as Senate Shifts," November 9, 2006.

———, "Fallon Resigns as Chief of U.S. Forces in Middle East," March 12, 2008.

———, "Obama: U.S. to Withdraw Most Iraq Troops by August 2010," February 27, 2009.

———, "The Iraq War: A Nine-Year Timeline," October 21, 2011.

———, "Saddam Hussein Fast Facts," October 17, 2013.

———, "Jalal Talabani Fast Facts," August 28, 2014.

———, "Saddam Hussein Trial Fast Facts," March 12, 2015a.

———, "Iraq Prison Abuse Scandal Fast Facts," March 27, 2015b.

———, "Jessica Lynch Fast Facts," April 15, 2015c.

———, "Operation Iraqi Freedom and Operation New Dawn Fast Facts," April 21, 2015d.

———, "Nuri al-Maliki Fast Facts," July 3, 2015e.

Cockburn, Patrick, "Who Is Whose Enemy?" *London Review of Books*, Vol. 30, No. 5, March 2008. As of August 12, 2016: http://www.lrb.co.uk/v30/n05/patrick-cockburn/who-is-whose-enemy

Cocks, Tim, and Muhanad Mohammed, "Iraq Regains Control of Cities as U.S. Pulls Back," Reuters, June 30, 2009. As of August 12, 2016: http://uk.reuters.com/article/uk-iraq-usa-troops-idUKLS34055920090630

Cohen, Eliot A., *Supreme Command: Soldiers, Statesmen, and Leadership in Wartime*, New York: Simon and Schuster, September 9, 2003.

Coles, Harry L., and Albert K. Weinberg, *Civil Affairs: Soldiers Become Governors*, Washington, D.C.: U.S. Army Center of Military History, 1992.

Colloton, Patrick, and Tommy Stoner, "Transition Teams and Operational Integration," *Infantry*, Vol. 95, No. 6, November–December 2006, pp. 32–41.

Cordesman, Anthony H., and Adam Mansner, *Iraqi Force Development: Conditions for Success, Consequences of Failure*, Washington, D.C.: Center for Strategic and International Studies, September 2007.

Council on Foreign Relations, "Terrorist Havens: Iraq," *CFR Backgrounder*, December 1, 2005. As of December 9, 2015:
http://www.cfr.org/iraq/terrorism-havens-iraq/p9513

CQ Transcriptions, "Iraq Briefing," *Washington Post*, October 24, 2006. As of August 12, 2016:
http://www.washingtonpost.com/wp-dyn/content/article/2006/10/24/AR2006102400481.html

———, "President Bush Addresses Nation on Iraq War," *Washington Post*, January 10, 2007. As of August 12, 2016:
http://www.washingtonpost.com/wp-dyn/content/article/2007/01/10/AR2007011002208.html

Crane, Conrad C., and W. Andrew Terrill, *Reconstructing Iraq: Insights, Challenges, and Missions for Military Forces in a Post-Conflict Scenario*, Carlisle Barracks, Pa.: Strategic Studies Institute, U.S. Army War College, 2003.

Dale, Catherine, *Operation Iraqi Freedom: Strategies, Approaches, Results, and Issues for Congress*, Washington, D.C.: Congressional Research Service, RL34387, February 22, 2008.

Damon, Arwa, "Shadowy Iraq Office Accused of Sectarian Agenda," CNN, May 1, 2007. As of November 21, 2016:
http://www.cnn.com/2007/WORLD/meast/05/01/iraq.office/

Davis, Daniel, *Dereliction of Duty II: Senior Military Leaders' Loss of Integrity Wounds Afghan War Effort*, January 27, 2012.

Davis, Timothy, *Building the Iraqi Army: Teaching a Nation to Fish*, thesis, Fort Leavenworth, Kan.: U.S. Army Command and General Staff College, 2005.

Defense Manpower Data Center, "DoD Personnel, Workforce Reports & Publications," webpage, undated. As of February 1, 2016:
https://www.dmdc.osd.mil/appj/dwp/dwp_reports.jsp

de Lira, Gerald, Jr., *The Anger of a Great Nation: Operation Vigilant Resolve*, thesis, Quantico, Va.: Marine Corps University, 2009.

Department of the Army, *The Army Training and Leader Development Panel Officer Study Report to the Army*, Arlington, Va., 2003. As of February 1, 2016:
http://handle.dtic.mil/100.2/ADA415810

———, *2008 Army Posture Statement Information Papers: Accelerate Army Growth*, 2008. As of February 1, 2016:
http://www.army.mil/aps/08/information_papers/transform/Accelerate_Army_Growth.html

———, *Commander's Guide to Operational Records and Data Collection*, Handbook No. 09-22, Fort Leavenworth, Kan.: Center for Army Lessons Learned, 2012.

———, *2013 Chief of Staff of the Army Leader Development Task Force Final Report*, Washington, D.C., June 14, 2013.

———, *2014 Army Strategic Planning Guidance*, Washington, D.C., 2014a. As of February 1, 2016:
http://www.g8.army.mil/pdf/Army_Strategic_Planning_Guidance2014.pdf

———, *The U.S. Army Operating Concept: Win in a Complex World*, TRADOC Pamphlet 525-3-1, Washington, D.C.: Headquarters, Department of the Army, October 31, 2014b.

———, "2013 Focus Areas," memorandum, August 14, 2015.

Diamond, Larry, "What Went Wrong in Iraq," *Foreign Affairs*, Vol. 83, No. 5, September–October 2004, pp. 34–56.

Djerejian, Edward P., and Frank G. Wisner, eds., *Guiding Principles for U.S. Post-Conflict Policy in Iraq*, Report of an Independent Working Group, Washington D.C.: Council on Foreign Relations and the James A. Baker III Institute for Public Policy of Rice University, 2002. As of November 25, 2015:
http://www.cfr.org/content/publications/attachments/Iraq_TF.pdf

Dobbins, James, Seth G. Jones, Benjamin Runkle, and Siddarth Mohandas, *Occupying Iraq: A History of the Coalition Provisional Authority*, Santa Monica, Calif.: RAND Corporation, MG-847-CC, 2009. As of August 12, 2016:
http://www.rand.org/pubs/monographs/MG847.html

Dobbins, James, John G. McGinn, Keith Crane, Seth G. Jones, Rollie Lal, Andrew Rathmell, Rachel Swanger, and Anga Timilsina, *America's Role in Nation-Building: From Germany to Iraq*, Santa Monica, Calif.: RAND Corporation, MR-1753-RC, 2003. As of August 12, 2016:
http://www.rand.org/pubs/monograph_reports/MR1753.html

DoD—See U.S. Department of Defense.

Dorman, Shawn "Desire to 'Serve My Country' Cited by Volunteers for Duty in Iraq," *Washington Post*, March 23, 2006. As of December 1, 2015:
http://www.washingtonpost.com/wp-dyn/content/article/2006/03/22/AR2006032202085.html

Druzin, Heath, "U.S. Forces Introducing Iraqis to High-Tech Tools," *Stars and Stripes*, August 4, 2009. As of December 1, 2015:
http://www.stripes.com/news/u-s-forces-introducing-iraqis-to-high-tech-tools-1.93765

Dubik, James M., *Building Security Forces and Ministerial Capacity: Iraq as a Primer*, Washington, D.C.: Institute for the Study of War, August 2009.

———, "A Closer Look at the 'Build Partner Capacity' Mission," *Army Magazine*, January 2012, pp. 14–16. As of August 12, 2016:
http://ausar-web01.inetu.net/publications/armymagazine/archive/2012/01/Documents/FC_Dubik_0112.pdf

Eisenstadt, Michael, and Jeffrey White, "Assessing Iraq's Sunni Arab Insurgency," *Military Review*, May–June 2006. As of December 18, 2015:
http://www.washingtoninstitute.org/policy-analysis/view/assessing-iraqs-sunni-arab-insurgency1

Erwin, Sandra, "An Army Under Stress: A Tale of Two Green Lines," *National Defense*, April 2006. As of February 1, 2016:
http://www.nationaldefensemagazine.org/archive/2006/April/Pages/defensewatch5377.aspx

Farrell, Stephen, "50 Die in Fight Between Shia Groups in Karballa," *New York Times*, August 29, 2007.

Fassihi, Farnaz, Greg Jaffe, Yaroslav Trofimov, Carla Anne Robbins, and Yochi J. Dreazen, "Early U.S. Decisions on Iraq Now Haunt American Efforts: Officials Let Looters Roam, Disbanded Army, Allowed Radicals to Gain Strength," *Wall Street Journal*, April 19, 2004. As of November 25, 2015:
http://www.wsj.com/articles/SB108232780526786049

Fastabend, David A., and Robert H. Simpson, "'Adapt or Die': The Imperative for a Culture of Innovation in the United States Army," *Army Magazine*, February 2004.

Feaver, Peter, "The Right to Be Right: Civil Military Relations and the Iraq Surge Decision," *International Security*, Vol. 35, No. 4, Spring 2011, pp. 87–125.

Feith, Douglas J., *War and Decision: Inside the Pentagon at the Dawn of the War on Terrorism*, New York: HarperCollins, 2008.

Felix, Kevin M., and Frederick D. Wong, "The Case for Megacities," *Parameters*, Vol. 45, No. 1, Spring 2015, pp. 19–32.

Ferguson, Charles H., *No End in Sight: Iraq's Descent into Chaos*, New York: Public Affairs, 2008.

Field Manual 3-0, *Operations*, Washington, D.C.: Headquarters, Department of the Army, 2001.

Field Manual 3-24, *Counterinsurgency*, Washington, D.C.: Headquarters, Department of the Army, December 2006. As of December 18, 2015:
http://usacac.army.mil/cac2/Repository/Materials/COIN-FM3-24.pdf

Field Manual 3-57, *Civil Affairs Operations*, Washington, D.C.: Headquarters, Department of the Army, 2011.

Field Manual 3-94, *Theater Army, Corps, and Division Operations*, Washington, D.C.: Headquarters, Department of the Army, 2014.

Field Manual 27-5/OpNav 50E-3, *United States Army and Navy Manual of Military Government and Civil Affairs*, Washington, D.C.: U.S. War Department and Navy Department, 1943.

Field Manual 41-10, *Civil Affairs Operations*, Washington, D.C.: Headquarters Department of the Army, 2000.

Field Manual 100-15, *Corps Operations*, Washington, D.C.: Headquarters, Department of the Army, 1996.

Filkins, Dexter, "US and Iraq Retake Ramadi One Neighborhood at a Time," *New York Times*, June 27, 2006.

Flaherty, Anne Plummer, "Gates Confirmed as Secretary of Defense," *Washington Post*, December 7, 2006.

FM—*See* Field Manual.

Folsom, Seth W. B., *The Highway War: A Marine Company Commander in Iraq*, Washington, D.C: Potomac Books, 2006.

Fontenot, Gregory, E. J. Degen, and David Tohn, *On Point: The United States Army in Operation Iraqi Freedom*, Fort Leavenworth, Kan.: Combat Studies Institute Press, 2004.

Fox News, "U.S.: Operation Matador a Success," May 15, 2005.

Franks, Tommy, and Malcom McConnell, *American Soldier*, New York: HarperCollins, 2004.

Freedburg, Sydney J., Jr., "Army Mulls Train and Advise Brigades: Gen. Milley," *Breaking Defense*, December 14, 2015. As of February 1, 2016:
http://breakingdefense.com/2015/12/army-mulls-train-advise-brigades-gen-milley/

Fritz, Jason, "Lessons Observed on Lessons Observed: IEDs, Advising, and Armor," *War on the Rocks*, February 3, 2014. As of February 1, 2016:
http://warontherocks.com/2014/02/lessons-observed-on-lessons-observed-ieds-advising-and-armor/

Frontline, "Saddam Hussein's Weapons of Mass Destruction," Public Broadcasting System, undated. As of December 9, 2015:
http://www.pbs.org/wgbh/pages/frontline/shows/gunning/etc/arsenal.html

———, "Interviews: Frederick W. Kagan," Public Broadcasting Service, February 26, 2004. As of August 12, 2016:
http://www.pbs.org/wgbh/pages/frontline/shows/invasion/interviews/kagan.html

———, "Interviews: Lt. Gen. Jay Garner (Ret.)," Public Broadcasting Service, August 11, 2006a. As of November 30, 2015:
http://www.pbs.org/wgbh/pages/frontline/yeariniraq/interviews/garner.html

———, "Inside the Green Zone," Public Broadcasting Service, October 17, 2006b. As of November 24, 2015:
http://www.pbs.org/wgbh/pages/frontline/yeariniraq/analysis/greenzone.html

———, "Key Controversies of the Post-War Period: Debaathification," Public Broadcasting System, October 17, 2006c. As of November 24, 2015:
http://www.pbs.org/wgbh/pages/frontline/yeariniraq/analysis/fuel.html

———, "Interviews: Richard Armitage," Public Broadcasting Service, December 18, 2007. As of November 1, 2015:
http://www.pbs.org/wgbh/pages/frontline/bushswar/interviews/armitage.html

Gallup, "Iraq," webpage, undated. As of November 5, 2015:
http://www.gallup.com/poll/1633/iraq.aspx

Gates, Robert M., "Remarks by Secretary of Defense Robert M. Gates at USGLC Tribute Dinner," U.S. Global Leadership Campaign, July 15, 2008. As of August 12, 2016:
http://www.usglc.org/USGLCdocs/USGLC_Remarks_by_Defense_Secretary_Gates.pdf

Gentile, Gian, David E. Johnson, Lisa Saum-Manning, Raphael S. Cohen, Shara Williams, Carrie Lee, Michael Shurkin, Brenna Allen, Sarah Soliman, and James L. Doty III, *Reimagining the Character of Urban Operations for the United States Army Past, Present, and Future*, Santa Monica, Calif.: RAND Corporation, RR-1602-A, 2017.

Gettleman, Jeffrey, "Enraged Mob in Fallujah Kills 4 American Contractors," *New York Times*, March 31, 2004.

Gibson, Chris, "Battlefield Victories and Strategic Success: The Path Forward in Iraq," *Military Review*, September–October 2006, pp. 47–58.

Gilmore, Gerry J., "Abizaid Set to Supplant Franks as CENTCOM Commander," DoD News, July 2, 2003.

Gordon, David Stott, "Military Governance: The Essential Mission of Civil Affairs," in Christopher Holshek and John C. Church, Jr., eds., *2014–2015 Civil Affairs Issue Papers: The Future of Civil Affairs*, Carlisle Barracks, Pa.: U.S. Army War College Press, 2015.

Gordon, Michael R., "The 2000 Campaign: The Military; Bush Would Stop U.S. Peacekeeping in Balkan Fights," *New York Times*, October 21, 2000. As of November 23, 2015:
http://www.nytimes.com/2000/10/21/us/the-2000-campaign-the-military-bush-would-stop-us-peacekeeping-in-balkan-fights.html?pagewanted=all

———, "The Former Insurgent Counterinsurgency," *New York Times*, September 2, 2007.

———, "Occupation Plan for Iraq Faulted in Army History," *New York Times*, June 29, 2008a. As of August 12, 2016:
http://www.nytimes.com/2008/06/29/washington/29army.html?pagewanted=all&_r=0

———, "U.S. Troop 'Surge' Took Place Amid Doubt and Debate," *New York Times*, August 31, 2008b. As of February 1, 2016:
http://www.nytimes.com/2008/08/31/world/americas/
31iht-31military.15759523.html?pagewanted=all

———, "In U.S. Exit from Iraq, Failed Efforts and Challenges," *New York Times*, September 22, 2012. As of September 4, 2015:
http://www.nytimes.com/2012/09/23/world/middleeast/failed-efforts-of-americas-last-months-in-iraq.html

Gordon, Michael R., and Bernard E. Trainor, *Cobra II: The Inside Story of the Invasion and Occupation of Iraq*, New York: Vintage Books, 2006.

———, *The Endgame: The Inside Story of the Struggle for Iraq, from George W. Bush to Barack Obama*, New York: Vintage Books, 2012.

Hajjar, Remi, "What Lessons Did We Learn (or Re-Learn) About Military Advising After 9/11," *Military Review*, November–December 2014, pp. 63–79.

Halchin, L. Elaine, *The Coalition Provisional Authority (CPA): Origin, Characteristics, and Institutional Authorities*, Washington, D.C.: Congressional Research Service, RL32370, June 6, 2005. As of October 21, 2015:
http://www.au.af.mil/au/awc/awcgate/crs/rl32370.pdf

Hanley, Charles J., "AP Enterprise: Former Iraqi Detainees Tell of Riots, Punishment in the Sun, Good Americans and Pitiless Ones," *San Diego Union Tribune*, November 1, 2003.

Harkins, Gina, "Shuttering of Elite Unit Spells End of 7-Year Mission for Marines," *Marine Corps Times*, July 4, 2014.

Headquarters Marine Corps, "Marines Raise American Flag over New U.S. Embassy in Iraq," July 1, 2004. As of April 28, 2017:
http://www.hqmc.marines.mil/News/News-Article-Display/Article/551856/marines-raise-american-flag-over-new-us-embassy-in-iraq/

Hendrickson, David C., and Robert W. Tucker, "Revisions in Need of Revising: What Went Wrong in the Iraq War," *Survival*, Vol. 47, No. 2, 2005, pp. 7–31.

Herrera, Rick, "Brave Rifles at Talafar," in William G. Robertson, ed., *In Contact: Case Studies in the Long War*, Vol. 1, Fort Leavenworth, Kan.: Combat Studies Institute, 2006.

Hersh, Seymour M., "Torture at Abu Ghraib," *New Yorker*, May 10, 2004.

Hill, Christopher R., "How the Obama Administration Ignored Iraq: One Ambassador's Story of an Exit Strategy Gone Wrong," *Politico*, October 2, 2014. As of March 3, 2016:
http://www.politico.com/magazine/story/2014/10/how-the-obama-administration-disowned-iraq-111565_Page3.html#ixzz41qcxclgp

Hooker, Richard D., Jr., and Joseph J. Collins, *Lessons Encountered: Learning from the Long War*, Washington, D.C.: National Defense University Press, September 2015.

Hosek, James, *How Is Deployment to Iraq and Afghanistan Affecting U.S. Service Members and Their Families? An Overview of Early RAND Research on the Topic*, Santa Monica, Calif.: RAND Corporation, OP-316-OSD, 2011. As of November 21, 2016:
https://www.rand.org/pubs/occasional_papers/OP316.html

Huntington, Samuel P., *The Soldier and the State: The Theory and Politics of Civil-Military Relations*, Cambridge, Mass.: Harvard University Press, 1957.

Independent Panel to Review Department of Defense Detention Operations, *The Schlesinger Report: An Investigation of Abu Ghraib*, New York: Cosimo, 2005.

Institute for the Study of War, "Baghdad Belts," webpage, undated. As of April 11, 2017:
http://www.understandingwar.org/region/baghdad-belts

———, "Anbar Province and Cities," November 13, 2016. As of April 11, 2017:
http://understandingwar.org/map/anbar-province-and-cities

International Crisis Group, "Iraq: Building a New Security Structure," Middle East Report No. 20, Baghdad/Brussels, December 23, 2003. As of March 28, 2019:
https://www.crisisgroup.org/middle-east-north-africa/gulf-and-arabian-peninsula/iran/iraq-building-new-security-structure

———, "The Next Iraqi War? Sectarianism and Civil Conflict," Middle East Report No. 52, February 27, 2006. As of March 28, 2019:
https://www.crisisgroup.org/middle-east-north-africa/gulf-and-arabian-peninsula/iraq/next-iraqi-war-sectarianism-and-civil-conflict

Iraq Body Count, "Civilian Deaths from Violence in 2007," webpage, January 1, 2008. As of January 27, 2016:
https://www.iraqbodycount.org/analysis/numbers/2007/

"Iraqi National Assembly Meeting," live coverage from Baghdad, C-SPAN, March 16, 2005.

JCS—*See* Joint Chiefs of Staff.

Johnson, David E., "Preparing Potential Senior Army Leaders for the Future: An Assessment of Leader Development Efforts in the Post–Cold War Era," Santa Monica, Calif.: RAND Corporation, IP-224-A, 2002. As of January 26, 2016:
http://www.rand.org/publications/IP/IP224/

———, *Hard Fighting: Israel in Lebanon and Gaza*, Santa Monica, Calif.: RAND Corporation, MG-1085-A/AF, 2011a. As of April 11, 2017:
http://www.rand.org/pubs/monographs/MG1085.html

———, "What Are You Prepared to Do? NATO and the Strategic Mismatch Between Ends, Ways, and Means in Afghanistan—and in the Future," *Studies in Conflict and Terrorism*, Vol. 34, No. 5, May 2011b, pp. 383–401.

———, "Failure to Learn: Reflections on a Career in the Post-Vietnam Army," *War on the Rocks*, January 24, 2014. As of February 1, 2016:
http://warontherocks.com/2014/01/failure-to-learn-reflections-on-a-career-in-the-post-vietnam-army/

———, "Fighting the 'Islamic State': The Case for US Ground Forces," *Parameters*, Vol. 45, No. 2, Summer 2015.

———, *The Challenges of the "Now" and Their Implications for the U.S. Army*, Santa Monica, Calif.: RAND Corporation, PE-184-A, 2016. As of August 12, 2016:
http://www.rand.org/pubs/perspectives/PE184.html

Johnson, David E., M. Wade Markel, and Brian Shannon, *The 2008 Battle of Sadr City: Reimagining Urban Combat*, Santa Monica, Calif.: RAND Corporation, RR-160-A, 2013. As of August 12, 2016:
http://www.rand.org/pubs/research_reports/RR160.html

Joint Chiefs of Staff, "Operation Iraqi Freedom (OIF) History Brief," briefing slides, May 14, 2003. As of August 12, 2016:
https://nsarchive.files.wordpress.com/2010/10/oif-history.pdf

Kagan, Frederick W., *Finding the Target: The Transformation of American Military Policy*, New York: Encounter Book, 2006.

Kagan, Kimberly, *The Surge: A Military History*, New York: Encounter Books, 2009.

Kaplan, Fred, "War-Gamed: Why the Army Shouldn't Be So Surprised by Saddam's Moves," *Slate*, March 28, 2003. As of December 18, 2015:
http://www.slate.com/articles/news_and_politics/war_stories/2003/03/wargamed.html

———, *The Insurgents: David Petraeus and the Plot to Change the American Way of War*, New York: Simon and Schuster, 2013.

Karadsheh, Jomana, and Octavia Nasr, "Iraqi Journalist Throws Shoes at Bush in Baghdad," CNN, December 15, 2008. As of November 4, 2011:
http://www.cnn.com/2008/WORLD/meast/12/14/bush.iraq/

Keller, Dennis E., *U.S. Military Forces and Police Assistance in Stability Operations: The Least-Worst Option to Fill the U.S. Capacity Gap*, Carlisle, Pa.: Army Strategic Studies Institute, Peacekeeping and Stability Operations Institute Paper, August 2010. As of November 21, 2016:
https://www.globalsecurity.org/military/library/report/2010/ssi_keller.pdf

Khalil, Ashraf, and Patrick J. McDonnell, "Iraq Violence Taking a Sectarian Twist," *Los Angeles Times*, May 16, 2005. As of January 29, 2016:
http://articles.latimes.com/2005/may/16/world/fg-sectarian16

Khazan, Olga, "Being a Foreign Service Officer Became Much, Much Harder After 9/11," *The Atlantic*, April 9, 2013. As of October 29, 2015:
http://www.theatlantic.com/international/archive/2013/04/being-a-foreign-service-officer-became-much-much-harder-after-9-11/274822/

Khedery, Ali, "Why We Stuck with Maliki—and Lost Iraq," *Washington Post*, July 3, 2014. As of November 4, 2015:
https://www.washingtonpost.com/opinions/why-we-stuck-with-maliki--and-lost-iraq/2014/07/03/0dd6a8a4-f7ec-11e3-a606-946fd632f9f1_story.html

Kilcullen, David, "Anatomy of a Tribal Revolt," *Small Wars Journal*, August 29, 2007.

Kirkpatrick, David D., "Graft Hobbles Iraq's Military in Fighting ISIS," *New York Times*, November 23, 2013. As of February 1, 2016:
http://www.nytimes.com/2014/11/24/world/middleeast/graft-hobbles-iraqs-military-in-fighting-isis.html

Knickmeyer, Ellen, and K. I. Ibrahim, "Bomb Shatters Mosque in Iraq," *Washington Post*, February 23, 2006. As of February 1, 2016:
http://www.washingtonpost.com/wp-dyn/content/article/2006/02/22/AR2006022200454.html

Knights, Michael, "No Go No More: The Battle for Sadr City," *Jane's Intelligence Review*, Vol. 20, No. 7, July 2008, p. 20–22.

Knowlton, William A., "Ethics and Decision-Making," address delivered at the U.S. Army War College, Carlisle Barracks, Pa., October 22, 1984.

Koladish, Luke, and Kat Briere, "New Command Marks Milestone in Iraq," U.S. Army, January 2, 2010. As of December 17, 2015:
http://www.army.mil/article/32437/

Koloski, Andrew W., and John S. Kolasheski, "Thickening the Lines: Sons of Iraq, a Combat Multiplier," *Military Review*, January–February 2009, pp. 41–53.

Korb, Lawrence, Brian Katulis, Sean Duggan, and Peter Juul, *How Does This End? Strategic Failures Overshadow Tactical Gains in Iraq*, Washington, D.C.: Center for American Progress, 2008.

Krepinevich, Andrew F., *Transforming the Legions: The Army and the Future of Land Warfare*, Washington, D.C.: Center for Strategic and Budgetary Analysis, January 14, 2004. As of February 1, 2016:
http://csbaonline.org/publications/2004/01/transforming-the-legions-the-army-and-the-future-of-land-warfare/

Kuehl, Dale, "Testing Galula in Ameriyah: The People Are the Key," *Military Review*, March–April 2009, pp. 72–79.

Lamothe, Dan, "Iraq Has Finally Started Using the F-16 Fighter Jet in Combat Operations," *Washington Post*, September 6, 2015. As of December 17, 2015:
https://www.washingtonpost.com/news/checkpoint/wp/2015/09/06/iraq-has-finally-started-using-the-f-16-fighter-jet-in-combat-operations/

Landler, Mark, "U.S. Troops to Leave Iraq by Year's End, Obama Says," *New York Times*, October 21, 2011. As of November 4, 2015:
http://www.nytimes.com/2011/10/22/world/middleeast/president-obama-announces-end-of-war-in-iraq.html?src=un&feedurl=http%3A%2F%2Fjson8.nytimes.com%2Fpages%2Fworld%2Fmiddleeast%2Findex.jsonp

Lardner, Richard, "Army Secretary Nominee Worried About Cuts to Army's Size," Associated Press, January 21, 2016.

Leonard, Henry A., J. Michael Polich, Jeffrey D. Peterson, Ronald E. Sortor, and S. Craig Moore, *Something Old, Something New: Army Leader Development in a Dynamic Environment*, Santa Monica, Calif.: RAND Corporation, MG-281-A, 2006. As of August 12, 2016:
http://www.rand.org/pubs/monographs/MG281.html

Leung, Rebecca, "Abuse of Iraqi POWs by GIs Probed," CBS News, April 27, 2004.

Logan, Joseph, "Last U.S. Troops Leave Iraq, Ending War," Reuters, December 18, 2011. As of December 17, 2015:
http://www.reuters.com/article/2011/12/18/us-iraq-withdrawal-idUSTRE7BH03320111218#kFiGvl51mMqYD18K.97

Lopez, C. Todd, "Army to Realign Brigades, Cut 40,000 Soldiers, 17,000 Civilians," U.S. Army, July 9, 2015. As of January 29, 2016:
http://www.army.mil/article/151992/Army_to_realign_brigades__cut_40_000_Soldiers__17_000_civilians/

MacFarland, Sean, and Niel Smith, "Anbar Awakens: The Tipping Point," *Military Review*, March–April 2008, pp. 41–52.

Malkasian, Carter, "Counterinsurgency in Iraq, May 2003–January 2007," in Daniel Marston, ed., *Counterinsurgency in Modern Warfare*, New York: Osprey Publishing, 2008.

Manea, Octavian, "The Philosophy Behind the Iraq Surge: An Interview with General Jack Keane," *Small Wars Journal*, Vol. 7, No. 4, April 5, 2011, pp. 24–26.

Mansfield, Edward D., and Jack Snyder, *Electing to Fight: Why Emerging Democracies Go to War*, Cambridge, Mass.: MIT Press, 2005.

Mansoor, Peter A., *Baghdad at Sunrise: A Brigade Commander's War in Iraq*, New Haven, Conn.: Yale University Press, 2008a.

———, "How the Surge Worked," *Washington Post*, August 10, 2008b. As of January 29, 2016:
http://www.washingtonpost.com/wp-dyn/content/article/2008/08/08/AR2008080802918.html

———, *Surge: My Journey with General David Petraeus and the Remaking of the Iraq War*, New Haven, Conn.: Yale University Press, 2013.

Margolick, David, "The Night of the Generals," *Vanity Fair*, April 2007. As of August 12, 2016:
http://www.vanityfair.com/news/2007/04/iraqgenerals200704

Marlatt, Greta E., *A Bibliography of Professional Military Education (PME)*, Monterey, Calif.: Naval Postgraduate School, October 2007. As of February 1, 2016:
http://edocs.nps.edu/npspubs/scholarly/biblio/Oct07-PME_biblio.pdf

Marquis, Jefferson P., Walter L. Perry, Andrea Mejia, Jerry M. Sollinger, and Vipin Narang, "Genesis of the War," in Walter L. Perry, Richard E. Darilek, Laurinda L. Rohn, and Jerry M. Sollinger, eds., *Operation IRAQI FREEDOM: Decisive War, Elusive Peace*, Santa Monica, Calif.: RAND Corporation, RR-1214-A, 2015, pp. 9–30. As of August 12, 2016:
http://www.rand.org/pubs/research_reports/RR1214.html

Martinez, Luis, "US May Have Wasted $8 Billion in Effort to Rebuild Iraq," ABC News, March 6, 2013. As of December 17, 2015:
http://abcnews.go.com/blogs/politics/2013/03/us-may-have-wasted-8-billion-in-effort-to-rebuild-iraq/

Matthews, Dylan, "How Important Was the Surge?" *The American Prospect*, July 25, 2008. As of January 29, 2016:
http://prospect.org/article/how-important-was-surge

McChrystal, Stanley, *My Share of the Task: A Memoir*, London: Penguin Books, 2013.

McMaster, H. R., *Dereliction of Duty: Johnson, McNamara, the Joint Chiefs of Staff, and the Lies That Led to Vietnam*, New York: HarperCollins, 1997.

McWilliams, Timothy S., and Nicholas J. Schlosser, *U.S. Marines in Battle: Fallujah*, Quantico, Va.: U.S. Marine Corps, 2014.

Metz, Steven, *Iraq and the Evolution of American Strategy*, Washington D.C.: Potomac Books, 2008.

Middle East Institute, "Wendy Chamberlain Interview Notes," April 18, 2007.

Millham, Matt, "Odierno Takes Command of Multi-National Corps-Iraq," *Stars and Stripes*, December 15, 2006.

Moaddel, Mansoor, Mark Tessler, and Ronald Inglehart, "Foreign Occupation and National Pride: The Case of Iraq," *Public Opinion Quarterly*, Vol. 72, No. 4, Winter 2008, pp. 677–705.

Mohammed, Aref, Jack Kimball, and Waleed Ibrahim, "Five Killed as U.S., Iraqi Troops Raid Border Village," Reuters, February 12, 2010. As of December 17, 2015:
http://www.reuters.com/article/2010/02/12/us-iraq-violence-iran-idUSTRE61B24Y20100212#iIU753YuqEMwmEx3.97

Moore, John C., "Sadr City: The Armor Pure Assault in Urban Terrain," *Armor*, November–December 2004, pp. 31–37. As of December 18, 2015:
http://www.westpointaog.org/file/ChristopherDeanNiningerNewsSadrCityArticlee.pdf

Montgomery, Gary W., and Timothy S. McWilliams, eds., *Al-Anbar Awakening*, Vol. 2: *Iraqi Perspectives: From Insurgency to Counterinsurgency in Iraq, 2004–2009*, Quantico, Va.: Marine Corps University Press, 2009.

Murphy, Cullen, and Todd S. Purdum, "Farewell to All That: An Oral History of the Bush White House," *Vanity Fair*, February 2009. As of April 11, 2017:
http://www.vanityfair.com/news/2009/02/bush-oral-history200902?currentPage=all&printable=true

Murphy, Jarrett, "Palestinians Get Saddam Charity Checks," CBS News, March 14, 2003. As of December 9, 2015:
http://www.cbsnews.com/news/palestinians-get-saddam-charity-checks/

Murray, Williamson, and Robert H. Scales, Jr., *The Iraq War: A Military History*, New York: Belknap, 2003.

Myers, Richard B., *Eyes on the Horizon: Serving on the Front Lines of National Security*, New York: Simon and Schuster, 2009.

Nagl, John A., *Institutionalizing Adaptation: It's Time for a Permanent Army Advisor Corps*, Washington, D.C.: Center for a New American Security, June 2007. As of February 1, 2016: http://www.cnas.org/files/documents/publications/Nagl_AdvisoryCorp_June07.pdf

National Commission on the Future of the U.S. Army, *Report to the President and the Congress of the United States, January 28, 2016*, Arlington, Va., 2016.

National Security Council, *National Strategy for Victory in Iraq*, November 30, 2005. As of October 27, 2015: http://www.washingtonpost.com/wp-srv/nation/documents/Iraqnationalstrategy11-30-05.pdf

———, "Highlights of the Iraq Strategy Review," briefing slides, January 2007. As of August 12, 2016: http://2001-2009.state.gov/documents/organization/78696.pdf

Nordland, Rod, "U.S. Soldiers, Back in Iraq, Find Security Forces in Disrepair," *New York Times*, April 14, 2015. As of February 1, 2016: http://www.nytimes.com/2015/04/15/world/middleeast/iraq-military-united-states-forces-camp-taji.html?_r=0

Obama, Barack, "My Plan for Iraq," *New York Times*, July 14, 2008. As of May 16, 2016: http://www.nytimes.com/2008/07/14/opinion/14obama.html?_r=0

———, "Responsibly Ending the War in Iraq," remarks as prepared for delivery, Camp Lejeune, N.C., February 27, 2009.

———, "Letter from the President—Authorization for the Use of United States Armed Forces in Connection with the Islamic State of Iraq and the Levant," White House, February 11, 2015.

"Obama Shifts US Focus from Iraq to Afghanistan Early in Presidency," Voice of America, January 14, 2014. As of March 3, 2015: http://www.voanews.com/content/obama-shifts-us-focus-from-iraq-to-afghanistan-early-in-presidency-81678877/111475.html

Office of the Historian, "Zalmay Khalilzad (1951–)," U.S. Department of State, Bureau of Public Affairs, undated. As of October 26, 2015: https://history.state.gov/departmenthistory/people/khalilzad-zalmay

Ollivant, Douglas A., *Rapid, Decisive, or Effective? The Applicability of Rapid Decisive Operations in the Enforcement of the Bush Doctrine*, Fort Leavenworth, Kan.: School of Advanced Military Studies, April 21, 2004. As of December 18, 2015: http://www.dtic.mil/dtic/tr/fulltext/u2/a427379.pdf

———, "Producing Victory: A 2007 Post-Script for Implementation," *Military Review*, March–April 2007, pp. 109–110.

Ollivant, Douglas A., and Eric D. Chewning, "Producing Victory: Rethinking Conventional Forces in COIN Operations," *Military Review*, July–August 2006, pp. 50–59.

Olsen, Howard, and John Davis, *Training U.S. Army Officers for Peace Operations: Lessons from Bosnia*, Special Report, Washington, D.C.: United States Institute of Peace, October 29, 1999.

Otterman, Sharon, "Iraq: Iraq's Prewar Military Capabilities," *CFR Backgrounder*, April 24, 2003. As of December 18, 2015:
http://www.cfr.org/iraq/Iraq-iraqs-prewar-military-capabilities/p7695

———, "Iraq: The Interim Constitution," *CFR Backgrounder*, March 8, 2004. As of August 12, 2016:
http://www.cfr.org/iraq/iraq-interim-constitution/p7672

Packer, George, "The Lesson of Tal Afar: Is It Too Late for the Administration to Correct Its Course in Iraq?" *New Yorker*, April 10, 2006. As of January 26, 2016:
http://www.newyorker.com/magazine/2006/04/10/the-lesson-of-tal-afar

Panzino, Charlsy, "Fort Benning to Stand Up Security Force Brigades, Training Academy," *Army Times*, February 16, 2017.

Partlow, Joshua, "Maliki's Office Is Seen Behind Purge in Forces," *Washington Post*, April 30, 2007. As of February 1, 2016:
http://www.washingtonpost.com/wp-dyn/content/article/2007/04/29/AR2007042901728.html

Perito, Robert M., "Iraq's Interior Ministry: Frustrating Reform," USIPeace Briefing, Washington, D.C.: United States Institute of Peace, May 2008.

———, *The Iraq Federal Police: U.S. Police Building Under Fire*, Washington, D.C.: United States Institute of Peace, Special Report No. 291, 2011. As of April 11, 2017:
https://www.usip.org/sites/default/files/SR291_The_Iraq_Federal_Police.pdf

Perry, Cal, "Milestone Elections Begin in Iraq," CNN, January 30, 2005. As of January 29, 2016:
http://www.cnn.com/2005/WORLD/meast/01/29/iraq.main/index.html?eref=sitesearch

Perry, Walter L., "Planning the War and the Transition to Peace," in Walter L. Perry, Richard E. Darilek, Laurinda L. Rohn, and Jerry M. Sollinger, eds., *Operation IRAQI FREEDOM: Decisive War, Elusive Peace*, Santa Monica: RAND Corporation, RR-1214-A, 2015, pp. 31–56. As of August 12, 2016::
http://www.rand.org/pubs/research_reports/RR1214.html

Perry, Walter L., Richard E. Darilek, Laurinda L. Rohn, and Jerry M. Sollinger, eds., *Operation IRAQI FREEDOM: Decisive War, Elusive Peace*, Santa Monica, Calif.: RAND Corporation, RR-1214-A, 2015. As of August 12, 2016:
http://www.rand.org/pubs/research_reports/RR1214.html

Perry, Walter L., Stuart E. Johnson, Keith Crane, David C. Gompert, John Gordon IV, Robert E. Hunter, Dalia Dassa Kaye, Terrence K. Kelly, Eric Peltz, and Howard J. Shatz, *Withdrawing from Iraq: Alternative Schedules, Associated Risks, and Mitigating Strategies*, Santa Monica, Calif.: RAND Corporation, MG-882-OSD, 2009. As of August 12, 2016:
http://www.rand.org/pubs/monographs/MG882.html

Petraeus, David H., "Lessons of History and Lessons of Vietnam," *Parameters*, Winter 2010–2011, p. 48–61. As of February 1, 2016:
http://strategicstudiesinstitute.army.mil/pubs/parameters/Articles/2010winter/Petraeus.pdf

———, "How We Won in Iraq," *Foreign Policy*, October 29, 2013. As of November 22, 2016:
http://foreignpolicy.com/2013/10/29/how-we-won-in-iraq/

Pfiffner, James P., "US Blunders in Iraq: De-Baathification and Disbanding the Army," *Intelligence and National Security*, Vol. 25, No. 1, March 2010, pp. 76–85.

Phillips, Macon, "President Barack Obama's Inaugural Address," White House, January 21, 2009. As of August 12, 2016:
https://www.whitehouse.gov/blog/2009/01/21/president-barack-obamas-inaugural-address

Pincus, Walter, "U.S. Seeks Contractors to Train Iraqi Military," *Washington Post*, May 4, 2008.

Pirnie, Bruce R., John Gordon IV, Richard R. Brennan, Jr., Forrest E. Morgan, Alexander C. Hou, Chad Yost, Andrea Mejia, and David E. Mosher, "Land Operations," in Walter L. Perry, Richard E. Darilek, Laurinda L. Rohn, and Jerry M. Sollinger, eds., *Operation IRAQI FREEDOM: Decisive War, Elusive Peace*, Santa Monica, Calif.: RAND Corporation, RR-1214-A, 2015, pp. 57–148. As of August 12, 2016:
http://www.rand.org/pubs/research_reports/RR1214.html

Pirnie, Bruce R., and Edward O'Connell, *Counterinsurgency in Iraq (2003–2006): RAND Counterinsurgency Study—Volume 2*, Santa Monica, Calif.: RAND Corporation, MG-595/3-OSD, 2008. As of August 12, 2016:
http://www.rand.org/pubs/monographs/MG595z3.html

Pitman, Todd, "Iraq's Sunni Sheiks Join Americans to Fight Insurgency," *San Diego Union Tribune*, March 25, 2007.

Pleitgen, Frederik, "Colonel: Iraqi Forces Still Need Help from U.S. Troops," CNN, July 2, 2007. As of August 12, 2016:
http://www.cnn.com/2007/WORLD/meast/07/01/pleitgen.surge/index.html?eref=rss_latest

Plummer, Anne, "Army Chief Tells President Restructuring Force Could Cost $20 Billion," *Inside the Army*, February 9, 2004.

Price, Jay, "War Leads to Changes in the 'Division Ready Brigade,'" *Knoxville News Sentinel*, March 21, 2007.

Quinlivan, James T., "Force Requirements in Stability Operations," *Parameters*, Winter 1995–1996, pp. 59–69.

———, "Burden of Victory: The Painful Arithmetic of Stability Operations," *RAND Review*, Vol. 27, No. 2, Summer 2003. As of February 1, 2016:
http://www.rand.org/pubs/corporate_pubs/CP22-2003-08.html

Rathmell, Andrew, Olga Oliker, Terrence K. Kelly, David Brannan, and Keith Crane, *Developing Iraq's Security Sector: The Coalition Provisional Authority's Experience*, Santa Monica, Calif.: RAND Corporation, MG-365-OSD, 2006. As of August 12, 2016:
http://www.rand.org/pubs/monographs/MG365.html

Rayburn, Joel, *Iraq After America: Strongmen, Sectarians, Resistance*, Stanford, Calif.: Hoover Institution Press, 2014.

Reynolds, Kevin P., "Insurgency/Counterinsurgency: Does the Army 'Get It?'" paper presented at the International Studies Association Annual Convention, Carlisle, Pa., February 28–March 3, 2007.

Rice, Condoleezza, *No Higher Honor: A Memoir of My Years in Washington*, New York: Crown Publishers, 2011.

Ricks, Thomas E., *Fiasco: The American Military Adventure in Iraq*, New York: Penguin Press, 2006a.

———, "In Iraq, Military Forgot the Lessons of Vietnam," *Washington Post*, July 23, 2006b. As of November 25, 2015:
http://www.washingtonpost.com/wp-dyn/content/article/2006/07/22/AR2006072200444.html

———, *The Gamble: General David Petraeus and the American Military Adventure in Iraq, 2006–2008*, New York: Penguin Press, 2009.

Robertson, Campbell, and Stephen Farrell, "Pact, Approved in Iraq, Sets Time for U.S. Pullout," *New York Times*, November 16, 2008. As of November 4, 2008:
http://www.nytimes.com/2008/11/17/world/middleeast/17iraq.html

Robinson, Linda, *Tell Me How This Ends: General David Petraeus and the Search for a Way out of Iraq*, New York: Public Affairs, 2008.

Roggio, Bill, "Operation Steel Curtain in Husaybah," *Long War Journal*, November 5, 2005. As of August 12, 2016:
http://www.longwarjournal.org/archives/2005/11/operation_steel_1.php

———, "Mahdi Army Uses 'Flying IEDs' in Baghdad," *Long War Journal*, June 5, 2008. As of December 17, 2015:
http://www.longwarjournal.org/archives/2008/06/mahdi_army_uses_flyi.php

———, "Al Qaeda Leader Abu Omar al Baghdadi Confirmed Captured: Prime Minister Maliki," *Long War Journal*, April 27, 2009. As of December 17, 2015:
http://www.longwarjournal.org/archives/2009/04/al_qaeda_leader_abu.php

———, "Iraqi, US Forces Kill 10 During Clash with Hezbollah Brigades Near the Iranian Border," *Long War Journal*, February 12, 2010. As of December 17, 2015:
http://www.longwarjournal.org/archives/2010/02/iraqi_us_forces_kill.php

———, "Analysis: ISIS, Allies Reviving 'Baghdad Belts' Battle Plan," *Long War Journal*, June 14, 2014. As of February 17, 2016:
http://www.longwarjournal.org/archives/2014/06/analysis_isis_allies.php.

Rogin, Josh, "Iraqi Ambassador: We Will Request U.S. Troop Extension 'in Our Own Sweet Time,'" *Foreign Policy*, August 25, 2011a. As of November 4, 2015:
http://foreignpolicy.com/2011/08/25/
iraqi-ambassador-we-will-request-u-s-troop-extension-in-our-own-sweet-time/

———, "Condoleezza Rice: We Never Expected to Leave Iraq in 2011," *Foreign Policy*, November 2, 2011b. As of November 4, 2015:
http://foreignpolicy.com/2011/11/02/condoleezza-rice-we-never-expected-to-leave-iraq-in-2011/

Ronco, "Decision Brief to Department of Defense Office of Reconstruction and Humanitarian Assistance on the Disarmament, Demobilization and Reintegration of the Iraqi Armed Forces," briefing, March 2003, provided to RAND.

Rosen, Nir, *Aftermath: Following America's Wars in the Muslim World*, New York: Nation Books, 2010.

Rubin, Alissa J., "Shiite Rivalries Slash at a Once Calm Iraqi City," *New York Times*, June 21, 2007.

———, "Iraq Marks Withdrawal of U.S. Troops From Cities," *New York Times*, June 30, 2009. As of August 12, 2016:
http://www.nytimes.com/2009/07/01/world/middleeast/01iraq.html

———, "Ahmad Chalabi and the Legacy of De-Baathification in Iraq," *New York Times*, November 3, 2015. As of November 25, 2015:
http://www.nytimes.com/2015/11/04/world/middleeast/
ahmad-chalabi-and-the-legacy-of-de-baathification-in-iraq.html?_r=0

Rudd, Gordon W., *Reconstructing Iraq: Regime Change, Jay Garner, and the ORHA Story*, Lawrence, Kan.: University of Kansas Press, 2011.

"Rumsfeld, Casey Hold Press Conference on Iraq," CNN Transcripts, June 22, 2006. As of August 12, 2016:
http://www.cnn.com/TRANSCRIPTS/0606/22/se.01.html

Rumsfeld, Donald, *Known and Unknown: A Memoir*, New York: Sentinel, 2011.

Russo, Richard, "The Gotham Division and Staff Sergeant Parker: Imagining the Future of Urban Warfare," *Small Wars Journal*, June 11, 2014.

Sambanis, Nicholas, "It's Official: There Is Now a Civil War in Iraq," *New York Times*, July 23, 2006. As of January 29, 2016:
http://www.nytimes.com/2006/07/23/opinion/23sambanis.html

Samuels, David, "A Conversation with Colin Powell," *The Atlantic*, April 2007. As of February 1, 2016:
http://www.theatlantic.com/magazine/archive/2007/04/a-conversation-with-colin-powell/305873/

Santayana, George, *The Life of Reason*, Vol. 1, New York: Charles Scribner's Sons, 1905.

Schiavenza, Matt, "After Cuba: The Only Three Countries That Have No Relations with the U.S." *The Atlantic*, July 1, 2015. As of October 29, 2015:
http://www.theatlantic.com/international/archive/2015/07/cuba-us-embassy-bhutan-relations/397523/

Schmitt, Eric, "U.S. to Intensify Its Training in Iraq to Battle Insurgents," *New York Times*, November 2, 2005. As of January 27, 2016:
http://www.nytimes.com/2005/11/02/world/middleeast/us-to-intensify-its-training-in-iraq-to-battle-insurgents.html?_r=0

"Secretary Rumsfeld Stepping Down," NBC News, November 8, 2006.

Shake, Kori N., *State of Disrepair: Fixing the Culture and Practices of the State Department*, Stanford, Calif.: Hoover Institution Press, 2012.

Shanker, Thom, "New Strategy Vindicates Ex-Army Chief Shinseki," *New York Times*, January 12, 2007. As of December 9, 2015:
http://www.nytimes.com/2007/01/12/washington/12shinseki.html

Shanker, Thom, and Stephen Farrell, "Odierno Replaces Petraeus as U.S. Commander in Iraq," *New York Times*, September 16, 2008.

Sisk, Richard, "U.S. Doubles Number of Advisers in Iraq as Forces Push into Mosul," Military.com, January 4, 2017.

Sly, Liz, "The Hidden Hand Behind the Islamic State Militants? Saddam Hussein's," *Washington Post*, April 4, 2015. As of November 24, 2015:
https://www.washingtonpost.com/world/middle_east/the-hidden-hand-behind-the-islamic-state-militants-saddam-husseins/2015/04/04/aa97676c-cc32-11e4-8730-4f473416e759_story.html

Sly, Liz, and Ahmed Ramadan, "Insurgents Seize Iraqi City of Mosul as Security Forces Flee," *Washington Post*, June 10, 2014. As of December 17, 2015:
https://www.washingtonpost.com/world/insurgents-seize-iraqi-city-of-mosul-as-troops-flee/2014/06/10/21061e87-8fcd-4ed3-bc94-0e309af0a674_story.html

Smith, Craig S., "Poor Planning and Corruption Hobble Reconstruction of Iraq," *New York Times*, September 18, 2005. As of December 1, 2015:
http://www.nytimes.com/2005/09/18/world/middleeast/poor-planning-and-corruption-hobble-reconstruction-of-iraq.html

Smith, M. L. R., and David Martin Jones, *The Political Impossibility of Modern Counterinsurgency: Strategic Problems, Puzzles, and Paradoxes*, New York: Columbia University Press, 2015.

Sonnenfeldt, Helmut, and Ron Nessen, "You Go to War with the Press You Have," Brookings Institution, December 30, 2004. As of August 12, 2016:
https://www.brookings.edu/opinions/you-go-to-war-with-the-press-you-have/

Spiegel, Peter, "Army Is Training Advisors for Iraq," *Los Angeles Times*, October 25, 2006. As of November 21, 2016:
http://articles.latimes.com/2006/oct/25/nation/na-advisors25

Spinner, Jackie, and Karl Vick, "Troops Battle for Last Parts of Fallujah," *Washington Post*, November 14, 2004.

Stolberg, Sheryl Gay, and Jim Rutenberg, "Rumsfeld Resigns as Secretary of Defense After Big Election Gains for Democrats," *New York Times*, November 8, 2006.

Taguba, Antonio M., *Article 15-6 Investigation of the 800th Military Police Brigade*, Department of the Army, May 27, 2004. As of February 1, 2016:
http://www.npr.org/iraq/2004/prison_abuse_report.pdf

"Taking on the Shia Militias," *The Economist*, January 24, 2007. As of February 1, 2016:
http://www.economist.com/node/8581764

Tan, Michelle, "101st Airborne to Deploy to Iraq, Kuwait," *Army Times*, November 16, 2015. As of February 1, 2016:
http://www.armytimes.com/story/military/careers/army/2015/11/06/101st-airborne-deploy-iraq-kuwait/74761852/

———, "Army Chief: Soldiers Must Be Ready to Fight in 'Megacities'," *Defense News*, October 5, 2016. As of April 11, 2017:
http://www.defensenews.com/articles/army-chief-soldiers-must-be-ready-to-fight-in-megacities

Tawfeeq, Mohammed, and Jomana Karadsheh, "Cease-Fire Reached in Baghdad's Sadr City," CNN, May 11, 2008. As of February 1, 2016:
http://www.cnn.com/2008/WORLD/meast/05/10/iraq.main/

Tenet, George, and Bill Harlow, *At the Center of the Storm: My Years at the CIA*, New York: HarperCollins, 2007.

Thiel, Joshua, "The Statistical Irrelevance of American SIGACT Data: Iraq Surge Analysis Reveals Reality," *Small Wars Journal*, April 12, 2011.

Thompson, Mark, "The Rise and Fall of 'General Peaches'," *Time*, November 14, 2012. As of February 1, 2016:
http://nation.time.com/2012/11/14/the-rise-and-fall-of-general-peaches/

"Timeline of Major Events in the Iraq War," *New York Times*, October 21, 2011.

Trumbull, Charles P., IV, and Julie B. Martin, "Elections and Government Formation in Iraq: An Analysis of the Judiciary's Role," *Vanderbilt Journal of Transnational Law*, Vol. 44, No. 331, 2011.

Tyson, Ann Scott, and Josh White, "Strained Army Extends Tours to 15 Months," *Washington Post*, April 12, 2007. As of November 21, 2016:
http://www.washingtonpost.com/wp-dyn/content/article/2007/04/11/AR2007041100615.html

United Nations, *World Statistics Pocketbook 2009*, Series V, No. 34, New York, 2010. As of February 1, 2016:
http://unstats.un.org/unsd/pocketbook/Pocketbook%202009.pdf

United Nations High Commissioner for Refugees, "Chronology of Events in Iraq, July 2004," September 28, 2004. As of August 12, 2016:
http://www.refworld.org/docid/415c66b84.html

United Nations Security Council, Resolution 1483 (2003) [on the Situation Between Iraq and Kuwait], New York, May 22, 2003a.

———, Resolution 1511 (2003) [on Authorizing a Multinational Force Under Unified Command to Take All Necessary Measures to Contribute to the Maintenance of Security and Stability in Iraq], New York, October 16, 2003b.

———, Resolution 1546 (2004) [on Formation of a Sovereign Interim Government of Iraq], New York, June 8, 2004.

United States of America and Republic of Iraq, "Agreement Between the United States of America and the Republic of Iraq on the Withdrawal of United States Forces from Iraq and the Organization of Their Activities During Their Temporary Presence in Iraq," status of forces agreement, November 17, 2008. As of August 12, 2016:
http://www.state.gov/documents/organization/122074.pdf

United States Institute of Peace, "Provincial Reconstruction Teams in Iraq," March 20, 2013. As of October 26, 2015:
http://www.usip.org/publications/provincial-reconstruction-teams-in-iraq-1

U.S. Agency for International Development, "The Office of Crisis Surge Support Staff," webpage, May 12, 2014. As of April 12, 2019:
https://www.usaid.gov/who-we-are/organization/bureaus/
bureau-democracy-conflict-and-humanitarian-assistance/office-crisis-surge-support

USAID—*See* U.S. Agency for International Development.

U.S. Army War College, "Directive Academic Year 2002: Core Curriculum Course 4: Implementing National Military Strategy," Carlisle Barracks, Pa., 2001.

———, "Directive Academic Year 2002: Core Curriculum Course 4: Implementing National Military Strategy," Carlisle Barracks, Pa., 2005.

"U.S. Captures, Renames Baghdad Airport," *USA Today*, April 3, 2003.

U.S. Central Command, "USCENTCOM Bids Farewell to Commander," MacDill Air Force Base, Fla., March 28, 2008.

U.S. Congress, 114th Congress, 1st Sess., National Defense Authorization Act for Fiscal Year 2016, Washington, D.C., S. 1356, January 6, 2015.

"U.S. Death Toll in Iraq Passes 3,000," *USA Today*, January 1, 2007. As of April 11, 2017:
http://usatoday30.usatoday.com/news/world/iraq/2006-12-31-us-death-toll-3000_x.htm

U.S. Department of Defense, *Functions of the Department of Defense and Its Major Components*, DoD Directive 5100.1, Washington, D.C., August 1, 2002.

———, *Measuring Stability and Security in Iraq*, Washington, D.C., July 2005.

———, *Measuring Stability and Security in Iraq*, Washington, D.C., May 2006a.

———, *Measuring Stability and Security in Iraq*, Washington, D.C., November 2006b.

———, *Measuring Stability and Security in Iraq*, Washington, D.C., December 2006c.

———, *Measuring Stability and Security in Iraq*, Washington, D.C., March 2007a.

———, *Measuring Stability and Security in Iraq*, Washington, D.C., September 2007b.

———, *Measuring Stability and Security in Iraq*, Washington, D.C., December 2007c.

———, *Measuring Stability and Security in Iraq*, Washington, D.C., March 2008a.

———, *Measuring Stability and Security in Iraq*, Washington, D.C., September 2008b.

———, *Measuring Stability and Security in Iraq*, Washington, D.C., June 2010a.

———, *Functions of the Department of Defense and Its Major Components*, DoD Directive 5100.01, Washington, D.C., December 21, 2010b.

———, *Sustaining U.S. Global Leadership: Priorities for 21st Century Defense*, Washington, D.C., January 2012.

———, *Quadrennial Defense Review 2014*, Washington, D.C., March 2014. As of February 1, 2016:
http://archive.defense.gov/pubs/2014_Quadrennial_Defense_Review.pdf

U.S. Department of Defense and Associated Press, "OIF Timeline/Significant Events," March 21, 2008. As of August 12, 2016:
http://www.mirecc.va.gov/docs/visn6/12_OIF_Timeline.pdf

U.S. Department of State and the Broadcasting Board of Governors, Office of the Inspector General, *Review of Staffing at U.S. Embassy Baghdad*, Report No. ISP-IQO-05-57, March 2005. As of December 1, 2015:
https://oig.state.gov/system/files/124639.pdf

Usher, Sebastian, "Baathist Mistake Corrected Amid Concern," BBC News, January 12, 2008. As of November 24, 2015:
http://news.bbc.co.uk/2/hi/middle_east/7185276.stm

U.S. Interagency Counterinsurgency Initiative, *U.S. Government Counterinsurgency Guide*, Washington, D.C., January 2009. As of December 18, 2015:
http://www.state.gov/documents/organization/119629.pdf

U.S. Senate, *Nominations Before the Senate Armed Services Committee, Second Session 110th Congress*, Committee on Armed Services, Washington, D.C., 2008.

Van Roosen, Hugh C., *Military Support to Governance*, Version 7-Draft, white paper, January 12, 2015.

Visser, Reidar, "An Unstable, Divided Land," *New York Times*, December 15, 2011. As of December 18, 2015:
http://www.nytimes.com/2011/12/16/opinion/an-unstable-divided-land.html?_r=0

von Drehle, David, and R. Jeffrey Smith, "U.S. Strikes Iraq for Plot to Kill Bush," *Washington Post*, June 27, 1993. As of December 9, 2015:
http://www.washingtonpost.com/wp-srv/inatl/longterm/iraq/timeline/062793.htm

von Zielbauer, Paul, "Iraqi Violence Ebbed in September, Reports Say," *New York Times*, October 2, 2007. As of February 1, 2016:
http://www.nytimes.com/2007/10/02/world/middleeast/02iraq.html

Ward, Celeste J., *The Coalition Provisional Authority's Experience with Governance in Iraq: Lessons Identified*, United States Institute of Peace, Special Report 139, May 2005. As of November 24, 2015:
http://www.usip.org/sites/default/files/sr139.pdf

West, Bing, *The Strongest Tribe: War, Politics, and the Endgame in Iraq*, New York: Random House, 2008.

West, Bing, and Ray Smith, *The March Up: Taking Baghdad with the United States Marines*, New York: Bantam, 2004.

White House, *National Security Strategy of the United States of America*, Washington, D.C., September 17, 2002.

———, "President Bush and Iraq Prime Minister Maliki Sign the Strategic Framework Agreement and Security Agreement," December 14, 2008. As of November 4, 2015:
http://georgewbush-whitehouse.archives.gov/news/releases/2008/12/20081214-2.html

Whitley, Albert, "Statement by: Major General Albert Whitley CMG, CBE, Senior British Land Advisor to the Commander the Coalition Forces Land Component Command (CFLCC) Kuwait and Iraq from November 2002 to May 2003; and Deputy Commanding General (with Particular Responsibility for Post Hostilities) DCG CFLCC, February 2003 to May 2003," in *Report of the Iraq Inquiry: Report of a Committee of Privy Counsellors*, London, 2010. As of August 12, 2016:
http://www.iraqinquiry.org.uk/media/96166/2011-01-25-Statement-Whitley.pdf

"Why Iraq's Army Crumbled," *The Economist*, June 21, 2014. As of November 23, 2015:
http://www.economist.com/news/middle-east-and-africa/21604629-politicisation-iraqs-security-forces-undermined-their-fighting-ability-why

Wilson, Scott, "A Different Street Fight in Iraq: U.S. General Turns to Public Works in Battle for Hearts and Minds," *Washington Post*, May 27, 2004. As of December 18, 2015:
http://www.washingtonpost.com/wp-dyn/articles/A58770-2004May26.html

Wing, Joel, "Rethinking the Surge in Iraq," *Musings on Iraq*, August 22, 2011.

Wolfowitz, Paul, "Rising Up," *New Republic*, Vol. 219, No. 23, December 7, 1998, pp. 12–14.

Woodward, Bob, *The War Within: A Secret White House History, 2006–2008*, New York: Simon and Schuster, 2008a.

———, "Why Did Violence Plummet? It Wasn't Just the Surge," *Washington Post*, September 8, 2008b. As of January 29, 2016:
http://www.washingtonpost.com/wp-dyn/content/article/2008/09/07/AR2008090701847.html

Wright, Donald P., and Timothy R. Reese, *On Point II: Transition to the New Campaign—The United States Army in Operation Iraqi Freedom, May 2003–January 2005*, Fort Leavenworth, Kan.: Combat Studies Institute Press, 2008.

Zakheim, Dov S., *A Vulcan's Tale: How the Bush Administration Mismanaged the Reconstruction of Afghanistan*, Washington D.C.: Brookings Institution Press, 2011.

Zeleny, Jeff, "Obama Calls for U.S. to Shift Focus on Terrorism," *New York Times*, August 1, 2007. As of March 3, 2016:
http://www.nytimes.com/2007/08/01/us/politics/01cnd-obama.html?_r=0

Ziemke, Erwin F., *The U.S. Army in the Occupation of Germany 1944–1946*, Washington, D.C.: U.S. Army Center of Military History, 2003.

Zucchino, David, *Thunder Run: The Armored Strike to Capture Baghdad*, New York: Grove Press, 2004.

———, "Why Iraqi Army Can't Fight, Despite $25 Billion in U.S. Aid, Training," *Los Angeles Times*, November 3, 2014. As of November 23, 2015:
http://www.latimes.com/world/middleeast/la-fg-iraq-army-20141103-story.html